LIBRARY IN A BOOK

GLOBAL TERRORISM

Revised Edition

Harry Henderson

■✓®

Facts On File, Inc.

Author's Note

This Library in a Book volume entitled *Global Terrorism* is the thoroughly revised second edition of *Terrorism*, a comprehensive reference and research handbook on terrorism, counterterrorism, and terrorist incidents around the world. Another Library in a Book volume entitled *Terrorist Challenge to America* focuses specifically on the events of September 11, 2001, their effects on the United States, and the subsequent domestic and foreign efforts by the United States to fight terrorism.

There is a small amount of overlap in that both books include general background and bibliographies about terrorism. This *Global Terrorism* title naturally also includes basic coverage of the terrorist attacks on the United States. However, the emphasis in *Global Terrorism* is on terrorism as a worldwide phenomenon, with materials relating to the major world trouble spots, as well as a more comprehensive historical summary. The two titles can therefore be viewed as complementary—together they provide both comprehensive global coverage and more detailed coverage from the point of view of the United States and its interests.

GLOBAL TERRORISM, REVISED EDITION

Copyright © 2004 by Harry Henderson

Maps and graphs copyright © 2004 by Facts On File, Inc.

Facts On File, Inc.
132 West 31st Street
New York NY 10001

Library of Congress Cataloging-in-Publication Data
Henderson, Harry, 1951–
    Global terrorism / Harry Henderson.
        p. cm.—(Library in a book)
    Rev. ed. of: Terrorism. c2001.
    includes index.
    ISBN 0-8160-5337-5 (hc)
    1. Terrorism—Research. I. Henderson, Harry, 1951– Terrorism. II. Title. III. Series.

HV6431. H43 2004
303.6′25—dc22   2003063126

Facts On File books are available at special discounts when purchased in bulk quantities for businesses, associations, institutions, or sales promotions. Please call our Special Sales Department in New York at (212) 967-8800 or (800) 322-8755.

You can find Facts On File on the World Wide Web at http://www.factsonfile.com.

Maps and graphs by Jeremy Eagle

Printed in the United States of America

MP Hermitage 10 9 8 7 6 5 4 3 2 1

This book is printed on acid-free paper.

CONTENTS

PART III
APPENDICES

PART I

OVERVIEW OF THE TOPIC

CHAPTER 1

INTRODUCTION: GLOBAL PERSPECTIVES ON TERRORISM

By the time this book is published, it will have been about three years since the morning of September 11, 2001, brought the global reach of terrorism into the streets and living rooms of America. Americans have seen the first stages of the "war on terrorism" declared by President George W. Bush play out in Afghanistan and Iraq, as well as on a smaller scale in nations as diverse as Colombia, Indonesia, the Philippines, Pakistan, and Yemen. U.S. intelligence agencies have been revamped and brought into closer cooperation with one another and with their foreign counterparts. Domestically, citizens of democracies such as the United States and Great Britain face new restrictions, particularly on immigration and air travel. New forms of electronic and biometric surveillance have been proposed. Changes in U.S. legal procedures for detaining and prosecuting suspects have raised the question of whether the civil liberties that characterize democratic societies might also become victims of the war on terrorism.

Understandably enough, the reaction to the devastating attacks on the United States has focused on Islamic terrorists in general and Osama bin Laden and al-Qaeda in particular. With the exception of Colombia, most military assistance and intervention since 2001 has aimed at Islamic terrorist groups or regimes believed to be supporting terrorism. However, enough time has now passed to perhaps allow for a more global perspective.

Terrorism operates through the global connections of communication and transportation that make the modern world possible. Terrorist groups often cooperate, and a few such as al-Qaeda have developed the ability to hit targets on the other side of the world. Actual and potential weapons ranging from the RPG (rocket-propelled grenade launcher) to the explosive-laden vest to exotic possibilities of biological, chemical, nuclear, or cybernetic attack are becoming the common property of terrorist or insurgent groups of all sorts. In turn, much of the tactics and technology of counterterrorism,

3

such as intelligence techniques and the "hardening" of infrastructure targets, is broadly applicable to any terrorist threat.

At the same time, however, the motivations and goals of terrorists are neither simple nor interchangeable. They are often local or regional in character. They draw upon specific ethnic and cultural conflicts (as in Northern Ireland or Israel/Palestine), the desire of particular groups for independence, or, increasingly, the apocalyptic imperatives of religion. Understanding the particular history of a conflict and how it has shaped motivations and attitudes is necessary not only to assess the risk posed by a particular group but also in order to try to change the conditions that create poverty or repression and drive people to consider terrorism.

When considering terrorism and counterterrorism in a global context one must ask and begin to try to answer many important questions:

- What are the defining characteristics of terrorism?
- How does terrorism differ from other organized uses of violence such as conventional war, guerrilla war, and organized crime?
- Have predominant motivations for terrorism changed in recent years? What makes the "new terrorism" more difficult to deal with than the "classic" form?
- What are the typical forms of organization, tactics, and weapons used by terrorists?
- What are terrorists seeking to communicate by their actions? How do they shape their attacks to maximize their impact?
- What new weapons are becoming accessible to terrorists? How do they change the equation?
- What are the proper roles in counterterrorist strategy for the military? Intelligence agencies? The police?
- How can potential terrorist targets be "hardened" to make them less attractive to terrorists and to minimize the damage if they are attacked?
- What would be necessary for the international community to truly create a global strategy against terrorism?

The first step in trying to answer these questions is to come up with a reasonable definition of terrorism.

DEFINING TERRORISM

As with pornography, one's first impulse may be to say, "I may not be able to define it, but I know it when I see it." If a suicide bomb demolishes a restaurant in Israel, an airliner is hijacked by people armed with box cutters and crashed into a building, or a cult releases deadly nerve gas into the Tokyo subway, virtually all observers will agree that a terrorist act has occurred. But how does one define terrorism?

To start with the most restrictive characterization, in order to make laws about terrorism, one needs a legal definition. Here is the one used by the U.S. government:

> *The term "terrorism" means premeditated, politically motivated violence perpetrated against noncombatant targets by subnational groups or clandestine agents, usually intended to influence an audience.*[1]

The key parts of this definition are that the violence is motivated by political considerations, that it targets noncombatants (not soldiers engaged in military action), and that its perpetrators are not themselves part of a government.

Political analyst, security counselor, and White House adviser Brian Jenkins gives a somewhat expanded version of this definition of terrorism, noting that

> *All terrorist acts . . . involve violence or the threat of violence, often coupled with specific demands. The targets are mainly civilians. The motives are political. The actions generally are designed to achieve maximum publicity. The perpetrators are usually members of an organized group, and unlike other criminals, they often claim credit for the act. (This is a true hallmark of terrorism.) And, finally, it is intrinsic to a terrorist act that it is usually intended to produce psychological effects far beyond the immediate physical damage. One person's terrorist is everyone's terrorist.*[2]

The problem with these definitions is not that they are inaccurate, as far as they go, but that they are not complete enough to explain how terrorism relates to other forms of violence or to violent action by government itself. Although governments (which consider themselves to have a monopoly on legitimate force) never define their own actions as terrorism, many analysts speak also of "state terrorism" in describing, for example, the use of death squads by authoritarian Latin American governments to eliminate the political opposition. As noted by linguist and activist Noam Chomsky:

> *The term terrorism has come to be applied mainly to "retail terrorism" by individuals or groups. Whereas the term was once applied to Emperors who molest their own subjects and the world, now it is restricted to thieves who molest the powerful. Extricating ourselves from the system of indoctrination,*

we will use the term 'terrorism' to refer to the threat or use of violence to in-
timidate or coerce (generally for political ends), whether it is the wholesale
terrorism of the Emperor or the retail terrorism of the thief.[3]

The discussion of terrorism, then, must encompass not only political violence initiated by groups fighting against governments, but also terroristic
actions taken by governments themselves. That is because while the focus
of this and most books on terrorism is on the acts of nongovernmental terrorist groups, the context for understanding these acts must include the actions of governments that often foster "retail" terrorism by the wholesale
state terrorism that they have inflicted on their own people.

TERRORISM VERSUS WAR

If war has been described as politics by other means, is terrorism simply war
by other means? Or can terrorism be distinguished from war? Both war and
terrorism, after all, can create innocent victims. As Brian Jenkins notes: "Although we may make moral distinctions between dropping bombs on a city
from 20,000 feet and car bombs driven into embassies by suicidal terrorists,
the world may not share that fine distinction."[4]

Some of the more radical pundits argue that the only difference between
war and terrorism is that war kills a lot more people, and wars are fought by
governments. This seems simplistic, however. In the international legal system that has developed in the past century, wars are supposed to be fought
according to certain rules. One expert in the field states the following:

The fundamental principle underlying the whole structure of the interna-
tional humanitarian law applicable in armed conflicts is that belligerents
shall not inflict on their adversaries harm out of proportion to the legitimate
goals of warfare . . . for instance, that belligerents shall not kill their prison-
ers for, having captured them, they have to that extent weakened the mili-
tary forces of the enemy, and killing them would add nothing to this result.

[this implies that] (1) distinction shall be made at all times between bel-
ligerents and civilian populations; (2) the civilian population, as well as ob-
jects of civilian character, shall not be made the object of deliberate attacks; (3)
in attacking military objectives, any unreasonable damage to the civilian pop-
ulation and objects of civilian character shall be avoided; (4) no weapons or
other means and methods of warfare shall be used which are calculated to
cause unnecessary or otherwise excessive suffering.[5]

These laws are clearly not observed by terrorists. It can be argued that
terrorist violence is not "out of proportion" to its goals, because the goals of

terrorism are different from those of warfare. Both the terrorists and the military want to force their opponents to submit to certain demands. The military accomplishes this by destroying the opponents' ability to resist or by making it clear that the costs to the enemy of continuing to resist are worse than those of accepting the terms offered for surrender. The terrorist, however, does not have the means to destroy the government's ability to resist, but only, perhaps, to create a demoralizing fear that destroys the people's willingness to back the government. Thus most militaries do not want to kill prisoners, not only because doing so is felt to be dishonorable and it does not further weaken the enemy force, but also because one does not want one's own soldiers to be killed after they are captured. The terrorist, on the other hand, may choose to kill precisely because doing so heightens the fear effect that he or she is trying to achieve.

Attacking civilians or causing unnecessary damage is supposed to be avoided in war. Many militaries, including that of the United States, have *generally* avoided deliberately attacking civilians, but even here there have been exceptions, such as the massacre at My Lai during the Vietnam War. But despite the claims made for "smart weapons," which can supposedly distinguish between civilian and military buildings, in cases such as the U.S. bombing of Serbia in 1999 and of Iraq in 2003, deciding to conduct such attacks implies willingness to accept some amount of "collateral damage" (damage to areas other than the intended target) and killing of civilians.

Therefore, the difference between war and terrorism is not always one of effect, but of goals and purposes. The killing of civilians may be an accidental outcome of war, but it is often viewed as necessary by the terrorist.

TERRORISM AND REVOLUTION

Terrorists and revolutionaries are both seeking radical political change. While some revolutionaries target mainly the government they are trying to overthrow and its facilities and military forces, others are less discriminating. (Indeed, even the American Revolution, which is often looked upon as a relatively chivalrous battle between redcoats and bluecoats, included considerable terrorism against British loyalists on the part of colonists who supported the revolt as well as punitive raids by British forces.)

Further, doctrines of revolution such as those that spring from Marxism-Leninism actually see a role for terror as part of the revolutionary process. Leon Trotsky noted the following:

> *A victorious war, generally speaking, destroys only an insignificant part of the conquered army, intimidating the remainder and breaking their will. The revolution works in the same way: it kills individuals, and intimidates*

thousands. In this sense, the Red Terror is not distinguishable from the armed insurrection of which it is the direct continuation.[6]

There are, however, some distinctions that can be made between terrorism and revolution. Revolution generally implies an activity that is more focused on specific objectives, broader based in its support, and more systematic in its efforts than terrorism. A revolution (as distinguished from a mere coup) implies some base of support and some ability to create a new government to replace the old. However, an earlier terrorist campaign may create the conditions for revolution (which is indeed the hope of most terrorists), and a revolution may be accompanied by terrorist acts, either incidentally or by policy.

TERRORISM AND GUERRILLA WARFARE

If the relationship of terrorism to revolution seems difficult to pin down, the distinction between terrorism and guerrilla (or "unconventional") warfare is even more problematic. According to the U.S. military, this type of warfare consists of the following:

A broad spectrum of military and paramilitary operations conducted in enemy-held, enemy-controlled, or politically sensitive territory. Unconventional warfare includes, but is not limited to, the interrelated fields of guerrilla warfare, evasion and escape, subversion, sabotage, and other operations of a low visibility, covert or clandestine nature. These interrelated aspects of unconventional warfare may be prosecuted singly or collectively by predominately indigenous personnel, usually supported and directed by (an) external source(s) during all conditions of war or peace.[7]

In the latter part of the 20th century, guerrilla operations aimed at established governments were common, particularly in Latin America, Africa, and Southeast Asia. These conflicts have frequently included such actions as the burning of villages, assassinations of government officials such as local mayors, and even wholesale massacres. Viewed in themselves, these are certainly terrorist acts and imply that guerilla war includes terrorism. But the relationship between the two is complex. According to an expert on guerrilla warfare:

To claim that guerrilla [warfare] is necessarily coupled with terrorism is certainly grossly inaccurate. A number of important guerrilla movements steadily refused to resort to terrorism . . . And yet . . . The fact is that most of the contemporary guerrilla movements either habitually, or at various stages of their activities, use terrorism, at least as a form of revolutionary tactics.[8]

Nevertheless, while guerrillas often use terrorism (and governments, in turn, use terroristic tactics against guerrillas and the people who may be supporting them), guerrilla organizations are different from typical terrorist groups. While guerrillas generally conduct raids rather than seek pitched battles, they are equipped similarly to regular light military units, and they usually have military weapons such as mortars, grenade or rocket launchers, heavy machine guns, or even light artillery. They view themselves as soldiers under military-style discipline. Guerrilla forces may number from hundreds to thousands, and to be successful, they must be supported by a significant number of people who provide supplies and often concealment, whether because they share the guerrillas' objectives or because they fear retaliation. Although guerrillas frequently also depend on outside help (particularly for heavy weapons and military advisers), they have ties to the indigenous community.

In conducting their war, guerrillas sometimes observe at least an approximation of the laws of war that are supposed to govern conventional armies. They can take and exchange prisoners or negotiate with enemy commanders.

Terrorist groups, on the other hand, are typically small (tens or at most, hundreds). Their typical actions are bombings, ambushes, assassinations, hijackings, and kidnappings. Their weapons of choice are the homemade bomb and the automatic pistol. Many terrorist groups have little support from or interaction with the surrounding population. They are not organized along military lines, but typically in small cells. (See "How Terrorist Groups Work" for an explanation of cells.) Their demands and negotiations, if conducted at all, are for things like ransoms, safe passage, or the freeing of imprisoned comrades.

These distinctions appear in sharp relief when one compares, for example, the Vietcong of the 1960s or the Afghani resistance fighters of the early 1980s with a much smaller and much more isolated group like the Weathermen of the early 1970s or even the German Red Army Faction of about the same period. But as noted above, guerrillas sometimes use terrorist tactics, and it becomes rather pointless to try to determine whether certain groups such as Peru's Shining Path are terrorist or guerrilla organizations. Further, a group such as Hezbollah combines elements of a popular movement, a guerrilla force, and a terrorist organization. Hezbollah launches regular rocket attacks against Israel, but also provides people in the community with an extensive network of social services.

STATE TERRORISM

As noted, governments themselves have often used terrorist-style tactics against their opponents, including killing, torture, or kidnapping followed by "disappearance." The most devastating state terror comes when an ideological

9

faction controls a totalitarian state and targets its political enemies for virtual extermination. For example, the Chinese cultural revolution under Mao Ze-dong beginning in the mid-1960s and the regime of Cambodian dictator Pol Pot starting in the mid-1970s represented radical attempts to reshape society by any means necessary. Millions of real or suspected political enemies were killed, "reeducated," or dispossessed. Eventually such movements end because they destroy the ability of society to sustain itself or provoke overwhelming reactions such as the Vietnamese invasion of Cambodia in 1979.

State terrorism can be more subtle when it is part of an ongoing struggle between a regime and insurgent forces. It is frequently a "chicken-and-egg" question whether state terrorism is a response to provocation by insurgent terrorists or guerrillas or a basic policy that itself creates and sustains the conditions for insurgency.

One thing is clear: The state terrorism of the 20th century, from Adolf Hitler, Joseph Stalin, and Mao Zedong to the death squads of Argentina and Guatemala, has killed many more people than nongovernmental terrorist groups have. Of course, this does not justify the latter terror, but it is part of the context needed to understand it.

THE DEVELOPMENT OF MODERN TERRORISM

The use of terror is evident as far back as history has been recorded. The massacre of the inhabitants of a captured city was a common feature of warfare until the last few centuries. A would-be conqueror could expedite conquest by proclaiming that cities that refused to yield immediately would be razed and their inhabitants killed. In battle, given the hand weapons and massed formations used, most casualties were inflicted only after one side broke and ran. The conduct of politics via assassinations was also commonplace and resulted, for example, in the short terms of office of many later Roman emperors.

Nongovernmental groups also practiced early forms of terrorism. The word *assassin*, for example, derives from the name of a 13th-century Islamic sect that is said to have partaken of hashish before carrying out stabbing attacks on its political enemies. Other cultures, too, have had groups of stealthy killers, such as Japan's ninjas.

REVOLUTION AND STATE

While terror may have been common in the ancient and medieval world, the idea of terrorism as a conscious political tactic can be traced to the late 18th century, the beginning of the modern age of revolutions, when terror was systematically linked to political philosophies. French revolutionaries such as Robespierre embraced terror as a tool for political transformation as part of a total revolution in society. One scholar of terrorism notes that

> *One of the original justifications for terror was that man would be totally reconstructed; one didn't have to worry about the kinds of means one was using because the reconstruction itself would be total and there would be no lingering after-effects. . . . [Modern] terrorism was initiated by people who had millennial expectations, who expected the world to be utterly transformed.*[9]

Ultimate principles can be held to require ultimate actions. To assert, as the American colonists and then the French did, that the individual has "inalienable" rights is to suggest that extreme means may be necessary to secure or preserve those rights. Insurgents who felt themselves sufficiently justified could view terror as a means to attaining the transcendent value of liberty. States such as Revolutionary France (and in the 20th century, Revolutionary Russia) could also embrace terror, claiming that it was necessary in order to preserve the revolution. As early as 1790, a British conservative, Edmund Burke, referred to the new French government as "the reign of terror."

TERRORISM AND ANARCHY

During the 19th century, several forces led to the development of terrorist groups in Europe (particularly Russia) and to a lesser extent, in the United States. The ideas of political democracy and liberalism were spreading. But at the same time, industrialization was displacing large masses of people from the rural economy to the factory, where harsh and exploitative working conditions were typical. When workers tried to organize to demand better conditions, the response was often brutal suppression by the government, the employer's private police, or both.

One response to this situation was Karl Marx's development of the idea of socialism. In socialism, the people would own and benefit from the means of production. Marx saw an inherent struggle between workers and capitalists that could only be resolved by a process of revolution. He did not advocate individual acts of terrorism, however, but rather thought in terms of a mass movement led by an enlightened "vanguard."

Another group known as anarchists sought more immediate and radical change. Anarchists focused not on the mass but on the individual. They did not trust any government. Some anarchists believed in using only peaceful means. Others, such as Peter Kropotkin, a Russian, promoted universal anarchist revolution carried out through violence. He also proclaimed a key idea of modern terrorism, the "propaganda of the deed." This meant that rather than just issuing proclamations that could be ignored by opponents and the general public, the revolutionary would do things that could not be ignored—such as setting off bombs. Kropotkin also recognized, as modern terrorists do, that the media is an extremely necessary and useful tool because it disseminates news about the terrorists' deeds and hence amplifies their terrifying effect. The early terrorists also knew that some stories would be bigger than others. Thus German-American anarchist Johan Most observed as early as the 1880s that "Everyone now knows, for example, that the more highly placed the one shot or blown up, and the more perfectly executed the attempt, the greater the propagandistic effect."[10]

Another anarchist, Karl Heinzen, a German, was even more explicit in his tactics. When the European revolutions of 1848 failed to dislodge conservative governments, he concluded that revolutionaries could not successfully confront the government directly. Instead, they had to create chaotic, confused conditions that would paralyze authorities. The method he recommended for achieving this goal was widespread, indiscriminate use of bombs. In Russia, bombing and assassination became a persistent tactic of anarchists seeking to overthrow the czar.

AWAKENING NATIONALISM

The early 20th century saw the awakening of many nationalist and revolutionary impulses. For example, many Jews began to embrace Zionism and its vision of a Jewish state in Palestine. Many of the Arab peoples in the Middle East developed a stronger sense of their own nationhood. Both sides began to rebel against British colonialism. Some of that rebellion began to take the form of terrorism. Similarly, ethnic minorities that had been kept in a second-class position in their own land, such as Irish Catholics, began to develop revolutionary or terrorist organizations. Meanwhile, the Soviet Union began to organize a network of communist parties in many countries, which all sought a "proletarian revolution."

POSTCOLONIALISM AND THE COLD WAR

Following World War II, Britain and France, while part of the victorious alliance, had been seriously weakened economically. They did not have the strength both to rebuild their own economies and to vigorously defend their overseas colonies. Indigenous populations throughout what became known then as the "Third World" were desperately poor, while European elites controlled most of the countries' wealth and resources. A combination of instability, desperation, and the attractiveness of democratic ideals led to the emergence of popular uprisings, often taking forms ranging from sporadic terrorism to large-scale guerrilla warfare. For example, the Islamic population in France's colony of Algeria began a bloody struggle for independence in the 1950s. These uprisings were aided by the widespread availability relatively inexpensive but lethal weapons, ranging from war-surplus grenades and mortars to the ubiquitous AK-47 automatic rifle.

In Latin America, where most nations were already independent, the struggle took a different form. From Mexico south to Chile, most countries were ruled by some form of oligarchy in which an elite of established families and wealthy industrialists controlled most of the national wealth. There too, guerrilla groups, usually inspired by communist or socialist ideas, took up arms against the governments.

The cold war between the United States and the western democracies on one side and the Soviet Union and the communist bloc on the other inevitably became bound up in the postcolonial struggles. Communism offered an appealing alternative to the desperately poor. To contain it, the United States tended to support the oligarchs who promised to keep order and protect the investments of U.S. and other foreign corporations. In the 1970s, Noam Chomsky told U.S. citizens that they were supporting brutal, repressive governments:

> *The military juntas of Latin America and Asia are our juntas. Many of them were directly installed by us or are the beneficiaries of our direct intervention, and most of the others came into existence with our tacit support, using military equipment and training supplied by the United States. . . . Terror in these states is functional, improving the "investment climate," at least in the short run, and U.S. aid to terror-prone states . . . is positively related to terror and improvement of investment climate and negatively related to human rights.[11]*

Meanwhile, the Soviet Union offered weapons, training, and advisers to the rebel groups—not just in the hope of installing communist governments, but because embroiling the West in "brushfire wars" might distract and weaken it in the global struggle for supremacy. (Indeed, after the reunification of Germany in 1990, it was revealed that the East German intelligence service had secretly funded many of the leftist terrorist groups in western Europe.) In the Western Hemisphere, the overthrow of the Cuban government by Fidel Castro in 1960 offered the Soviets a base from which to encourage leftist revolutions and guerrilla wars throughout Central and South America.

The "proxy war" of terrorism and rebellion offered practical advantages to leaders on both sides of the Iron Curtain. As one contemporary observer noted, "the truth is, at a time when it is difficult to mobilize great masses of people without provoking a global conflict with irreparable damage, terrorism tends to become more and more a substitute for war."[12]

13

The result, according to terrorism expert Walter Laqueur, was that the cold war created a crescendo of terrorism around the world:

Multinational terrorism reached its climax in the early 1970s, involving close cooperation between small terrorist groups in many countries, with the Libyans, the Algerians, the North Koreans and the Cubans acting as pay-masters, suppliers of weapons and other equipment as well as coordinators. . . . The Soviet Union supported a number of terrorist movements such as some Palestinians and African groups and the exile Croats; mostly such assistance would be given through intermediaries so that its origins would be difficult to prove and any charges of complicity could be indignantly denied.”[13]

Two of the world's most persistent hotbeds of terrorism can also be de-scribed as legacies of colonialism. In the Middle East, contradictory British colonial policies begun during World War I had set Jews and Palestinians on a collision with each others' interests. After Israel had repeatedly demon-strated its military strength, Islamic extremists turned to terrorism as a weapon against the Jewish state and its American and European allies. Northern Ireland, too, was essentially a colony created by British policy since the 16th century. Some members of the Catholic population, frus-trated by their lack of rights and economic opportunity, turned to terrorism and the Irish Republican Army (IRA) in the 1970s.

Often joined with ideology, nationalism and ethnicity can provide a pow-erful bond that can sustain terrorist activity not only through solidarity but by denying ambiguity or the possible humanity of the opponent. As an Irish observer, Ed Cairns of the University of Ulster, has noted:

The practice of dividing people into "us" and "them" is so deeply ingrained that it's almost unconscious. It's as if there's a computer in the back of the head of every person who lives in Northern Ireland that's programmed to work out what side another person is on.[14]

Thus the wellsprings of later 20th century and early 21st century terror-ism are complex, deriving from the struggle against colonialism, the inspi-ration of communist or socialist ideology, and the bonds of nationalism, ethnicity, and religion. Often these factors are mixed together in the same movement. The IRA, for example, sometimes used Marxist rhetoric, yet represented an ethnic group that was defined in part by religion.

TERRORISM IN THE WESTERN DEMOCRACIES

Terrorist and revolutionary activity was not confined to the developing na-tions, however. The 1960s also saw a leftist movement, mostly on the part of intellectuals and students, in both Western Europe and the United States. In France, the movement also spread to the working class, while in the United States, despite the efforts of activists, it remained confined mainly to the student antiwar effort, the civil rights movements, and black and brown power movements.

Groups such as Germany's Red Army Faction, France's Action Directe, and Italy's Red Brigades based their ideology on Marxism-Leninism, emphasizing action against the government and capitalists in urban population centers. From roughly 1970 to the mid-1980s, they carried on extensive bombing campaigns as well as some shootings and kidnappings. In the United States, groups such as the Weathermen and New World Liberation Front carried on similar activities, but on a smaller scale.

From the mid-1980s through the first years of the 21st century, the focus of terrorism in the Western democracies seemed to shift from the Left to the Right. As Walter Laqueur observes:

> *Left-wing ideology was virtually all-pervasive in the 1970s, and this was reflected in the propaganda of nationalist groups such as the IRA, the Basque separatist group ETA, and the Palestinian terrorists—for example in anti-imperialist slogans and calls for working-class solidarity, and so on. . . .*
>
> *During the 1980s, left-wing terrorism petered out, a trend that coincided with the collapse of the Soviet bloc, though it was not caused by the collapse. Instead, the terrorist initiative in Western countries such as the United States, and also Germany and Turkey, moved to the extreme right. Yesterday's theories about the progressive character of terrorism ceased to make sense and became, in fact, embarrassing. The burning of a hostel housing foreign guest workers in Germany could hardly be described any longer as a liberating act. Neither could the[first] bombing of the World Trade Center in New York or the bombing of a government building in Oklahoma City be interpreted as a prologue to a revolution that would help the masses. The old wisdom about one person's terrorist being another person's freedom fighter was no longer heard.[15]*

In the future, ideological terrorism may come from both the Right and Left in response to globalism. The Left opposes economic globalism—the control of the world's economic resources by multinational corporations—and decries what it sees as the inability of democratic governments to hold the economic behemoths accountable. The Right views political globalism in the form of the United Nations and other institutions as a threat to the sovereignty of countries, regions, and localities. Extremists on both sides have shown their willingness to use violence in order to be heard.

Global Terrorism

THE NEW TERRORISM

In the early 1990s the fall of the Soviet Union, the end of the cold war, and some glimmerings of peace in Northern Ireland and even in the Middle East had begun to suggest that the era of large scale terrorism might be drawing to an end. By the end of the decade, however, experts such as Walter Laqueur began to sound the alarm about a "new terrorism" that was strikingly different from traditional terrorism in both motives and methods. According to Laqueur:

> *Traditional terrorism, whether of the separatist or the ideological (left or right) variety, had political and social aims, such as gaining independence, getting rid of foreigners, or establishing a new social order. Such terrorist groups aimed at forcing concessions, sometimes far-reaching concessions, from their antagonists. The new terrorism is different in character, aiming not at clearly defined political demands but at the destruction of society and the elimination of large sections of the population. In its most extreme form, this new terrorism intends to liquidate all satanic forces, which may include the majority of a country or of mankind, as a precondition for the growth of another, better, and in any case different breed of human. In its maddest, most extreme form it may aim at the destruction of all life on earth, as the ultimate punishment for mankind's crimes.[16]*

During the 1990s groups such as Japan's Aum Shinrikyo cult (which used Sarin nerve gas in the Tokyo subway) showed that the potential for apocalyptic terrorism existed. The same fanaticism that cults such as the Branch Davidians or Heaven's Gate brought to their self-immolation could be as easily turned to the destruction of others.

Al-Qaeda, the most devastatingly successful modern terrorist group, also shares some of the characteristics of postmodern terrorism. While not quite apocalyptic, it is certainly absolutist. Al-Qaeda seeks the imposition of its distorted version of Islam through a theocracy in Egypt, Saudi Arabia, and the other countries of the Middle East. It views Israel, the United States, and Russia as "satans" that must be utterly destroyed. Moderate governments are viewed almost as vehemently.

The new terrorism of fanatics poses difficult problems for counterterrorism. Because such groups are not interested in political gains or such things as money or the freedom of prisoners, negotiation with them can be fruitless. And according to Canadian strategic analyst Ron Purver,

> *What makes these groups especially dangerous is that they may not be constrained by some of the political disincentives—fear of alienating potential*

supporters or of unleashing massive government retribution, etc.—that may have operated in the past in the case of more traditional terrorist groups.[17]

The most troubling aspect of the new terrorism its potential access to weapons of mass destruction (WMD)—chemical, biological, or even nuclear. With such weapons any terrorist attack can be an unprecedented disaster. Because the new terrorist groups do not experience the constraints of traditional political terrorist groups, they may feel little inhibition against the use of such weapons.

WHO IS THE TERRORIST?

Because terrorism like any human activity is ultimately carried out by individuals, it is necessary to look at individual motivation. Although the ideologies and motives that inspire terrorism and the role of terrorism in particular conflicts differ considerably, scholars have tried to identify some more or less universal characteristics of terrorists and the structure and operation of terrorist groups. These continue to operate (with some distinctions) even with the "new terrorism."

As David Rapoport notes, the terrorist is someone who has made radical decisions about issues that society would generally prefer to avoid:

The terrorist acts in an environment where the society has a good deal of ambivalence about the cause the terrorist is concerned with. Society is unwilling to come to grips with the cause the terrorist is proposing, but will ignore the cause unless it finds it cannot do so. What the terrorist does is indicate that he is willing to die or sacrifice himself for the cause. . . . One problem with contemporary definitions of terrorism, because they focus on the killing, is that they really can't see why somebody like the IRA, for example, would engage in hunger strikes; how that really performs the same functions, and even performs it better than killing does sometimes. . . . Whether the violence is inflicted on oneself or on others, it's the striking character of the act which, first of all, calls attention and secondly . . . galvanizes latent emotions.[18]

However, the line between peaceful and violent response to social conditions is not always a bright one. Most people who are not pure pacifists can visualize some conditions under which they would use force to resist or change what they consider to be intolerable conditions. As Douglas Pike has concluded:

What seems more to the point is not language but thought pattern, world view, philosophy of politics . . . what are the limits of force, irrational violence, terror, in that ascending order, in bringing about social change? All of us fall somewhere along this force-violence-terror continuum. Toward one end are those who believe that less rather than more is justified; toward the other are those who advocate more on grounds of imperative need or as principle . . .[19]

However, where terrorists have chosen to place themselves on the continuum of violence is a product of personality and psychology as well as commitment to ideology. According to political sociologist I. L. Horowitz's study of the biographies of terrorists, one can draw some general conclusions about the attitudes of people who engage in terrorism and the beliefs or expectations they have about the results of their actions:

1. *A terrorist is a person engaged in politics who makes little if any distinction between strategy and tactics on one hand, and principles on the other. . . .*

2. *A terrorist is a person prepared to surrender his own life for a cause considered transcendent in value. . . .*

3. *A terrorist is a person who possesses both a self-fulfilling prophetic element and a self-destructive element*

4. *A terrorist is a person for whom all events are volatile and none are determined. . . .*

5. *A terrorist is a person who is (a) young; (b) most often of middle class family background; (c) usually male; and (d) economically marginal. . . .*

6. *A terrorist performs his duties as an avocation. . . .*

7. *The terrorist distinguishes himself from the casual homicide in several crucial respects: he murders systematically rather than at random; he is symbolic rather than passionate . . . and his actions are usually well planned rather than spontaneous. Terrorism is thus primarily a sociological phenomenon; whereas homicide can be more easily interpreted in psychological terms. . . .*

8. *The terrorist by definition is a person who does not distinguish between coercion and terrorism because he lacks access to the coercive mechanisms of the state.*

9. *A terrorist is a person who, through the act of violence, advertises and dramatizes a wider discontent. . . .*

10. *A terrorist believes that the act of violence will encourage the uncommitted public to withdraw support from a regime or institution, and hence make wider revolutionary acts possible by weakening the resolve of the opposition.*

11. *A terrorist may direct his activities against the leadership of the opposition by assassinating presidents and power holders. . . . Other terrorists*

> *may direct their activities against the symbols of establishment and agencies. . . .*

12. *A terrorist does not have a particularly well-defined ideological persuasion.*[20]

An important part of a terrorist's psychology is the attitude toward the group. As is well known, being in a group can add a dimension of intensity to any activity. In speaking of revolutionary groups, Arthur Koestler makes an observation that is equally applicable to terrorists:

> *The total identification of the individual with the group makes him unselfish in more than one sense. . . . It makes him perform comradely, altruistic, heroic actions—to the point of self-sacrifice—and at the same time behave with ruthless cruelty toward the enemy or victim of the group. In other words, the self-assertive behavior of the group is based on the self-transcending behavior of its members, which often entails sacrifice of personal interests and even of life in the interest of the group. To put it simply: the egotism of the group feeds on the altruism of its members.*[21]

The growing use of suicide bombing (first used extensively by the Tamil Tigers but now featured by the al-Aqsa Martyrs Brigade and other groups against Israel) is also a characteristic of modern terrorism that draws upon the ability to psychologically manipulate (usually young) idealists. Although terrorists in the past have sometimes been willing to blow themselves up, what is distinctive about today's suicide terrorism is its systematic organization. Walter Laqueur points out that

> *The suicide terrorist is only the last link in a chain. There is no spontaneous suicide terrorism. The candidates are chosen by those in charge of the organization. The suicide terrorists are organized and trained—receiving intelligence information to guide them—and eventually given the arms and explosives to carry out their mission. The people who guide the suicide terrorists have their political agenda. They organize the missions not as a purposeless manifestation of despair but to attain a certain political aim.*[22]

HOW TERRORIST GROUPS WORK

The terrorist group may offer psychological reinforcement to the individual, but it also serves more immediately practical purposes. Although individuals (such as Theodore Kaczynski, the Unabomber, or Oklahoma City bombers Timothy McVeigh and Terry Nichols) can sometimes strike grievous blows, a sustained terrorist campaign requires organization and resources.

Global Terrorism

According to counterterrorism specialist James Fraser, a "classic" terrorist group is organized something like a pyramid. At the very top are a few leaders who make the overall policy and plans. Below them is a somewhat larger group of terrorists who actually carry out attacks. This is called the *active cadre*. Members of the active cadre often specialize in particular activities, such as intelligence or surveillance, bomb-making, or communications. The next lower and broader level of the pyramid is composed of the "active supporters." These people are crucial for the sustained operation of the terrorist campaign, because they provide intelligence and warning, weapons and supplies, communications, transportation, and safe houses. Finally, there is a diffuse group of "passive supporters" who agree with the goals of the terrorist group, help spread their ideas, and provide money and other support.

The neatness of this organizational scheme is somewhat misleading, however. Most terrorist groups are small, with fewer than 50 members. The same individuals may play several roles or shift rapidly from one role to another. Most terrorist groups receive little public support, and so do not have access to the resources needed to mount a major campaign.

Terrorist groups face very difficult challenges. First of all, they have to keep their members' identity and/or whereabouts secret. After all, the police or army generally has more than enough force to overwhelm any terrorists they can locate. Since the 19th century, terrorists have used a specialized structure that seeks to preserve secrecy. The active terrorists are divided into groups of about five people, called cells. Each cell is usually organized for a particular role, such as tactical assault or intelligence. Generally the members of a cell do not know anyone outside the cell. Communications are maintained by the cell leader, who might communicate with only one other cell leader. When an operation is planned, leaders can link several cells together operationally into a "column," so that intelligence, support, and combat functions can be brought to bear.

The cell system seeks to preserve secrecy by limiting the amount of information authorities can learn. If a cell member is captured and interrogated, he or she ideally knows only the identities of other people in the same cell. But the same compartmentalization that serves secrecy also makes communication within, and coordination of, the group very difficult. If something in an operation starts to go wrong, or the police mount a raid or sweep, it may be hard to alert the group members to abort or change the operation or to evacuate and go into hiding.

Especially in a large group such as the Provisional Irish Republican Army, because most members lack direct access to the leadership, they cannot always verify the authenticity of orders or give feedback to the leaders. It is fairly easy for one or a few leaders and the chain of command that reports to them to splinter or split off, creating a new faction.

An even more amorphous type of organization can be found in some modern terrorist groups such as radical antiabortion and Christian fundamentalist groups and ecoterrorists such as the Earth Liberation Front (ELF) and Animal Liberation Front (ALF). These groups hardly even exist as organizations. Individuals or small groups of individuals carry out actions in the name of the group. Proclamations are often communicated via web sites run by uninvolved sympathizers. Because there are no identified leaders, it is especially hard for authorities to track down such groups.

How competent are terrorists at their trade? Although intelligence experts have identified mistakes in "tradecraft" and communications security on the part of al-Qaeda's September 11 attack team, it must be said that they only identified them after the twin towers had been destroyed. Al-Qaeda had been competent enough to achieve its purpose.

If a terrorist group finds itself pinned down in a sustained conflict, however, it is likely to lose. Compared to soldiers in a conventional military unit, members of a terrorist group may individually have high morale (indeed, the impetus of fanaticism can go beyond normal morale). But the terrorist group usually lacks the systematic discipline and training of a military unit, even if it calls itself an army and adopts military nomenclature.

HOW TERRORISTS COMMUNICATE

Unlike homicidal maniacs, terrorists kill for a reason. That reason is to communicate a message that will instill fear in the enemy government and demoralize it. Thus

> *Terrorism . . . can cause enormous problems for democratic governments because of its impact on the psychology of great masses of citizens. . . . Terrorist bombings, assassinations, and hostage-taking have, in nations with a free press, the ability to hold the attention of vast populations.[23]*

Given the importance to terrorists that their actions "send a message" that will compel opponents to respond, students of communications theory can usefully examine terrorism from the perspective of the problems with successful communication. Thus Philip A. Karber suggests the following:

> *As a symbolic act, terrorism can be analyzed much like other mediums of communication, consisting of four basic components: transmitter (terrorist), intended recipient (target), message (bombing, ambush) and feed-back (reaction of target). The terrorist's message of violence necessitates a victim, whether personal or institutional, but the target or intended recipient of the*

communication may not be the victim. . . . Terrorism is subject to many of the same pathologies and disruptions suffered by more conventional forms of communication. These include lack of fidelity in the medium of transmission (the choice of victim conveys wrong message to target), background noise (competing events obscure the message), target distortion (recipient misinterprets the meaning of the one signal and fails to regulate output to changing circumstances or target feedback). . . .

However, if terrorism is to be conceived of as "propaganda of the deed," we must devise a content analysis of symbolic violence.[24]

In a world of 24-hour cable news and the Internet, the terrorist can be sure that news of any significant attack will be spread almost instantly, complete with graphic pictures of the carnage. The relationship between terrorism and the media is complex, however. The media is not simply a mirror or even a passive amplifier; it both reflects and shapes the public response. The public response to terror is usually begins with shock and rage and continues with a demand that something be done to prevent future attacks. Thus following the 1995 Oklahoma City bombing, public anxiety and outrage were translated in a year or so into the passage by Congress of an antiterrorism act that gave the government new legal tools and correspondingly diminished civil liberties. The same happened even more quickly and on a larger scale following the September 11, 2001, attacks.

A venerable strategy of terrorists is to provoke the government into repressive measures in the hope that this in turn will cause unrest or revolt. When the terrorist group is small and local, this strategy has more often than not backfired, resulting in the destruction of the terrorists themselves. However, when terrorism is international in scope, such a definitive conclusion is unlikely. Rather, there is likely to be an ebb and flow of activity, with some groups being suppressed (at least for a time) only to have others emerge.

COUNTERTERRORISM

Counterterrorism can be defined as the attempt to prevent terrorism or at least reduce its frequency and severity. Understanding the terrorist's psychology, motivations, organization and goals is an important part of this effort. Another part is the use of intelligence, including surveillance, eavesdropping, informers, and devices to detect bombs and weapons, such as those in airports.

INTELLIGENCE

The first line of defense against terrorists is the attempt to find out who they are and what they are up to. This can be done through eavesdropping or monitoring telephone or computer communication, giving rewards for information, sending undercover agents to infiltrate terrorist groups, or using paid informants. But none of these tools can be 100 percent effective, nor are they always used in timely fashion.

As the initial shock of the September 11, 2001, attacks began to wear off, the question of whether the attacks could have been detected and prevented naturally arose. What clues, had they been shared and acted upon in time, might have led perhaps to the team of 20 hijackers being rounded up before they could board the four planes? As both secret congressional committees and the media began to try to "connect the dots" they found clues that in retrospect many would say should have alerted the FBI and CIA that something big was in the offing.

Al-Qaeda was already suspected of conducting an escalating series of increasingly ambitious attacks, including the embassy bombings in Africa and the attack on the warship U.S.S. *Cole*. There were warnings that al-Qaeda was infiltrating people into the United States and setting up "sleeper cells" who were trained and ready to be activated. There were reports of students apparently of Middle East extraction in flight schools—students who seemed more interested in steering jetliners than in landing them.

Of course patterns are always much easier to see in hindsight. Each warning, each bit of "chatter" found in eavesdropped communications that now seems to point to the attacks on the World Trade Center and Pentagon was embedded in a sea of other items suggesting other targets and types of attacks.

The more important lessons that might be drawn have to do with how intelligence is gathered and shared. In the wake of September 11 institutional and legal barriers have been relaxed to allow the FBI (primarily a domestic law enforcement agency) and the CIA (an intelligence agency restricted to foreign intelligence) as well as other agencies to share intelligence and try to put pieces of the puzzle together in "real time." Cooperation with foreign intelligence agencies such as those of Great Britain, Germany, Italy, and even Pakistan has also improved.

What kind of data is most likely to prove useful in identifying and tracking terrorists? According to Paul Wilkinson of the Centre for the Study of Terrorism and Political Violence at the University of St. Andrews, the vital items include:

- *data on the activities of groups and individuals suspected of involvement in terrorism;*
- *information concerning the forgery or falsification of travel documents;*
- *intelligence on trafficking in explosives, weapons, or nuclear, biological, or chemical material which could be used by terrorists, and on activities*

by individuals or groups pointing to the possibility of terrorists using chemical, biological, radiological and nuclear (CBRN) attacks or threats;

- *information on the use of sophisticated communications technology by terrorist groups, for example the use of encryption, and*

- *intelligence on links between terrorists and international organised crime, especially using drug trafficking.*[25]

HOMELAND SECURITY

Besides trying to improve intelligence the United States and other developed countries have also responded to the threat of global terrorist activity by giving higher priority to domestic security efforts. In the United States this effort resulted in 2002 in the establishment of a Department of Homeland Security that has taken over the function of many federal agencies, including the Immigration and Naturalization Service, the Secret Service, and the Coast Guard (but not the FBI).

Any domestic security effort has two basic parts. The first is improved coordination of intelligence efforts (as described earlier) and the attempt to turn intelligence into meaningful warnings or interventions that might anticipate and block terrorist attacks. In 2002–2003 there was some success in arresting alleged terrorist cells or support networks, but the official color-coded terror threat levels were widely seen to be less than useful, as were the several rather nonspecific warnings that were issued after September 11, 2001.

The effectiveness of creating new bureaucracies and realigning existing ones is always difficult to assess. In the United States the existence of three separate levels of law enforcement (federal, state, and local) also complicates matters. The government has attempted to enlist citizens in efforts to watch for and report suspicious activity, but both the value and propriety of such snooping has been questioned. After all, such activities have generally been associated not with democracies but with totalitarian societies.

HARDENING THE TARGET

The second part of homeland security is improving the protection of infrastructure—the facilities that make transportation, the provision of necessities such as power and water, and the activities of daily life possible. If the government's intelligence services cannot uncover a pending attack, perhaps the target can be made difficult for the terrorist to penetrate. This generally means the installation of detection or screening systems. But what does one protect, and how much? Counterterrorists (and the governments they work for) do not have unlimited resources. Spending money to guard against one thing means not having it to use against something else.

The issue of airport security is a classic example of this dilemma. Because of the devastating effect of using hijacked airliners as flying bombs, much of the recent hardening efforts have focused on airports. A new Transportation Security Agency was established and responsibility for passenger and baggage screening was taken from the airlines and turned over to federal employees.

Strengthening security could take the form of improved training for airport personnel, in addition to the deployment of new technology. For example, a scanning device called the CTX 5000, deployed in some airports in the late 1990s, uses the same three-dimensional imaging technique as a hospital CAT scan, making it much easier to identify weapons or other suspicious objects. Other devices under development will be able to chemically "sniff" for vapors given off by explosives.

However, there are prices to be paid for such new advances in both cost and convenience. The new detectors are still very expensive. Another proposal, requiring that every bag be matched to verify that its owner is on board, is gradually being implemented. In many airports in Europe and the Middle East, passengers go through not one or two screenings but a dozen or more. It is unlikely that U.S. travelers, who place such a premium on convenience and speed, would accept such a situation even in the present climate.

The practice of using "profiles" (sets of characteristics that correlate with a "typical" terrorist) raises important questions. While the specific criteria used are kept secret, some obvious examples might include origin, destination, and method of payment (cash payment is considered suspicious). However, representatives of ethnic groups frequently associated in the public mind with terrorism (such as Arab Americans) have suggested that ethnicity is being used implicitly as a criterion, although authorities deny this.

Some of the techniques used to try to keep terrorists out of airports can also be applied to other major public facilities such as transit stations, power plants, office complexes, and even entertainment venues. Surveillance cameras are already common, particularly in British cities. Authorities are now experimenting with computerized facial recognition systems that could potentially identify suspected terrorists from the facial images caught in cameras. Another approach is to require positive identification for access, through the use of biometric devices that would compare identifying characteristics (such as facial or hand geometry or retinal patterns) with stored database records.

WEAPONS OF MASS DESTRUCTION

The fact that no system of surveillance, intelligence and hardening can be expected to prevent all attacks becomes more significant when one considers potential terrorist weapons that could be both harder to detect than a hijacked airliner and far more deadly. Starting in the late 1990s experts began to warn of the potential for terrorists obtaining and using weapons of mass destruction (WMD), such as chemical, biological, and nuclear or radiological weapons.

Chemical weapons are clearly available to terrorist groups, either through "homebrew" means or rogue states. In Japan, Aum Shinrikyo deliberately focused on recruiting people with the necessary technical skills for its 1995 nerve gas attack on the Tokyo subway, and it explored a range of chemical, biological, and even radiological options.

The story is much the same with biological agents. Until recently, it has been fairly easy for terrorists to order pathogens (disease microbes) simply by posing as medical researchers. In 1995, Larry Wayne Harris, a white supremacist, was convicted of having obtained three vials of bubonic plague bacteria using a fake letterhead.

The mysterious (and as yet unsolved) mail-borne anthrax attacks that killed four people in October 2001 are suspected to be the work of a single individual. While not terribly effective, the anthrax attacks caused considerable psychological stress and economic damage to the Postal Service, as well as shutting down Congress for several days.

Biological attack need not be particularly high tech. In 1984, members of the Rajneesh cult in Oregon faced the prospect of a local vote to restrict the use of the land on their commune. Two of the cultists decided to sidetrack the voters from the polls. They cultured a batch of *Salmonella* (bacteria that can cause serious food poisoning) and then spread the material into salad bars and coffee creamers at 10 local restaurants and in supermarket produce bins. More than 750 people became ill, though no one died.

Compared to a traditional bomb, a chemical or biological weapon (CBW) may be potentially more deadly, but it can also be more dangerous to the user and less reliable. People untrained in the safe handling of such materials may well kill themselves before they have the opportunity to kill others. The delivery of chemical and biological weapons requires that they be dispersed in such a way that many people will be exposed. A rocket or bomb with a CBW warhead may be ineffective because the explosion of the warhead destroys the toxic agent, disperses it prematurely, or unfavorable winds intervene.

Because terrorists may try to avoid these problems by introducing toxic agents directly into a city water supply or a building's air supply, guarding these points of entry can provide some security against attack. Other prevention measures include the closer tracking of the distribution of biological agents, the development of new, inexpensive detection systems, and the stockpiling of vaccines in case a more virulent disease such as smallpox is unleashed by terrorists. In general good public health measures are also good antiterrorism measures.

Terrorists have traditionally favored attacks on discrete, highly visible, symbolic targets, such as public buildings or officials. They have generally sought to kill or maim people directly. However, a "new terrorist" or an unfriendly foreign power that seeks to strike a truly crippling blow against a nation may well target its vital if less visible infrastructure instead. As Thomas W. Franzier, president of GenCon, a conference dealing with genetics and biological resources notes:

> *The U.S. has around a five-day supply of foods for the table. If food shipments were interrupted, it would be only a matter of a few days until many kinds of foods become unavailable. Hoarding would occur with an effective attack on a critical infrastructure such as the national power grid or telephone grid. And introducing a deadly zoonotic [animal-affecting] pathogen into a large number of meat animals could destroy domestic and foreign markets for that species. Attacking critical infrastructures with biological agents is quite feasible today.*[26]

Nuclear terrorism is the biggest nightmare for most people. A nuclear explosion, after all, would fulfill the most fanatic terrorist's apocalyptic desires in the most visible possible way. But nuclear weapons are even more difficult for terrorists to handle than biological or chemical ones are. With so many nuclear warheads being stored under conditions of uncertain security in the former Soviet Union, it is possible terrorists might be able to buy or steal a ready-made nuclear weapon. But nuclear warheads have complex safety interlocks, and it has been proposed that the weapons be fitted with devices that would allow them to be remotely destroyed or disabled if terrorists obtain them. U.S. agencies since the 1990s have sought closer coordination between U.S. and former Soviet scientists and engineers in order to secure the nuclear stockpiles.

Building a nuclear weapon from stolen fissionable material is also possible but would require considerable training. Refining the fissionable material from uranium is possible, given the resources of a rogue state. The United States used Saddam Hussein's alleged attempt to develop nuclear weapons as one of the reasons to justify removing him from power in April 2003 (though little evidence for such a program was found.) As of fall 2003 North Korea's announcement that it would become a nuclear weapons–owning state was causing considerable consternation, especially because that nation is also developing missiles with increased range. But the consequences to a nation giving terrorists access to a nuclear weapon would be so severe that such a scenario seems unlikely.

A perhaps more likely threat is that terrorists will create a "radiological weapon," also known as a "dirty bomb." Such a weapon would not create the devastating explosion of a nuclear weapon, but, rather, would use conventional explosives to scatter radioactive materials (such as waste from a nuclear reactor or a radiation source from a medical device) over a large area. Since such nuclear waste is currently stored at many nuclear power plants and medical facilities, it is quite plausible that terrorists could obtain some, and it would then be a simple matter to create a bomb that would disperse it.

Experts believe that such a weapon would be mainly psychological in effect. Many Americans have a fear of radiation that is out of proportion to its actual danger. The Federation of American Scientists has estimated that such a bomb, perhaps containing a radiation source from a food irradiation machine, if exploded in Manhattan might increase the chance of death from cancer for persons exposed to the most concentrated radiation by 1 in 100. Given that everyone's chance of eventually dying from cancer is already about 25 in 100, this would mean simply raising it to 26. Most deaths would likely be from the explosion itself.

However, a "dirty bomb" attack might also have considerable economic impact. If current EPA regulations were enforced after an attack, large areas might be declared uninhabitable and might not be able to be decontaminated to a sufficient degree.

Given that terrorists can probably obtain weapons of mass destruction, how likely is it that they would in fact do so? Jonathan B. Tucker and Amy Sands, two researchers at the Center for Nonproliferation Studies at the Monterey Institute of International Studies in Monterey, California, believes that the relatively small number of chemical and biological attacks, mostly outside the United States, may be because

> *Historically, traditional terrorist organizations have eschewed chemical or biological agents for several reasons, including unfamiliarity with the relevant technologies, the hazards and unpredictability of toxic agents, moral constraints, concern that indiscriminate casualties could alienate current or future supporters, and fear that a mass-casualty attack could bring down the full repressive power of the affected government on their heads.*[27]

This implies that the future risk of terrorist attacks with weapons of mass destruction may be dependent on whether the nature of terrorists and their motives is indeed changing as Walter Laqueur suggested. Brian Jenkins believes that there are

> *two kinds of situations that lead entities that use violence to abandon the constraints of moral and political order that stop them from using weapons of*

mass destruction. The first is connected with ethnic or racial conflicts where the goal is genocide. The second happens when these entities put themselves on the fringe of the political and social systems and enter into religious fanaticism, believing sincerely that they have the mandate of God.[28]

The various types of mass destruction terrorist attacks generally require similar types of response on the part of federal and local authorities. Mock WMD attack drills have now become almost as commonplace in major cities as traditional disaster exercises. Experts in emergency medicine write articles on the training of "first responders" in mass attack situations. As Seattle, Washington, fire chief A. D. Vickery notes:

The public safety first responder needs to be taught and provided necessary equipment to manage a situation (such as in a weapons of mass destruction incident that could involve biological or chemical weapons). This includes confining and isolating an incident; detecting, decontaminating and treating large numbers of people on the scene; organizing regional capabilities; and having initial capabilities within the city or town for about 24 hours until federal assistance can arrive.[29]

CYBERTERRORISM

Perhaps the least tangible terrorist attack is one that targets information systems that have become essential to all aspects of modern life. Computer users have become familiar in recent years with computer viruses and worms such as Blaster that can spread like wildfire through networks and hamper computer operations or even destroy data. The Internet has also proven to be vulnerable, not only to hackers or crackers who can steal sensitive financial or other information, but to a simple brute force approach called a "denial of service attack." In February 2000, major commercial web sites such as Amazon.com, Yahoo!, and eBay were bombarded by a flood of information requests that had been launched from programs that had been spread earlier via a virus. The information flood made it difficult or impossible for users to buy things on the web and thus cost the online merchants at least some short-term cash flow.

Since that time a seemingly never ending succession of "evolving" viruses have taken advantage of flaws in computer operating software or exploited the carelessness or gullibility of users that leads them to open unfamiliar e-mail attachments. Microsoft and other vendors have fought back by trying to provide software "patches" promptly to block the attacks, as well as software that scans for and blocks viruses and firewalls that detect and block unauthorized Internet activity.

While not being able to buy a product online or get one's e-mail immediately is a relatively minor inconvenience, attacks on the computers that control critical functions such as power and air traffic control could cause more direct economic damage and even loss of life. On the other hand, these critical computers tend to be more closely guarded and isolated from direct access via the Internet. The ease of entry into such systems is probably overrated, but the massive power outage in the northeastern United States and Canada in August 2003 reminds people that the power grid is sensitive to even relatively minor disruptions.

A variety of computer security measures have been proposed and are being implemented to varying degrees:

- Improving national monitoring centers that give early warning of attacks
- Increasing the number of highly trained computer security experts and investigators
- Training system administrators and users in how to recognize hacker attacks and the "social engineering" techniques hackers often use to trick people into revealing their passwords
- Creating more "intelligent" software that can act as a cyber "immune system," automatically adapting to, targeting, and neutralizing viruses. Indeed, it might be possible to create "benign" viruses that, like vaccines, could protect systems from infection.

Another aspect of cyberterrorism is the use of computer systems and the Internet by terrorists themselves. Many of the groups certified as terrorists by the U.S. Department of State have their own web sites, which they use to spread their message. Freely available encryption programs offer terrorists the opportunity to coordinate their operations using e-mail that is difficult for the government or any outsider to read. The National Security Agency (NSA) is rumored to be using massive quantities of supercomputing power to crack codes being used on the web. An international surveillance program called Echelon was recently revealed by civil libertarians. Echelon apparently has the capability to process and screen massive amounts of communications including satellite transmissions, cell phone calls, and computer messages.

The federal government fought an unsuccessful battle in the mid-1990s to restrict the export and use of the most secure encryption systems. As a practical matter, there is no way to prevent the spread of either information or software on the worldwide, decentralized Internet. Further, businesses demand high-quality encryption to protect their data. Another government proposal, the Clipper Chip, would have offered such encryption built into the PC itself, but at a price—the government would have a key that it could use to unlock any message, presumably after having obtained a court order. But civil libertarians have waged a major campaign against this proposal, and a related proposal to require that encryption users provide a copy of their code key in a "key escrow" from which the government could retrieve it. Libertarians believe that potential for government abuse of such snooping abilities is simply too great to permit their use.

FIGHTING THE WAR ON TERRORISM

There are basically three kinds of tools that might be used carry the battle to terrorists around the world. The criminal law and legal system can be used to prosecute terrorist suspects. The military can be used to destroy terrorist infrastructure (bases, training camps, and so on) or to punish or overthrow regimes that sponsor terrorism. Finally, diplomatic efforts and international cooperation can be pursued in the hope that nations can work together to prevent the free movement of terrorists around the world as well as improving the often desperate economic and political conditions that often inspire insurgency and terrorism. However, each of these tools has both shortcomings and potentially serious negative effects.

BALANCING SECURITY AND LIBERTY

Major terrorist attacks often lead to attempts to expand the legal powers of the government to investigate, apprehend, and detain terrorist suspects. Each time this happens there is a renewed debate on whether measures touted as necessary and effective for fighting terrorism would also sacrifice too much of the fundamental liberties proclaimed by the constitutions of the United States and those of most developed democracies—freedom of expression and association, personal privacy, and the right to due process of law in criminal proceedings.

At least initially, a majority of the population tends to go along with proposed new antiterrorism measures. For example a survey by the Institute for Social Research in March 2002 (that is, about six months after the September 11 attacks) found that seven in 10 Americans were willing to give up at least some of their civil liberties if it would improve security.

Since the 1970s the FBI had been restricted in its ability to investigate domestic political and cultural groups because of its history of infiltrating and disrupting such groups in the 1960s. There was also supposed to be a bright line between the FBI's pursuit of intelligence in the domestic sphere and the CIA in the international arena. After the September 11 attacks the administration suggested that this wall between the two agencies had been one of the things preventing them from "connecting the dots" and forestalling the terrorists.

New guidelines promulgated in 2002 allow for the two agencies to share information, and for foreign intelligence to be used in domestic criminal prosecutions. Further, the FBI can now investigate groups that it believes might have some connection to terrorism, without having the kind of specific information that would be needed to get a warrant. Critics fear that the result will be secret, unaccountable, wide-ranging intrusions into communities such as Arab Americans. The result might be a "chilling effect" on groups that fear hidden informers and a reluctance to engage in demonstrations or other legitimate political activities. This would threaten both freedom of association and freedom of expression.

Surveillance has also been made easier and more flexible. Instead of requiring specific permission to tap particular communications devices, a "roving wiretap" warrant now allows tapping and tracing any means of communication used by a suspect, whether cell phone, land line, or e-mail. While that seems reasonable granted the realities of modern communications technology and granted that someone is a legitimate suspect in the first place, the upshot is that this wider net is likely to inadvertently draw into its net communications from third parties. E-mail and Internet surveillance is also broader under the new guidelines, potentially compromising the privacy of Internet users who have nothing to do with the investigation, and "chilling" web site operators. "Sneak and peak" warrants, which allow surveillance without informing the subject for weeks or even months, are now easier to obtain.

A more serious concern to many legal experts is the blurring of the line between foreign intelligence gathering (covered by the Foreign Intelligence Surveillance Act of 1978) and domestic criminal investigation. FISA's standards for initiating surveillance are less restrictive than those for obtaining a regular criminal warrant. Now, apparently, as long as a "significant purpose" of an investigation is obtaining foreign intelligence, the FISA standard can be used, and domestic law enforcement agencies may be tempted to conjure up some sort of intelligence connection to what are properly domestic crimes.

There are also wider-ranging surveillance projects that are not directed to particular individuals and do not require warrants. The Terrorism Information Awareness program being organized by DARPA (Defense Advanced Research Projects Agency) proposes to use sophisticated data mining and pattern recognition techniques to sift through huge quantities of data. According to the Electronic Privacy Information Center:

The project calls for the development of "revolutionary technology for ultra-large all-source information repositories," which would contain information

> *from multiple sources to create a "virtual, centralized, grand database." This database would be populated by transaction data contained in current databases such as financial records, medical records, communication records, and travel records as well as new sources of information. Also fed into the database would be intelligence data.[30]*

When combined with the vast amount of communications monitoring being done, many libertarians believe this poses a serious threat to personal privacy. Since a majority of the public both wants security and values privacy in an age where technology has made it increasingly precarious, a collision between these two fundamental concerns seems inevitable.

Finally, there is the criminal prosecution of suspected terrorists. There has always been a tension between the priorities inherent in the criminal law in most modern democracies and the perceived necessity to confront the terrorist threat. Ordinary criminals certainly are a threat to society, and the courts and the political system do have to strike a balance between that threat and the desire to prevent the conviction of innocent people. However, while many people may accept the notion that an ordinary criminal who murders another person might go free because of the strict adherence to the rights of the defendant and the rules of evidence, many of these same people feel differently if the person who might go free is someone who may have killed dozens, hundreds, or even thousands of people—and is likely to try to do so again. Thus where terrorist suspects are concerned, there is considerable pressure to set aside or shortcut the traditional safeguards built into the legal system.

In the USA PATRIOT Act and various guidelines promulgated in 2002, the ability to prosecute people for giving material aid to terrorists or harboring them has been widened, as has the scope of regulations concerning money laundering. The use of conspiracy charges against terrorism suspects is also increasingly common—in part to pile on charges that might be negotiated away in return for cooperation. (This appears to have been the case with the "American Taliban," John Walker Lindh.) Conspiracy charges have been a powerful tool against organized crime, but are more problematic when used against dissident groups. One danger is that people who share some of the ideas of, for example, a radical Islamic group but do not condone or directly support terrorism might find themselves faced with numerous conspiracy charges potentially adding up to tens of years in prison.

Courts have ruled that the president as commander in chief of the armed forces has the power to hold terrorists captured in Afghanistan and other areas of military conflict indefinitely without trial because they are "unlawful combatants" rather than regular soldiers who follow the normal usages of war. Because the government believes that terrorism suspects might be able to pass vital information about the investigation to terrorist groups, some suspects such as Zacarias Moussaoui (believed to be a major organizer of the September 11 hijackers) have been given only limited access to lawyers, and their lawyers in turn have been provided only limited access to information that they believe is necessary for mounting an effective defense. (Another case, that of Yaser Esam Hamdi, involves a suspect who might have a claim to American citizenship but is also being treated as an enemy combatant.) It has also been proposed that certain terrorism suspects be tried by military tribunals rather than civilian courts. Proponents cite the need for security and safeguarding sensitive information, but critics question the independence and objectivity of such tribunals, as well as the more limited legal rights given to defendants.

As for prosecuting terrorist suspects in the regular U.S. courts, a study released in December 2003 by researchers at Syracuse University suggests that not many major terrorists are being taken out of circulation. Of the 6,400 "terrorism-related" cases referred to the Justice Department for prosecution, about a quarter were dropped without filing charges. There have been only 879 convictions as of December 2003, which included 184 for crimes specifically involving "international terrorism." However even among these, which are presumably the most serious cases, 80 received no jail time, 91 were sentenced to a year or less, and 10 got from one to five years in prison. Only three persons were sentenced for more than five years.

Defenders of the legal offensive in the war on terrorism argue that some potentially serious threats may have been disrupted by arresting and holding people who may have had at least minor involvement with terrorist groups. However, civil libertarians point to the injustice in holding people for many months, disrupting their lives and families, only to eventually deport them, release them, or convict them on minor charges.

THE MILITARY OPTION

Since the fall of the Soviet Union around 1990, the United States has been the world's undisputed military superpower. No other nation has the ability to transport complete armies virtually anywhere on the globe while controlling the sea and air. Technology has also given the United States weapons of amazing precision, such as cruise missiles, "smart bombs," and pilotless drone aircraft—as well as a web of satellite and aerial sensors to survey battlefields and search for fugitives.

Less than a month after the twin towers fell in New York, U.S. forces were striking with missiles and bombs against the Taliban, the radical Islamic government in Afghanistan that had been providing facilities and cover for al-Qaeda. The military effort continued with the skillful use of small Special Forces contingents that linked up with and helped direct anti-

Taliban Northern Alliance forces. By the end of November 2001 the Taliban had been removed from power and plans for establishing a new Afghan government were underway.

In April 2003 the effort to remove Iraq's Saddam Hussein seemed to proceed with equal swiftness. There was little large-scale resistance to the U.S. invasion, although small groups of *fedayeen* loyal to Hussein launched numerous hit-and-run attacks to little effect. By May 1 Baghdad and other major cities were in U.S. or British hands, and President Bush had declared "major combat" to be at an end.

Unfortunately, the attempt to provide security, stability, and recovery for the people of Afghanistan and Iraq has been far more difficult. By mid-2003 Afghanistan's government under Hamid Karzai was far from establishing control over the many competing warlords or local leaders, and resurgent Taliban forces, reinforced from across the border with Pakistan, were launching increasingly large attacks in remote, mountainous southern Afghanistan.

As for Iraq, the well-planned military campaign evidently was not accompanied by an equally well-planned campaign to win the peace. Following the overthrow of Saddam Hussein there was first widespread looting, which, combined with the country's aging and decrepit infrastructure, kept much of Baghdad without electricity. Working telephone systems were also scarce. The U.S. forces were late in guarding key infrastructure, and they did not have the equipment to improvise a communications network or to provide power generation for hospitals and other vital facilities. The result was that a civilian populace that initially seemed glad to have gotten rid of a brutal and oppressive regime became increasingly disappointed and restive.

As summer 2003 wore on, Hussein's Baath Party loyalists and apparently also incoming al-Qaeda operatives began to launch devastating terrorist attacks. In the month of August alone powerful explosions destroyed first the headquarters for the United Nations in Baghdad and then the country's holiest Shiite mosque, the latter attack killing a revered cleric and enraging the Shiite population that had been persecuted by Hussein.

While it is too soon to know whether stable, relatively prosperous, and democratic regimes might yet emerge in Afghanistan and Iraq, it seems clear that the military can be a useful tool for disrupting terrorist infrastructure or removing regimes that promote terrorism. But without a well thought out and sustained plan for the aftermath, the result is likely to be the creation of conditions that can and will be exploited by terrorists.

GLOBAL COOPERATION AGAINST TERRORISM

In the months following September 11, 2001, the United States received widespread sympathy from most of the world's nations. The leaders of the developed democracies in particular recognized that a global terrorist network, in successfully targeting the political and economic capitals of the world's only superpower, was also demonstrating that it could strike any nation that it viewed as an enemy. Such values as free markets, cultural pluralism, and democracy seemed to be anathema to Osama bin Laden and his followers and sympathizers. In turn, many people in Western nations agreed that the terrorists had declared war on civilization itself.

Intelligence cooperation between the United States, Great Britain, and the European democracies has been generally good. Authorities in Britain, Germany, Italy, and other countries have uncovered suspected al-Qaeda cells and provided valuable information about how the terrorist network is organized, as well as some of its plans. Countries such as Russia, China, and India have also expressed willingness to cooperate in the war against terrorism, although antiterrorist rhetoric can also be used to justify other interests (such as Russia's battle against Chechnyan separatists).

In the Islamic world the situation is, not surprisingly, more complicated. Bordering on Afghanistan, Pakistan's cooperation was vital in the battle against the Taliban and al-Qaeda in 2001–02. But Pakistani president Pervez Musharraf has had to continually balance the need to accommodate pressure from the United States with the sentiments of the populace, which tends to be sympathetic to the Islamist cause. Saudi Arabia is in a rather similar position: The nation's elite is traditionally allied with the United States as a moderating influence in the region, but some of the nation's richest families have been accused of funneling money to terrorist groups (Osama bin Laden is a Saudi expatriate).

In countries such as the Philippines and Colombia, the United States has provided aid and military advisers to fight against regional terrorist groups. This is a traditional way to leverage one's resources in carrying out a campaign at a relatively low level, but as one remembers from Vietnam, there is always the potential to be drawn into an increasingly expensive commitment to a failing government.

The overall policy as articulated by President George W. Bush has been that the United States can no longer tolerate any nation building weapons of mass destruction (nuclear, chemical, or biological) that might be provided to terrorists. The proposition is that any such development will be preempted: with the cooperation of the international community if possible, but unilaterally if necessary.

Such a policy has the advantage of clarity and the support of many Americans who have vivid memories of September 11. When the United States intervened militarily in Afghanistan, it received widespread support from many nations, including basing and overflight rights. In this case the connection to the September 11 terrorists seemed clear and the need to remove a regime that had fostered that terrorism seemed obvious.

Iraq, however, would be the next test of the new policy of pre-emption. Here things were much less clear and much more troubling to many of America's allies. The war was justified by President Bush and British prime minister Tony Blair because Iraq was said to have chemical and biological weapons and to be rapidly developing nuclear weapons. Although no such weapons were found after the war, even assuming Iraq had them, it was not clear why there was a need to go to war immediately rather than ratcheting up the pressure and sanctions and pushing for more robust inspections. Besides, it seemed inconsistent to treat North Korea, a state that very probably actually does have a few nuclear bombs, relatively mildly, while relentlessly attacking Iraq.

Similarly, another justification given for attacking Iraq was the atrocities that Saddam Hussein had committed on his own people. Indeed, most people and nations would agree that Hussein's human rights record is execrable. But atrocities at least as bad had been committed in Rwanda without significant response by the United States, and many other countries around the world still have repressive dictatorships.

Finally, another justification developed in the run up to the war was that Iraq had ties to al-Qaeda and other terrorist groups. It is definitely true that Saddam Hussein has repeatedly paid "compensation" to families of Palestinian suicide bombers. There is also evidence of some al-Qaeda members visiting Baghdad, and of terrorist camps in Iraq (but not in an area that was under the control of Hussein's government). Again, however, the question was why Iraq should be singled out so urgently when other countries such as Syria have had at least as close a connection to terrorists.

The upshot was that the allies who had cooperated so readily in Afghanistan generally opposed the war in Iraq (with the notable exception of Great Britain under Tony Blair.) France, Germany, and Russia in particular expressed strong opposition, and the United States was unable to obtain a resolution of support from the UN Security Council.

By late 2003 the United States seemed to be at a new crossroads in the war against terrorism. Increasingly strident voices were being heard from Congress and even from within the administration, urging that unilateral pre-emption be replaced by a new effort to develop stronger global cooperation. There are many potential obstacles, however. If the United States should experience another major attack, pre-emption might again be justified, at least in domestic political terms. The United Nations, meanwhile, has shown itself to be effective in some areas such as providing humanitarian aid and peacekeeping, but it is not clear that it can be decisive and agile enough to cope with global terrorism.

TERRORISM IN THE 21ST CENTURY

It should be clear that there is no one simple cause for terrorism in the world today and no magic bullet that can stop it from continuing to happen. There appear to be two broad types of terrorism today: systematic terrorism that arises from political, economic, or cultural grievances, and "idiosyncratic" terrorism such as that practiced by religious apocalyptic groups or groups motivated by absolute views on some particular issue (such as antiabortion, environmentalism, or animal rights). The latter forms of terrorism are not amenable to a political or economic development approach. The only relevant approaches there are those that apply to all terrorist threats: intelligence, hardening potential targets, and rigorous criminal prosecution.

For addressing the large-scale systematic terrorism in the Middle East, Southeast Asia, and Central and Latin America, however, an understanding of the dislocations being caused by economic globalism and disparate development can be very useful. Thomas P. M. Barnett of the U.S. Naval War College has developed a strategic approach from mapping the flows of economic activity, communications, and media in the modern world. His world map features three distinctive areas. In the "functioning core" of the United States and other developed and developing countries, relatively free markets, economic growth, and liberal institutions function. In the "nonintegrating gap" characteristic of many countries in Africa, the Middle East, and elsewhere, few or none of the benefits of the global economy have penetrated, and societies are characterized by repressive regimes and widespread, seemingly intractable poverty. Between these two regions lies a sort of seam or fault line through which terrorists and other sources of violence and disruption tend to flow.[31]

This model suggests that the long-term strategy for reducing systematic global terrorism is to shrink the gap between the functioning and dysfunctional areas of the world by providing economic aid, training, and other means to create growing economies that offer hope to people. This analysis is not unlike the liberal strategy that led to the development of the Peace Corps and other programs as a way to reduce the appeal of communism during the cold war. The potential value of creating growth and hope is as obvious now as it was then and extends well beyond the benefits of reducing terrorist activity. But now as then the will and the means to transform about a third of the world remain elusive.

What other conclusions can one draw about the nature of modern global terrorism and the responses it requires? The following would probably be among those found in a consensus of expert opinion:

- As shown on September 11, 2001, the people and infrastructure of the developed world are vulnerable to attacks that can cause massive casualties and disruption.
- Also as shown on that terrible day, terrorists can be perceptive in finding weaknesses, such as the vulnerability of airliners, and innovative in realizing that airliners could be turned into suicide cruise missiles.
- Global terror networks such as al-Qaeda have the resources and patience to coordinate attacks over a wide area.
- The "old terrorism" based on ideology or national aspirations is susceptible (as in Northern Ireland, Spain, and Sri Lanka) to developing peace processes that provide a plausible alternative to violence.
- The "new terrorism" such as that of apocalyptic or radical fundamentalist movements (such as al-Qaeda) is much less susceptible to being brought into some sort of negotiation or peace process.
- The worst possible combination would be radical "new terrorists" and weapons of mass destruction. International cooperation is needed to prevent states from developing such weapons; systems must be developed to detect them before they are deployed; emergency responders must be trained to deal with the results of their use.
- There are a number of ways to harden potential terrorist targets, but risk can only be reduced, not eliminated.
- The growing disparity between developed and developing nations that can take advantage of global trade on the one hand and nations seemingly stalled in poverty and isolation will be one of the most powerful engines driving terrorism in coming years.
- Other possible "engines" of future terrorism include dislocation from environmental change (global warming) and population and immigration pressures.

If the United States and other democratic nations are to bring the threat of global terrorism under control, they will need to have a perspective that addresses both global and regional issues, as well as an integration of domestic security efforts and international cooperation. The international community will have to create a new paradigm that, while borrowing appropriately from military and law enforcement approaches, also includes diplomacy and better understanding of other cultures. Underlying social and economic issues will also have to be addressed.

---

[1] 22 U.S.C. 2656f(d).

2 Brian Jenkins, quoted in Jacob W. F. Sundberg, "Introduction to International Terrorism—The Tactics and Strategy of International Terrorism," in Magnus D. Sandbu and Peter Nordbeck, eds. *International Terrorism: Report from a Seminar Arranged by The European Law Students Association 1987*. [Lund]: Juristförlaget i Lund: Distribution, Akademibokhandeln i Lund, 1989.

3 Noam Chomsky, quoted in Jay M. Shafritz, et al. *Almanac of Modern Terrorism*, New York: Facts On File, 1991, p. 264.

4 Brian Jenkins, quoted in Jay M. Shafritz, et al. *Almanac of Modern Terrorism*, p. 256.

5 Frits Kalshoven. *The Law of Warfare: A Summary of Its Recent History and Trends in Development*. Leiden: A. W. Sijthoff, 1973, pp. 27–29.

6 Leon Trotsky. *Against Individual Terrorism*. New York: Pathfinder Press, 1974, pp. 3–4.

7 U.S. Dept. of Defense, Joint Chiefs of Staff. *Dictionary of Military and Associated Terms (Incorporating the NATO and IADB Dictionaries)*. Washington, D.C., 1 April 1984, p. 164.

8 Edward Kossoy. *Living with Guerrilla: Guerrilla as a Legal Problem and a Political Fact*. Geneva: Librarie, Droz, 1976, p. 328.

9 Interview with David Rapoport, cited in Alex P. Schmid and Albert J. Jongman, et al. *Political Terrorism*. Rev. ed. New York: North-Holland, 1988, p. 22.

10 Johan Most. *Freiheit*, September 13, 1884. Reprinted in W. Laqueur, ed. *The Terrorism Reader*. New York: New American Library, 1978, p. 100.

11 Noam Chomsky and E. S. Herman. *The Political Economy of Human Rights*, vol. 1, *The Washington Connection and Third World Fascism*. Nottingham: Spokesman, 1979, pp. 16–17.

12 Robert Thompson, *Revolutionary War in World Strategy 1945–1969*. London: Secker & Warburg, 1970, p. 4.

13 Walter Laqueur. *Terrorism*. London: Weidenfeld and Nicolson, 1977, p. 53.

14 Quoted in Annie Murphy Paul, "Dispatch from Derry," *Psychology Today*, vol. 31, Nov.–Dec. 1998, p. 28ff.

15 Walter Laqueur. *The New Terrorism: Fanaticism and the Arms of Mass Destruction* pp. 106–107.

16 Walter Laqueur.. *The New Terrorism*, New York: Oxford University Press, 1999, p. 81.

17 Quoted in Jose Vegar, "Terrorism's New Breed," *Bulletin of the Atomic Scientists*, vol. 54, March–April 1998, p. 50ff.

18 I. L. Horowitz, quoted in Schmid and Jongman, p. 22.

19 Douglas Pike, "The Viet-Cong Strategy of Terror," cited in Schmid and J. Jongman, p. 16.

20 I. L. Horowitz, "Political Terrorism and State Power," *Journal of Political and Military Sociology* I (1973), pp. 147–157

21 Arthur Koestler, *The Ghost in the Machine.* London: Hutchinson, 1967, pp. 243, 251.

22 Walter Laqueur, *No End to War: Terrorism in the Twenty-First Century.* New York: Continuum, 2003, p. 91.

23 Heymann, Philip B. *Terrorism and America: A Commonsense Strategy for a Democratic Society.* Cambridge: MIT Press, 1998, p. 9.

24 Philip A. Karber, "Urban Terrorism" Baseline Data and a Conceptual Framework," *Social Science Quarterly 52* (December 1971), pp. 527–533.

25 Paul Wilkinson. "Current and Future Trends in Domestic and International Terrorism: Implications for Democratic Government and the International Community." *Strategic Review for Southern Africa*, November 2002, pp. 106–112.

26 James P. Lucier, "We Are What We Eat—and That Makes the United States Vulnerable." *Insight on the News*, vol. 14, November 16, 1998, p. 6.

27 Jonathan B. Tucker and Amy Sands, "An Unlikely Threat," *Bulletin of the Atomic Scientists*, vol. 55, July 1999, p. 46.

28 Vegar, Jose, "Terrorism's New Breed," p. 50ff.

29 Juan Otero and Deborah Rigsby, "NLC Explains Local Role, Need for 'First Response' to Terrorism." *Nation's Cities Weekly*, vol. 21, September 7, 1998, p. 1ff.

30 Electronic Privacy Information Center. "Terrorism Information Awareness." Available online. URL: http://www.epic.org/privacy/profiling/tia/ Updated on May 30, 2003.

31 See Thomas P. M. Barnett. "The Pentagon's New Map." *Esquire*, March 2003, pp. 227–228.

CHAPTER 2

SURVEY OF INTERNATIONAL TERRORISM

This chapter presents a regional overview of terrorism in Northern Ireland, Europe, Israel and Palestine, the Middle East as a whole, Africa, Central Asia, East Asia, the Asia-Pacific region, Latin America, and the United States (both imported and indigenous groups). Each section begins with a brief description of the region's major conflicts and developments as they have related to terrorist activity since the 1960s. This is followed by an alphabetical listing of terrorist groups that play (or have played) a significant role in terrorist activities in that region.

NORTHERN IRELAND

Until the late 1990s the conflict in Northern Ireland between Protestant and Catholic groups had been used as an example of the kind of seemingly intractable situation that gives rise to an endless cycle of terrorism and communal violence. However, recent developments have given considerable cause for hope for a peaceful settlement.

The roots of what came to be called the "Troubles" in Northern Ireland began in the 16th century when Henry VIII, king of England, established the Protestant Church of England as the official state church, and Catholics were persecuted and often deprived of civil rights. When Henry tried to establish Protestantism in Ireland, the Catholic population rebelled. The situation was exacerbated when Henry's daughter Elizabeth I encouraged the settlement of English Protestants in a large section of Northern Ireland. Many of the Irish living in what became known as the Plantation of Ulster were displaced. Because the newcomers (mainly Scottish and English) were also ethnically different from the Irish, the bitter conflict that ensued combined two of humankind's most thorny issues—religion and ethnicity.

During the 17th century, things got steadily worse. Expansion of the English settlement continued, and the Irish revolted. The revolt was put down by Oliver Cromwell, whose forces massacred thousands of Irish Catholics. In 1688, when the Catholic James II was forced off the British throne by William of Orange after a short three-year reign, James II used Ireland as a base for his attempt to retake the throne. The Protestant supporters of William defended the town of Derry from the Catholic forces until the English army could break the siege. In 1690, William finally defeated James at the battle of the Boyne river. About a hundred years later, the Protestants began to call themselves "Orangemen," after William, and have celebrated their victory at the Boyne with an annual parade.

GROWTH OF IRISH NATIONALISM

The 18th century ended with a revolt by the Irish nationalist Thomas Wolfe Tone, who tried to unite both Protestants and Catholics against the foreign rule of Britain. Although the revolt failed, it strengthened Irish nationalism. In the 19th century, Irish nationalists resisted British attempts to unite all of Ireland with what had become Great Britain, and the people of Ireland suffered the terrible potato famine of 1845–48, which disproportionately killed Irish Catholics, who were generally poor, and forced many others to emigrate, many to the United States. Meanwhile, the Protestants consolidated their power in Northern Ireland. Called Unionists, they believed that only uniting Ireland with Britain could give the island a successful economy. They were opposed by the Republicans, who sought an independent Irish state.

By the late 19th century, an organization called the Irish Republican Brotherhood (originally formed by Irish immigrants in New York City) was waging a campaign of bombing and assassination against the British, not unlike that of the modern Irish Republican Army (IRA). During World War I, the British, in part to keep the Irish from aiding Germany, promised "home rule" to Ireland. But some Republicans either did not believe the British or did not want to wait, while Unionists wanted no part of any Irish Republic dominated by the Catholics of the south. On Easter Monday in 1916, a full-scale Republican rebellion, today known as the Easter Rebellion or Easter Rising, broke out in Dublin, led by several thousand armed followers of Patrick Pearse and James Connolly. However, the lightly armed rebels were no match for a British force that arrived with artillery and forced the rebels to surrender. But Pearse created from the rebellion a force whose name would later become ominous: the Irish Republican Army. When the British reacted to the rebellion with a wave of executions and imprisonments, the IRA vowed to carry on the struggle.

REPUBLICANS AND THE IRA

By a 1921 treaty, the British tried for a compromise: Southern Ireland became an independent state, while predominately Protestant Northern Ireland continued to be ruled and protected by Britain until some future time when it could be peacefully joined to the Irish Republic. Of course, most Unionists did not want to be part of the south and demanded continued British protection. Meanwhile, although many moderates accepted the division of Ireland at least temporarily, the extreme Republicans represented by the IRA did not. The IRA fought the new Irish government, demanding that the Republic fight for a united, independent Ireland. However, the Republican movement was split in 1932 when one of its main leaders, Eamon de Valera, took over the Irish government. As the IRA began to wane in the south, the Unionists in the north and the British were locked into a tight embrace, with the British allowing the Unionists some measure of self-rule and the ability to keep themselves firmly separate from the south.

By the 1930s, what was left of the IRA had split in two. A moderate wing, following the agenda of the Sinn Féin political party, sought to persuade the north to unite with the south on socialist principles. The other wing, however, held to the old Republican demand to drive the British out of Northern Ireland, creating an Irish Republic on nationalist principles. This more militant faction formed the Provisional Wing of the IRA, which by the 1950s was carrying out small-scale terrorist activities in the north.

THE "TROUBLES" BEGIN

By the 1960s, the Catholics in Northern Ireland had become frustrated; for decades they had been denied access to economic opportunities and fair treatment by authorities. A new movement emerged that focused not so much on republicanism as on civil rights. At first the violent wing of the IRA, having engaged in sporadic terrorism earlier in the decade, played only a marginal role in the new struggle. But when Catholics marched for civil rights, better housing, and education, they were viciously attacked by the Protestant-controlled police (the Royal Ulster Constabulary, or RUC) and by police reservists (called B-Specials) who functioned as a sort of Protestant paramilitary group.

During summer 1969, Catholic civil rights demonstrators trying to march from Londonderry to Belfast were tear-gassed and beaten by the RUC and the B-Specials. On August 15, the Protestants added insult to injury by holding their traditional "Apprentice Boys" or Orangemen parade. Many of the police joined the parade, and the Protestants armed themselves with sticks, rocks, and Molotov cocktails. Belfast and Londonderry (Derry for short) were swept by fires and rioting. When the British army arrived to quell the disturbances, it made matters worse by openly siding with what many of the

44

soldiers viewed as fellow Protestant English countrymen. This bitterly disappointed Catholics who had hoped the army would play a neutral, peacekeeping role and perhaps even protect them from abuses by the RUC and B-Specials. Increasingly, they saw the IRA as their only alternative.

Temporarily patching up its internal differences, the IRA declared war on the British army, vowing to drive it out of Northern Ireland through waves of bombings, assassinations, and other violent actions. In response to the renewed terrorism, in 1973 Britain enacted the Emergency Powers Act, which, while supposedly reforming the existing Special Powers Act, still allowed the police to arrest persons and hold them without trial and to conduct secret trials and trials without a jury. Such measures were viewed by the British as necessary to prevent terrorists from intimidating witnesses. Supporters believed the measures were necessary for dealing with the emergency created by the Provisional IRA terrorists (who by 1969 had split from the moderate wing of the IRA), while opponents saw them as just another way to institutionalize the oppression of the Catholics.

Besides supporting the police, British military (including the elite Special Air Service and intelligence units) played an independent role in fighting the IRA. Gradually, however, British frustration with the seemingly intractable situation led to a policy under Prime Minister Margaret Thatcher of "Ulsterization"—increasingly, letting the Irish solve their own problems, replacing British forces with an expanded RUC without the B-Specials and other ties to Protestant groups. During the 1980s, effective intelligence and the use of secret testimony by Irish informants (called "supergrasses" for "snakes in the grass") led to the imprisonment of many IRA activists and to protests by human rights groups.

QUEST FOR PEACE

Despite its attacks, the mainstream IRA increasingly concluded that it could not defeat the British. Meanwhile, ordinary Irish people in both the Catholic and Protestant communities exerted pressure for a peace settlement.

During the 1990s, peace seemed tantalizingly close. On August 31, 1994, the official IRA announced a cease-fire and said it was ready to join peace negotiations. The Combined Loyalist Military Command followed suit. Some smaller extremist factions (such as one calling itself the Real IRA) continued their attacks. In 1996 the peace process was derailed when the IRA cease fire ended with a massive explosion in Canary Wharf, London.

However, peace efforts resumed. In the "Good Friday Agreement" of April 10, 1998, voters in both Northern Ireland and the Irish Republic approved a new legislative assembly for Northern Ireland that included both Catholics and Protestants. Authorities in the north and south also cooperated in making regional policies in areas such as transportation and the environment. On August 15, however, an IRA splinter group set off a car bomb in Omagh, killing 28 people.

In 1999, the peace process seemed to falter again when the IRA and Protestant groups bickered about disarmament or the "decommissioning" of weapons. The following year, when the Ulster Unionist Party (UUP) under David Trimble refused to participate in the decommissioning process, the British intervened and temporarily restored direct rule, and the IRA agreed to put its weapons "completely and verifiably beyond use." During 2001 the assembly was restored after negotiations. Observers have noted that the September 11, 2001, attacks on the United States and the mounting of a new global American antiterrorist effort has exerted pressure on both sides in the Northern Ireland conflict to eschew terrorism. In particular, support for the Provisional IRA (PIRA) by Irish Americans has apparently declined.

Both Sinn Fein and the pro-agreement Democratic Unionist Party (DUP) registered gains in the 2001 parliamentary elections. Perhaps in response, in 2002 there was scattered violence by IRA and Unionist splinter groups. As of mid-2003 the number of violent incidents had fallen considerably, but authorities are concerned about possible bombing plots by the Real IRA and Continuity IRA.

GROUPS IN NORTHERN IRELAND

Continuity IRA   This rather shadowy radical republican group is believed to often cooperate with the Real IRA (see below). However, in August 2003 the group denied allegations in trial testimony by U.S. FBI agent David Rupert that the Continuity IRA had worked with the Real IRA in the 1998 Omagh bombing that almost derailed the peace process. Police were also investigating the Continuity IRA in mid-2003 for possible plots to bomb police stations and the actual bombing of a Dublin transit station.

Irish Republican Army (IRA)   The principal militant organization dedicated to the removal of the British-run Northern Ireland government and the unification of Northern Ireland with the Irish Republic in the south. The IRA emerged from the Easter Rising of 1916, and the pressure IRA guerrillas exerted against the British helped encourage the formation of the Irish Free State that became the current state of Ireland. However, Irish Republicans split between those willing to accept a divided Ireland (with the Irish Free State in the south and the north remaining British) and those insisting on a republic encompassing all of Ireland. The IRA sided with the latter group during the Irish civil war of 1921–23, but were defeated by former IRA leader Michael Collins, who led the Free State forces. The IRA began a new bombing campaign against the British in both Northern Ireland and southern Ireland in the 1930s. In 1939 the organization was banned by the Irish Free State, which became the Republic of Ireland in 1949. The IRA then focused on Northern Ireland. Following the failure of military actions against the British up to the early 1960s, the IRA turned for a time to civil disobedience and nonviolent action. More militant members objected to this moderate approach and formed the Provisional Irish Republican Army (see that entry for more details). The political wing of the modern IRA is known as Sinn Féin. See the entry on Sinn Féin for more details.

Loyalist Volunteer Force (LVF)   Formed in 1996 as an extremist offshoot of the Ulster Volunteer Force, the LVF has launched vicious attacks on both Catholic and Protestant leaders who support the Northern Ireland peace process. However, the group declared a cease-fire and gave up some of its weapons in 1998.

Provisional Irish Republican Army (PIRA)   This organization, also called the Provisional Wing of the Irish Republican Army, was formed in 1969 when the IRA split into two groups. By 1972, the "official" IRA had renounced terrorism, and the Provisional Wing became the main vehicle for those who wanted to carry on a violent struggle against British rule in Northern Ireland. Gradually the older members of the PIRA, motivated by Republican nationalism, gave way to a younger generation that looked toward leftist ideology that emphasized political action over terrorism. The "Provos" carried on a protracted campaign of violence into the early 1990s, seeking to keep world attention focused on Northern Ireland while sapping the will of the British people to maintain their rule in the province. Most PIRA attacks have taken place in Northern Ireland, against British security forces and officials, using well-honed techniques of bombing and ambush. The British, in turn, have kept up relentless pressure on the PIRA through the use of investigators and informants. (Informants discovered by the PIRA are often brutally tortured and killed.) The PIRA has been sustained by widespread nationalist sentiment among the Catholic population of Northern Ireland and by support raised through robberies, donations from sympathizers in the United States, and weapons and other help from Libya. The PIRA and the Basque group ETA have also developed a long-standing cooperation. However, the PIRA has maintained a cease fire for several years as part of the overall North Ireland peace process and has begun to "decommission" weapons in such a way that they could not be easily used.

Real IRA   A small, violent wing of the radical Republican 32-County Sovereignty Movement, the Real IRA, founded in 1998, seeks to remove all British forces from Northern Ireland and unite it with the Irish Republic. The group bitterly opposes the Northern Ireland peace process, including the adoption by Sinn Féin in September 1997 of the Mitchell Principles of democracy and nonviolence. The group claimed responsibility for the car bomb attack in Omagh, Northern Ireland, on August 15, 1998, which killed 29 persons and injured 220, and is believed to be responsible for numerous generally small bombings as well as shootings.

Sinn Féin ("We, Ourselves") Founded in 1900 by Irish nationalist Arthur Griffith, Sinn Féin began as a movement to promote Gaelic culture in the face of British influence. Following the British suppression of the Easter Rebellion (a failed insurrectional attempt to end British rule in Ireland that was held on Easter Monday, 1916) during World War I, Sinn Féin became the rallying point for political organization by Irish nationalists. Following election victories in 1918, Sinn Féin set up an Irish parliament known as the Dáil Éirann, which declared Irish independence, a status recognized by the British with the establishment of the Irish Free State in southern Ireland. When republican leader Eamon de Valera entered the Irish parliament in 1927 and most Irish seemed to be reconciled to the permanent division of the island, Sinn Féin essentially disbanded. However, with the resurgence of the Irish Republican Army in the 1960s, Sinn Féin reemerged as the political wing of the IRA. When the IRA split into "official" and provisional wings, Sinn Féin mirrored this split, with Gerry Adams becoming leader of the radical provisional wing of Sinn Féin in 1983. During the years of rampant terrorism, Sinn Féin, although not recognized by the British as a legitimate political party, provided a means for the more peacefully inclined to support Irish nationalism, a conduit for support for the IRA, and a way for the British to communicate indirectly with the IRA. During the peace process of the late 1990s, Sinn Féin won representation in a democratically elected assembly intended to share ruling power between Catholics and Protestants in Northern Ireland.

Ulster Defense Association (UDA) An outlawed Protestant paramilitary and vigilante organization in Northern Ireland, the UDA was formed in the early 1970s and has tens of thousands of members. The group is the most powerful Protestant group in the violent conflict in Northern Ireland and has unofficial ties with the Royal Ulster Constabulary. The group has been implicated in many beatings, killings, and kidnappings of Catholics.

Ulster Volunteer Force (UVF) A group of armed Protestant nationalists in Ulster, Northern Ireland, formed in 1966. The UVF took its name from a popular home-rule organization in existence earlier in the century. The UVF violently attacked the Irish Republican Army and its suspected sympathizers in the early 1970s, conducting numerous bombings. In 1976 the organization claimed to renounce violence.

EUROPE

Europe in a sense is the birthplace of modern terrorism (both the state terrorism of the French Revolution and the theories of violent anarchism). In the latter part of the 20th century, Europe has seen both ideology-based terrorism (both Left and Right) and terrorism based on nationalism or ethnicity. Since the fall of the Soviet Union and the end of the cold war, the predominant source of terrorism has changed from ideology to nationalism.

LEFTIST TERRORISM

Since the 19th century, European anarchists, socialists, or communists have sometimes carried on a violent struggle against the capitalist system, particularly in times when workers suffered harsh economic and social conditions. The student movements that erupted in the late 1960s in most of the western world included a considerable component of marxist thought and combined the traditional appeal to the working class with a new struggle against American imperialism as typified by the war in Vietnam. Inevitably, for a relatively small number of extremists, protests and politics were not enough—especially when the political gains were limited.

A number of leftist terrorist groups were formed in the late 1960s and early 1970s, including Germany's Red Army Faction (RAF), France's Action Directe, and Italy's Red Brigades. Some of the extremists, such as the Baader-Meinhof gang, the forerunner of the RAF, combined criminal motivations with leftist ideology. (The gang decided that bank robbery would make a satisfactory funding source. While Ulrike Meinhof showed dedication to her communist principles, her partner in crime, Andreas Baader, lived an upscale lifestyle with some of the robbery proceeds.)

In many ways the RAF's fate was typical of that of other European leftist terrorists. During the 1970s the RAF engaged in a series of bombings, robberies, and murders. As German police arrested and jailed RAF leaders, other members tried to use terrorism to gain their freedom. A series of murders, including the killing of the pilot of a hijacked airliner in October 1977, caused even many committed leftists to reject the group. While the RAF tried to gain exposure by participating in the anti-NATO agitation of the 1980s, it never regained its earlier prominence. The fall of the Berlin Wall and the reunification of Germany removed the communist East German government that had secretly supported many leftist European terrorists and that offered sanctuary when things became too hot.

Similarly, changing politics undermined support for the Red Brigades in Italy, despite the group's effective organization, which combined the advantages of decentralized cells with the ability to launch coordinated attacks. In

1999, the group apparently resurfaced, killing Italian government labor adviser Massimo D'Antona, and, in 2003, another adviser, Marco Biagi.

RIGHT-WING TERRORISM

If the 1970s was the decade of the Left in Europe, the 1980s saw right-wing terrorism predominate. Europe's generally strong economic growth diminished the appeal of leftist ideology. While the economic trends culminating in the 1990s with the European Union and its single currency seemed to be bringing about the triumph of globalism over nationalism, fear of a loss of national identity amid a growing influx of immigrants from countries such as Turkey, as well as the stress caused by the need to integrate millions of former East Germans, fueled a modest resurgence of German nationalism and, in more extreme form, neofascism or neo-Nazism. During the early 1990s, German neo-Nazis, who had started by fighting in the streets against leftists, switched their focus to beating immigrants, tourists, and Jews.

In France, the moderate right wing took control of parliament in 1986 and a coalition government was formed under Jacques Chirac. In the 1988 election, the more radical right-wing candidate Jean-Marie Le Pen, whose National Front party ran on an anti-immigration platform, did surprisingly well in the first round of voting. Austria, too, saw a right-wing resurgence in 1999 when Jorg Haider's Freedom Party scored electoral victories and forced its inclusion in the ruling coalition. However, these gains proved short-lived.

Although more extreme forms of the sentiments that have led to right-wing gains have sometimes been expressed in terrorist activity, large-scale, organized right-wing terrorism comparable to the leftist terrorism of the 1980s did not emerge in Europe during the 1990s. Resurgent fear of Islamic terrorism following the 2001 attacks on the United States has led to some anti-immigrant violence, which, along with any significant economic downturn, might fuel a resurgence of right-wing terrorism.

ETHNIC-BASED TERRORISM

Besides ideological conflicts, long-standing grievances of ethnic minorities have also been a source of European terrorism. In Spain since the 1950s, the Basques, a unique ethnicity completely separate from the dominant Spanish, have sought an independent homeland within Spain. The Basque Nation and Liberty Party (Euzkadi Ta Askatasuna, or ETA) evolved from a political group into a terrorist group when Basque aspirations were brutally repressed by Spanish dictator Francisco Franco's regime in the early 1960s. The ETA and its more militant offshoot (ETA-M) carried on a terror campaign that reached its peak in the late 1970s, financing its efforts mainly through kidnappings and bank robberies. During the 1980s, however, more liberal Spanish policies allowed Basque nationalists to express their views more openly through the political process, and support for the ETA declined. Increasingly, the ETA began to be seen as a marginal group by even the Basques themselves. The ETA signed a peace accord with other parties in 1998. However, in 1999, claiming that it had been betrayed by Spanish officials, the group resumed terrorist attacks, including a focus on the tourist industry in 2002.

In general, as of 2003 there is not much indigenous terrorist activity in Europe, but police in the United Kingdom, Germany, Italy and other countries have investigated, uncovered, and arrested numerous persons allegedly connected to al-Qaeda and other outside terrorist groups. If there should be significant economic disruption, the potential for indigenous ideological, ethnic or nativist (anti-immigrant) terrorism remains.

Finally, it should be noted that Turkey, a country that has growing political and economic ties to Europe, is covered in the Middle East section of this survey. This is because, with regard to international terrorism, Turkey is being increasingly drawn into the battle between radical Islamic terrorists and secular regimes and Western interests in the region.

GROUPS IN EUROPE

Action Directe (AD)   A French marxist terrorist organization founded in 1979, the group specialized in bombing banks, businesses, and other targets that it associated with capitalism and imperialism. In August 1985, the group turned its attention to military targets and claimed joint responsibility with Germany's Red Army Faction for a bombing at the U.S. Air Force base in Rhein-Main, West Germany, that killed two American soldiers. Action Directe then became part of an umbrella group called the Anti-Imperialist Armed Front (AIAF), which called international workers to combat the "Americanization of Europe." In 1985, Action Directe assassinated French general René Audran and the next year killed Georges Besse, chairman of the Renault automobile company. Following these actions, however, an intensive police investigation led to the arrest of many of Action Directe's key leaders, and the group faded away.

Euzkadi Ta Askatasuna (ETA, Basque for "Basque Fatherland and Liberty")   ETA is a radical Basque separatist organization. Originally an offshoot of a Basque nationalist party during the 1950s, by the early 1960s ETA had given up on peaceful politics and begun terrorist actions against the Spanish government. Many ETA supporters looked to the marxist-based insurgents in developing nations for inspiration, and a more militant faction called ETA-M (for "military") emerged in the 1970s and carried out some of the worst Basque terrorist attacks of that and the following decade. In 1968, the ETA assassinated Meliton Manzanas, police chief in the city of San Sebastian. In 1973, ETA assassinated Luis Carrero Blanco, the prime minister of Spain. In a stream of shootings and bombings during the 1970s and 1980s more than 800 people died. The more moderate political faction renounced violence. ETA is believed to have forged links with other terrorist organizations, such as the IRA, as well as the governments of Libya and Cuba. Despite a decline in influence after the 1980s, the ETA's ability to tap into a broad base of Basque nationalist sentiment has enabled the group to survive punishing blows from Spanish authorities. In September 1998 the ETA declared a "unilateral cease-fire," and in 1999 signed an accord. By 1999, after what it says was bad faith by the Spanish government, the group was again staging large-scale attacks.

Grupo de Resistencia Antifascista, Primero de Octubre (GRAPO, Spanish for "Antifascist Resistance Group, October 1") This small Spanish Maoist group was formed in 1975 with a focus on removing U.S. and NATO facilities from Spain and creating a communist state. The group was secretive, though it was believed to have ties to Action Directe in France and the Red Brigades in Italy. GRAPO was active through the 1980s, bombing U.S. cultural and military facilities and shooting police officials. Its attacks culminated in 1990 with the bombing of the Madrid Stock Exchange, the Constitutional Court, and the Economic Ministry. However, police sweeps resulted in the arrest of most of the group's leadership, rendering it inactive for the rest of the 1990s.

P2 This shadowy group has been linked to right-wing, neofascist, and Masonic groups in Italy. It may have been implicated together with the Red Brigades and the Mafia in the kidnapping of former Italian prime minister Aldo Moro in 1978. In 1980 the uncovering of a P2 membership list that included many prominent Italian military, government, and police officials led to the downfall of the Italian government and severely strained relations between Italy and NATO.

Popular Forces of April 25 (FP-25, in Portuguese, "Forças Populares do 25 Abril") This Portuguese leftist group sought to overthrow the Portuguese government and replace it with a marxist state. More immediately, it sought to break all ties between Portugal and the United States and NATO. During the mid-1980s the group enacted bombings, rocket attacks, and assassination attempts, including attacks on the U.S. embassy in Portugal and a NATO headquarters outside Lisbon. In 1986 the group appeared under a new name, "Armed Revolutionary Organization."

Red Army Faction (RAF, in German, "Rote Armee Faktion") One of the largest European leftist terrorist organizations, the RAF emerged out of the widespread radical student movements of the late 1960s. Dominated in its early years by the mercurial terrorists Andreas Baader, Ulrike

Meinhof, and Gudrun Ensslin, the group was also known as the Baader-Meinhof Gang. The group began in 1968 with attacks on West German corporate facilities. During the 1970s, the RAF forged links in an emerging international terror network that included the major Palestinian groups, who provided the RAF with training. In turn, RAF members carried out operations on behalf of the Palestinians, including the 1975 seizure of the OPEC ministers in Vienna. In 1977, however, a failed hijacking led to the suicide of Baader, Ensslin, and another jailed member. The group then turned its attention back to domestic targets including businesses and NATO facilities. Despite frequent arrests of key leaders, the RAF's well-educated, trained, and highly motivated core membership kept the organization effective into the 1990s. Another reason for the group's robustness emerged in 1990 when records of the former East German intelligence service revealed that the RAF had been trained and closely supervised by the East German interior ministry.

Red Brigades (BR, in Italian, "Brigate Rosse") Like many European leftist terrorist groups, the Red Brigades emerged from the radical student activism of the late 1960s. It was founded in 1970 by a small group of young Italian communists. In the mid-1970s, the group began a brutal campaign of kidnapping and violent attacks, including "kneecapping" victims (breaking or shooting their kneecaps, thus crippling them). The main targets were people considered to be important figures in the establishment or ruling class, including judges and other officials, police, and the military. During the 1980s the group began to target NATO officials, kidnapping and then releasing U.S. deputy commander of NATO Brigadier General James Dozier. The group also expressed its solidarity and cooperation with the major Palestinian terrorist groups. In the late 1970s and early 1980s (and again in 1987), Italian police managed to sweep up many BR leaders and their extensive weapons caches. Combined with an internal split in 1984, these events led to the group's decline, though it surface again in 1999 and 2003 with assassinations of two Italian labor advisers.

Revolutionary Cells (RZ, in German, "Revolutionaere Zellen") A left-wing German terrorist group formed in 1973, its leaders vowed to strike fear into the heart of the ruling class through shooting, bombing, and taking hostages. The group bases its organization and methods on urban guerrilla tactics, with small cells operating independently against local targets. Its ability to disguise its members as ordinary citizens and its skill with time-delayed bombs and other weapons made the Revolutionary Cells a difficult problem for West German authorities in the late 1980s.

Revolutionary Organization 17 November (in Greek, "Epanastatiki Organosi 17 Noemvri") This small, marxist Greek radical group, active mainly during the 1970s, was named to commemorate the killing of a demonstrator in Athens in 1973. The group's terrorist attacks (typically, shootings from ambush) targeted U.S. and NATO officials and Greeks associated with them. The group called for the severing of all ties between Greece and NATO.

Terra Lliure (in English, "Free Land")   This group sought the establishment of an independent Catalan state in Spain's Catalonia region. Formed in the 1970s, Terra Lliure undertook a terror campaign in the early 1980s, mainly targeting banks and tourism-related businesses such as travel agencies with small bombs. In 1987 the group claimed credit for bombings of the U.S. consulate general's office in Barcelona as well as a United Service Organizations (USO) club.

ISRAEL AND PALESTINE

In the three-cornered conflict that erupted just before World War II, both the Arabs and the Jews wanted independence from British rule, but neither was willing to join the other in an independent Palestine. The Arabs revolted against the British, and they and the Jews also fought each other.

By the end of World War II, it was clear that the British had little enthusiasm or resources for continuing their role as protector of Palestine. Thousands of Jews, refugees of the Holocaust, began to smuggle themselves into Palestine past the British authorities. Seeing the influx as threatening to their future self-determination, Palestinian Arabs began to arm themselves and prepare for full-scale fighting against the Jews as soon as the British pulled out. In turn, a Jewish terrorist group, the Irgun, attacked British soldiers and Palestinians. The dual objectives of the Irgun were to make it too painful for the British to remain and to intimidate and drive out Palestinian Arabs.

One possibility for settlement was a partition of Palestine into separate Jewish and Palestinian states. The British liked this idea, and the United Nations agreed and proclaimed the partition on May 15, 1948. Amid great rejoicing, the Jews declared the establishment of the new state of Israel on their side of the partition line. Palestinian and neighboring Arab forces immediately invaded the new Jewish state, which defended itself and prevailed.

While the struggle between Arabs and Jews in Palestine remained the fulcrum of unrest in the Middle East, the Arab world itself was being pulled in different directions. All of Israel's Arab neighbors proclaimed their willingness to join together to "drive Israel into the sea." In 1967, however, Israel's armed forces struck crushing blows at both Egypt and Syria in the Six-Day War. In October 1973, Egypt under President Anwar Sadat and Syria made a surprise attack on Israel during the Jewish Yom Kippur holiday. They achieved remarkable success at first, with Egyptian forces driving the Israelis deep into the Sinai while Syria, attacking from the Golan Heights, almost made it to Jerusalem.

Because military success had restored Arab self-respect, Sadat was powerful enough to seek better relations with both Israel and the United States (earlier, he had been aligned with the Soviets). Israel, under Prime Minister Menachem Begin, wanted peace but also insisted on controlling enough territory to allow the nation to defend itself in some depth from any future attacks. In the Camp David Peace Accords, mediated by U.S. president Jimmy Carter, Israel agreed to give up the Sinai in exchange for peace with Egypt.

Egypt, Saudi Arabia, and Jordan tacitly agreed that Israel was there to stay and decided to focus on their own economic development. But "rejectionists," such as in Syria and Iran, refused to compromise with Israel. (Sadat was killed by rejectionists in 1981.)

The Palestinians were caught in the middle of the Arab-Israeli struggle. Many of them had fled during Israel's wartime expansion and were living in squalid refugee camps, stuck in a political limbo without civil rights or hope for the future.

Some joined or supported the Palestine Liberation Organization (PLO), led by Yasir Arafat and founded in 1964. But the PLO suffered setbacks. In 1970, forces of Jordan's King Hussein, who was pursuing a moderate policy toward Israel, expelled the PLO. The more militant wing of the PLO killed 11 Israeli athletes at the 1972 Olympic Games in Munich, Germany— marking the growing international reach of terrorist activities.

Meanwhile, the PLO shifted its guerrilla operations to Lebanon, who together with other radical Islamic groups launched constant rocket bombardments and raids across the Israeli border, accompanied by suicide bombings and assassinations. They also began to attack targets in Israel, Lebanon, and even western Europe that were associated with Israel or the United States. In 1982, however, Israel invaded Lebanon, destroying much of the PLO infrastructure but also becoming embroiled in an endless battle between armed militias and other groups—destroying much of Beirut.

Yasir Arafat's position as PLO leader was challenged from two directions in the late 1980s. Relocating in Tunis, he concluded that terrorism would never bring about a Palestinian state. In 1988, Arafat implicitly recognized Israel's right to exist, renounced terrorism, and sought to reinvent himself as a peacemaker and political spokesperson for the Palestinian people in the international community.

THE INTIFADA

While militant PLO members rejected Arafat and formed an organization called Hamas, in 1987 Palestinian youths began a remarkable movement that became known as the Intifada. They demonstrated throughout the Israeli-occupied territories, demanding self-government, and despite frequent clashes between rock-throwing youths and Israeli troops shooting rubber bullets, Israel could not suppress the uprising. Arafat, equally caught by surprise, could not co-opt it for his own purposes.

As world opinion began to swing in favor of the Intifada, Arafat emerged as the only Palestinian leader who had the international stature to negotiate with Israel and to seek American help. By 1994, the Israelis were willing to take the first steps toward Palestinian autonomy, and a quasi-national Palestinian Authority was empowered to handle domestic affairs in the Palestinian territories.

As in Northern Ireland, the road to peace remained rocky and uncertain. A series of peace agreements signed between Israel and Arab parties successively failed. Arab extremists continued to make terrorist attacks, while right-wing Israelis resisted the peace process. In 1995, Israeli prime minister Yitzhak Rabin was assassinated by an Orthodox Jewish fanatic. Some Israeli settlers in the occupied territories said they would violently resist their areas coming under Palestinian control.

In 2000 President Bill Clinton convened a summit at Camp David but failed to reach an agreement after intense negotiations. By fall 2000 growing Palestinian frustration at the slowness of progress toward statehood and reaction to Israeli right-wing leader Ariel Sharon's visit to the Temple Mount (Haram ash Sharif) had triggered a second *intifada* with large-scale clashes in which Israel responded to attacks by attacking Palestinian police stations and other facilities and bulldozed the houses of those believed responsible for terrorist attacks. The Mitchell Report released in 2001 called for a halt to the violence and an end to the building of new Israeli settlements, but it was essentially ignored.

The terrorist attacks of September 11, 2001, temporarily diverted the attention of the United States from the Israel/Palestine issue. However, in 2003 a new "road map to peace" was proposed by the George W. Bush administration. A new cease-fire between Israel and the main Palestinian groups lasted less two months, however. By summer new suicide bombings by the al-Aqsa Martyrs Brigade and rocket attacks by Hamas from across the Gaza Strip were being met by military incursions plus a stepped-up program of targeted killings of Hamas leaders from the air with rockets.

GROUPS IN ISRAEL AND PALESTINE

al-Aqsa Martyrs Brigade This small but potent group operates in small cells and specializes in suicide bomb attacks against Israeli soldiers, civilians and settlers. In January 2002 they introduced the first female suicide bomber. The pace of the attacks increased in 2003.

Democratic Front for the Liberation of Palestine (DFLP) A Marxist-Leninist Palestinian group founded in 1968, the DFLP opposed the efforts of the Palestine Liberation Organization as being too moderate and lacking "class consciousness." The DFLP specialized in attacking Israelis, both within Israel and in the occupied territories. In May 1974, DFLP terrorists disguised as Israeli soldiers killed 27 Israelis and wounded 134 in a school in Ma'alot, Israel. During the later 1970s and 1980s they conducted minor bombings and unsuccessful hostage-taking attempts.

al-Fatah (Harakat al-Tahrir al Filistini, Palestine Liberation Movement) Founded in 1957, al-Fatah is the largest organization in the umbrella group PLO (Palestine Liberation Organization). Al-Fatah has been led since 1964 by Yasir Arafat. However, in the 1990s Arafat renounced violence and moved into mainstream politics as leader of the Palestine Authority and the nascent Palestinian state. During the 1960s al-Fatah mounted guerrilla raids into Israel from bases in Jordan. In September 1970, Jordan's King Hussein attacked and expelled al-Fatah from the country, and the group established new bases in Lebanon and Syria. The expulsion also resulted in the more militant Black September faction splitting off from al-Fatah; the split also proved to be useful to Arafat, who could support terrorism at arm's length through al-Fatah while preserving deniability by claiming the PLO was not responsible. During the 1970s, al-Fatah expanded its terrorist activities to western Europe and also provided a sort of international training school for terrorists. In 1982, Israel invaded Lebanon, forcing al-Fatah to abandon its bases there. The group dispersed to Tunisia, Algeria, South Yemen, and other countries, but in the late 1980s it began to infiltrate into Lebanon again.

Hamas (Islamic Resistance Movement, in English, "Courage") Hamas emerged in 1987 as a radical offshoot of the Palestinian branch of the Muslim Brotherhood. Its growth coincided with that of the Intifada, or Palestinian uprising against the Israeli occupation. Hamas demands not only a Palestinian state, but one "from the Mediterranean Sea to the Jordan river," which would of course eliminate Israel. The group engages in both political and terrorist activities, with its main base of operations in the Gaza Strip and portions of the West Bank. Its specialty is suicide bomb attacks against military and civilian targets in Israel, but it has also attacked Palestinians it views as Israeli collaborators. In fall 2000, the group claimed responsibility for a Jerusalem car bombing amid renewed clashes between Israelis and Palestinians. Since then Hamas has specialized in rocket attacks against Israeli military installations as well as attacks against Israeli cities from the Gaza Strip, now using longer-range rockets. Israel has retaliated by killing Hamas leaders by rockets from the air, vowing to work their way down a list of those responsible for terrorism.

Jewish Defense League (JDL)   This militant Jewish group was founded in Brooklyn, New York, in 1968, by Rabbi Meir Kahane. It started out as a sort of neighborhood crime watch or vigilante group, but by the 1970s it was carrying out violent actions against groups it considered to be oppressing Jews, attacking targets associated with the Soviet Union or Arab/Palestinian groups. The group is believed by some observers to be responsible for two attacks in 1985 on offices of the American-Arab Anti-Discrimination League.

Palestine Islamic Jihad   This group originated among militant Palestinians in the Gaza Strip in the 1970s. Its goals include the destruction of Israel and the replacement of Arab governments that are deemed to be too moderate. In recent years the group has attacked people and facilities within Israel.

Palestine Liberation Organization (PLO)   This umbrella organization for Palestinian nationalist groups has been recognized by the Arab nations as "the sole, legitimate representative of the Palestinian people" and has been increasingly seen around the world as a legitimate political institution that will serve as the foundation for an independent Palestinian state. The PLO was originally founded in 1964 as a nonmilitant organization. Following the disastrous defeat of the Arab participants in the Six-Day War in 1967, however, Yasir Arafat and his al-Fatah organization then forged the PLO into a weapon to be used directly against Israel. In the late 1960s, the PLO carried out guerrilla raids into Israel while functioning as a kind of quasi-state with local autonomy within Jordan. In 1970, Jordan's King Hussein expelled the Palestinian guerrilla groups, which established new bases in Lebanon and Syria. Following the 1973 Arab-Israeli war, the PLO split into moderate and militant factions, with the moderate faction announcing its willingness to accept a Palestinian state in the West Bank and Gaza Strip and the militant, or rejectionist faction still demanding the total destruction of the state of Israel.

Since the mid-1970s, the moderate, mainstream PLO gained increasing legitimacy both in the Arab world and farther afield through participation in the United Nations. The situation was complicated, however, by the civil war in Lebanon that started in 1975 and the Israeli invasion of Lebanon in 1982, when PLO forces split between those loyal to Arafat and those loyal to Syria. In 1988, however, the PLO took on a new role when King Hussein of Jordan transferred his claims to the territory occupied by Israel to the PLO, and the Palestine National Council (the PLO's policy-making body) accepted United Nations Resolutions 242 and 338, as Arafat officially accepted Israel's right to exist. The PLO was removed from the U.S. State Department's roster of terrorist groups soon after.

Popular Front for the Liberation of Palestine (PFLP)   A Marxist-Leninist guerrilla organization founded by George Habash in 1967 as a leftist alternative to the Islamic nationalist al-Fatah. Between 1968 and

1970, the PFLP undertook a campaign of aircraft hijackings, mainly targeting Israel's El Al airline. The campaign culminated with the near-simultaneous hijackings of three airliners in September 1970, forcing them to land at Dawson's Field in Jordan, where they were subsequently destroyed. The PFLP also worked with the Red Army Faction in the Massacre at Israel's Lod Airport that resulted in 25 deaths. However, the PFLP hijacking in 1976 of an Air France plane to Entebbe, Uganda, failed after Israeli forces successfully raided on the airport. Similarly, a 1977 hijacking was thwarted by a rescue raid by West German commandos. The PFLP also recruited and worked with the infamous terrorist Carlos "the Jackal" (Ilyich Ramírez Sánchez). Later, the PFLP spearheaded the opposition to Yasir Arafat's moderate pronegotiation stance within the PLO. Recently (in 2001) the PFLP assassinated the Israeli tourism minister in retaliation for Israel having killed its secretary general.

Popular Front for the Liberation of Palestine–General Command (PFLP–GC)   A splinter group of the PFLP founded in 1968 by Ahmed Jabril, this faction was resolutely committed to the destruction of Israel and specialized in cross-border raids against Israeli citizens. The PFLP–GC has worked and trained Armenian and European terrorist groups. The group accumulated a variety of sophisticated weapons including Soviet AS-7 antiaircraft missiles, antitank missiles, artillery, and even motorized hang gliders used to carry raiders. The PFLP–GC has hijacked airliners, bombed planes and buses, and set off bombs in Jerusalem and other parts of Israel. Its most spectacular success may have been its exchange of three captured Israelis for 1,150 Palestinian prisoners held in Israel. The group has also been linked to the bombing of Pan Am flight 103 in December 1988.

Popular Struggle Front (PSF, Palestine Popular Struggle Front)   This Palestinian terrorist group broke from the Palestine Liberation Organization in 1974, joining "rejectionists" who opposed any moves toward settlement of the Arab-Israeli conflict. During the 1970s, the group engaged in hijackings and kidnappings, including the abduction of U.S. Army Colonel Ernest R. Morgan in Beirut. The group also launched bomb and rocket attacks against targets in Israel, leading to retaliatory attacks by the Israeli air force against PSF bases. In 1991, the group rejoined the PLO.

MIDDLE EAST

Along with Northern Ireland, the Middle East is the region most often associated with terrorism. At the crossroads of Europe, Africa, and Asia and endowed with a plentiful supply of the modern world's most vital resource, oil, it seems inevitable that this area would be the focus of a variety of conflicts.

The modern situation in the Middle East is the result of several developments. Following World War I, the remnants of the Turkish Ottoman Empire that had ruled the area for hundreds of years were displaced by British and French forces that sought to control the area. Meanwhile, European Jews had developed a strong movement called Zionism, with the goal of reestablishing of the biblical Jewish state in what was now Palestine. Just as the British had tried to pacify the Irish during World War I by promising them home rule, in the Balfour Declaration of November 2, 1917, they promised the Jews who had begun to settle in Palestine in increasing numbers that they could have their state. At the same time, the British sought to retain their alliance with Arab nations against Germany's ally, Turkey, by promising Arabs that they too could have self-determination after the war. Meanwhile, in the Sykes-Picot agreement of 1916, both the British and the French agreed to carve out spheres of influence in the Middle East and proposed to share Iran with Russia. There would be no way to fulfill all three of these agendas.

Following the war, the British drew boundaries to create what would eventually become the modern Arab nations of Syria, Jordan, Egypt, Saudi Arabia, Iraq, Iran, and Libya. They then chose rulers for the new states from the traditional ruling families in the Arab world. The British kept a close eye on these clients rulers and while the Islamic world did develop a pan-Arabist movement, the attempt at unification made little headway amid the long-standing rivalries among many of the ruling families. In 1922, the British received a mandate from the League of Nations to rule the Protectorate of Trans-Jordan, which included Palestine with its predominately Arab population and a significant minority of Jewish settlers. (The central conflict between Israel and the Palestinians is covered in the preceding section.)

In 1979, a fundamentalist Shiite Muslim government inspired by Ayatollah Khomeini overthrew the U.S.-backed shah in Iran. Emphasizing a relatively minor element of Islam, the *jihad* or holy war, the Iranians and other Shiite fundamentalists attacked not only Israel but also the United States, whose globe-girdling secular culture threatened to undermine what they saw as the purity of their faith. But the fundamentalists have had an equally significant agenda of seeking to overthrow moderate Islamic or secularist governments and replace them with a system of strict religious law (*sharia*).

Elsewhere in the Islamic world, Iraq's ruler, Saddam Hussein, remained a persistent thorn in the side of the West. Many believed he was still pursuing the development of weapons of mass destruction despite his defeat by a coalition of Western and moderate Arab military forces in the Persian Gulf War of 1990–91.

During the 1990s a wealthy Saudi expatriate named Osama bin Laden, who had gained experience in organizing resistance to the Soviet-backed government in Afghanistan in the 1980s, developed al-Qaeda, or "the

Base," a group dedicated to attacking American interests, seeing the United States even more than Israel as the new spearhead of a "crusade" against Islam. Working from bases in Afghanistan but organized into cells around the world, al-Qaeda stepped up the pace of its attacks, bombing two U.S. embassies in Africa in 1998, assaulting the U.S. destroyer *Cole* in Aden harbor, Yemen, in 2000, and finally, orchestrating the attacks by hijacked airliners that on September 11, 2001, destroyed the World Trade Center in New York and damaged the Pentagon.

The U.S. response to those attacks put great pressure on governments in the region to renounce terrorism and to cooperate at least to some extent in the campaign against the Afghani Taliban and al-Qaeda. Following the more or less successful conclusion of that campaign, the United States, Great Britain, and a small coalition of other nations attacked Iraq in 2003 and overthrew Saddam Hussein. However, the instability in postwar Iraq may be giving al-Qaeda and other terrrorist groups new causes and new opportunities to establish themselves. The situation in Turkey, the bridge between the Middle East and Europe, has also become complicated. The Kurds, too, form a distinct ethnic minority. The Kurdistan Workers' Party (PKK) had a Marxist-Leninist ideological base, but it later appealed to the more popular sentiment of nationalism. PKK leaders went to Lebanon, where they trained with experienced Islamic terrorists. Returning to Turkey and backed by Syria, the PKK waged guerrilla war, massacring thousands of Turkish villagers. During the 1990s, however, the PKK announced it was seeking a peaceful political solution in negotiation with the Muslim government that had come to power in Turkey. PKK leader Abdullah Ocalan was seized by Turkish agents in February 1999, tried, and sentenced to death (with execution suspended as of mid-2003), From prison, Ocalan initiated a peace effort, and the group expressed interest in achieving a political solution. However, the group says it retains the right to use violence and has continued some training.

In late 2003 radical Islamic terrorism apparently also made itself felt in Turkey. A shadowy group called the Great Eastern Islamist Raiders' Front (IBDA-C), probably linked to al-Qaeda, claimed responsibility for attacks in November on two synagogues and a British bank and consulate. Some Turkish leaders have also accused the Turkish Hezbollah of involvement, but the present status of this organization is unclear.

GROUPS IN THE MIDDLE EAST

Abu Nidal Organization (ANO)   A loose coalition of organizations founded and operated by terrorist leader Sabri al-Banna (Abu Nidal), who broke with the Palestine Liberation Organization in 1974. (The ANO designation is used by the U.S. State Department, not the terrorists themselves.) The organization has operated under other names such as the Arab Revolutionary Council, Fatah Revolutionary Council, and Black September. Since the 1980s, organizations under this umbrella have conducted more than 100 terrorist actions in more than 20 countries, killing about 900 people. Actions include attacks on passengers in airports in Vienna and Rome in December 1985 and the massacre of worshippers at an Istanbul synagogue in 1986. In 1993, six members of the organization were arrested, convicted, and given long prison terms. The organization was dormant during the remainder of the decade, and in January 2002 Abu Nidal died in an explosion in Beirut, Lebanon.

Arab National Youth Organization for the Liberation of Palestine (ANYOLP) The ANYOLP was a radical offshoot that broke away from the Popular Front for the Liberation of Palestine in 1972. The group engaged in hijackings and violent attacks, such as one on an Israeli diplomat in Cyprus in April 1973. Israel's retaliatory raid on Beirut led to the death of several PLO leaders and the breakup of the ANYOLP.

Armed Islamic Group (GIA, in French, "Groupe Islamic Armée") An Algerian Islamic extremist group, the GIA seeks to replace the secular Algerian regime with an Islamic state. When the Algerian government refused to recognize the election victory of the Islamic Salvation Front in 1992, the GIA began a campaign of terrorist attacks, often massacring village inhabitants. In September 1993, the GIA began to target foreigners in Algeria and had killed more than 100 by early 2000. In 1994, the GIA hijacked an Air France flight to Algiers, and it has also been linked to 1995 bombings in France.

Black September A terrorist organization founded primarily to seek revenge for the expulsion of militant Palestinian groups by the Jordanian army in 1970, Black September assassinated Wasfi al-tal, the prime minister of Jordan, in 1971. In 1972, the group claimed credit for the massacre of Israeli athletes at the Munich Olympics. According to observers, Black September, rather than being a true independent group, served as a vehicle for Abu Nidal and other al-Fatah leaders to carry out terrorist acts without taking direct responsibility for them.

Fatah Revolutionary Council *See* **Abu Nidal Organization**

Great Eastern Islamist Raiders' Front (IBDA-C) Formed in the 1970s, this obscure group has sought the overthrow of Turkey's secularist government and its replacement by a Sunni Muslim regime—although the group also includes a strange admixture of radical leftist ideology. The group has apparently recently formed ties with al-Qaeda. In November 2003 the IBDA-C claimed credit for major attacks on two synagogues and a British bank and consulate, all in Istanbul.

Hezbollah (in English, "The Party of God")   A radical Shiite organization founded in 1978, Hezbollah is dedicated to the establishment of fundamentalist Islamic rule in Lebanon and elsewhere. Hezbollah drew most of its inspiration and much of its backing from the fundamentalist revolution and regime in Iran, starting in 1979. Most of the group's terrorist activity targets U.S. and Israeli interests, including actions carried out under the rubric of "Islamic Jihad." Hezbollah terrorists bombed the U.S. embassy and Marine barracks in Lebanon in October 1983 and the U.S. embassy annex in Beirut in September 1984. They also held foreign hostages in Lebanon during the 1980s. By 2000 the group had apparently stepped up efforts to train Palestinians in guerrilla tactics.

Irgun (Irgun Zvai Leumi, in English, "National Military Organization")   An Israeli terrorist group founded in 1938, Irgun conducted terrorist attacks against the Palestinians and the British occupation authorities. The group's two most devastating attacks were the bombing of the King David Hotel (which housed British offices) on July 22, 1946, which killed 90 people—many not involved with the British, and the massacre of Arab villagers at Deir Yassin on April 9, 1948, an action conducted with the Stern Gang. Irgun leader Menachem Begin later became prime minister of Israel.

Islamic Group (IG, in Arabic, "Al Gama'at al-Islamaya")   A large, militant Islamic organization based in Egypt since the late 1970s, IG's spiritual leader is Sheikh Omar Abdel Rahman, who was convicted and imprisoned in the United States in connection with the 1993 World Trade Center bombing and various assassination plots. Starting in 1992, the Islamic Group began to attack foreign tourists in Egypt, hoping to hurt the nation's economy and destabilize the secularist government of Hosni Mubarak. The group also claimed credit for a 1995 assassination attempt against the Egyptian leader. In November 1997, terrorists from the group killed 58 tourists at Luxor, Egypt.

Islamic Jihad   The actual nature of this group has been hard to determine. Its name has surfaced mainly in connection with terrorist actions such as the April 1983 bombing of the U.S. embassy in Beirut and the bombings later that year of the U.S. Marine Corps barracks in Beirut and the barracks for the French peacekeepers. However, "Islamic Jihad" may simply be an umbrella term used by radical Shiite organizations such as Hezbollah when they feel it is safer to not claim direct responsibility for an action.

Kurdistan Workers' Party (PKK)   A Kurdish insurgent group in Turkey, based on Marxist-Leninist ideology, the PKK began in 1984 as a rural guerrilla group but then expanded into urban areas. In 1993, in response to severe government repression of the Kurdish minority, the PKK began to expand its attacks on government facilities to include Turkish diplomats and businesses throughout western Europe, as well as attacking Turkey's tourist industry by targeting foreign tourists. In 1995, the Turkish army began a military campaign against PKK bases in northern Iraq, and in 1999 Turkish authorities captured PKK leader Abdullah Ocalan, who was sentenced to death (this sentence was suspended). These events severely weakened the PKK's power. Encouraged by a conciliatory Ocalan, the group turned in a peaceful direction in 2002, changing the name of the political arm to the Kurdistan Freedom and Democracy Congress. However, the group retains the ability to launch terrorist attacks through its military wing, the People's Defense Force.

Muslim Brotherhood (Ikwhan) The Muslim Brotherhood is an Islamic fundamentalist group that seeks to replace secular governments in the Muslim world with theocratic governments that would be ruled according to Muslim law (*sharia*). There are actually several separate regional Muslim Brotherhood groups in Egypt, Syria, and other countries. The groups are active in domestic politics, where they are opposed by secularist governments or Muslims who disagree with their radical agenda. For example, when Syrian president Hafez al-Assad decided to enter the Lebanese civil war on the side of the Maronite Christians, Muslim Brotherhood radicals attacked al-Assad's younger brother Rifaat as well as police stations and offices of the ruling Baath party. Al-Assad cracked down on the group, which unsuccessfully attempted to assassinate him.

al-Qaeda (al-Quaida, in English, "The Base") A group established by Saudi Arabian millionaire Osama bin Laden around 1990, al-Qaida recruited mainly Arabs who had fought in Afghanistan against the Soviet invasion in the early 1980s. In February 1998, bin Laden issued a statement calling upon Muslims to kill U.S. citizens throughout the world. The group bombed the U.S. embassies in Nairobi, Kenya, and Dar es Salaam, Tanzania, on August 7, 1998, killing more than 300 people and injuring more than 5,000 others. The United States retaliated with a cruise missile attack that damaged but did not destroy the group's training camp in Afghanistan. Bin Laden's operatives are also suspected in the October 12, 2000, bombing of the U.S. destroyer *Cole*, which killed 17 sailors. Following the attacks on the World Trade Center and Pentagon on September 11, 2001, U.S. officials declared bin Laden to be the "prime suspect" in the attacks. Using air attacks and U.S. Special Forces in conjunction with Northern Alliance forces, the U.S. coalition killed many al-Qaeda and Taliban fighters and destroyed much of al-Qaeda's infrastructure in Afghanistan. However, the group probably has a significant but unknown number of cells in many countries including the United States, potentially being able to launch new terrrorist attacks. Meanwhile, al-Qaeda has worked closely with other groups such as Jemaah Islamiyah in Indonesia.

Stern Gang A Zionist terrorist group founded by Abraham Stern in the early 1940s. The group became known as Lehi after Stern's death in

1942. One of the group's major leaders, Yitzhak Shamir, later became prime minister of Israel. Two notorious actions by the Lehi group were the 1948 killing of the United Nations mediator for Palestine, Count Folke Bernadotte, who had been branded as "anti-Zionist," and the massacre that same year of more than 200 Palestinian civilians at the village of Deir Yassin, in which Irgun also participated.

AFRICA

Several dimensions of conflict in Africa have led to armed insurgency and outbreaks of terrorism. Geopolitically, the continent can be divided into two parts. Northern Africa, including Libya, Algeria, and Tunisia, is tied culturally to the Middle East through the common bond of Islam and has participated in the same dynamics that have motivated terrorism in the Middle East. The 1998 bombings of the U.S. embassies in Kenya and Tanzania by terrorists connected to Osama bin Laden also showed that Africa could be a theater for international as well as regional terrorism.

Algeria gained its independence from France through a bloody insurrection in the 1950s and early 1960s that saw much terrorism on both sides. Playing out a conflict common throughout the Islamic world, Islamic fundamentalists have unleashed terror against the moderate government since 1992. The government's failure to recognize the electoral victories of Islamist parties has only added fuel to the flames.

Libya, under Muammar al-Qaddafi, provided bases and support for many international terrorist groups (both Islamic and European) in the 1970s and early 1980s, but later seemed to be seeking closer ties with the West. (In 2003 Libya signed an agreement taking responsibility for the Pan Am 103 bombing in 1988, agreeing to pay compensation to victims.)

In sub-Saharan Africa, the principal dynamic in the 1950s and 1960s was the struggle of black majorities to gain independence from white-minority colonialist governments. This was complicated by the support given by the Soviets during the cold war to left-leaning guerrilla groups and the support of western governments and corporations for authoritarian black leaders who could protect investments (such as oil production in Nigeria).

Weak, unbalanced economies, undemocratic leadership, and a general neglect by the developed world continues to create the conditions for insurgency and civil war through much of Africa. Indeed, the violence has typically been on the larger scale of guerrilla war (Mozambique), factional struggle (Sierra Leone) and Liberia, and near-genocidal ethnic conflict (Rwanda) rather than the actions of small terrorist groups.

Southern Africa continues to deal with the legacy of the vicious struggle between South Africa's white minority apartheid government and black insurgents represented by the African National Congress (ANC) and other groups—a struggle that was also carried out by proxy in Mozambique, where RENAMO (Resistência Nacional Moçambicana, or Mozambique National Resistence), backed by the South Africa and Rhodesian white regimes, fought through the 1980s against leftist FRELIMO guerrilla forces supported by the ANC. Yet despite the high crime rate, sporadic terrorism, and the unmet basic needs of millions of poor blacks, South Africa, under an ANC government since 1990, has avoided the chaos that many feared would ensue after the apartheid government ended.

GROUPS IN AFRICA

African National Congress (ANC)   The major antiapartheid organization in South Africa, the ANC fought the apartheid regime by both political and guerrilla means. In 1961, following the Sharpesville massacre, the ANC formed a military offshoot, the Umkhonto we Sizwe ("Spear of the Nation"), headed by Nelson Mandela. During the 1960s and 1970s the guerrilla attacks generally avoided hurting innocent civilians. In 1986, however, the organization took a more militant turn when acting ANC president Oliver Tambo encouraged attacks on government facilities and officials and upon civilians viewed as supporters of the white regime. With the establishment of majority black rule in the 1994 elections in which Nelson Mandela became president of South Africa, the ANC has struggled to transform itself from an opposition group to the leading party in a government of national unity.

Eritrean Liberation Front (ELF)   A Muslim separatist group founded in 1958, the ELF seeks independence for Muslim Eritrea from Ethiopia. In 1971 a more militant faction called the Eritrean People's Liberation Front emerged and became dominant. (There was also a guerrilla unit designated the Eritrean Liberation Army.) The ELF has hijacked several Ethiopian Airlines flights.

FLN (in French, "Front de Liberation Nationale," in English, "National Liberation Front")   Founded in 1954, the FLN carried on a violent campaign consisting mainly of bombings against Algeria's French colonial rulers. The French settlers, through the OAS, retaliated with violent reprisals. The bloody fighting ended with the establishment of the independent Algerian state in 1962.

Islamic Salvation Front (FIS, in Arabic, "Jabha al Islamiyah li-Inqadh")   This group was the main fundamentalist Islamic party in Algeria. After the group won majorities in the 1991 elections, secular military leaders staged a coup on January 11, 1992, canceling follow-up elections and ruling by decree. Government forces cracked down on the FIS, arresting thousands of supporters. Throughout the 1990s, the FIS responded with armed attacks on Algerian officials and military, as well as terrorist attacks against civilians; eventually more than 100,000 people died in the conflict. In June 1999 the government and the FIS signed a cease-fire and amnesty agreement.

OAS ("Secret Army Organization") An organization of French and other European settlers in Algeria, the OAS fought against native Algerian nationalists who were seeking to overthrow French rule. In the early 1960s, the OAS took violent action to disrupt peace negotiations between the nationalists and the French government, killing the mayor of Evian, France, the site of the talks. Many members of the French military violently opposed the French decision to grant Algeria independence, and the OAS joined with four former French generals in an unsuccessful attempt to seize Algiers in April 1961. Their ensuing campaign of violence was met with equal violence by the Algerian National Liberation Front (FLN), and most Europeans fled the country.

RENAMO (in Portuguese, "Resistência Nacional Moçambicana") or Mozambique National Resistance (MNR) The MNR was formed in the 1970s after Portugal granted independence to Mozambique and a leftist government sympathetic to the African Nationalist Congress took power. The anticommunist MNR was sponsored by the apartheid regime in South Africa and the white government of Rhodesia. Its goal was to destabilize the Mozambican government and to fight FRELIMO, the leftist Mozambican guerrilla movement that was aiding the African National Congress in South Africa. In 1982 the MNR changed its name to RENAMO and began to expand its activities into the nearby countries of Zimbabwe (formerly Rhodesia), Malawi, and Zambia. During the 1980s RENAMO guerrillas used brutal tactics including assassination and kidnapping of government officials and relief workers as well as outright massacres, such as the killing of more than 400 civilians in the town of Homoine. In the early 1990s RENAMO's fortunes declined when the African National Congress took over the South African government, drying up the group's major source of aid. RENAMO and the Mozambican government began to negotiate and signed an accord in 1992. Both RENAMO and FRELIMO participated in UN-supervised elections in 1994; despite disputes over the 1999 election, large-scale violence did not recur.

Zimbabwe African People's Union (ZAPU) The ZAPU was founded in 1961 and led by Joshua Nkomo. It fought for black liberation against the white-run government of what was then known as Rhodesia. During the 1970s the group carried out frequent attacks against Rhodesia's white settlers and blacks whom it viewed as enemy collaborators. The group eventually lost out militarily and politically to its larger black rival, ZANU (Zimbabwe African National Union).

CENTRAL ASIA

While it is difficult to generalize over such a wide area, most terrorism in central Asia seems to stem from the conflict between ethnic or religious groups.

The breakup of the Soviet Union resulted in a number of independent Muslim republics in the volatile region bordered by Europe, Asia, and the Middle East. The Russians became concerned about the threat of terrorist or separatist activity resulting from the extension of Muslim influence. In the 1990s, Russia became embroiled in a war to suppress separatists in Chechnya, a mountainous Caucasian republic. The first Russian military efforts were unsuccessful, but a renewed effort following the Moscow bombings in 1999 succeeded in gaining a precarious control. However, Chechen terrorists continued to strike within Russia itself, following the October 2002 Moscow theater takeover with attacks in 2003 and a suspected subway bombing in February 2004.

In India, the sporadic conflict between Muslims and Hindus that has existed ever since the British partitioned the subcontinent into the mostly Hindu India and the mostly Muslim Pakistan has expressed itself in a number of actions, including the February 2000 hijacking of an Afghani jet on a domestic flight out of Kabul, and its diversion to an airport outside London. By that time the main focus of the conflict was the Indian province of Kashmir, which Muslims want to make either an independent state or part of Pakistan.

Pakistan became a linchpin of the region for the new war on terrorism following the September 11, 2001, attacks. The United States pressured Pakistan for intelligence and aid in identifying and neutralizing al-Qaeda and Taliban members in the area, as well as during the military operations in Afghanistan that followed. At the same time, however, Pakistani president Pervez Musharraf has had to keep in mind the largely Islamic population's support for the Taliban. The Pakistan border has remained rather porous; in 2003 Taliban fighters who had been scattered in the earlier fighting may be regrouping and coming back into Afghanistan.

Besides the Hindu-Muslim conflict, the Sikhs, a religious minority who live mainly in northern India, have also been in violent conflict with the Hindu majority. Demanding a separate state and reacting to Indian government actions such as the 1984 attack on one of Sikism's holiest temples (the Golden Temple of Amritsar), Sikh terrorists assassinated Indian prime minister Indira Gandhi in October 1984 and were accused of the bombing of an Air India jet in June 1985 that resulted in 329 deaths.

For many years Sri Lanka (formerly British Ceylon) has been the scene of a persistent terrorist campaign by a group known as the Tamil Tigers that seeks independence for the Tamil minority (the majority in the country are Sinhalese). Despite some victories by the Sri Lankan military, the insurgency continued. However, in 2002 the Tamil Tigers and the government signed a comprehensive cease-fire.

GROUPS IN CENTRAL ASIA

Armenian Revolutionary Army   This Armenian nationalist organization surfaced suddenly in 1983 to claim credit for the murder of two Turkish diplomats in Brussels. Later that year, the group seized the Turkish embassy in Lisbon. The terrorists blew up the building, killing themselves and two of their hostages. It remained unclear whether the group had any real existence or was a cover name.

Armenian Secret Army for the Liberation of Armenia (ASALA)   An organization of Armenian nationalists founded in 1975, ASALA seeks an end to discrimination against and mistreatment of Turkey's Armenian minority. Its goal is the formation of an independent state in the traditional Armenian homeland in eastern Turkey, northern Iran, northern Iraq, and the former Soviet Armenian republic. The group was fueled by anger among many Armenians who feel that the West favors Turkey for geopolitical purposes and continues to ignore the 1915 Turkish genocide of Armenians that claimed an estimated 1.5 million victims. The group has engaged in several terrorist bombings including a 1983 attack on Orly Airport in Paris. By the end of the 1980s the organization was in decline, and many Armenian nationalists now oppose terrorism as being counterproductive.

Harakat ul-Mujahadeen (HUM)   This radical Muslim group is based in Pakistan but operates mainly in Kashmir, an area disputed between Muslim Pakistan and majority Hindu India. The group has attacked Indian troops and tourists in Kashmir and has been linked to some kidnappings. The HUM is believed to be part of Osama bin Laden's network. Its terrorist training bases in Afghanistan were damaged by U.S. cruise missile attacks in 1999.

Kashmiri Liberation Front   This is a separatist group representing Muslim Kashmiris who want independence from Hindu-dominated India. This and other separatist groups receive covert support from Muslim Pakistan, which also claims the Kashmir region and has fought repeated military skirmishes with India.

Tamil Tigers (Liberation Tigers of Tamil Eelam or LTTE)   The Tamil Tigers are a Sri Lankan separatist guerrilla organization founded in 1972. The island nation of Sri Lanka (Ceylon) has seen bitter conflict between the Hindu Tamil minority and the Buddhist Sinhalese majority. The Tigers seek an independent Tamil state in the northern and eastern parts of the island. The group is distinctive in its "pioneering" use of suicide bombers, a tactic later widely adopted by some Palestinian groups. Despite receiving antiterrorist aid and troops from India in the late 1980s, the Sri Lankan government was unable to defeat the Tigers, who have proven able to mount substantial attacks. The result was a bloody stalemate that ended in 2002 with the signing of a comprehensive cease-fire.

EAST ASIA

The major countries of east Asia have not experienced much terrorism. China's government keeps a close rein even on peaceful dissident groups. Japan, perhaps the Asian nation most like the industrial West socioeconomically, has had its own indigenous left-wing terrorist groups, including the Japanese Red Army, but as with European groups such as the Red Army Faction, leftist terrorism has not been a major concern in recent years.

Rather than a resurgence from the right, however, the mid-1990s witnessed the emergence of the idiosyncratic terror cult Aum Shinrikyo, which made the first large-scale chemical weapons terrorist attack when it released Sarin nerve gas into the Tokyo subway. Japanese police arrested the cult's leader and have cracked down on the group's widespread facilities.

Another potential Asian terrorist trouble spot is North Korea. North Korea's communist government has long carried out sporadic state-sponsored terrorism against South Korea and has developed ballistic missiles and is now believed to have a few nuclear weapons. North Korea's economy is very weak, and its leaders began in the late 1990s to seek better cooperation both with South Korea and the United States. In a possible breakthrough in June 2000, the presidents of the two Koreas had a cordial meeting and expressed hopes for closer cooperation and eventual unification. However, by 2002–03 North Korea's rhetoric had again grown bellicose, with North Korea demanding a nonaggression pact from the United States in exchange for its abandoning its nuclear program.

GROUPS IN EAST ASIA

Aum Shinrikyo (Aum Supreme Truth, now Aleph) A Japanese religious cult established in 1987 by Soko Asahara, who formed a grandiose plan to take over the world. When the plan failed to materialize, Asahara gradually emphasized apocalyptic elements, including an Armageddon that he claimed would be triggered by the United States. Using the cult's considerable financial resources and technically trained members, the group began to research and develop chemical, biological, and even nuclear weapons. On March 20, 1995, cult members released Sarin, a nerve gas, into the Tokyo subway, killing 12 people and injuring more than 5,000. Despite the arrest of its leader, the cult continued to recruit members in the late 1990s, though the group remains under close police surveillance. In 2000 the group, under new leadership, had changed its name to Aleph and has claimed to renounce violence.

Chukaku-Ha (in English, the "Nucleus") A Japanese leftist extremist group, Chukaku-Ha seeks to overthrow Japan's constitutional monarchy and to sever ties with the United States. While the group is primarily political, it does have a terrorist wing that has focused on attacking infrastructure and property rather than killing. In 1988, the group attacked the Japanese National Railway to protest its privatization, as well as attacking the construction site for the Tokyo International Airport at Narita.

Japanese Red Army (JRA, in Japanese, "Nippon Sekigun") This small but extremely violent Japanese left-wing terrorist group was founded in 1971 as an offshoot of radical student movements of the late 1960s. Its founder, Fusako Shigenobu, linked up with Palestinian terrorists and went with a group of followers to train in Lebanon. The JRA first became known to the world when it hijacked a Japanese airliner in 1970. It also carried out terrorist acts in the Middle East on behalf of the Popular Front for the Liberation of Palestine, such as the massacre at Lod Airport in Israel in 1972. In September 1974, the JRA seized the French embassy in the Hague and held 12 hostages until the French government freed an imprisoned comrade. Since the late 1970s, the JRA no longer seems to operate as a distinct group, but its members continued to carry out terrorist acts individually or under the umbrella name Anti-Imperialist International Brigade.

ASIA–PACIFIC

This wide-ranging region, characterized by scattered islands and a diversity of small ethnic groups, has become a new terrorist trouble spot in the 2000s.

Surprisingly to many people, Indonesia has more Muslims than any other country. In 1999 separatists in East Timor achieved independence after a bloody struggle. Meanwhile bitter ethnic conflict between Muslims and Christians flared up after the overthrow of the dictator Suharto. Many indigenous tribes such as the Dayak also fought bitter battles characterized by the wielding of machetes and sometimes even cannibalism.

The most recent and dangerous terrorist erruption, however, is the growth of Jemaah Islamiyah. This group has close ties to al-Qaeda and seeks to create a great Islamic state throughout the Asia-Pacific region. In October 2002 the group set off a huge bomb in Bali, killing at least 200 people and wounding more than 300 more.

The other major terrorist trouble spot in the region is the Philippines. There the Abu Sayyaf, another group believed to have ties to al-Qaeda, has kidnapped numerous persons, including a number of foreign journalists and missionaries.

GROUPS IN ASIA–PACIFIC

Abu Sayyaf   This group is a radical Islamic separatist group in the Philippines, with ties to al-Qaeda. It had split from the Moro Liberation Front in the 1990s. The group's political agenda, however, seems less important than its desire to raise money by kidnapping and extortion. Its victims have included a number of foreign tourists, journalists, and missionaries; the latter including Gracia and Martin Burnham. (Gracia was rescued by commandos, but Martin died in the firefight.)

Jemaah Islamiyah (JI)   This Islamic group seeks to create a regional government following radical Islamic principles. The group has close ties to al-Qaeda and has launched major attacks, notably the Bali nightclub bombing in October 2002. Its leader, Abu Bakir Bashir, and other plotters of the Bali attack were arrested and tried in 2003 on numerous charges. Sentences are pending.

Komando Jihad   This group, founded by Ali Moertopo in 1977, was a Muslim separatist group in Indonesia. Its terrorist activities included a 1980 hijacking of an Indonesian airliner, which was foiled by a raid by government forces. Many Komando Jihad terrorists were imprisoned in the 1980s and released in the 1990s.

Moro Liberation Front (MLF, Moro National Liberation Front)   This is a Muslim separatist group seeking a separate state for Muslims in the islands of Mindanao and the Sulu Archipelago in the southern Philippines. The group has received support from both Libya's Muammar al-Qaddafi and Iran. The group mainly conducted guerrilla operations, but in 1975 it hijacked two Philippine airliners. (The second hijacking resulted in the death or capture of the hijackers.) Government counterterrorism efforts and internal disputes weakened the group. In 1986 the new Philippine president, Corazon Aquino, signed a truce agreement with the MLF.

New People's Army (NPA)   A Maoist guerrilla group in the Philippines, associated with the Communist Party of the Philippines. During the 1970s and early 1980s the group grew, spreading its influence from its rural roots into the cities. The repressive activities of the Marcos regime brought new supporters to the movement. The group engaged in relatively small-scale terrorist activities, primarily against government officials and police. In the late 1980s the group underwent internal splits and purges that weakened it, and the overthrow of the Marcos regime offered democratic alternatives, although continuing poverty still fueled unrest. In 2001-02 the group began again to target U.S. military personnel.

LATIN AMERICA

The story of terrorism in Latin America is woven from persistent strands. The countries in South America (as well as Mexico) were founded by Spanish and Portuguese, starting in the 16th century. The conquest of extensive indigenous societies (the Aztec, Maya, and Inca) created a continually exploited underclass of Indian peoples. Colonialism ensured that a European elite and its descendants controlled vast lands worked by impoverished native peoples.

The invasion of Spain by Napoleon in the early 19th century triggered liberal, revolutionary sentiments in members of the Latin American elite who also looked for inspiration to the first American revolution, which had given birth to the United States in 1776. Despite brutal countermeasures by Spain, a series of successful revolutions swept Latin America, led by José de San Martín and Bernardo O'Higgins in the south, Simón Bolívar in the north. A successful revolution in Mexico overthrew European rule in 1821. But despite the idealism of leaders such as Bolívar, who sought to create something like a United States of the Americas, the new countries went their separate ways.

By the 20th century, the predominant influence on Latin America was its powerful northern neighbor, the United States. Ever since the United States had claimed the Western Hemisphere as its "manifest destiny," and thus off limits to Europeans in the preceding century, American businesses and corporations had invested a lot of capital in South and Central America. They pressed the federal government to protect their interests with military force, including the U.S. Marines on occasion. Most Latin American countries remained poor and poorly governed. Typically, the military or a military-backed oligarchy brutally suppressed any political opposition.

Following World War II, the poor nations in Africa and Asia that had been ruled by Europeans struggled for independence and, with less success, economic self-sufficiency. During the cold war, the Soviets generally supported insurgencies and guerrilla groups that at least claimed to represent the poor, while the United States, in the name of stability and the checking of worldwide communism, usually sided with the ruling oligarchs.

The revolution that brought Fidel Castro to power in Cuba in 1959 gave leftist insurgents a beachhead in the Western Hemisphere. Castro's victory inspired charismatic guerrilla leaders such as his compatriot Che Guevara, French revolutionary theorist and exponent of terrorism Frantz Fanon, and the Brazilian Carlos Marighella. To these thinkers, terrorism was not a blind striking out against injustice, but a weapon that, combined with guerrilla war in the countryside, could destabilize oligarchic governments. Much of their thinking, including the use of terrorism to trigger government repression that could in turn inspire a general uprising, would become the common currency of terrorist groups around the world.

Other than in Cuba, leftist insurgents achieved long-term results only in Nicaragua, where in 1979 the leftist Sandinistas overthrew U.S.-backed dictator Anastasio Somoza, a staunch anticommunist. The Sandinistas were then attacked by the contras, U.S.-backed guerrillas, and they were defeated in a 1990 election by a U.S.-backed moderate candidate, Violeta Chamorro.

In Chile, the brief reign of the leftist government of Salvador Allende was overthrown in 1973 by the U.S.-backed Augusto Pinochet. In Chile, as in Argentina, right-wing "death squads" unleashed state terrorism on insurgents, political opponents, and random citizens. Similar tactics were also used in Guatemala and El Salvador. Some hope for democracy emerged, however, when Patricio Aylwin Azócar, leader of a democratic coalition, was elected president of Chile. While Pinochet still had a powerful position as head of the army, he stepped down in 1998. Later that year, he was arrested in London on charges of brutality against Spanish citizens in Chile during his regime. The British eventually declined to extradite him on grounds of his poor health, but he may still face charges in Chile.

In Colombia, the continuing three-sided struggle between the government, leftist rebels, and drug lords has brought calls for increased American aid, which opponents doubt would have any effect on the drug problem, and could involve the United States in a Vietnam-like quagmire.

Peru's Sendero Luminoso (Shining Path) became known for its unusual and ruthless tactics. The teachings of its founder, Abimael Guzmán, are based on a Maoist model, focusing on gaining control of rural areas and ruthlessly eliminating opponents using both guerrilla and terrorist tactics. Guzmán's arrest and successful campaigns by the Peruvian military had largely destroyed the Shining Path by the mid-1990s.

Latin America continues to struggle with poverty, insurgency, and outbreaks of terrorism, though economic growth in areas, such as Brazil, and the possibility of reform in others, such as Mexico, have brought some hope.

GROUPS IN LATIN AMERICA

Bandero Roja (GBR, in English, "Red Flag") Was a small Venezuelan leftist guerrilla and terrorist group that operated mainly during the late 1970s and early 1980s. It primarily targeted wealthy business owners, kidnapping them for ransom and demanding protection money. In 1981 the group carried out its best-known action, the simultaneous hijacking of three domestic airliners, demanding the release of prisoners plus a ransom of $10 million. Following the failure of negotiations, some of the group then fled to Cuba, while others were arrested or killed by government forces.

Cinchoneros Popular Liberation Movement (MPL)   This small Honduran leftist group was the armed wing of the People's Revolutionary Union, a communist splinter group. (Cinchoneros was the nickname of Serapio Romero, a Honduran peasant rebel apparently executed in the 19th century.) The group financed itself through robberies and kidnappings, as well as receiving support and cooperation from Cuba and Salvadoran FMLN guerrillas. In 1980, the MPL hijacked a Honduran Airlines jet in an unsuccessful attempt to win freedom for 15 Salvadoran leftists imprisoned in Honduras. In 1982, the MPL raided an economic conference in San Pedro Sula, taking 105 hostages. Again failing to win their demands, they traded the hostages for safe passage to Cuba. The group conducted other attacks into the late 1980s.

Extraditables   The terrorist arm of the Colombian drug cartels, the Extraditables emerged in the 1980s. By the end of the decade they had killed 261 people and wounded more than 1,200 in about 200 separate attacks, including the bombing of an Avianca airliner in November 1989 and the truck bombing of the Bogotá police headquarters the same month. The purpose of the terrorism was to pressure the Colombian government to back down from its antidrug efforts and to refuse to extradite drug lords to the United States.

Frente Farabundo Martí de Liberación Nacional (FMLN, in English, "Farabundo Martí National Liberation Front")   FMLN is the umbrella organization for the five major Salvadoran left-wing guerrilla groups that fought to overturn the government of El Salvador during the 1980s. During that time the group received extensive support from Cuba and the Sandinista regime in Nicaragua. The group used terrorism as a core part of its strategy to destabilize the Salvadoran government and prevent the establishment of a Western-style democracy. As with many other guerrilla groups, FMLN has used kidnapping and extortion (which it refers to as "taxes") to raise money in areas it controls.

Fuerzas Armadas de Liberación Nacional (FALN, in English, "Armed Forces of National Liberation")   A militant Puerto Rican separatist organization, FALN has conducted terrorist bombings in both the United States and Puerto Rico. Its best-known attacks were the bombing of five New York City banks on October 26, 1974, and the bombing of Fraunces Tavern in New York's Wall Street area, which killed four people and wounded more than 60. The group was disrupted in April 1980 by the arrest of 11 members in Evanston, Illinois, during an attempted armed robbery. The FALN set off additional bombs in New York on December 31,

1983, targeting the FBI, police, and court offices; the group largely became inactive in the 1980s. This group should not be confused with the Venezuelan FALN, a marxist guerrilla group active in the 1960s and early 1970s.

Fuerzas Armadas Revolucionarias de Colombia (FARC, in English, "Revolutionary Armed Forces of Colombia")   The largest leftist guerrilla movement in Colombia, FARC was established in 1966 by the Colombian Communist Party as its military wing, and the organization had close relations with the Soviet and Cuban governments. During the 1980s, FARC conducted bombings of Colombian government targets as well as U.S.-owned businesses in Colombia and carried out killings and kidnappings. A May 1984 cease-fire ended large-scale military actions but did not stop the terror campaign. FARC has also cooperated with drug interests, offering protection in exchange for money to purchase weapons and supplies, and it has also kidnapped people for ransom, including the abduction of a U.S. Peace Corps worker, who was released after a $250,000 ransom was received. In 1998, FARC began sporadic peace negotiations with the Colombian government, but they ended abruptly in February 2002, when the group hijacked an airliner, kidnapping a Colombian senator in the process.

Fuerzas Revolucionarios Populares Lorenzo Zelaya (FRP-LZ, in English, "Lorenzo Zelaya Popular Revolutionary Forces")   The FRP-LZ was a Honduran Marxist-Leninist group which sought to overthrow the Honduran government. Active mainly during the early 1980s, the FRP-LZ targeted Honduran government facilities (such as the National Assembly), U.S. diplomats, and diplomats from Argentina, Chile, and Peru (countries that the group accused of supporting U.S. interests). In 1982 the group hijacked a Honduran airliner. The hijackers failed to win their demands for $1 million and the release of 32 political prisoners, but they were allowed to flee to Cuba after releasing their hostages. The arrest and defection of the group's leader, Efraín Duarte Salgado, in 1983 led to the group's disintegration.

Movimiento 19 de Abril (M-19, in English, "Movement of April 19")   A Colombian rebel group that combined leftist, nationalist, and populist appeals for the overthrow of the Colombian establishment and an end to U.S. imperialism. The group was active through the 1970s and 1980s, financing its plans with robberies and extortion of (and sometimes cooperation with) drug traffickers. The group also received training and support from Cuba, Nicaragua, and Libya. In 1980, M-19 seized 15 diplomats and 16 other hostages at the embassy of the Dominican Republic, freeing them after 61 days in exchange for ransom and safe passage to Cuba. The group's largest attack was the 1985 seizure of the Justice Ministry building in Bogotá, involving about 500 hostages, including members of the Supreme Court and Council of State. Government forces counterattacked, killing the terrorists, but 11 Supreme Court justices and 50 other hostages died in the fighting. The M-19 also carried on a running skirmish with the drug cartels. In the 1990s, M-19 signed several accords with the government and began to function as a regular political party.

Movimiento Revolucionario do Octobre 8 (MR-8, in English, "Revolutionary Movement of October 8")   MR-8 was a Brazilian terrorist organization that was particularly active in the 1960s and 1970s. It was affiliated with the Brazilian Communist Party. It conducted numerous attacks, of which the most famous was the kidnapping of U.S. ambassador Charles Elbrick in 1969.

Movimiento Revolucionario Tupac Amaru (MRTA, in English, "Tupac Amaru Revolutionary Movement")   A Marxist-Leninist guerrilla movement founded in Peru by radical university students and intellectuals in 1983, the MRTA is named after Tupac Amaru, an 18th-century anticolonialist leader. The group has emphasized a traditional marxist approach (as opposed to the Maoist approach of Peru's Shining Path). During the 1980s, the MRTA specialized in attacks on U.S. representatives and businesses and raised money through extortion of businesses and offering protection to drug traffickers. During the 1990s, many members were arrested and the group seemed to be in decline. However, in December 1996, MRTA terrorists seized the Japanese embassy in Lima, taking hundreds of hostages. Government forces retook the embassy and freed the captives, and MRTA mounted no further major attacks during the decade.

Puerto Rican Nationalists   Throughout much of the 20th century the Puerto Rico Nationalist Party sought independence of the island from the United States. The party's most important leader, Pedro Albizo Campos, failed to win popular support in a 1932 election, and was subsequently imprisoned for plotting to overthrow the U.S. government. Freed and repatriated after World War II, Campos again attempted to gain political support, but the Nationalist Party did poorly in the 1948 election. Campos and the more radical nationalists abandoned politics in favor of terrorist action. In 1950 they attacked both the governor's house in Puerto Rico and Blair House in Washington, D.C., where President Harry Truman was staying during White House renovations. In 1954, armed Puerto Rican nationalist terrorists fired into the chambers of the U.S. House of Representatives, wounding five representatives.

Sendero Luminoso (in English, "The Shining Path")   A Peruvian Maoist-inspired terrorist group founded by Abimael Guzmán Reynoso in 1969, Sendero Luminoso has been one of the most unpredictable and vicious terrorist groups. The group is rural-based and has sought to enlist the support of the native Quechua people through appeals to their heritage and traditions. With little support from Cuba or other outside forces, the group provides for its needs mainly through bank robberies and extortion ("war taxes"). Ironically, although the group has attacked Peruvian officials and foreign diplomats, the majority of its violence has been directed against the very peasants it claims to be fighting for, brutally punishing people suspected of collaborating with the authorities. In the 1990s the group went into decline with the arrest of its leader, Abimael Guzmán, in 1992, the arrest of other leaders in 1995, and a government amnesty for members who agreed to renounce terrorism.

Tonton Macoutes (in English, "bogeyman," Volunteers for National Security) Tonton Macoutes was an unofficial militia sponsored and used by Haitian dictator François "Papa Doc" Duvalier to eliminate enemies and silence dissent via state terror. After Duvalier was deposed in 1985, the Tonton Macoutes offered its services to another president, Henri Namphy. In 1988 the Tonton Macoutes attacked a church service in Port-au-Prince that included dissenters, killing nine persons, wounding 77, and setting fire to the church. The church's pastor, Jean-Bertrand Aristide, survived the attack, however, and rallied supporters to fight the Tonton Macoutes. In 1990, Aristide briefly served as president, was deposed, and then was restored to office in 1994 with the aid of international forces. The decade ended with a new spate of political violence.

Tupamaros (Movimiento de Liberación Nacional, or MLN, in English, "National Liberation Movement") Tupamaros is a Uruguayan guerrilla and terrorist group founded in the early 1960s by Raul Sendic Antonaccio. Like the MRTA, the MLN derived its name from Tupac Amaru, an 18th-century Peruvian Indian chieftain who fought the Spanish. The group began its activities by robbing and attacking banks and other institutions, but by the mid-1960s it had broadened its base in the capital of Montevideo, gaining influence through propaganda exposing government corruption and by employing the Robin Hood–like tactic of giving the proceeds of robberies to the poor. In 1970 the Tupamaros kidnapped and killed USAID official Daniel A. Mitrione. The following year they kidnapped the British ambassador. The Uruguayan government successfully suppressed the group in 1972, but the battle also resulted in the reactionary imposition of military government until 1984. In 1985 the new civilian government declared an amnesty for Tupamaros prisoners, and Sendic, the founder, entered mainstream politics.

UNITED STATES AND CANADA

Until the Oklahoma City bombing of 1995 and, especially, the attacks on the World Trade Center and the Pentagon in 2001, the United States had suffered less from terrorism than many other developed nations. However, political and economic violence have deep roots in U.S. history.

During the first half of the 19th century, the bitter battle over slavery saw terrorism on both sides, such as the violence over Kansas statehood that gave rise to the term *bleeding Kansas*. Following the Civil War, southern whites brutally repressed the freed blacks. Race remained a persistent source of terrorism in the United States.

In the later 19th and early 20th century, labor struggles were another major source of terrorism. In many industries the guns and clubs of private police forces were used to break up strikes and union organizations, and the municipal and state police often sided with the companies against the strikers. In turn, labor radicals such as the more militant members of the International Workers of the World (IWW) engaged in some sabotage and bombings.

In addition to the largely peaceful civil rights and antiwar movements, the social upheaval of the 1960s also spun off a variety of leftist terrorist groups. Their causes ranged from black power (Black Panthers, Black Liberation Army, some Black Muslims) to leftist anti-imperialism (the Weathermen, New World Liberation Front, and others) to the bizarre (Symbionese Liberation Army). However, the end of the Vietnam War and the prosperity of the 1980s led to a diminishment of left-wing terrorism in the United States.

In the late 1980s and 1990s, most terrorism came from the right wing. Its motivations included white supremacy (as with the Aryan Nations and the Ku Klux Klan, as well as Christian Identity groups that espoused a theology of whiteness) as well as a more generalized populist revolt against what many people, particularly in rural areas, perceived to be a too-powerful federal government that served alien economic interests. By the late 1980s this sentiment had found its widespread expression in the founding of numerous militias. (Although most militias did not engage in overt violence, some fringe elements did. The Oklahoma City bombing, however, was the work of two men who had no real involvement with organized militia groups.)

The comprehensive counterterrorist program that followed the September 11, 2001, attacks has probably suppressed most indigenous terrorist activity with the exception of environmental and animal rights terrorism (see below). The anthrax attacks the following month remain unsolved, although expert opinion leans toward it being the work of a lone wolf with no connection to foreign terrorism. In May 2003 radical antiabortion terrrorist Eric Rudolph, believed to be responsible for the 1996 Olympic Park bombing as well as several clinic attacks, was finally captured after eluding authorities in rural North Carolina for several years.

Canada has had little terrorist activity, with the exception of some "spillover" activity from U.S. groups and the activities of some radical French Quebec separatists, which has diminished as Quebec has gained greater autonomy.

A few other issues have also caused persistent terrorism. Radical antiabortion groups have bombed women's health clinics and killed personnel. Buildings presumed to be associated with Jews or gays have also been attacked.

Even the Earth and its animals have found terrorist advocates. Ecoterrorists under the name Earth Liberation Front have destroyed lumber company facilities and even a Colorado ski resort. A related group, animal rights activists, such as the Animal Liberation Front, have freed laboratory animals and attacked facilities involved with animal or genetic research. In recent years the groups have stepped up their attacks. The ELF has targeted sport utility vehicles (SUVs) in dealer parking lots as well as newly built apartment complexes, while the ALF continues to attack animal research facilities.

GROUPS IN THE UNITED STATES AND CANADA

Animal Liberation Front (ALF)/Earth Liberation Front (ELF)   Radical animal rights and environmental organizations starting in 1978 created a shadowy activist network. The group has no formal structure and may act under either name or both. It has conducted several attacks on research and food facilities in Great Britain and the United States, notably the lacing of Mars candy bars with rat poison in 1984 and the destruction of a livestock-disease research laboratory at the University of California, Davis, in 1987. In October 1999 the same group, under the name Earth Liberation Front, claimed responsibility for arson that caused $12 million in damage to a Vail, Colorado, ski resort. Later major targets included an egg farm, a horticultural research station involved with genetic engineering, and a McDonald's restaurant. Lately, the group (as ELF) has been burning down newly built apartment complexes and torching SUVs in dealer parking lots. So far, the group has targeted only property and no one has been injured.

Armed Resistance Unit   A small U.S. left-wing organization that claimed credit for the November 6, 1983, bombing of the Senate wing of the U.S. Capitol building. The group stated that the attack was in protest of the U.S. invasion of Grenada. The group faded away; it may have been a cover name for the United Freedom Front.

Aryan Nations   A loose coalition of U.S. white supremacist, anti-Semitic radical right-wing groups. The organization was founded by Richard Girnt Butler in 1974 and attracted followers from the Ku Klux Klan and other racist groups. It seeks the formation of a "white homeland" in the northwest United States. Although it does not directly conduct terrorist operations, some observers suspect it is a haven or supporter of terrorist groups such as the Order as well as individual terrorists. By 2000 successful legal action by the Southern Poverty Law Center had resulted in the group's losing its compound and much of its resources.

Black Liberation Army An extremist U.S. Black Power group, the Black Liberation Army killed eight law enforcement officers between 1971 and 1973. A massive FBI effort led to the arrests of most of the group's leaders, and the group disintegrated.

Black Panther Party The most prominent U.S. Black Power group, the Black Panthers were founded in 1966 in Oakland, California, by Huey Newton and Bobby Seale. The Panthers attempted to be both a grassroots community organization, running schools and breakfast programs, and an urban guerrilla force that targeted law enforcement officers. In the late 1960s and early 1970s a series of violent confrontations with police and a massive FBI effort led to the death, arrest, or exile of most of the organization's leading members.

Covenant, the Sword, and the Arm of the Lord A U.S. white supremacist group, affiliated with Aryan Nations, this group was active in the 1980s. In 1985 police uncovered a weapons cache and training camp.

Front de Libération du Québec (FLQ, in English, "Quebec Liberation Front") This violent separatist group bombed Canadian government and public facilities in the province of Quebec during the 1960s. On October 5, 1970, the group kidnapped British trade commissioner James R. Cross in Montreal and demanded $500,000 and the release of 23 FLQ prisoners for his return. When Canadian prime minister Pierre Trudeau refused to negotiate, the group kidnapped another official, Quebec's minister of labor and immigration, Pierre Laporte, and strangled him to death. Police found the kidnappers' hideout and negotiated for Cross's release in exchange for safe passage to Cuba.

Ku Klux Klan (KKK) A white supremacist, racist group, the KKK, was originally founded in the United States during the post–Civil War Reconstruction period as a way to intimidate and suppress the newly freed blacks and their white political allies. The group had a resurgence in the 1920s and it broadened its agenda to include anti-immigrant, anti-Catholic, and anti-Semitic activities. Klansmen sought to strike terror into their victims by wearing white sheets and hoods and burning crosses, and the group carried out hundreds of lynchings early in the 20th century. Starting in the 1980s, however, successful lawsuits brought by Morris Dees of the Southern Poverty Law Center and other plaintiffs bankrupted and dispersed the major Klan organizations, and the group is now more of a symbol of hatred than an active terrorist force.

New World Liberation Front (NWLF) A U.S. left-wing group, mainly active in California during the 1970s, the NWLF conducted numerous, mostly small bombings against public utilities, particularly targeting International Telephone and Telegraph (IT&T), which it accused of helping to overthrow the leftist Allende government in Chile.

The Order   A violent, white supremacist, neo-Nazi organization, the Order had a brief but violent career in the mid-1980s. It was founded in 1983 by Robert Matthews, who died in a shootout with police in Puget Sound, Washington, in December 1984. The group raised money through robbery, notably an attack on a Brinks armored car outside Ukiah, California, in June 1983, which yielded $3.6 million, at that time the largest armored car robbery in U.S. history. The Order declared that its goal was to overthrow the U.S. government, which it claimed was "occupied" or controlled by secret Zionist forces, and to establish an independent "white nation" in the northwestern United States. The group assassinated Denver radio talk-show host Alan Berg (who was Jewish) in 1984 and bombed a Seattle theater and a synagogue in Boise, Idaho. Successful investigation by the FBI and subsequent prosecution essentially destroyed the group by 1987.

Posse Comitatus (in English, "Power of the County")   A U.S. right-wing organization founded in 1969, it was one of the earliest expressions of a generalized movement on the radical right that rejected federal authority, taxation, and courts, insisting that only local, county-level authorities were legitimate. Although it has not carried out terrorist actions as a group, members have been implicated in shoot-outs with police and attacks on government facilities and officials.

Symbionese Liberation Army (SLA)   A tiny, idiosyncratic, California-based left-wing terrorist group, the SLA surfaced with the killing of Oakland education superintendent Marcus Foster and the kidnapping and subsequent brainwashing of newspaper heiress Patricia Hearst in 1974. The SLA tried to build its image in the minority community by demanding ransom in the form of food distribution to the poor, but the group had no real popular support. On May 17, 1974, a gun battle and a fire killed six members of the small group, effectively destroying it.

United Freedom Front (UFF)   The UFF was a small but active American radical left-wing organization that attacked U.S. military installations and major corporations during the early 1980s. A major effort by federal and local law enforcement agencies led to the arrest and imprisonment of virtually the entire group.

Weather Underground (popularly known as the Weathermen)   The Weather Underground was a violent Marxist terrorist group formed in Chicago in 1969 by members of Students for a Democratic Society (SDS) who wanted a more militant, revolutionary program. (The name comes from a line in a Bob Dylan song: "You don't need a weatherman to know which way the wind blows.") The Weathermen conducted numerous bombings and arson attacks for about a year. In March 1970, however, seven of the group's top leaders were killed in an apparently accidental explosion in a New York City apartment they had been using for assembling bombs.

ACRONYMS FOR OTHER TERRORIST GROUPS

AIM	American Indian Movement
ALF	Arab Liberation Front (part of the PLO) (Middle East)
BLA	Black Liberation Army (United States)
BSO	Black September Organization (Middle East)
CSA	The Covenant, the Sword, and the Arm of the Lord (United States)
ELN	Ejército de Liberación Nacional (National Liberation Army) (used by a Colombian and a Bolivian group)
FAL	Frente Argentino de Liberación (Argentine Liberation Front) (Argentina)
FAL	Fuerzas Armadas de Liberación (Armed Forces of Liberation) (member of FMLN, El Salvador)
FNLC	Front de la Libération Nationale de la Corse (Corsican Liberation Front (Corsica)
FRC	Fatah Revolutionary Council (Abu Nidal Organization; Middle East)
FRELIMO	Mozambican Liberation Front (Mozambique)
FSLN	Frente Sandinista de Liberación Nacional (Sandinista National Liberation Front) (Nicaragua)
LEHI	Lohame Herut Israel, also called Stern Gang (Israel)
MIR	Movimiento de la Izquerda Revolucionaria (Movement of the Revolutionary Left) (Chile, Peru, and Venezuela)
NAYLP	National Arab Youth for the Liberation of Palestine (Middle East)
NORAID	Irish Northern Aid Committee (Northern Ireland, United States)
NSWPP	National Socialist White People's Party (neo-Nazi, United States)
PDFLP	Democratic Front for the Liberation of Palestine (Middle East)
PLF	Palestine Liberation Front (Middle East)
RENAMO	Resistência Nacional Moçambicana (Mozambique National Resistance) or MNR (Mozambique)
UFF	Ulster Freedom Fighters (Northern Ireland)
UNITA	União Nacional para a Independência Total de Angola (National Union for the Total Independence of Angola) (Angola)
WAR	White Aryan Resistance (United States)
ZAF	Zapata Armed Front (Mexico)

CHAPTER 3

THE LAW AND TERRORISM

The already complex law of terrorism has become increasingly problematic in the wake of the September 11, 2001, attacks. In addition to the normal criminal law, international agreements and the law of war can come into play, depending on where suspects are apprehended, their immigration or combatant status, and what they are accused of doing.

FEDERAL LEGISLATION

Federal law is found in the United States Code. There are a number of provisions in the U.S. Code that relate to persons suspected of belonging to groups that use terrorism or advocate the overthrow of the U.S. government.

Definition of Terrorism

18 U.S. Code Sec. 2331 defines "international terrorism" as follows:

(1) the term "international terrorism" means activities that
(A) involve violent acts or acts dangerous to human life that are a violation of the criminal laws of the United States or of any State, or that would be a criminal violation if committed within the jurisdiction of the United States or of any State;
(B) appear to be intended—
(i) to intimidate or coerce a civilian population;
(ii) to influence the policy of a government by intimidation or coercion; or
(iii) to affect the conduct of a government by assassination or kidnapping; and

(C) occur primarily outside the territorial jurisdiction of the United States, or transcend national boundaries in terms of the means by which they are accomplished, the persons they appear intended to intimidate or coerce, or the locale in which their perpetrators operate or seek asylum.

Domestic Terrorism

Sedition can be described as advocacy or action aimed at overthrowing the government. Terrorism conducted within the United States (such as by U.S. extremist groups) falls generally under the category of seditious conspiracy, which is defined in 18 U.S.C. Sec. 2384:

> *If two or more persons in any State or Territory, or in any place subject to the jurisdiction of the United States, conspire to overthrow, put down, or to destroy by force the Government of the United States, or to levy war against them, or to oppose by force the authority thereof, or by force to prevent, hinder, or delay the execution of any law of the United States, or by force to seize, take, or possess any property of the United States contrary to the authority thereof, they shall each be fined under this title or imprisoned not more than twenty years, or both.*

While the preceding refers to action, certain speech or expression can also be considered sedition, as when one

> *knowingly or willfully advocates, abets, advises, or teaches the duty, necessity, desirability, or propriety of overthrowing or destroying the government of the United States or the government of any State, Territory, District or Possession thereof, or the government of any political subdivision therein, by force or violence, or by the assassination of any officer of any such government.*

The core controversy in many sedition cases has to do with whether speech, however extreme, is so closely connected to action (or to inciting to action) as to constitute sedition. In the current atmosphere of the war on terrorism, the related question is when association with or nonviolent aid to certain groups amounts to conspiracy to engage in terrorist acts.

In practice, the sedition laws (including those passed during the McCarthy era of the Cold War, such as the Smith Act of 1940 and the McCarran Act of 1950) are not generally enforced against persons who simply advocate the overthrow of the government. During the 1950s and 1960s, the Supreme

Court gradually broadened the protections afforded by the First Amendment in such a way that mere belief, advocacy, or discussion was not illegal. Some knowledge of and participation in actual activity aimed at the overthrow of the government was required. However, recent cases stemming from later antiterrorist laws tend to suggest that immigrants or aliens in the United States have less protection, and can be kept out (or deported) for engaging in advocacy or other behavior that would be protected if done by U.S. citizens.

IMMIGRATION ACT

In general, aliens who engage in terrorist activities as defined in Sec. 1182 of the Immigration and Naturalization Act are excludable and deportable. Terrorist activity is defined as follows:

(I) The highjacking [sic] or sabotage of any conveyance (including an aircraft, vessel, or vehicle).
(II) The seizing or detaining, and threatening to kill, injure, or continue to detain, another individual in order to compel a third person (including a governmental organization) to do or abstain from doing any act as an explicit or implicit condition for the release of the individual seized or detained.
(III) A violent attack upon an internationally protected person (as defined in section 1116(b)(4) of title 18) or upon the liberty of such a person.
(IV) An assassination.
(V) The use of any—
  (a) biological agent, chemical agent, or nuclear weapon or device, or
  (b) explosive or firearm (other than for mere personal monetary gain), with intent to endanger, directly or indirectly, the safety of one or more individuals or to cause substantial damage to property.
(VI) A threat, attempt, or conspiracy to do any of the foregoing.

[As used in this chapter] [of the U.S. Code], the term "engage in terrorist activity" means to commit, in an individual capacity or as a member of an organization, an act of terrorist activity or an act which the actor knows, or reasonably should know, affords material support to any individual, organization, or government in conducting a terrorist activity at any time, including any of the following acts:

(I) The preparation or planning of a terrorist activity.
(II) The gathering of information on potential targets for terrorist activity.
(III) The providing of any type of material support, including a safe house, transportation, communications, funds, false identification,

weapons, explosives, or training, to any individual the actor knows or has reason to believe has committed or plans to commit a terrorist activity.
(IV) The soliciting of funds or other things of value for terrorist activity or for any terrorist organization.
(V) The solicitation of any individual for membership in a terrorist organization, terrorist government, or to engage in a terrorist activity.

Prosecuting Terrorism

Equally important with defining terrorism is establishing the legal mechanisms for investigating terrorist acts and prosecuting the alleged perpetrators. Three key laws passed in 1978, 1996, and 2001 establish this legal framework, with proposed modifications likely to be considered soon.

FOREIGN INTELLIGENCE SURVEILLANCE ACT (1978)

The Foreign Intelligence Surveillance Act (FISA) arose from the need to provide a way for intelligence agencies to conduct surveillance of suspected spies or terrorists without falling into the systematic violation of the rights of dissenting citizens as had happened in the 1960s and early 1970s.

The FISA provides a legal procedure for obtaining authorization for surveillance, electronic eavesdropping/wiretapping, or surreptitious entry. Because making a public application for surveillance in court could tip off the people being investigated, the warrants authorizing surveillance are issued by a secret panel consisting of seven federal district judges. In order to get a warrant, the person being investigated must be "a foreign power or an agent of a foreign power." In addition, if the target is a U.S. citizen or permanent resident alien, there must be "probable cause to believe that the U.S. person's activities may or are about to involve a violation of the criminal statutes of the United States." Although evidence gathered under FISA must be gathered primarily for "an intelligence purpose," the evidence may be used later in a criminal prosecution. Under the USA PATRIOT Act of 2001 both the categories of persons subject to these provisions and the types of surveillance that may be use have been broadened. Meanwhile, further expansions of investigative and prosecutorial powers have been requested (often called PATRIOT II) but have met with significant opposition.

ANTITERRORISM ACT OF 1996

The Antiterrorism and Effective Death Penalty Act of 1996 has added or revised many provisions of the U.S. code that define terrorist activity and that deal with related matters such as deportation of immigrants and the regulation of chemical and biological weapons as well as explosives.

The following is a summary of the provisions that deal directly with terrorism (material in quotes is from the legislative summary, provided to Congress, and available through the Library of Congress Thomas Service).

Jurisdiction for Lawsuits Against Terrorist States

Title II, Subtitle B gives victims of foreign terrorism greater ability to sue a foreign government that sponsored the terrorist attack, in cases where "money damages are sought against a foreign government for personal injury or death caused by an act of torture, extra judicial killing, aircraft sabotage, hostage taking, or the provision of material support or resources to terrorists," subject to a 10-year statute of limitations. (Such lawsuits have generally been barred on grounds of "sovereign immunity" in the past.) However, the right to sue can be limited in cases in which "the Attorney General certifies will interfere with a criminal investigation or prosecution, or a national security operation, related to the incident that gave rise to the cause of action, subject to specified restrictions."

Assistance to Victims of Terrorism

Title II, Subtitle C, entitled the Justice for Victims of Terrorism Act of 1996, amends the Victims of Crimes Act of 1984 to provide money for states "(1) to provide compensation and assistance to State residents who, while outside U.S. territorial boundaries, are victims of a terrorist act or mass violence and are not eligible for compensation under the Omnibus Diplomatic Security and Antiterrorism Act of 1986; and (2) for eligible crime victim compensation and assistance programs to provide emergency relief, including crisis response efforts, assistance, training, and technical assistance, for the benefit of victims of terrorist acts or mass violence occurring within the United States and funding to U.S. Attorney's Offices for use in coordination with State victims compensation and assistance efforts in providing emergency relief."

Prohibitions on International Terrorist Funding

Title III, Subtitle A amends "the Immigration and Nationality Act (INA) to authorize the Secretary of State, in consultation with the Secretary of the Treasury (Secretary) and the Attorney General, to designate an organization as a terrorist organization upon finding that the organization is a foreign organization that engages in terrorist activity and such activity threatens the security of U.S. nationals or U.S. national security." The procedures for such designation are then given.

Section 303 sets "penalties for knowingly providing, or attempting or conspiring to provide, material support or resources to a foreign terrorist organization. Requires any financial institution that becomes aware that it has possession of, or control over, any funds in which a foreign terrorist organization or its agent has an interest, to retain possession of or maintain control over such funds and report to the Secretary the existence of such funds, with exceptions. Establishes civil penalties for knowingly failing to comply with such provision."

Prohibition on Assistance to Terrorist States

Title III, Subtitle B "[i]mposes penalties upon U.S. persons who engage in a financial transaction with a country knowing or having reasonable cause to know that such country has been designated under the Export Administration Act as a country supporting international terrorism." Existing language is amended in section 323 so that "humanitarian assistance to persons not directly involved in violations" is no longer an exception to the prohibition, but "medicine or religious materials" are allowed.

Sanctions Against Terrorist Nations

The ability of the President to impose sanctions on terrorist states is substantially enhanced.

Section 324 affirms the President's power to "use all necessary means, including covert action and military force, to destroy international infrastructure used by international terrorists."

Section 325 "[a]mends: (1) the Foreign Assistance Act of 1961 to authorize the President to withhold assistance to the governments of countries that aid (including providing military equipment to) terrorist states, with exceptions by presidential waiver when in the national interest; and (2) the International Financial Institutions Act to direct the Secretary to instruct the U.S. executive director of each international financial institution to oppose assistance by such institutions to terrorist states."

Subsequent sections define various types of assistance affected by the legislation and appropriate a small amount of funds for assistance to foreign countries in developing counterterrorism programs.

Terrorist and Criminal Alien Removal and Exclusion—
Subtitle A: Removal of Alien Terrorists

This section provides additional powers to remove or exclude aliens who are associated with terrorism.

Title IV, Subtitle A "Directs the Chief Justice of the United States to publicly designate five district court judges from five of the U.S. judicial circuits to constitute a court with jurisdiction to conduct removal proceedings."

A controversial provision allows for the use of secret (classified) testimony in courts closed to the public ("in camera"). Further, it

> *"Allows a single judge of the removal court, in determining whether to grant an application, to consider, ex parte and in camera, in addition to the information contained in the application: (1) other (including classified) information presented under oath or affirmation; and (2) testimony received in any hearing on the application of which a verbatim record shall be kept."*

Exclusion of Members and Representatives of Terrorist Organizations

Title IV, Subtitle B "[m]akes being a member or representative of a foreign terrorist organization a basis for exclusion from the United States under the INA."

Modification to Asylum Procedures

Title IV, Subtitle C "[p]rohibits the Attorney General from granting asylum to an alien excludable as a terrorist unless the Attorney General determines that the individual seeking asylum will not be a danger to U.S. security." It has various provisions that limit the rights of such aliens to appeal.

Nuclear Weapons Restrictions

Title V, Subtitle A "[r]evises Federal criminal code provisions regarding prohibited transactions involving nuclear materials to cover specified actions involving nuclear byproduct material and actions knowingly causing substantial damage to the environment."

Expands jurisdiction by making such prohibitions applicable where an offender or victim is a U.S. national or a U.S. corporation or other legal entity. Repeals a requirement for jurisdiction that at the time of the offense the nuclear material must have been in use, storage, or transport for peaceful purposes.

Modifies the definition of "nuclear material" to mean material containing any plutonium (currently, with an isotopic concentration not in excess of 80 percent plutonium 238)."

Section 503 "[d]irects the Attorney General and the Secretary of Defense to jointly conduct a study and report to the Congress on the number and extent of thefts from military arsenals of firearms, explosives, and other materials that are potentially useful to terrorists."

The Law and Terrorism

Biological Weapons Restrictions

Title V, Subtitle B "[a]mends the Federal criminal code to include within the scope of prohibitions regarding biological weapons attempts, threats, and conspiracies to acquire a biological agent, toxin, or delivery system for use as a weapon. Authorizes the United States to obtain an injunction against the threat to engage in prohibited conduct with respect to such prohibitions.

Expanded definitions of biological agents and related items are given. Biological weapons are included in the category of "weapons of mass destruction" as used elsewhere in federal law.

The Secretary of Health and Human Services is directed to develop a list of biological agents that have potential to be dangerous weapons, to develop safety procedures and procedures for the use and access to such materials."

Chemical Weapons Restrictions

Title V, Subtitle C specifies criminal penalties for any person who "without lawful authority, uses or attempts or conspires to use a chemical weapon against: (1) a U.S. national while such national is outside the United States; (2) any person within the United States; or (3) any property that is owned, leased, or used by the United States, whether the property is within or outside of the United States." It also provides for studying the feasibility of developing a test facility for studying the effects of chemical weapons.

Implementation of Plastic Explosives Convention

Title VI: Implementing a treaty commitment, this provision generally requires that all plastic explosives be manufactured with a "detection agent" or taggant included. It also prohibits "any person (other than a U.S. agency or the National Guard of any State) possessing any plastic explosive on the effective date of this Act from failing to report to the Secretary the quantity of such explosives possessed, the manufacturer or importer, and any identification marks."

Criminal Law Modifications to Counter Terrorism

Title VII, Subtitle A provides increased penalties for "(1) conspiracies involving explosives; (2) specified terrorism crimes, including carrying weapons or explosives on an aircraft; and (3) the use of explosives or arson."

Subtitle B expands jurisdiction over persons involved with offenses committed while aboard an aircraft in flight, as well as over persons involved with bomb threats. It also specifies increased criminal penalties.

Section 725 adds chemical weapons to the legal category of "weapons of mass destruction."

Section 726 "[a]dds terrorism offenses to the money laundering statute."

91

Section 727 "Sets penalties for: (1) killing or attempting to kill any U.S. officer engaged in, or on account of, the performance of official duties or any person assisting such an officer or employee; and (2) threatening to assault, kidnap, or murder former Federal officers and employees."

Section 728 "Includes among the aggravating factors for homicide that the defendant intentionally killed or attempted to kill more than one person in a single criminal episode."

Section 732 specifies research into tagging explosives or making them inert, as well as the regulation of the use of fertilizer in making explosives.

USE OF MILITARY IN DOMESTIC TERRORIST ATTACK

A provision added to the 1997 Defense Appropriations Act (10 U.S.C. 382) allows the use of the U.S. military in response to an attack using a biological or chemical weapon of mass destruction.

ROVING WIRETAP PROVISIONS (1999)

Provisions in the Intelligence Authorization Act for 1999 expanded the ability of federal agents to use court-ordered wiretaps. Rather than specifying a particular phone or other instrument, agents can follow the suspect and tap whatever instruments he or she is likely to use. These provisions are opposed by civil libertarians and privacy advocates who feel they weaken the Fourth Amendment, which requires that searches be conducted specifically.

LIMITATIONS ON COUNTERTERRORISM

An executive order signed by President Reagan (executive order 12333, December 4, 1981) provides that "No person employed by or acting on behalf of the United States Government shall engage in, or conspire to engage in, assassination." This remains in force. However, "assassination" is generally interpreted as the intentional targeting of a specific person. As the attacks on Muammar al-Qaddafi in Libya in 1986, Osama bin Laden in Afghanistan in 1999, and Saddam Hussein in 2003 seem to indicate, bombing or shooting missiles at an area where a foreign leader is likely to be residing is not interpreted as an attempt at assassination.

MILITARY TRIBUNALS AND THE LAW OF WAR

In 2002 the administration proposed that people such as al-Qaeda or Taliban fighters captured during military action in Afghanistan or elsewhere be tried by military tribunals. (As of mid-2003 no such trials have taken place.) The power to conduct military tribunals is generally held to flow from the president's constitutional role as commander in chief of the armed forces.

A related matter has been the designation of certain suspects as *"unlawful combatants,"* a term applied to terrorists or others who use weapons without following the normal usages of war (such as not being in uniform, deliberately targeting civilians, and so on). The best known case is that of Yaser Esam Hamdi, an American-born Taliban fighter who has tried (so far unsuccessfully) to demand a trial but is being held indefinitely as an unlawful combatant. The problem with this designation is that the war on terrorism has no defined end. (In November 2003 the Supreme Court agreed to determine whether prisoners held at Guantánamo Bay, Cuba, should have recourse to the courts.)

The response to terrorist attacks within the United States has also been to re-examine the possible use of the military as part of the response. The use of military forces within the United States has generally been restricted by the Posse Comitatus Act (18 USC 1385), passed during the post–Civil War Reconstruction era (1878). This law generally prohibits the use of military personnel for domestic law enforcement activities except where explicitly authorized by the Constitution or by Congress. However, the military has sometimes provided "assistance" or advisers (as at the Waco siege), and urgent needs such as the "war on drugs" and now the "war on terrorism" have been cited as justification for modifications to the Posse Comitatus Act.

USA PATRIOT ACT OF 2001

This law, whose full title is "Uniting and Strengthening America by Providing Appropriate Tools Required to Intercept and Obstruct Terrorism," is the major legal response to the attacks of September 11, 2001. It broadens surveillance and other intelligence-gathering powers and provides additional legal weapons to prosecutors as well. A full summary can also be obtained from the Library of Congress THOMAS site. Some key provisions include the following:

- The president can freeze U.S. assets of any country, organization, or person upon determining that there is a threat to U.S. national security.

- Foreign intelligence information can be more freely shared between federal agencies, easing for example the traditional legal barriers between the CIA as foreign intelligence agency and the FBI's role in domestic intelligence and counterintelligence.

- It is now easier for the government to "trap and trace" communications and extends these activities to e-mail and other computer-based communications, including stored files.

- "Roving" surveillance can be authorized; it is not tied to a particular communications device but follows the target whatever devices are used.

- Anti–money laundering requirements previously applied only to banks and other financial institutions are extended to securities brokers and dealers. The law also prohibits various practices used to conceal the source of funds.

- The legislation expands the ability to deport aliens associated with terrorist groups or who advocate or otherwise support terrorist actions.

- Terrorist activity now comes under the category of "racketeering," allowing application of the RICO (Racketeer Influenced and Corrupt Organizations) statute.

- The law increases penalties for terrorist activity as well as defining "harboring a terrorist" as a crime and removing the statute of limitation for terrorist activity that "resulted in or created a foreseeable risk of death or serious bodily injury to another person."

- The "knowing possession" of a biological agent or toxin for other than legitimate purposes such as medical research is prohibited.

Many of these provisions are controversial and are currently being subjected to litigation as well as reconsideration in Congress.

TERRORISM AND INTERNATIONAL TREATIES

The United States is party to a number of multilateral international treaties that involve subjects directly related to terrorism. A selection of such treaties is presented, organized by subject.

CITATIONS

Citations following some treaty titles refer to the following:

Bevans Bevans, Charles. *Treaties and Other International Agreements of the United States of America, 1776–1949.* Washington, D.C.: U.S. Department of State, 1968–76.

LNTS *Treaty Series: Publications of Treaties and International Engagements Registered with the Secretariat of the League.* Geneva: League of Nations, 1920–46.

TIAS   *Treaties and Other International Acts Series.* Washington, D.C.: Government Printing Office, 1946.

UNTS   *United Nations Treaty Series.* New York: United Nations, 1946/47– . This can be accessed online at http://untreaty.un.org/ENGLISH/series/simpleunts.asp.

UST   *United States Treaties and Other International Agreements.* Washington, D.C.: U.S. Department of State, 1952– .

Aviation and Hijacking

CONVENTION ON INTERNATIONAL CIVIL AVIATION. DONE AT CHICAGO DECEMBER 7, 1944; ENTERED INTO FORCE APRIL 4, 1947. 61 STAT. 1180; TIAS 1591; 3 BEVANS 944; 15 UNTS 295.

This treaty resulted in the creation of the International Civil Aviation Organization (ICA). It established the general framework for international standards for the operation of civil aviation, to which later agreements would add provisions specifically relating to hijacking, sabotage, and other terrorist acts.

CONVENTION ON OFFENSES AND CERTAIN OTHER ACTS COMMITTED ON BOARD AIRCRAFT. DONE AT TOKYO SEPTEMBER 14, 1963; ENTERED INTO FORCE DECEMBER 4, 1969.

This treaty did not specify particular criminal acts, but gave an aircraft's pilot in command the authority to act if he or she had "reasonable grounds" to believe that an act has been or is about to be committed which is a threat to "safety" or "good order and discipline on board the aircraft". Such actions can include restraining the threatening passenger and calling upon the assistance of crew or passengers.

CONVENTION FOR THE SUPPRESSION OF UNLAWFUL SEIZURE OF AIRCRAFT (HIJACKING). DONE AT THE HAGUE DECEMBER 16, 1970; ENTERED INTO FORCE OCTOBER 14, 1971.

This treaty covers the procedures for the detention and investigation of persons accused of having unlawfully seized or attempted to seize an aircraft, including cooperation between the nation in which the person is apprehended, the state where the aircraft is registered, and the state where the accused person resides.

CONVENTION FOR THE SUPPRESSION OF UNLAWFUL ACTS AGAINST THE SAFETY OF CIVIL AVIATION (SABOTAGE). DONE AT MONTREAL SEPTEMBER 23, 1971; ENTERED INTO FORCE JANUARY 26, 1973. 24 UST 564; TIAS 7570.

This treaty is directed at a variety of forms of destruction or sabotage that would compromise the safety or operation of the civil aviation system, specified as: "Unlawfully and intentionally to perform an act of violence against a person either when that person is on board an aircraft in flight and the act is likely to endanger the safety of the aircraft or that person is at an airport serving international civil aviation and the act is likely to cause serious injury or death, to destroy an aircraft in service or to so damage it as to make flight unsafe or impossible; to place or cause to be placed on board an aircraft in service by whatever means a substance likely to destroy it or so to damage it that it cannot fly or that its safety in flight is likely to be endangered; to destroy, damage, or interfere with the operation of air navigation facilities if it is likely to endanger the safety of an aircraft in flight; to communicate knowingly false information thereby endangering the safety of such an aircraft; to destroy or damage the facilities or an airport serving international civil aviation or damage aircraft not in service located on such an airport or disrupt the services of such an airport."

PROTOCOL FOR THE SUPPRESSION OF UNLAWFUL ACTS OF VIOLENCE AT AIRPORTS SERVING INTERNATIONAL CIVIL AVIATION, SUPPLEMENTARY TO THE CONVENTION OF SEPTEMBER 23, 1971. DONE AT MONTREAL FEBRUARY 24, 1988; ENTERED INTO FORCE AUGUST 6, 1989; FOR THE UNITED STATES NOVEMBER 18, 1994.

This is a supplementary protocol to the Montreal Convention above.

Biological and Chemical Weapons

PROTOCOL FOR THE PROHIBITION OF THE USE IN WAR OF ASPHYXIATING, POISONOUS, OR OTHER GASES, AND OF BACTERIOLOGICAL METHODS OF WARFARE. DONE AT GENEVA JUNE 17, 1925; ENTERED INTO FORCE FEBRUARY 8, 1928; FOR THE UNITED STATES APRIL 10, 1975. 26 UST 571; TIAS 8061; 94 LNTS 65.

This is the original treaty against the use of poison gas (which had been extensively employed by both sides in World War I), and bacterial agents. In general, the treaty was adhered to during World War II.

CONVENTION ON THE PROHIBITION OF THE DEVELOPMENT, PRODUCTION, AND STOCKPILING OF BACTERIOLOGICAL (BIOLOGICAL) AND TOXIN WEAPONS AND ON THEIR DESTRUCTION. DONE AT WASHINGTON, LONDON, AND MOSCOW APRIL 10, 1972; ENTERED INTO FORCE MARCH 26, 1975. 26 UST 583; TIAS 8062; 1015 UNTS 163.

This treaty prohibits the development, production, and stockpiling of bacteriological and toxin weapons and requires the destruction of existing stockpiles.

CONVENTION ON THE PROHIBITION OF THE DEVELOPMENT, PRODUCTION, STOCKPILING, AND USE OF CHEMICAL WEAPONS AND ON THEIR DESTRUCTION, WITH ANNEXES. DONE AT PARIS JANUARY 13, 1993; ENTERED INTO FORCE APRIL 29, 1997.

This treaty provides a rigorous schedule for the destruction of chemical weapons stockpiled by signatory nations (more than 135 nations have ratified the treaty). It has been ratified by more than 140 nations.

INTERNATIONAL COVENANT ON CIVIL AND POLITICAL RIGHTS. DONE AT NEW YORK DECEMBER 16, 1966; ENTERED INTO FORCE MARCH 23, 1976; FOR THE UNITED STATES SEPTEMBER 8, 1992.

This fundamental document, ratified by more than 140 nations, specifies civil and political rights including political and social self-determination, and equal and due process in legal proceedings. The agreement prohibits torture and scientific experimentation without a person's consent, as well as slavery. Theoretically, at least, it would prevent extrajudicial antiterrorism measures, though a clause in the agreement does allow for its abrogation "in time of public emergency."

Maritime

PROTOCOL FOR THE SUPPRESSION OF UNLAWFUL ACTS AGAINST THE SAFETY OF FIXED PLATFORMS LOCATED ON THE CONTINENTAL SHELF. DONE AT ROME MARCH 10, 1988; ENTERED INTO FORCE MARCH 1, 1992; FOR THE UNITED STATES MARCH 6, 1995.

This agreement declares it to be an offense to seize, destroy, or attempt to destroy fixed maritime platforms (such as oil rigs on the continental shelf) or to attack occupants of such facilities.

CONVENTION FOR THE SUPPRESSION OF UNLAWFUL ACTS AGAINST THE SAFETY OF MARITIME NAVIGATION. SIGNED AT ROME MARCH 10, 1988; ENTERED INTO FORCE MARCH 1, 1992; FOR THE UNITED STATES MARCH 6, 1995.

Similar to laws against sabotage of civil aviation, this agreement deals with offenses where an individual or individuals seize a ship, attack personnel on board, damage a ship, or otherwise interfere with its safe navigation and operation. It specifies the taking into custody of persons suspected of such offenses, and the cooperation of the nation where the arrest is made, the nation to whom the ship is registered, and the nation where the suspects reside, and encourages the promotion of extradition for such offenses.

Nuclear Materials

CONVENTION ON THE PHYSICAL PROTECTION OF NUCLEAR MATERIALS, WITH ANNEX. DONE AT VIENNA OCTOBER 26, 1979; ENTERED INTO FORCE FEBRUARY 8, 1987.

This treaty, signed by 45 nations, restricts the transport of nuclear materials to or through nonsignatory nations, and provides standards for protecting the integrity of shipments and recovering them in case of theft. Signatories are required to criminalize the theft or fraudulent obtaining of nuclear materials or the use of such materials in attacks or threatened attacks, and to make these extraditable offenses. The treaty was further affirmed in 1992.

TREATY ON THE NON-PROLIFERATION OF NUCLEAR WEAPONS. DONE AT WASHINGTON, LONDON AND MOSCOW JULY 1, 1968; ENTERED INTO FORCE MARCH 5, 1970.

This treaty, among other things, requires that "Each nuclear-weapon State Party to the Treaty undertakes not to transfer to any recipient whatsoever nuclear weapons or other nuclear explosive devices or control over such weapons or explosive devices directly, or indirectly; and not in any way to assist, encourage, or induce any non-nuclear-weapon State to manufacture or otherwise acquire nuclear weapons or other nuclear explosive devices, or control over such weapons or explosive devices." By attempting to restrict the possession of nuclear weapons to those nations already having them, the treaty attempts to make development of nuclear weapons by "rogue states" (some of whom support terrorism) less likely.

Terrorism (General)

CONVENTION TO PREVENT AND PUNISH THE ACTS OF TERRORISM TAKING THE FORM OF CRIMES AGAINST PERSONS AND RELATED EXTORTION THAT ARE OF INTERNATIONAL SIGNIFICANCE. DONE AT WASHINGTON FEBRUARY 2, 1971; ENTERED INTO FORCE OCTOBER 16, 1973.

This treaty requires that signatories take "all the measures that they may consider effective, under their own laws, and especially those established in this convention, to prevent and punish acts of terrorism, especially kidnapping, murder, and other assaults against the life or physical integrity of those persons to whom the state has the duty according to international law to give special protection, as well as extortion in connection with those crimes." It provides for the extradition or prosecution of offenders.

CONVENTION ON THE PREVENTION AND PUNISHMENT OF CRIMES AGAINST INTERNATIONALLY PROTECTED PERSONS, INCLUDING DIPLOMATIC AGENTS. DONE AT NEW YORK DECEMBER 14, 1973; ENTERED INTO FORCE FEBRUARY 20, 1977. 28 UST 1975; TIAS 8532; 1035 UNTS 167.

This treaty deals with attacks or kidnapping against government officials or diplomats, who are "internationally protected persons."

INTERNATIONAL CONVENTION AGAINST THE TAKING OF HOSTAGES. DONE AT NEW YORK DECEMBER 17, 1979; ENTERED INTO FORCE JUNE 3, 1983; FOR THE UNITED STATES JANUARY 6, 1985. TIAS 11081.

This treaty deals with the taking of hostages "in order to compel a third party, namely, a State, an international intergovernmental organization, a natural or juridical person, or a group of persons, to do or abstain from doing any act as an explicit or implicit condition for the release of the hostage." Signatories are required to take measures against groups in their territory who may be planning such hostage-taking, to facilitate the freeing and repatriation of hostages, and to extradite or prosecute alleged hostage-takers.

INTERNATIONAL CONVENTION FOR THE SUPPRESSION OF THE FINANCING OF TERRORISM. ADOPTED BY THE GENERAL ASSEMBLY OF THE UNITED NATIONS IN RESOLUTION 54/109 OF DECEMBER 9, 1999.

This agreement defines and prohibits terrorist acts and prohibits individuals from participating in such acts or providing funds or other resources to groups known to be terrorist.

Torture

CONVENTION AGAINST TORTURE AND OTHER CRUEL, INHUMAN OR DEGRADING TREATMENT OR PUNISHMENT. DONE AT NEW YORK DECEMBER 10, 1984; ENTERED INTO FORCE JUNE 26, 1987; FOR THE UNITED STATES NOVEMBER 20, 1994.

Article 5 of the Universal Declaration of Human Rights and Article 7 of the International Covenant on Civil and Political Rights provide that no one shall be subjected to torture or to cruel, inhuman, or degrading treatment or punishment. This agreement requires signatories to take legal measures to prevent the use of torture within its territory. Torture may not be justified under any circumstances, even national emergency. The prosecution and extradition of persons accused of committing acts of torture is specified.

CONVENTION RELATIVE TO THE PROTECTION OF CIVILIAN PERSONS IN TIME OF WAR. DATED AT GENEVA AUGUST 12, 1949; ENTERED INTO FORCE OCTOBER 21, 1950; FOR THE UNITED STATES FEBRUARY 2, 1956. 6 UST 3516; TIAS 3365; 75 UNTS 287.

This agreement requires the humane treatment of civilians and also combatants whose injuries or other circumstances have removed them from active combat. Hospitals and other facilities for the treatment of such persons are not to be attacked.

COURT CASES

The cases described below deal with key legal issues involving terrorism and counterterrorism. (It should be noted that as of this writing, a number of challenges to the 1996 Antiterrorism and Effective Death Penalty Act and USA PATRIOT Act of 2001 were still working their way through the courts.)

Some of these issues include:

- Can mere advocacy of the forceful overthrow of the U.S. government be outlawed, or does the advocacy have to be accompanied by some substantial action in furtherance of that goal?
- Can mere membership in a group associated with terrorism or revolution be outlawed, or is some active participation in a conspiracy required?

- Do immigrants (or potential immigrants) have the same rights as U.S. citizens with regard to the First Amendment (freedom of association or advocacy) and the Fifth Amendment (due process of law)?
- Can persons captured as "unlawful combatants" during an anti-terrorist military action be tried in military courts even if they are U.S. citizens?

Note that the trials of defendants such as Timothy McVeigh or Theodore Kaczynski are not included below because they are not of great legal interest, although they may be of great human interest.

EX PARTE QUIRIN, 317 U.S. 1 (1942)

Background

This case arose when eight German saboteurs were landed from a submarine—four in Long Island and four in Florida. Although they had lived in the United States previously, they had returned to Germany in the 1930s, and all but one acknowledged German citizenship. They were under German military orders to attempt to disrupt or destroy key installations involved with the U.S. economy and war effort. The saboteurs proved to be quite inept, and they were quickly swept up by the FBI, which turned them over to the U.S. military for trial. The saboteurs filed habeas corpus petitions. The petitions were denied by the D.C. District Court and the matter came to the Supreme Court for review. The Court held a special session to consider the petition in an expedited manner.

Legal Issues

The attorneys for the accused Germans argued that the military did not have jurisdiction because the regular U.S. courts were open and available for trial, and in the Civil War case of *Ex Parte Miligan* the Supreme Court had ruled that military tribunals could only be used within the United States in places where regular courts were not in session.

Decision

The Court rejected the habeas petition. The opinion first noted that

> The Constitution thus invests the President as Commander in Chief with the power to wage war which Congress has declared, and to carry into effect all laws passed by Congress for the conduct of war and for the government and regulation of the Armed Forces, and all laws defining and punishing offences against the law of nations, including those which pertain to the conduct of war.

Applying the laws of war, the Court noted that

The . . . enemy combatant who without uniform comes secretly through the lines for the purpose of waging war by destruction of life or property, are familiar examples of belligerents who are generally deemed . . . to be offenders against the law of war subject to trial and punishment by military tribunals.

Because the Germans were subject to the law of war and had violated it, the military jurisdiction was upheld.

Impact

By upholding military jurisdiction over an "unlawful combatant" serving an enemy of the United States, *Quirin* has been cited as a strong precedent for upholding the use of military tribunals for trying terrorists captured by the U.S. military.

YATES V. UNITED STATES, 354 U.S. 298 (1957)

Background

In 1951, 14 persons including the appellant were charged with violating the Smith Act through their membership in the Communist Party in California.

Legal Issues

Although in *Dennis v. United States* (1951) the Court had already ruled that membership in a communist organization that advocated the overthrow of the government of the United States was not protected by the First Amendment, Yates argued that his activities did not involve the direct or immediate overthrow of the government. He may have expressed opinions about what would be desirable in the future but did not advocate that any specific action be taken against the government.

Decision

The Court overturned Yates's conviction. It ruled that to violate the Smith Act (and lose protection under the First Amendment), a person had to advocate some concrete action, not just express an abstract opinion.

Impact

By distinguishing between opinion and advocacy and between indefinite advocacy and immediate advocacy, this decision broadened First Amendment protections.

A number of other cases raise various nuances. In *Scales v. United States* (1961) the Court upheld the 1950 McCarren Act's prohibition of "knowing" and "active and purposeful membership" in an organization that seeks to overthrow the U.S. government.

In *Noto v. United States* (1961) the Court turned to the question of when an organization itself (the Communist Party in this case) actually advocated the overthrow of the U.S. government in a concrete and direct way.

In *Brandenberg v. Ohio* (1969) the Court addressed a domestic terrorism case involving threats by Ku Klux Klan members against African Americans and against government officials that they said sought to "suppress the White, Caucasian race." The Court ruled that even such vehement language could only be criminalized if it is intended to produce and is likely to produce "imminent lawless action."

The combination of these three rulings sets a high threshold for criminalizing membership in even organizations with extreme political views, and in advocacy of such views. However, today when there are often close connections between merely militant and actively terrorist groups, the questions has again become complicated—see the entry for *Kiareldeen v. Reno* (1999).

RENO V. AMERICAN-ARAB ANTI-DISCRIMINATION COMMITTEE, 97-1252 (1999)

Background

In 1987, the Immigration and Naturalization Service (INS) began deportation proceedings against seven Palestinians and a Kenyan on the grounds that they were advocates of "doctrines of world communism" in violation of the cold war–era McCarran Act. When the constitutionality of this law was questioned, prosecutors replaced the McCarran Act–related charges with other charges relating to involvement with groups that engage in destruction of property or terrorist attacks.

The INS sought to deport these aliens because they had been distributing literature and carrying out other work for the Popular Front for the Liberation of Palestine (PFLP), which has engaged in both terrorist and political activities.

Legal Issues

The defendants argued that the First Amendment protected their rights of association and political advocacy, and thus they could not be deported solely on grounds of their association with a particular group. They claimed they were engaged in lawful political activity and had no involvement with terrorism. They argued that the immigration laws were being enforced selectively against persons whose political views were considered objectionable by the authorities, and they objected to the use of secret testimony or evidence that was not disclosed to the defense.

Decision

The district court upheld the appellants, noting that the PFLP did engage in a range of peaceful activities. The circuit court of appeals affirmed the ruling and further, it asserted that "Because of the danger of injustice when decisions lack the procedural safeguards that form the core of constitutional due process, . . . the use of undisclosed information in adjudications should be presumptively unconstitutional. Only the most extraordinary circumstances could support one-sided process."

The Supreme Court, however, ruled on a matter of procedure that Congress had denied, in a 1996 immigration law, the right to appeal such immigration decisions in federal court. In response to the claim of selective prosecution, the Court ruled that an "alien unlawfully in this country has no constitutional right to assert such a claim as a defense against his deportation." The Court did not address the question of the use of secret evidence or proceedings.

Impact

Apparently, the First Amendment does not give immigrants protection for being targeted based on their views, as it would for U.S. citizens. On the other hand, the appeals court had expressed serious misgivings about the use of secret evidence, which were left unresolved by the Supreme Court and remain largely unresolved in 2003.

KIARELDEEN V. RENO, 71 F. SUPP. 2D 402, 419 (D.N.J. 1999)

Background

Hany Kiareldeen, a Palestinian resident of the United States since 1990 and a student at Rutgers University, married a U.S. citizen in 1997 and applied for permanent residency status. In March 1998, however, Immigration and Naturalization Service (INS) and FBI agents arrested Kiareldeen, charging him with having stayed in the country too long after completing his studies. He was detained without bail. In removal proceedings Kiareldeen acknowledged that he had overstayed his visa, but that he had earlier asked for a "discretionary adjustment" of his status based on a claim for political asylum (he faced the threat of persecution or torture if he returned to his homeland). The INS, however, presented secret evidence to the judge that claimed that Kiareldeen was a member of a Palestinian terrorist group and thus a threat to U.S. national security.

At the conclusion of the first removal hearing, the judge ordered a reconsideration of whether Kiareldeen should continue to be detained pending conclusion of the legal process. At the second removal hearing, the judge determined that "[a]n evaluation of the evidence by a person of ordinary prudence and caution cannot sustain a finding that this respondent has engaged in terrorist activity." On April 2, 1999, the judge ordered that Kiareldeen's immigration status be adjusted and that he be freed on $1,500 bail pending completion of the proceedings.

The government appealed to the Board of Immigration Appeals (BIA), which stayed the order for Kiareldeen's release and then voted 2-1 to deny his release. The FBI announced that it had closed its criminal investigation, and although Kiareldeen had never been charged with any crime, he remained in INS detention. After another hearing, the BIA then reversed its ruling and ordered that Kiareldeen be freed, but the government appealed to the attorney general's office for review. Meanwhile, however, a habeas corpus petition that Kiareldeen had previously filed came before a federal district court in New Jersey.

Legal Issues

In the habeas petition, Kiareldeen argued that the use of secret evidence and hearings was not authorized by any of the immigration statutes. Further, he argued that even if the evidence were authorized, it would be unconstitutional under the Fifth Amendment, which guarantees due process of law in criminal proceedings.

The main legal issue is whether the use of secret evidence is permissible under the U.S. Constitution. Civil libertarians argue that the constitutional right to confront one's accusers and the state's evidence cannot be exercised if evidence (and even witnesses) are presented in secret. Defenders of the practice argue that in certain circumstances evidence must be kept secret in order to protect vital intelligence sources, while at the same time dangerous terrorists must be prevented from entering the country.

Decision

Judge William Walls granted the habeas petition, ruling that Kiareldeen was being held without justification, and freed him after 19 months of detention. He began by addressing the use of secret evidence:

The Law and Terrorism

[T]he court does not ignore the warnings of [the Rafeedie and Anti-Discrim-
ination Committee cases]. . . . Minimally, these cases teach that the INS'
reliance on secret evidence raises serious issues about the integrity of the ad-
versarial process, the impossibility of self-defense against undisclosed charges,
and the reliability of government processes initiated and prosecuted in dark-
ness. . . . Review of the Service's [INS] procedures involving Kiareldeen
leads the court to believe that the petitioner's case is an example of the dan-
gers of secret evidence.

The court noted that the unclassified summaries that the INS had provided to the defense were inadequate, because they were not specific enough for the defense to determine what evidence needed to be rebutted or countered. "Use of secret evidence creates a one-sided process by which the protections of our adversarial system are rendered impotent. [Kiareldeen] has been compelled by the government to attempt to prove the negative in the face of anonymous slurs of unseen and unsworn informers."

The court then responded to the government's assertion that it had an overriding interest in protecting national security. It replied that "even if the interest is deemed to be the unarguably weighty one of national security, as the government maintains, the court must inquire whether that interest is so all-encompassing that it requires that [Kiareldeen] be denied virtually every fundamental feature of due process." The court noted that the FBI had closed its investigation, leaving Kiareldeen in legal limbo. "Under these circumstances, the government's claimed interest in detaining [Kiareldeen] cannot be said to outweigh [his] interest in returning to freedom. . . . [T]he government's reliance on secret evidence violates the due process protections that the Constitution directs must be extended to all persons within the United States, citizens and resident aliens alike." The court made similar conclusions about the government's use of hearsay evidence and evidence from unsworn witnesses. The court granted the habeas petition, and a three-judge immigration panel granted Kiareldeen permanent residency status.

Impact

The lower courts seem to be increasingly concerned about and suspicious of the government's use of secret evidence and testimony, even when a person is accused of being a dangerous terrorist and a threat to national security. Another district court, in *Rafeedie v. INS*, had already come to a similar conclusion. On the other hand, in *Reno v. American-Arab Anti-Discrimination Committee*, the Supreme Court had refused to extend First Amendment rights to noncitizens. The question remains whether the Court, confronted with arguments based on fundamental due process and the Fifth Amendment, might agree with lower courts that the use of secret evidence is unacceptable. As of late 2003, the Supreme Court has not yet resolved this issue.

HAMDI V. RUMSFELD, U.S. COURT OF APPEALS, 4TH CIRCUIT, NO. 02-6895 (2002)

Background

Like "American Taliban" John Walker Lindh, Yaser Esam Hamdi is an American citizen who went to Afghanistan to fight for the Taliban. He was captured by U.S. forces and initially held at Guantánamo Bay, in Cuba, though when authorities learned he had been born in Louisiana and might still be able to claim American citizenship, he was transferred to the naval brig at Norfolk, Virginia.

After a writ of habeas corpus was filed, the District Court ruled that "Hamdi must be allowed to meet with his attorney because of fundamental justice provided under the Constitution." The government moved to block the meeting and the court of appeals issued a stay and agreed to hear the government's appeal.

Legal Issues

The fundamental issue is whether the usual legal rights available to American citizens can be set aside in favor of the president's power to declare a person to be an "unlawful combatant" subject to the exclusive jurisdiction of a military tribunal.

Decision

The appeals court opined that the district court had been too hasty in ignoring the government's prerogatives in times of active military hostilities. In particular, the government asserted the right to hold an "enemy combatant" without trial or counsel for the duration of the hostilities. Further, the district court had not properly considered the government's argument that allowing Hamdi access to counsel might allow the passage of sensitive information to terrorists.

The appeals court expressed great deference to the power of the executive branch in wartime matters. It directed:

Upon remand, the district court must consider the most cautious procedures first, conscious of the prospect that the least drastic procedures may promptly resolve Hamdi's case and make more intrusive measures unnecessary. Our Con-

The Law and Terrorism

stitution's commitment of the conduct of war to the political branches of American government requires the court's respect at every step. Because the district court appointed counsel and ordered access to the detainee without adequately considering the implications of its actions and before allowing the United States even to respond, we reverse the court's June 11 order mandating access to counsel and remand the case for proceedings consistent with this opinion.

In subsequent appeals Hamdi's detention as an unlawful combatant continued to be upheld as of mid-2003.

Impact

The government has been able to arrange that prisoners such as Lindh and Hamdi are brought into the jurisdiction of a Circuit that is widely believed to be conservative and favorably inclined toward upholding the government position. Like the case of Lindh, this case may well be resolved by plea bargain. If not, it will be interesting to see if the Supreme Court upholds the government position in such sweeping terms.

U.S. v. ARNAOUT (U.S. DISTRICT COURT, NORTHERN DISTRICT OF ILLINOIS, EASTERN DIVISION, NO. 02 CR 892 (2003)

Background

Enaam Arnaout, a Syrian-born U.S. citizen, was charged with raising money through his Islamic charitable organization, the Benevolence International Foundation (BIF), for use by al-Qaeda as well as for Islamic militant groups in Chechnya and Bosnia. The indictment laid out what it alleged was a "pipeline" of associations with al-Qaeda operatives by which Arnaout and the BIF funneled money and supplies to various groups. Indeed, according to prosecutors, e-mails, photos, and documents seized in the BIF's Bosnia offices showed that Arnaout had been communicating directly with Osama bin Laden.

Arnaout was charged with perjury (for filing false declarations to the government) and racketeering fraud, alleging that he had defrauded donors to the BIF by concealing the fact that some of their money was being used to support militants and terrorists rather than for charitable purposes.

Legal Issues

Much of the government's evidence against Arnaout was filed in the form of a detailed document called a proffer. The proffer quoted documents and other evidence purporting to show links between BIF and al-Qaeda, as well as citing an al-Qaeda operative who allegedly was told by bin Laden in 1993 that the BIF was one of al-Qaeda's funding channels. However, many of these alleged links were tenuous and the authors of most of the documents or statements could not be verified or made available for questioning. Although second-hand (hearsay) material is allowed in certain cases where obtaining direct testimony is impracticable, the prosecution must still show that a "preponderance of the evidence" links the defendant to the alleged conspiracy.

Decision

The federal judge ruled that the proffer did not meet the required standards of proof and was "devoid of analysis linking proffered hearsay to a specific conspiracy." She also ruled that the prosecutor could not, in his opening statement, link Arnaout to one particular alleged al-Qaeda operative, Mohamed Loay Bayazid, because the relevant evidence had not been supplied to the defense in a timely manner.

Although the prosecution could theoretically prepare new filings of statements by the co-conspirators, they realized that the judge's decision made it very unlikely that they would be able to sustain the charges relating to aiding al-Qaeda. The government therefore agreed to a plea bargain in which Arnaout pleaded guilty only to a single count of racketeering conspiracy involving using money raised under false pretenses to supply boots and uniforms to Muslim fighters. Arnaout was subsequently sentenced to 11 years in prison.

Impact

This case shows that it can be hard for prosecutors to prove illegal ties or activities involving individuals and terrorist groups. In many such cases the main evidence comes from documents that cannot be independently verified and co-conspirators who are not available to testify. The result in this case suggests that even the somewhat relaxed standards of conspiracy law may still be too hard to meet. This situation, combined with frustration at not being able to effectively prosecute terrorist networks may lead to laws that relax the standards of evidence even further, in turn creating concern about potential abuses (as has already been the case with other aspects of RICO when applied to "nontraditional" conspiracies).

CHAPTER 4

CHRONOLOGY

This chapter presents a chronology of selected terrorist attacks and other developments in the history of terrorism since 1946. This starting date was chosen because it marks the beginning of the postcolonial cold war period that shaped the environment for modern terrorism.

1946

- *January 7:* The Jewish terrorist group Irgun blows up the King David Hotel in Jerusalem, which had contained the principal government offices for the British mandate of Palestine. The blast killed 91 people, including 17 Jews and 46 non-British citizens.

1947

- Unrest in Palestine continues, as Jewish terrorists attack British soldiers. Typically, they kill the soldiers and booby-trap their bodies. The terrorists' objective is to force the British to hand over Palestine to the Jewish settlers.

1948

- *April 9:* Members of the Jewish terrorist organizations Irgun and Lehi (also known as the Stern Gang at that time) kill more than 200 Arab men, women, and children, in the Palestinian village of Deir Yassin, near Jerusalem. This and other terrorist attacks drive many Palestinian Arabs out of what will become the state of Israel.
- *September 17:* Count Folke Bernadotte of Sweden, who had been serving as United Nations mediator for Palestine between Israel and the Arabs, is killed along with French colonel André Serot by three members of the Jewish terrorist Stern Gang.
- *December 28:* Egyptian Prime Minister Mahmoud Fahmy el-Nokrashy Pasha is assassinated by a member of the extremist Muslim Brotherhood who is frustrated at Egypt's inability to destroy the Israeli state.

1950

- *November 1:* Puerto Rican nationalists get into a gun battle with White House Police and Secret Service personnel outside Blair House (the vice presidential mansion across the street from the White House, where President Harry Truman is in temporary residence). Their attempt to assassinate the president is unsuccessful.

1951

- *July 20:* King Abdullah I of Jordan is assassinated by a Palestinian gunman while visiting his father's tomb.

1954

- *March 1:* Four Puerto Rican nationalists in the visitors' gallery of the U.S. House of Representatives open fire on members of Congress. Five representatives are wounded, and all four terrorists are captured alive.

1955

- *August 20:* In Algeria, the insurgency against the French colonial government intensifies. The terrorist group FLN (Front de Libération Nationale, the National Liberation Front) murders and then mutilates 37 European men, women, and children in what becomes known as the Philippeville massacre.

1956

- *March 15:* Violence in Algeria continues, and the procolonial terrorist group OAS (Secret Army Organization) seizes and kills six men.
- *October 21–22:* Directed by Saadi Yacef, FLN assassins murder 49 people in Algeria.

1959

- *August 31:* Basque separatists found the "Basque Fatherland and Liberty Movement," whose initials in Basque are ETA.

1960

- *March 20:* Beginning a new era of state terrorism against the black population, in the township of Sharpesville, South Africa, police open fire on a civil rights demonstration and kill 69 blacks, including many women and children. In response, the African National Congress abandons nonviolent action in favor of more militant means.

Chronology

1963

- **November 27:** Venezuelan FALN insurgents kidnap a U.S. Army military attaché in Venezuela and demand the release of 70 political prisoners. The Venezuelan government releases the prisoners and the U.S. hostage is freed.

1966

- **October:** In the United States, the Black Power movement is on the rise. The Black Panthers are formed by Huey Newton and Bobby Seale. The group engages in community and political action but also becomes involved in violent clashes with police.

1968

- **July 28:** Three hijackers belonging to the Popular Front for the Liberation of Palestine-General Command (PFLP-GC) seize an Israeli El Al airliner flying from Rome to Tel Aviv and force it to land at Dar al-Bayda Airport in Algiers, taking 48 hostages. The terrorists release the 23 non-Israeli hostages. On September 1, the 25 Israeli hostages are released in exchange for 16 Arab prisoners in Israeli jails.
- **November 22:** A car bomb explodes in the Jewish sector in Jerusalem, killing 12 people.
- **December 28:** In apparent retaliation for attacks on its airliners, Israeli commandos attack the Beirut National Airport in Lebanon, destroying 13 airliners belonging to three Arab-owned airlines.

1969

- **July 18:** Palestinian terrorists bomb the Jewish-owned Marks and Spencer department store in London.
- **July 29:** Two members of the PFLP hijack an El Al jet on its way to Tel Aviv. They order the plane diverted to Damascus, where they release the passengers unharmed but destroy the plane. Syria, however, detains 6 Israeli passengers until December, when it exchanges them for 13 Syrians and 58 Egyptians held in Israeli prisons.
- **September 4:** The U.S. ambassador to Brazil, Charles Elbrick, is abducted in Rio de Janeiro by MR-8 (Revolutionary Movement of October 8) and affiliated terrorists. He is freed after the Brazilian government agrees to release 15 political prisoners.

1970

- **February 21:** Swissair flight 330 explodes shortly after takeoff from Geneva. The PFLP-GC under Ahmed Jabril claims responsibility.

- *March 31:* Nine members of the leftist terrorist group Japanese Red Army, led by Kozo Okamoto, hijack a Japan Air Lines flight from Tokyo to Kukuoka. They demand to be flown to P'yongyang, the North Korean capital.
- *June 24:* The Quebec separatist group Front De Libération du Québec (FLQ) sets off a bomb at the Defense Ministry in Ottawa.
- *July 22:* In Lebanon, five members of the Popular Struggle Front hijack an Olympic Airways flight from Beirut to Athens. After several weeks of negotiations mediated by the International Red Cross, the incident ends peacefully after the Greek government releases seven Palestinians held in Greek jails.
- *July 31:* In Uruguay, Tupamaros guerrillas kidnap a U.S. official, Daniel A. Mitrione, and Aloisio Gomide, a Brazilian diplomat. Mitrione is found dead but Gomide is released the following February after his family pays a ransom. In the following months the Tupamaros conduct several other kidnappings of diplomats and win the freedom of a number of prisoners.
- *September 6:* In a coordinated wave of hijackings, the PFLP seizes four planes in midair (a fifth attempt, on an El Al plane, is foiled by Israeli security personnel). Three of the planes are diverted to a field outside Amman, Jordan, while one is destroyed on the runway at Cairo. After three weeks of negotiations the hijackers release their collection of more than 400 hostages in exchange for the release of 8 Palestinians held in Western jails. The hijackings prove to be the last straw for King Hussein of Jordan, who has his army expel the PFLP guerrillas from the country.
- *October:* In Quebec, the FLQ (Front de Libération du Québec, Quebec Liberation Front) kidnaps a British trade official, demands ransom (which is refused), and finally releases him in exchange for passage to Cuba. A few days later the FLQ kidnaps and kills Pierre Laporte, Quebec's minister of labor.

1971

- *January 30:* Two members of the Kashmiri Liberation Front hijack an Indian Airlines flight to Lahore, Pakistan. When India refuses their demand for the release of 36 prisoners, they destroy the plane.
- *March 1:* The leftist terrorist group Weather Underground sets off a bomb that causes heavy damage to a wing of the U.S. Senate office building.
- *December 4:* In Northern Ireland, the loyalist terrorist group UVF (Ulster Volunteer Force) claims responsibility for a bomb attack that kills 15 people in a Belfast pub.

Chronology

1972

- *January 27:* A new U.S. terrorist group, the Black Liberation Army, surfaces when it kills two New York City police officers.
- *January 30:* In what becomes known as Bloody Sunday, British troops in Londonderry fire on a Catholic demonstration, killing 13 marchers.
- *February 22:* Five Palestinian hijackers seize a German Lufthansa airliner flying from New Delhi to Greece. They divert the plane to Aden, South Yemen, and release their hostages in exchange for a $5 million ransom. South Yemeni authorities in turn release the hijackers after taking $1 million of the ransom money.
- *May 8:* Four members of Black September seize a Sabena airliner on the ground at Lod Airport in Tel Aviv, hoping to trade the plane for the freedom of 317 *fedayeen* (Arab fighters) being held in Israeli jails. However, Israeli commandos recapture the plane, killing two of the hijackers. One passenger also dies in the battle.
- *May 11:* The German Red Army Faction carries out six bombing attacks against U.S. Army personnel in Frankfurt. One serviceman is killed and 11 are injured.
- *May 30:* In an ominous example of cooperation between disparate terrorist groups, the Japanese Red Army, working on behalf of the PFLP, launches a machine gun attack in the passenger terminal at Lod Airport in Tel Aviv, killing 25 people and wounding 76. Two terrorists are killed and the third captured.
- *July 8:* In retaliation for the massacre at Lod Airport the preceding month, Israeli agents in Lebanon assassinate Ghassan Kanafani, a leader of the PFLP.
- *July 21:* The Troubles in Northern Ireland worsen when the Provisional Wing of the Irish Republican Army (PIRA) sets off a total of 22 bombs in the Belfast area, killing 11 people and wounding more than 100.
- *September 5:* In one of the most shocking terrorist incidents of modern times, 8 Black September terrorists kill 11 Israeli athletes and coaches at the Olympic Games in Munich, Germany. Five of the terrorists are killed.
- *October 29:* Black September terrorists win the release of the three comrades captured in Munich by hijacking a Lufthansa flight from Beirut to Ankara, Turkey. The hijackers and the Munich terrorists meet in Libya, where they receive an enthusiastic reception. However, Israeli agents will hunt them relentlessly in years to come.
- *November 8:* Seven members of the Eritrean Liberation Army hijack an Ethiopian plane in an attempt to win the release of jailed comrades. Security personnel aboard the plane counterattack, however, and six of the

seven hijackers are killed. The plane is damaged by a grenade blast during the battle, but it lands safely, with nine passengers injured.

1973

- *March 1:* Eight Black September terrorists seize the Saudi Arabian embassy in Khartoum, Sudan. They make a variety of demands, including the release of the surviving gunman from the Lod Airport massacre in 1972 and freedom for Red Army Faction leaders imprisoned in West Germany. When their demands are refused, they murder U.S. ambassador Claude Noel and two other diplomats.
- *August 5:* In Greece, two gunmen from the Arab Nationalist Youth Organization for the Liberation of Palestine attack passengers disembarking from a TWA flight from Tel Aviv. Five people are killed and 55 wounded.
- *September:* The PIRA carries out an extensive bombing campaign throughout the London area.
- *December 17:* Five members of ANYOLP (the Arab Nationalist Youth Organization for the Liberation of Palestine) kill 33 Pan Am passengers on the ground at Italy's Leonardo da Vinci Airport. They then hijack a Lufthansa jet, divert it to Kuwait, and surrender, whereupon they are turned over to the Palestine Liberation Organization (PLO).

1974

- *February 3:* The PIRA bombs a bus carrying British soldiers and their families, killing 12 people.
- *February 4:* Patricia Hearst, heiress of the Hearst publishing family, is kidnapped by members of the Symbionese Liberation Army (SLA) from her apartment in San Francisco. In the coming months she is brainwashed and transformed into "Tanya" and participates in robberies carried out by the terrorist group.
- *April 11:* Gunmen from the PFLP-GC attack the Israeli settlement of Qiryat Shemona, killing 18 settlers and wounding 16 others. The terrorists demand the release of 100 Palestinians being held in Israeli jails, but Israeli troops carry out an assault and kill them.
- *April 13:* In the Philippines, the New People's Army kills three U.S. Navy personnel near the Subic Bay naval base.
- *May 15:* Gunmen from the DFLP (Democratic Front for the Liberation of Palestine) seize a school in the village of Ma'alot, taking more than 100 students and teachers hostage. Israeli forces retake the school, but 27 children die during the gun battle.
- *May 17:* Los Angeles police attack an SLA safe house, killing six SLA members.

Chronology

- *June 17:* The PIRA bombs the Tower of London, killing one tourist and injuring more than 40.
- *August 4:* The Italian fascist group Black Order claims credit for setting off a bomb on an Italian train traveling from Bologna to Munich. Twelve people are killed and about 50 wounded.
- *September 7:* A TWA airliner explodes just after taking off from the Athens airport. The attack is linked to ANYOLP.
- *September 13:* The ETA bombs a Madrid cafe frequented by workers in the nearby national police headquarters. Twelve people are killed and more than 80 wounded.
- *October 6:* Starting a terror campaign, the Fuerzas Armadas de Liberación Nacional (FALN), a Puerto Rican separatist group, bombs five banks in New York City.
- *November 9:* The German Red Army Faction assassinates West German Supreme Court president Günther Drenkman in his home in Bonn.
- *November 21:* The PIRA bombs two pubs in Birmingham, killing 21 people and wounding almost 200.

1975

- *January 24:* Puerto Rican FALN terrorists explode a bomb in New York's historic Fraunces Tavern, killing four patrons and wounding 60.
- *January 29:* The U.S. State Department headquarters in Washington, D.C., is badly damaged by a bomb planted by the Weather Underground.
- *February 25:* In Argentina, Montoneros terrorists kidnap John P. Egan, U.S. honorary consul to the city of Córdoba. He is found murdered two days later.
- *March 1:* Kurdish nationalists hijack an Iraqi Airways flight and divert it to Teheran, Iran, while engaging in a gun battle with Iraqi security forces aboard the plane. The hijackers surrender to Iranian authorities, who execute them on April 7.
- *April 7:* Three members of the Moro Liberation Front hijack a Philippine Airlines flight. They release the passengers in Manila but continue to hold the plane's crew and an airline executive hostage. They later free their hostages and are granted asylum in Libya. A similar hijack attempt the following month ends with three hijackers and 10 passengers dead after a gun battle with Philippine troops. The other three hijackers are captured and later executed.
- *April 17:* In Cambodia, one of modern history's worst reigns of state terror begins when the Khmer Rouge–controlled government forces city populations into the countryside, where many will die of starvation.
- *August 4:* A terrorist squad from the Japanese Red Army (JRA) takes over the U.S. consulate and the Swedish embassy in Kuala Lumpur, Malaysia.

They threaten to destroy the buildings and kill their 52 hostages if their demand for freedom for seven imprisoned JRA members in Japan is not met. The Japanese government agrees to the demands, and five of the seven prisoners willingly join the hostage-takers in Tripoli, Libya.

- *September 15:* Terrorists from the Black September group occupy the Egyptian embassy in Madrid, seize six diplomats, and demand that Egypt withdraw from its ongoing peace talks with Israel in Geneva, Switzerland, and repudiate agreements that had already been reached. The terrorists take their hostages to Algiers and release them without winning their demands.
- *December 21:* PFLP terrorists led by Ilyich Ramírez Sánchez (a.k.a. Carlos the Jackal) storm into an OPEC conference in Vienna, taking 81 hostages. They free the hostages in exchange for $50 million and a flight to safety in Algiers.
- *December 23:* In Athens, CIA station chief Richard Welch is assassinated by members of the Greek marxist group Revolutionary Organization 17 November.

1976

- *January 4:* In Northern Ireland, five Catholics are killed in two attacks by Protestant gunmen. The next day, gunmen from the IRA remove 10 Protestants from a bus in Armagh and execute them by the side of the road.
- *May 23:* Molluccan terrorists seize a Dutch school and a passenger train and use their hostages to demand that the Dutch government pressure Indonesia to give their region independence. The hostages at the school are freed four days later, but the train is stormed by Dutch marines who kill six terrorists. Two hostages also die.
- *June 27:* Seven terrorists from the PFLP and the Red Army Faction (RAF) hijack an Air France flight from Tel Aviv to Paris, diverting it to Entebbe, Uganda, where they are apparently aided by Ugandan dictator Idi Amin's soldiers. The hijackers demand the release of 53 terrorists who are being held in French, Swiss, Israeli, and Kenyan jails. But a planeful of Israeli commandos mount a daring raid and rescue most of the passengers, killing the terrorists and some Ugandan soldiers.
- *July 21:* Christopher Ewart-Biggs, British ambassador to Ireland, dies when his car passes over a land mine apparently planted along his route by the PIRA.
- *August 11:* PFLP gunmen attack an airport terminal in Istanbul, Turkey, killing four El Al passengers and wounding 20.

1977

- *March 9:* A Hanafi Muslim terrorist group seizes three buildings in Washington, D.C., holding 134 people hostage. The group surrenders peacefully two days later.

- *August 3:* The Puerto Rican separatist group FALN bombs two New York office buildings, killing one person.
- *September 5:* The RAF kidnaps German businessman Hans-Martin Schleyer after killing his driver and three bodyguards. They demand freedom for 11 imprisoned comrades, while their allies, the PFLP, hijack a Lufthansa jet and divert it to Mogadishu, Somalia. The situation unravels the following month, when German commandos recapture the plane and rescue the passengers. Many of the RAF prisoners commit suicide in their cells, and the RAF kills Schleyer in retaliation.
- *September 28:* The Japanese Red Army hijacks a Japan Air Lines plane and demands $6 million ransom and the freeing of nine prisoners. The Japanese government agrees to the demand and the hostages are released in batches as the plane makes several stops, ending up in Algeria, where the terrorists surrender.
- *December 4:* A hijacked Malaysian airliner crashes in Singapore during landing. Unidentified terrorists had apparently shot the pilot and copilot.

1978

- *February 17:* In Northern Ireland, the PIRA bombs the La Mon Restaurant, killing 12 and wounding more than 20.
- *March 16:* Red Brigades terrorists (possibly with the aid of the P2 group and the Mafia) kidnap Aldo Moro, former Italian prime minister and president of the Christian Democratic Party. The terrorists demand the release of 13 of their imprisoned comrades. The Italian government refuses to comply, and Moro's body is found in the trunk of a car parked on a Rome street.
- *April 11:* Eleven al-Fatah guerrillas make an amphibious landing outside the port of Haifa and hijack a passing bus in an attempt to reach Tel Aviv. Israeli security forces intercept the bus outside the capital. In the ensuing gun battle 25 passengers and nine terrorists are killed.

1979

- *February 12:* In Rhodesia, guerrillas from the Zimbabwe African People's Union use a Soviet-made surface-to-air missile to shoot down an Air Rhodesia plane, killing all 59 people aboard.
- *February 14:* The U.S. ambassador to Afghanistan, Adolph Dubs, is kidnapped and murdered by Muslim terrorists.
- *March 5:* In Spain, the Maoist urban guerrilla group GRAPO kills General Agustín Muñoz Vázquez in Madrid to protest Spain's entry into NATO.
- *March 22:* The PIRA reaches beyond the British Isles to assassinate Sir Richard Sykes, the British ambassador to the Netherlands, in front of his

home in The Hague. Sykes had formerly been the British ambassador to the Republic of Ireland at Dublin.

- *May 26:* A group of Ku Klux Klan (KKK) members attacks civil rights marchers in Decatur, Alabama. Two civil rights workers and two Klansmen are killed.
- *May 26:* Egypt and Israel sign the Camp David Peace Accord. Israel hands the Sinai back to Egypt. Islamic extremists begin to target Egyptian president Anwar Sadat.
- *June/July:* A wing of the Basque ETA group begins a "tourist war," bombing Spanish coastal tourist resorts. Only two people are injured, but the bombings cause extensive property damage.
- *August 27:* The PIRA assassinates Louis, Earl Mountbatten; his grandson; and another person by setting off a remote-control bomb hidden aboard their fishing boat in Donegal Bay, Ireland. The same day, the PIRA sets off two bombs near Warrenpoint, Ireland, killing 19 people, mostly British soldiers.
- *November 3:* During an anti-Klan rally in Greensboro, North Carolina, five U.S. communists are killed in an attack by a KKK group.
- *November 4:* Ayatollah Khomeini's Revolutionary Guards seize the U.S. embassy in Teheran, holding 53 U.S. personnel hostage. What became known as the Iranian Hostage Crisis drags on for 444 days.

1980

- *March 24:* The Roman Catholic archbishop of El Salvador, Oscar Romero, is assassinated by a right-wing death squad during mass.
- *April 30:* Members of an Iranian anti-Khomeini splinter group seize the Iranian embassy in London, holding more than 20 hostages and demanding international attention to the plight of Iran's Arab minority. The British government refuses to negotiate, and six days later, the Special Air Service Regiment (SAS) elite counterterrorism force assaults the building. All five terrorists are killed, but two hostages also die.
- *August 2:* A right-wing terrorist group bombs the railway station in Bologna, Italy, killing 84 people and causing a large number of injuries.
- *September 26:* The hijacking of a Yugoslav aircraft by Croatian separatists fails when the hostages fake a fire and escape to safety.
- *December 7:* The Venezuelan group Bandera Roja simultaneously hijacks three Venezuelan domestic airliners, demanding the release of seven prisoners and a ransom of $10 million. Their demands fail, and they fly to Havana and surrender to Cuban authorities.
- *December 31:* The PFLP takes credit for a bomb blast in the Norfolk Hotel in Nairobi, Kenya. Sixteen people are killed and 80 injured; and the historic building is devastated.

Chronology

1981

- *May 13:* Turkish-born terrorist Mehmet Ali Agca attempts to assassinate Pope John Paul II as the pontiff is entering St. Peter's Square in Rome. Although the pope is shot twice and seriously wounded, he makes a complete recovery. Agca is convicted and sentenced to life in prison. In 2000 he is pardoned by Italy (at the pope's urging) but is imprisoned in Turkey for another past murder.
- *August 31:* A car bomb set off by the RAF injures 18 U.S. citizens and two West Germans at the U.S. Air Force base at Ramstein. Two weeks later, the RAF makes an unsuccessful attempt to assassinate General Frederick Kroesen, chief commander of U.S. forces in Europe.
- *October 6:* President Anwar al-Sadat of Egypt is assassinated by Muslim extremists while he is watching a military parade. Eight other people are also killed.
- *October 20:* Following an unsuccessful armored car robbery near Nyack, New York, in which two policemen and a security guard are killed, Weather Underground fugitive Kathy Boudin is arrested and turned over to the FBI.
- *November 28:* As part of its attempt to topple the government of Syrian President Hafez al-Assad, the Muslim Brotherhood sets off a bomb in Damascus, killing 64 people.
- *December 17:* U.S. Army general and NATO commander for southern Europe James Lee Dozier is kidnapped by Red Brigades terrorists from his home in Verona, Italy. He is held for 42 days but is then freed in a successful raid by Italian counterterrorism forces.

1982

- *February 2:* Syrian president Hafez al-Assad strikes back at the Moslem Brotherhood, attacking its bases in the city of Hamah. More than 20,000 people die in the fighting.
- *June 3:* In London, the Black June group, instigated by Abu Nidal, seriously wounds Israel's ambassador to Britain, Shlomo Argov. A few days later Israel launches a full-scale invasion of Lebanon to root out terrorist bases.
- *July 20:* In London, the PIRA sets off a bomb in Hyde Park during the ceremonial changing of the guard. Two hours later, a second bomb goes off at a band concert in Regent's Park. Eleven people are killed in the two attacks.
- *August 7:* Armenian terrorists use a hand grenade and machine gun to kill seven people and wound more than 70 at the Esenboga Airport in Ankara, Turkey.
- *August 9:* Terrorists believed to be from the Abu Nidal group attack a Jewish restaurant and a synagogue in Paris, killing six people and wounding 27.

- **September 14:** The newly elected president of Lebanon, Bashir Gemayel, is assassinated by a bomb at his Beirut headquarters. His killer is Habib Tanios Chartouny, a member of the Syrian Social Nationalist Party.
- **September 16:** Christian Phalangists allied with the Israeli occupation force in Lebanon massacre from 800 to 1,000 people in the Sabra and Shatila refugee camps outside Beirut.
- **September 17:** Members of the Cinchoneros Popular Liberation Movement, a Honduran leftist terrorist group, kill one person and take 105 hostages at an economic conference in San Pedro Sula. They demand the release of nine prisoners held in Honduran jails and the expulsion of foreign military advisers. Their demands are refused, but they gain asylum in Cuba.
- **December 6:** A tavern in Ballykelly favored by British security forces is bombed by the Irish National Liberation Army. Seventeen people are killed, 11 of them soldiers.

1983

- Throughout the year, the Revolutionary Cells group carries out 19 bombings against government facilities in West Germany.
- **April 18:** A suicide truck bombing kills 49 people and injures 120 at the U.S. embassy in Beirut. The group Islamic Jihad claims responsibility.
- **July 27:** A group called the Armenian Revolutionary Army seizes the Turkish embassy in Lisbon, Portugal. The terrorists blow up the building, killing themselves and two of their hostages.
- **August 21:** Benigno Aquino, Jr., leader of the opposition to President Ferdinand Marcos of the Philippines, is assassinated at Manila airport shortly after landing. His death is quickly linked to Marcos supporters.
- **September 16:** Puerto Rican FALN separatists rob a Wells Fargo armored car terminal in West Hartford, Connecticut, escaping with $7.2 million.
- **October 9:** A bombing during a South Korea delegation visit to Burma kills 19 people. South Korean president Chun Doo Hwan is slightly delayed and narrowly escapes the bombing. The bombers are suspected to be North Korean agents.
- **October 23:** In one of the worst terrorist attacks directed against U.S. forces, 241 U.S. servicemen are killed when a suicide truck bomb is driven into the U.S. Marine Corps barracks in Beirut. Another explosion moments later kills 58 at a French barracks. Islamic Jihad claims responsibility. Despite a very similar attack on the U.S. embassy the previous April, U.S. authorities had taken few security precautions.
- **December 17:** The PIRA sets off a bomb in a crowd of Christmas shoppers in front of Harrods department store in London, killing five people and wounding 90.

Chronology

- *December 31:* The Puerto Rican separatist group FALN sets off bombs in New York City, attacking police, FBI, and federal court facilities.

1984

- *January 18:* Malcolm H. Kerr, president of the American University in Beirut, is killed by Islamic Jihad gunmen. The following month Frank Regier, a professor at the university, is kidnapped by Hezbollah.
- *March 16:* William Buckley, the CIA Beirut station chief, is kidnapped. Although his body is never found, he is believed to have been kidnapped, tortured, and killed by Islamic Jihad, which claimed responsibility for "executing" Buckley.
- *June 5–6:* Indian troops assault the Golden Temple of Amritsar, a stronghold of Sikh extremists. Hundreds of people are killed, including Sikh leader Jarnail Singh Bhindranwale.
- *June 18:* Alan Berg, a controversial Denver talk show host who is Jewish, is murdered by members of the neo-Nazi white supremacist group the Order.
- *July:* The Spanish terrorist group GRAPO explodes 15 bombs in several Spanish cities during the summer, causing extensive property damage to the French consulate, General Motors, and a French bank. The group demands an end to Spain's involvement with NATO and the United States.
- *August–September:* Trying to prevent people from voting against them in an upcoming referendum, members of the Rajneesh cult in Oregon contaminate salad bars with *Salmonella*. About 750 people get sick from this early attempt at bioterrorism.
- *September 20:* A truck bomb explodes at the U.S. embassy annex in East Beirut. A shadowy group called Islamic Jihad claims credit for the attack. Twenty-three people (including two U.S. citizens) are killed, and more than 60 are injured.
- *October 12:* The PIRA bombs a Brighton hotel where important British officials are staying, narrowly missing Prime Minister Margaret Thatcher. Sir Anthony Barry, a member of Parliament, is killed, and several cabinet officials and Conservative Party leaders are injured.
- *October 31:* Indian prime minister Indira Gandhi is assassinated by two of her bodyguards, who are Sikhs. The killing is in retaliation for the earlier Indian attack on the Golden Temple of Amritsar.
- *November:* During the next three months, the communist New People's Army in the Philippines will murder two mayors, a deputy mayor, and a police chief.
- *December 3:* Islamic Jihad hijacks a Kuwaiti airliner and kills two U.S. representatives of USAID. The Islamic Jihad members go to Iran and receive virtual asylum.

- *December 11:* The first of several bombings by European leftist terrorists (including Red Army Faction, Communist Combatant Cells, and Action Directe) damage NATO fuel pipeline facilities near Verviers, Belgium.
- *December 25:* Antiabortion terrorists simultaneously bomb three abortion clinics in Pensacola, Florida.

1985

- *March 16:* Terry A. Anderson, an Associated Press correspondent in Lebanon, is kidnapped by Islamic Jihad.
- *June 9:* Thomas M. Sutherland, acting Dean of Agriculture at the American University in Beirut, is also kidnapped by Islamic Jihad.
- *June 14:* Hezbollah terrorists hijack a TWA flight on its way to Rome and divert it to Beirut. They beat and kill U.S. Navy diver Robert Dean Stetham. The plane flies back and forth between Algiers and Beirut, with hostages being freed at each stop. The leader of the terrorists, Mohammed Ali Hamadei, is eventually convicted and sentenced to life in prison.
- *June 23:* An Air India flight mysteriously blows up on its way from Toronto to London, killing all 329 people on board. The wreckage is found off the coast of Ireland. Both the Kashmir Liberation Army and the Dashmesh Regiment, a Sikh group, claim responsibility. (The two groups are both obscure and their status is hard to determine.)
- *July 10:* French "counterterrorist" agents blow up the Greenpeace ship *Rainbow Warrior* in Auckland, New Zealand. The ship had been preparing to lead a flotilla to protest French nuclear tests.
- *August 8:* The RAF sets off a car bomb at the U.S. Air Force base at Rhein-Main, West Germany, killing two people and injuring 17. The previous day, the terrorists had killed an off-duty U.S. serviceman and used his identification to gain entry to the base.
- *October 7:* The Italian cruise ship *Achille Lauro* is hijacked by four terrorists from the PFLP, whose goal is unclear. Their brutal murder of Leon Klinghoffer, an elderly wheelchair-bound Jewish man, arouses public outrage. The terrorists receive long prison terms.
- *October 25:* Terrorists from the right-wing group RENAMO kidnap and murder two Jesuit priests in Mozambique as part of their campaign against missionaries and aid workers.
- *November 6:* The Colombian terrorist group M-19 seizes the Palace of Justice in Bogotá, taking 500 hostages including Supreme Court justices and members of the Council of State. Security forces retake the building next day in a bloody fight that takes the lives of all 20 or so terrorists, 11 Colombian soldiers, 11 Supreme Court justices, and 50 other hostages.

- *November 23:* Four members of an Abu Nidal splinter group hijack an EgyptAir jet flying from Athens to Cairo. They force the plane to land in Malta and free 13 female hostages. When the Maltese refuse to refuel the plane, the terrorists begin shooting their remaining hostages one by one. Egyptian commandos recapture the plane, but 57 people (including commandos, terrorists, and passengers) die in the gun battle and a fire that breaks out on the plane.
- *December 11:* A Sacramento, California, computer store owner is killed by a package bomb. This is the first fatality to be attributed to the Unabomber.
- *December 23:* Terrorists from the African National Congress set off a bomb in a shopping center in Durban, South Africa, killing five people and wounding 48.
- *December 27:* Abu Nidal terrorists kill 18 holiday travelers in the Rome and Vienna airports.

1986

- *April 5:* A bomb explosion in the crowded La Belle Disco in West Berlin kills 3 people (including 2 U.S. soldiers) and injures more than 200. U.S. government investigators link the bombing to Libya, and on April 15 the U.S. Air Force conducts a retaliatory bombing raid on two Libyan cities.
- *May 3:* The Liberation Tigers of Tamil Eelam (also known as the Tamil Tigers) destroy an Air Sri Lanka plane, killing 17 people. Four days later, a bomb explodes in Colombo, the capital of Sri Lanka, killing 14 and wounding more than 100.
- *June 18:* About 200 prisoners belonging to Peru's Shining Path group riot in a prison outside Lima and are killed by authorities. About a week later Shining Path guerrillas bomb a tourist train near the Inca ruins of Machu Picchu, killing eight and injuring 40.
- *July 14:* In Spain, the Basque ETA kills 10 Civil Guard cadets with a truck bomb, wounding 56 bystanders.
- *September 5:* Abu Nidal terrorists attempt to hijack a Pan Am plane at Karachi Airport, Pakistan. When their efforts are thwarted, they open fire, killing 20 passengers.
- *September 6:* Two Abu Nidal terrorists kill 21 people in an Istanbul synagogue, then commit suicide.
- *October 25:* ETA terrorists kill General Rafael Garrido Gil, the military governor of the Basque province of Guipuzcoa, together with his wife and son, by blowing up their car.
- *December 25:* Iranian-sponsored terrorists attempt to hijack an Iraqi airliner, but the plane crashes in Saudia Arabia, killing 62 of the 107 people aboard, including two of the four hijackers.

1987

- *January 20:* Terry Waite, the personal emissary of the Archbishop of Canterbury, is abducted in Lebanon by Islamic Jihad while on a mission to seek the release of hostages.
- *February 21:* French police arrest the four top leaders of Action Directe in a farmhouse outside the city of Orléans, dealing a crushing blow to the terrorist group.
- *March 23:* The PIRA sets off a car bomb outside an officers' club at the British army base at Rheindahlen, injuring more than 30 people. Most of the people hurt are West Germans, however, not British military personnel.
- *April:* In a series of attacks, the Liberation Tigers of Tamil Eelam (Tamil Tigers) blow up four buses and the central bus station in Colombo, Sri Lanka, killing more than 200 people.
- *September:* Shining Path terrorists step up their efforts in Peru, setting off car bombs in Lima, killing 40 civilians in two villages in Tocache province, and assassinating leftist APRA (Alianza Popular Revolucionaria Americana) party leader Nelson Pozo.
- *October 1:* An Israeli air raid on the PLO's Tunis headquarters destroys the building and kills 65 people, many of whom are innocent bystanders.
- *November 8:* In Enniskillen, Northern Ireland, PIRA terrorists bomb a military ceremony, killing 11 people and wounding 60.
- *November 25:* In Zimbabwe, suspected members of the black guerrilla organization Zimbabwe African People's Union (ZAPU) murder 16 people (including 10 children) working on a farm run by Pentecostal missionaries. All victims but one are white.
- *November 29:* A bomb planted by two North Korean agents destroys South Korean airlines flight 858, killing 115 passengers and crew.
- *December 8:* The first Intifada, a widespread campaign against the Israeli occupation of Palestine, begins.
- *December 11:* An ETA bomb attack on an apartment complex in Zaragosa that houses Spanish Civil Guard members kills 11 people and wounds 40.

1988

- *March 11:* Sinhalese terrorists kill 17 Tamils in apparent retaliation for an earlier attack by the Tamil Tigers that had killed 39 Sinhalese.
- *April 5:* Hezbollah terrorists supported by Iran hijack a Kuwaiti airliner and demand the release of 17 Shiite terrorists from prison. Negotiations fail, and the terrorists murder two hostages.
- *April 12:* Yu Kikumura, a member of the Japanese Red Army, is arrested in a rest area off the New Jersey Turnpike. His car contains three power-

ful bombs and other munitions. U.S. authorities believe he was preparing to bomb a U.S. facility in retaliation for the U.S. attack on Libya in April 1986. (The Japanese Red Army does make a successful retaliatory attack two days later against a USO club in Naples, Italy, killing a U.S. Navy enlisted woman and four other people.)

- *April 16:* Israeli agents kill Khalil al-Wazir, an al-Fatah commander also known as Abu Jihad.
- *May 11:* A suicide car bomb driven by an Abu Nidal terrorist kills two people and wounds 17 outside the Israeli embassy in Nicosia, Cyprus. The attack is said to be in retaliation for the killing of Khalil al-Wazir.
- *May 15:* Abu Nidal terrorists attack the Acropole Hotel and the British Sudan Club in Khartoum with grenades and automatic weapons, killing eight and wounding 21.
- *July 11:* In Greece, Abu Nidal terrorists set off a bomb aboard the cruise ship *City of Poros*, killing nine people and injuring 100. A second bomb explodes prematurely, killing two terrorists in their car.
- *September 7:* Police in Rome arrest 21 suspected members of the Red Brigades, seriously disrupting the group.
- *September 11:* In Port-au-Prince, Haiti, members of the Tonton Macoute militia attack a church service. The attack, apparently aimed at dissident priest Jean-Bertrand Aristide, kills nine people and injures 77.
- *October 26:* Police raid an apartment in Neuss, Germany, used by the PFLP-GC, seizing plastic explosives and a pressure-sensitive detonator used for blowing up planes in flight. However, they later release most of the arrestees, citing lack of evidence, and fail to find the bomb that prosecutors would later charge was used later to destroy Pan Am flight 103.
- *December 21:* Pan Am Flight 103 explodes as it is flying over Scotland, killing all 259 people on board and scattering wreckage over the village of Lockerbie, which kills 11 people on the ground. Investigators suspect the bomb was planted by the PFLP-GC, led by Ahmed Jabril.

1989

- *February 14:* Noted Indian-born British author Salman Rushdie goes into hiding after the Ayatollah Khomeini declares that Rushdie's novel *The Satanic Verses* is blasphemous, and issues a *fatwa*, or religious order, authorizing Rushdie's execution.
- *April:* The Tamil Tigers and other militant groups kill more than 100 people in Sri Lanka with bomb attacks.
- *April 3:* Members of the Animal Liberation Front break into a research facility at the University of Arizona and free more than 1,200 rabbits, mice, frogs, and other animals. They then set fire to the laboratory and a nearby administration building.

- **September 19:** A plane of the French airline UTA explodes shortly after takeoff in Chad, killing all 171 people aboard. Islamic Jihad terrorists take credit for the bombing, saying that it is in retaliation for Israel's kidnapping of Hezbollah leader Sheikh Abdel Karim Obeid.
- **November 11:** More than 1,000 FMLN guerrillas launch an offensive against El Salvador's capital city, San Salvador. The Salvadoran army eventually drives the guerrillas out of the city.
- **November 16:** Six Roman Catholic priests and two employees are dragged from their rooms in the José Simeón Cañas University of Central America and executed by a right-wing death squad. The Salvadoran government will later charge nine military personnel with the killings.
- **November 27:** The Extraditables, the terrorist arm of the Medellín drug cartel, blow up an Avianca plane in midair, killing all 107 people on board. The group claims it destroyed the plane to kill five police informants said to be among the passengers.
- **November 30:** A remote-controlled bomb kills Alfred Herrhausen, head of Germany's powerful Deutsche Bank, as his limousine passes through a Frankfurt suburb. The RAF claims responsibility for the attack.
- **December 6:** A truck bomb set off by the Extraditables kills more than 50 people and injures 250 in front of the headquarters of the Colombian police.
- **December 13:** An Italian court dismisses charges against 168 members of the Red Brigades, saying that the group was not a serious security threat.
- **December 16:** Colombian troops and police strike back at the Medellín cartel, killing drug lord José Gonzalo Rodríguez Gacha, his son, and 15 henchmen.
- **December 16:** Terrorists apparently motivated by race hatred send mail bombs to people associated with civil rights enforcement, killing Judge Robert S. Vance of the 11th Circuit Court and civil rights attorney Robert Robinson of Savannah, Georgia. Two more bombs, sent to the Circuit Court and to an office of the National Association for the Advancement of Colored People (NAACP) in Jacksonville, Florida, are disarmed.

1990

- **January 7:** Terrorists working for the Medellín cartel kidnap more than 20 wealthy Colombians over a one-week period. They hope to turn the nation's elite against the war on drugs.
- **March 9:** More than a thousand members of the Colombian M-19 terrorist group turn over the weapons to authorities. Their leader, Carlos Pizarro León-Gómez, renounces violence and becomes a candidate for president, but he is assassinated on April 26.
- **March 28:** British police discover five people at Heathrow Airport who are attempting to smuggle nuclear weapons components to Iraq.

Chronology

- *April 6:* In Peru, Shining Path guerrillas kill 24 people in the village of Alto Pauralli. Fifty villagers are killed in Sonomoro six days later.
- *April 19:* Sikh terrorists are believed to be responsible for the bombing of a bus near the northern Indian city of Pathanakot. Thirteen people are killed and 42 wounded.
- *May 5:* FBI agents in Florida arrest members of Pablo Escobar's Medellín cartel who were attempting to purchase 24 Stinger anti-aircraft missiles capable of shooting down airliners.
- *May 21:* An apparently deranged Jewish gunman kills seven Palestinians in the Gaza Strip. The attack causes renewed unrest in the occupied territories.
- *May 24:* A car bomb set off by Medellín cartel terrorists in front of Medellín's Inter-Continental Hotel kills 11 people and wounds 25.
- *May 24:* Two members of the radical environmental group Earth First! are injured by a bomb placed under the front seat of their car. Police claim that the activists were planning to use the bomb to disrupt logging operations, but the activists believe that it was planted by lumber interests. No charges are filed.
- *June 30:* As the East German communist government that had sheltered them falls, the identities of 10 RAF terrorists are revealed, and they are arrested by the new united German government. The fall of other Eastern European communist governments produces similar problems for the RAF and the infamous terrorist known as Carlos the Jackal.
- *July 14:* Tamil Tigers terrorists kill 35 Muslims after dragging them from passenger buses near the city of Kalmunai, Sri Lanka.
- *September 6:* Reports from Amnesty International and the Brazilian Institute for Social and Economic Analysis charge that death squads operated by the Brazilian government have killed hundreds of homeless children whom they regarded as nuisances.
- *October 9:* In India, People's War Group terrorists lock a railroad coach and set fire to it, killing 47 passengers.
- *October 11:* In the northern Spanish province of Galicia, an organization called the Guerrilla Army of the Free Galician People bombs a disco, killing three people and wounding 46.
- *October 19:* Three members of the white supremacist Aryan Nations group are convicted of conspiring to bomb a Seattle disco frequented by gays.
- *October 24:* The IRA attempts a new terrorist tactic: forcing a person they consider to be a British collaborator to make a suicide bomb attack, by holding the bomber's family hostage. Of three such attacks, one in Londonderry succeeds, killing five soldiers and the bomber and wounding 26 others.

■ *November 5:* Meir Kahane, leader of the extremist Jewish Defense League (JDL), is assassinated in New York. A year later, Arab terrorist El Sayyid Nosair is tried for the killing. He is convicted only of the charge of assault with a deadly weapon.

1991

■ *February 7:* IRA gunmen fire shots into British Prime Minister John Major's residence while he is meeting with his cabinet. There are no injuries.
■ *February 18:* IRA terrorists bomb Victoria and Paddington railway stations in London, killing one person and injuring 40.
■ *August–December:* The remaining six U.S. hostages (including Terry Waite) held in Lebanon by Islamic Jihad are released. The remains of William Buckley and Colonel William R. Higgins are returned to the United States.

1992

■ *January 11:* Secular military leaders stage a coup in Algeria, preventing the newly elected Islamic fundamentalist legislators from taking power. The secularists conduct a massive crackdown on the fundamentalist Islamic Salvation Front, which responds to the state terror with ongoing terrorist attacks.
■ *March 17:* Islamic Jihad claims credit for the car bombing of the Israeli embassy in Buenos Aires, killing 20 and wounding more than 200. The attack is a reprisal for Israeli air raids on Hezbollah bases.
■ *June 29:* Algerian president Muhammad Boudiaf is assassinated by members of the Armed Islamic Group.
■ *July 16:* The Shining Path begins a new offensive against the Peruvian government with two car bomb attacks in Lima, killing 18 people and wounding more than 140.
■ *August 31:* Randall Weaver, a white separatist who had fled to a remote cabin in Ruby Ridge, Idaho, after being charged with selling an illegal gun to federal agents, surrenders after a long siege. During the siege by federal forces, Weaver's wife, Vicki, is killed by a federal sniper while carrying their infant son. Weaver's older son, Sam, and Deputy Marshal William Degan had died in an earlier gun battle. Weaver is eventually acquitted of most charges, but his case becomes a rallying cry for right-wing antigovernment extremists.
■ *September 13:* Abimael Guzmán, the founder of Shining Path, and his top lieutenants are captured by Peruvian security forces while holding a meeting in Lima.

Chronology

- *October 9:* A Russian nuclear engineer is arrested just before selling a large quantity of highly enriched uranium to terrorists. The material could have been used to make a nuclear bomb.

1993

- *January 25:* A gunman, later identified as Pakistani terrorist Mir Aimal Kansi, opens fire with an automatic weapon on employees waiting to enter the CIA headquarters at Langley, Virginia. He kills two people and wounds three. He is captured more than three years later after an intensive investigation and a raid by FBI and CIA agents in Pakistan. A Virginia jury convicts him of capital murder.
- *February 26:* The World Trade Center in New York is bombed by followers of Egyptian fundamentalist spiritual leader Sheikh Omar Abdel Rahman, who drove a van containing a 1,200-pound bomb into one of the building's underground parking garages, killing six persons and injuring more than 1,000. Four persons are convicted by a federal jury on March 4, 1994, while two others remain at large.
- *April 1:* The United States indicts four Palestinian terrorists associated with the Abu Nidal organization for plotting to blow up the Israeli embassy in Washington, D.C.
- *April 19:* The federal siege of the compound of the Branch Davidian sect ends when the building explodes in flames after a tank assaults it and injects tear gas. Seventy-three people die, including cult leader David Koresh and many children. Authorities claim that the Branch Davidians had set fire to their own building, but critics accuse the FBI of having caused the disaster. As with Ruby Ridge, Waco becomes a battle cry for the extreme right-wing in America, who consider it another example of state-sponsored terrorism.
- *September 13:* A major Israeli-Palestinian peace agreement is signed in Washington, D.C., by Israeli prime minister Yitzhak Rabin and PLO chairman Yasir Arafat. Radical groups such as Hamas on the Palestinian side and Israeli ultranationalists launch terrorist attacks in an attempt to disrupt the peace process.
- *December 2:* Pablo Escobar, fugitive head of the Medellín drug cartel and organizer of a narcoterrorist bombing and kidnapping campaign against Colombian officials, is tracked down and killed in a gun battle with Colombian security forces in Medellín.

1994

- *February 25:* Baruch Goldstein, a militant follower of Rabbi Meir Kahane, opens fire on a group of Palestinian Muslims praying at the Tomb of the Patriarchs in Hebron, Israel. He kills about 30 people and wounds approximately 150. In response, riots break out in the occupied territories and negotiations on Palestinian autonomy are temporarily suspended.

- **March 14:** Nidal Ayyad, Ahmad Ajaj, Mohammad Salameh, and Mahmud Abouhalima are convicted on all four counts for their roles in the bombing of the World Trade Center in February 1993.
- **May–August:** In three separate incidents, German police seize nuclear materials being smuggled to European terrorists, possibly for eventual construction of a nuclear bomb.
- **August 15:** The notorious terrorist Carlos the Jackal (Ilyich Ramírez Sánchez) is captured in the Sudan by French counterterrorist agents. He is swiftly extradited to France for trial.
- **August 31:** The IRA agrees to a cease-fire, though some extremists continue terrorist attacks.

1995

- **January 22:** Islamic Jihad terrorists claim credit for a bombing outside a military camp in Israel. Nineteen people (including 18 Israeli soldiers) are killed, and another 65 injured.
- **January 30:** A car bomb explodes in Algiers, killing 42 people and injuring about 300 others.
- **February 6:** The trial of Sheikh Abdel Rahman and 11 other Islamic terrorists for the World Trade Center bombing and related conspiracies begins in U.S. Federal Court in New York City.
- **February 7:** Ramzi Ahmed Youssef, accused mastermind of the World Trade Center bombing, is arrested in Islamabad, Pakistan, and flown to the United States to stand trial.
- **March 20:** Members of the apocalyptic religious terrorist cult Aum Shinrikyo release deadly Sarin nerve gas into the Tokyo subway system. Twelve people are killed and about 5,000 injured to varying degrees. Japanese authorities begin a massive hunt for the terrorists and their leaders.
- **April 2:** Terrorists from the Hamas group accidentally set off a bomb in Gaza while assembling it. Eight people are killed and 30 wounded.
- **April 19:** A massive truck bomb explosion demolishes the Alfred P. Murrah Federal Building in Oklahoma City in the worst domestic terrorist attack in U.S. history to date. The blast kills 168 people, including children in a day care center. Two days later, Timothy McVeigh and Terry Nichols are charged with the bombing. They are not connected to any known terrorist group.

Chronology

- **June 26:** An attempt by radical Islamic gunmen to kill Egyptian president Hosni Mubarak during his visit to Addis Ababa, Ethiopia, fails, but two Ethiopian policemen and two terrorists are killed, and many bystanders are injured.
- **September 19:** The *Washington Post* publishes a rambling, anonymous 35,000-word anti-industrial manifesto by a person claiming to be responsible for the Unabomb attacks. The writer had offered to cease the attacks if it was published. Authorities hope that someone will be able to identify the person by his writing style.
- **October 1:** In one of the most important terrorist trials in U.S. history, 10 Islamic fundamentalist terrorists are convicted in a New York federal court of conspiracy to destroy U.S. public buildings and structures. Their spiritual leader, Sheikh Omar Abdel Rahman, is convicted of directing the conspiracy and also of conspiring to assassinate Egyptian president Hosni Mubarak. El Sayyid Nosair is convicted of the 1990 murder of Rabbi Meir Kahane (earlier, in state court, he had been convicted only of assault with a deadly weapon).

1996

- **February 14:** Believing that the "Unabomber Manifesto" had been written by his brother Theodore, David Kaczynski contacts the FBI. Theodore Kaczynski is arrested at his Montana cabin on April 3.
- **June:** A truck bomb kills 19 U.S. personnel and wounds 500 at a military camp in Dhahran, Saudi Arabia. Hani al-Sayegh is arrested in Canada and held for the attack. A controversy over the adequacy of U.S. military security develops, but the investigation bogs down due to lack of cooperation by Saudi Arabia.
- **July 27:** In the midst of the 1996 Summer Olympics, a pipe bomb goes off in Atlanta's Centennial Olympic Park, killing one person and injuring 112. Guard Richard Jewell, who had reported a suspicious knapsack and helped other guards clear the area before the explosion, is first hailed as a hero but then becomes the FBI's chief suspect. Although he is later cleared, his life and reputation are disrupted and he sues various media organizations for reckless reporting. The bombing is eventually linked to antiabortion terrorist Eric Robert Rudolph.
- **December 18:** MRTA (Tupac Amaru) terrorists seize the Japanese embassy in Lima, Peru, taking 490 hostages, including many prominent international diplomats. They release 225 of the hostages as a Christmas gesture and enter into prolonged negotiations with authorities, demanding the release of imprisoned comrades.

Global Terrorism

1997

- **January 16:** Two bombs explode at an abortion clinic in Atlanta, Georgia. The first bomb causes only property damage, but when investigators and reporters reach the scene, a second bomb injures six people. Eric Robert Rudolph is sought for both this attack and the Olympic Park bombing.
- **January 20:** Islamic terrorists in Algeria attack a village, killing 36 residents, some of whom are decapitated. The same terrorists then go to Algiers, where they set off a bomb that kills more than 30 people and wounds many more.
- **February 28:** A gay/lesbian bar in Atlanta, Georgia, is bombed, injuring five people. This attack is also linked to Eric Robert Rudolph.
- **March 21:** A suicide bomb attack on a Tel Aviv cafe kills five people including the terrorist and wounds many more. It also interrupts ongoing Israeli-Palestinian peace negotiations.
- **April:** White supremacist and microbiologist Larry Wayne Harris is sentenced to probation and community service for illegally obtaining bubonic plague cultures. He had claimed to be doing research to protect the United States from biological attack, but authorities suspected him of plotting an attack of his own.
- **April 22:** After months of fruitless negotiation with the MRTA, Peruvian troops burst into the Japanese embassy in Lima, freeing the diplomatic hostages. All 14 terrorists, one soldier, and one hostage are killed.
- **June 13:** A federal jury in Denver sentences Timothy McVeigh to death for the 1995 Oklahoma City bombing. His coconspirator, Terry Nichols, receives a life sentence.
- **June 29:** FBI agents in Pakistan arrest Mir Aimal Kansi, accused of a shooting on January 25, 1993, which killed two people and injured three outside the CIA headquarters in Langley, Virginia.
- **July 30:** Two bomb-carrying terrorists kill themselves and 13 bystanders in a crowded Jerusalem market. Another 150 people are injured. It is unclear whether the bombing was a suicide attack or an accident, but Hamas takes credit for the attack.
- **September 4:** Another Hamas suicide bomb attack on a Jerusalem market kills the three bombers and one bystander while injuring another 200 people.
- **September 23:** In Algeria, terrorists from the Islamic Salvation Front carry out a number of attacks, killing 85 and injuring 67 persons.
- **September 30:** Israel, hoping to aid the peace process, releases 20 terrorists from prison, including Sheikh Ahmed Yassin, founder of Hamas.

Chronology

- **November:** A terrorist campaign against the Egyptian government by the Islamic Group (Al-Gama'at al-Islamiyya) culminates in the killing of 58 tourists in Luxor.
- **December 24:** Carlos the Jackal (Ilyich Ramírez Sánchez) is convicted in Paris of murder and kidnapping and sentenced to life in prison.

1998

- **January 29:** An unknown terrorist bombs an abortion clinic in Birmingham, Alabama, killing off-duty police officer Robert Sanderson and injuring a nurse.
- **April 10:** A historic peace agreement is ratified by voters in both Northern Ireland and the Republic of Ireland. It calls for a Northern Ireland legislative council made up of both Protestants and Catholics, and the sharing of decision-making power between Northern Ireland and the Republic in areas such as transportation and the environment.
- **May 4:** Accepting a plea bargain, Theodore Kaczynski, the Unabomber, is sentenced to four consecutive life terms for his mail bombings. Kaczynski had sought to represent himself and had resisted any attempt by his attorneys to mount an insanity defense.
- **August 7:** In nearly simultaneous attacks, the U.S. embassies in Nairobi, Kenya, and Dar es Salaam, Tanzania, are bombed. The explosion in Kenya is larger, and destroys a building next door to the embassy after the truck carrying the bomb is turned away by an alert guard. Twelve U.S. citizens and 250 Kenyans are killed, and thousands of people are wounded. The explosion in Tanzania is considerably smaller but kills 10 people and wounds several times that number. The attacks are soon linked to terrorist multimillionaire Osama bin Laden, who is indicted in absentia.
- **August 15:** Slow but steady peace progress in Northern Ireland is threatened by a car bomb explosion in Omagh that kills 28 people and wounds 220. The perpetrators, a splinter group called the Real IRA, had given authorities a bomb warning with misleading information which caused bystanders to be evacuated in the direction of the bomb. The terrorists are vigorously condemned by the mainstream IRA, Sinn Féin, and Protestant groups.
- **August 20:** In retaliation for the earlier attacks on U.S. embassies in Africa, President Clinton orders cruise missile attacks on a pharmaceutical plant reportedly linked to terrorist nerve gas production in Khartoum, Sudan and Osama bin Laden's terrorist training camp in Afghanistan. Although bin Laden's camp is damaged, he escapes without injury. Later reports suggest that the pharmaceutical plant was actually just a pharmaceutical plant.
- **October 19:** A fire set by ecoterrorists causes $12 million in property damage to prime ski resort areas on Vail Mountain, Colorado. A group

calling itself the Earth Liberation Front (believed to be the same as the Animal Liberation Front) claims responsibility for the blaze, demanding an end to expansion of the facilities.

- *November 4:* A New York federal court returns indictments against Osama bin Laden and other members of the al-Qaeda group in connection with the bombings of the two U.S. embassies in Africa.

1999

- *August:* Jordan expels Hamas, arresting four members and closing the militant Islamic group's offices.
- *September–October:* A series of bomb blasts in Moscow are linked by authorities to Chechen terrorists who were demanding independence for the former Soviet Caucasian republic. Russian authorities respond with random police sweeps, curtailment of civil liberties, confused announcements, and a renewed military offensive in Chechnya.
- *September 6:* Israel's Supreme Court rules that government interrogators cannot be authorized to use torture or physical pressure beyond that "inherent in the interrogation process itself," even to get information about a pending terrorist attack.
- *December 14:* Ahmed Rassam, an alleged Algerian terrorist, is arrested for plotting to smuggle explosives into Port Townsend, Washington. Another Algerian, Abdelmajid Dahoumane, remains at large. The two are indicted on January 20, 2000, by a Seattle grand jury. The U.S. government announces a $5 million bounty for Dahoumane's capture. The authorities link the two suspects to the Armed Islamic Group.
- *December 31:* Ecoterrorists set fire to a genetic research facility partly funded by Monsanto Corporation at Michigan State University. The fire causes $400,000 in damages, and the Earth Liberation Front claims responsibility.

2000

- *February:* A federal jury in Washington state convicts a group of Freemen and Washington State Militia members of weapons charges but deadlocks on charges that they had conspired to blow up radio towers, a bridge, and a train tunnel to stop UN troops from "invading" from Canada.
- *February 14:* During this week hackers launch "denial of service attacks" that tie up major Internet commerce sites such as Yahoo! and eBay. While not tied to particular terrorist groups, the attacks illustrate the vulnerability of the growing U.S. e-commerce sector to cyberterrorism.
- *March:* U.S. officials consider whether to lift a ban on U.S. citizens traveling to Libya. Libya's decision to hand over two men suspected of in-

volvement in the 1988 bombing of Pan Am Flight 103 over Lockerbie, Scotland, has led to improved relations between the two nations, and the United States has suspended sanctions against Libya.

- *April 20:* Jordan puts 28 alleged terrorists on trial for plotting to attack U.S. and Israeli tourists in Jordan over the New Year's holiday.
- *August 12:* A bomb explodes in an underpass at Moscow's Pushkin Square, killing at least eight persons and injuring more than 90. Some Russian officials attribute the bombing to Chechen terrorists, while others are more reticent.
- *August 18:* Libya, seeking to participate in an Eastern Mediterranean summit, agrees to pay $25 million to Muslim rebels in the Philippines in exchange for the ransom of 16 hostages.
- *October:* Weeks of widespread violence follow right-wing Israeli politician Ariel Sharon's visit to the Temple Mount (called Haram ash Sharif by Muslims). Israeli helicopter gunships attack Palestinian headquarters and Hamas claims responsibility for a Jerusalem car bombing. More than 170 people are killed, mostly Palestinians.
- *October 12:* A suicide boat attack blows a gaping hole in the side of the U.S. Navy destroyer *Cole* while the ship is taking on fuel in Aden harbor, Yemen. The attack kills 17 sailors.
- *October 30:* Basque ETA terrorists set off a large bomb that kills a Spanish judge, his driver, and a bodyguard. Sixty passengers aboard a nearby bus are also injured. A growing wave of ETA attacks has shattered the cease-fire signed earlier in the year.
- *November 6:* The arrest of four suspects in the U.S.S. *Cole* bombing is said to reveal links between the attackers and Islamic Jihad, and suspicion grows that the attack was masterminded by terrorist organizer Osama bin Laden.

2001

- *January 31:* Abdelbaset Ali Mohmed al-Megrahi is found guilty of the bombing of Pan Am Flight 103 by a Scottish court. However, the other defendant, Al Amin Khalifa Fhimah, is not convicted.
- *March 30:* The ELF claims credit for the burning of 30 sport utility vehicles at an auto dealership in Eugene, Oregon.
- *May 29:* A U.S. federal district court finds four of Osama bin Laden's followers guilty of conspiring to kill Americans, including victims of the embassy bombings in Africa. They will later be sentenced to life in prison.
- *April 5:* The Animal Liberation Front (ALF) claims credit for a $1.5 million fire at a National Food Corp. egg farm in Arlington, Washington.

- *May 21:* An ALF arson attack causes $5.6 million damage to the University of Washington's Center for Urban Horticulture, which was a major center of research on genetically altered plants.
- *June 11:* Convicted Oklahoma City bomber Timothy McVeigh is executed by lethal injection after a plea for additional time to examine previously undisclosed evidence is denied.
- *September 8:* The ALF and ELF jointly claim credit for the $500,000 torching of a McDonald's restaurant.
- *September 11:* In nearly simultaneous attacks, hijacked jetliners are crashed into the twin towers of the World Trade Center in New York City, which soon collapse. A third plane crashes into the Pentagon, heavily damaging the building. A fourth plane crashes in a field in Pennsylvania after a group of passengers battle the hijackers. The estimated death toll is approximately 2,900. U.S. officials soon name Osama bin Laden as "prime suspect" in the attacks.
- *September 20:* Addressing a joint session of Congress, President George Bush tells Americans to expect a difficult, protracted struggle and announces the creation of a new cabinet-level office for "homeland security."
- *September 20:* The ALF claims credit for a $1 million fire at Coulston Foundation's White Sands Research Center in Alamogordo, New Mexico.
- *September 22:* First anthrax cases begin to appear in New York City. Unknown terrorists are suspected of mailing several letters containing spores.
- *October:* Anthrax toll rises to 12 skin cases, 10 inhaled. Four of the latter die. Congress and Postal Service are disrupted.
- *October 4:* An editor at the tabloid *The Sun* is diagnosed with inhaled anthrax, a disease last seen in the United States in 1976.
- *October 7:* U.S. and British forces begin air strikes against Taliban and al-Qaeda targets in Afghanistan. Meanwhile, a tape by Osama bin Laden praises the September 11 attacks and vows that Americans will have no security until Palestinians gain their rights and "all infidel armies leave the land of Muhammad."
- *October 10:* The FBI releases a list of the 22 most wanted terrorists.
- *October 12:* A letter sent to NBC anchor Tom Brokaw tests positive for anthrax.
- *October 15:* Another anthrax-laden letter is addressed to Senate majority leader Tom Daschle.
- *October 17:* The U.S. House of Representatives is closed for five days to test for anthrax.
- *October 26:* President Bush signs the USA PATRIOT Act, giving the government expanded powers for investigating and detaining terrorist suspects.

Chronology

- *November 9:* Northern Alliance forces aided by U.S. Special Forces capture the key Afghan city of Mazur-i-Sharif.
- *November 13:* Allied forces seize control of the Afghan capital, Kabul.
- *November 19:* President Bush signs a law providing for reinforcing airliner cockpit doors and providing for more armed marshals on flights.
- *November 25:* U.S. Marines establish a base near Kandahar, a third key Afghan city.
- *December 13:* Zacarias Moussaoui is ordered to stand trial on multiple conspiracy charges in connection with the September 11 attacks.
- *December 22:* An interim Afghan government under Hamid Karzai is sworn in.
- *December 22:* Richard Reid, a British citizen, attempts to detonate a bomb in his shoe while on an American Airlines flight from Paris to Miami. He is subdued by flight attendants and passengers.
- *December 27:* Defense Secretary Donald Rumsfeld announces that captured al-Qaeda and Taliban fighters will be transported to a remote facility at Guantánamo Bay, Cuba.

2002

- *January 16:* U.S. troops begin counterterrorism training for Filipino soldiers, reflecting an expanded U.S. effort to fight terrorism in the Philippines.
- *January 24:* John Walker Lindh, an American citizen who had joined the Taliban in Afghanistan, is charged with conspiracy to kill Americans and to provide "material resources" to terrorists.
- *January 27:* Wafa Idris, an ambulance worker at the Ramallah refugee camp, becomes the first female suicide bomber for the al-Aqsa Martyrs Brigade, killing one person in Jerusalem and wounding 40.
- *January 29:* In his State of the Union Address, President George W. Bush refers to Iran, Iraq, and North Korea as an "Axis of Evil" that is fostering terrorism and seeking weapons of mass destruction.
- *January 29:* The ELF claims a $250,000 arson attack at the University of Minnesota's Microbial and Plant Genomics Research Center, which had been under construction.
- *February 22:* The government of Sri Lanka (Ceylon) announces a formal cease-fire with the Tamil Tigers (LTTE), which will be followed by peace talks in September.
- *February 22:* Daniel Pearl, a reporter for the *Wall Street Journal* who had been kidnapped in January by Pakistani terrorists, is revealed to have been brutally murdered.

- *March 2:* U.S. forces launch Operation Anaconda, the first ground attack in Afghanistan using regular forces, in the Shar-i-Kot valley south of Kabul. Over the next 10 days the operation will kill several hundred Taliban and al-Qaeda fighters.
- *March 29:* Federal authorities announce they will seek the death penalty against September 11 attack conspirator Zacarias Moussaoui.
- *April 30:* Federal authorities arrest Enaam Arnaout, director of the Benevolence International Foundation, an Illinois-based Muslim charity. Attorney General John Ashcroft accuses Arnaout of being a close ally of Osama bin Laden who has used his group to funnel funds to terrorists.
- *May 10:* A bomb kills 42 people during a Victory Day celebration in the republic of Dagestan. Although no one claims responsibility, Islamic militants are suspected.
- *May 31:* U.S. authorities try to block American-born terrorism suspect Yaser Esam Hamdi from speaking to his attorney, arguing that sensitive information about the investigation might be passed to terrorists.
- *June 10:* U.S. authorities arrest Jose Padilla, a former Chicago gang member who had converted to Islam. They accuse him of plotting to build a radioactive "dirty bomb" for use against an American city. They designate him an "unlawful combatant," with reduced legal rights.
- *June 11:* The new Loya Jurga, or grand council, meets in Afghanistan to set up the country's new permanent government.
- *June 15:* Zacarias Moussaoui, who is representing himself, refuses to enter a plea, angrily denying the court's jurisdiction. Federal Judge Leonie Brinkema enters a plea of not guilty for him.
- *June 28:* President Bush authorizes a $10 million grant of emergency military assistance to fight terrorism in the Philippines.
- *July 12:* The Fourth Circuit Court of Appeals rules that Yaser Esam Hamdi can be denied access to an attorney because of his status as an "unlawful combatant" who can be detained for the duration of hostilities.
- *July 15:* John Walker Lindh strikes a plea bargain, pleading guilty only to aiding the Taliban and carrying explosives (grenades). He will later be sentenced to 20 years in prison.
- *July 17:* The House of Representatives issues the report of its investigation into intelligence efforts prior to September 11, 2001. It faults the FBI, CIA, and NSA for lack of effective cooperation and inability to properly recognize and act on threats.
- *August 29:* Four Detroit men (three of them airport employees) are indicted for allegedly being part of an al-Qaeda "sleeper operational combat cell."

Chronology

- *September 13:* Five men of Yemeni descent are arrested in Lakawana, New York, and are charged with giving "material support" to al-Qaeda. A sixth suspect is arrested in Bahrain.
- *October 4:* Four men in Portland, Oregon, are charged with aiding the Taliban and al-Qaeda by preparing to participate in a jihad against the United States.
- *October 12:* A huge blast in Bali, Indonesia, kills more than 180 people, many of whom are tourists from Australia and various Western countries. The attack will eventually be linked to the Jemaah Islamiya terrorist group, led by Hambali (Riduan Isamuddin). The group also has ties to al-Qaeda.
- *October 24:* Two suspects, John Allan Muhammad and 17-year-old John Lee Malvo, are arrested for a string of Washington, D.C.–area sniper attacks that had killed 10 people and wounded four. The two are not believed to be associated with a terrorist group.
- *November 25:* President Bush signs legislation creating the Department of Homeland Security, which merges numerous federal agencies and will coordinate intelligence efforts against terrorism.
- *November 26:* President Bush signs a law requiring insurance companies to cover losses to domestic property caused by foreign terrorists. However, the federal government is to pay most of any losses exceeding $10 billion.
- *November 27:* President Bush appoints Henry Kissinger to head a commission investigating the causes of the September 11, 2001, attacks. However, Kissinger will later resign after refusing to name his consulting clients, and he will be replaced by former New Jersey governor Thomas Keane.
- *December 13:* President Bush begins a program to inoculate 500,000 military personnel against smallpox; up to 10 million health care and emergency workers may follow.
- *December 21:* North Korea disconnects monitoring devices from its nuclear facilities, apparently beginning to reprocess its plutonium supply to create several nuclear weapons.
- *December 27:* Suicide bombers destroy the headquarters of Chechnya's Russian-controlled government, killing at least 90 people.

2003

- *January 5:* British police arresting five terror suspects find traces of the toxin Ricin in a London apartment.

- ***January 5:*** Starting another bad year for suicide bombing, two simultaneous attacks in a crowded Tel Aviv street kill 22 people and injure many more. The al-Aqsa Martyrs Brigade claims responsibility.
- ***February 28:*** Stepping up the pressure, President Bush tells Iraqi leader Saddam Hussein that he must go into exile if he wants to avoid war.
- ***March 2:*** Nineteen accused members of the leftist terrorist group November 17 are put on trial in Greece.
- ***March 4:*** A bomb in the airport at Davao kills 21 people. Philippine officials believe that the Moro Islamic Liberation Front is responsible for the attack.
- ***March 5:*** A suicide bomb attack on a bus in Haifa kills 15 people, breaking a relative lull in the violence. Israel retaliates by launching an incursion into Gaza and seizing some Palestinian facilities.
- ***March 19:*** Mahmoud Abbas accepts the new position of prime minister of Palestine, a post created by a reluctant Yasir Arafat.
- ***March 20:*** The U.S. opens an air offensive against Iraq with a "decapitation" attack on a building where they believed Saddam Hussein and other Iraqi leaders were meeting. The fate of Hussein remains unknown.
- ***March 21:*** Major air and ground attacks on Iraq begin. During the next week U.S. and coalition forces approach Baghdad. There is little large-scale action by the Iraqi military, but irregular groups of *fedayeen* fighters mount ambushes and inflict casualties.
- ***March 25:*** Several hundred U.S. troops begin a hunt for Taliban fighters in the countryside around Kandahar, Afghanistan, following discovery of a large cache of weapons.
- ***April 2:*** A bomb kills 16 at a ferry terminal in Davao. Again, the attack is blamed on the Moro Islamic Liberation Front.
- ***April 5:*** U.S. forces enter Baghdad, having already taken a position in the airport. Two days later British forces enter the important port of Basra.
- ***April 9:*** Saddam Hussein's Baathist government falls in Baghdad, but widespread looting breaks out and much of the city's buildings and infrastructure are vandalized.
- ***April 11:*** Ten suspects in the bomb attack on the U.S. destroyer *Cole* escape from a military prison in Aden, Yemen, with conflicting stories about their method of escape. Authorities later round up and arrest relatives and other people linked to the escapees.
- ***April 13:*** President Bush warns Syria not to harbor fleeing officials from Saddam Hussein's regime. He also accuses Syria of supporting Arab fighters who have been attempting to aid Hussein's regime against Coalition forces, and of developing chemical weapons.

Chronology

- *April 14:* U.S. Supreme Court justice Stephen Breyer urges attorneys to challenge cases where terrorism suspects are denied access to counsel or the government claims that civilian courts do not have jurisdiction. He suggests that such vigorous advocacy might pressure the government to look for ways to fight terrorism that are compatible with constitutional principles.
- *April 14:* In a plea bargain, James Ujaama, an African-American Muslim living in Seattle, pleads guilty to conspiring to provide cash, computers, and other assistance to the Taliban. Charges of helping to set up a terrorist training camp are dropped. Ujaama agrees to help authorities investigate the activity of radical London-based cleric Abu Hamza al-Masri.
- *April 14:* Indonesian prosecutors indict Abu Bakar Bashir, a prominent Muslim cleric. The leader of the radical group Jemaah Islamiyah, Bashir is accused of terrorist activities including the bombing of churches in December 2000 and a plot to blow up the U.S. embassy in Singapore.
- *April 15:* The U.S. captures the notorious terrorist Abu Abbas, who had been convicted in absentia by Italy for the 1985 hijacking of the cruise ship *Achille Lauro* in which American Leon Klinghoffer had been killed.
- *April 16:* One month after the beginning of the war against Iraq, the Pentagon announces that the major fighting has ended. Meanwhile, the Department of Homeland Security lowers the terrorism threat level from orange (high) to yellow (elevated).
- *April 18:* The first class of airline pilots are ready to graduate from a training course that will allow them to carry handguns in the cockpit.
- *April 30:* The United States presents Israeli prime minister Ariel Sharon and Palestinian prime minister Mahmoud Abbas with the "road map," a plan designed to create a cease-fire and ramp down tensions between the two sides, leading to the creation of a Palestinian state by 2005.
- *May 12:* A series of suicide car bombings in Riyadh, Saudi Arabia, targets foreign residents. Seven Americans are confirmed killed; accurate casualty figures for Saudis and other nationals are not immediately available. U.S. Secretary of State Colin Powell is visiting the country and condemns the attacks, which he says have the hallmarks of an al-Qaeda operation.
- *May 12:* A suicide truck bomb attack kills 41 people in a government compound in Russian-controlled Chechnya. It is believed to be the work of separatists who have refused to cooperate with the Moscow-drafted peace plans.
- *May 12:* Trials begin for Islamic militants accused of the massive October 2002 bombing attacks in Bali, Indonesia. The first defendant, Amrozi bin Nurhasyim, is accused of obtaining a minivan and bomb-making materials.

- *May 16:* A series of apparently coordinated suicide car bombings kills at least 39 people in Casablanca, Morocco. The toll includes 10 of the bombers; at least 60 people are wounded. The attack adds to the growing concern that a revived al-Qaeda was planning numerous operations against "soft targets" associated with American and European interests.
- *May 31:* Accused 1996 Atlanta Olympic Park bomber Eric Robert Rudolph is apprehended by police in a rural North Carolina town. Also accused of other bombings including attacks on abortion clinics, Rudolph had been the object of one of the most protracted and extensive manhunts in FBI history.
- *June 2:* A report by the Inspector General of the Justice Department criticizes the detention and treatment of illegal immigrants, many of whom were found to have no links to terrorism.
- *June 10:* Four members of Jemaah Islamiyah are arrested for allegedly planning to bomb embassies and resorts in Thailand.
- *June 11:* The "road map" threatens to be derailed when several attacks on Israeli soldiers are followed by a suicide bus bombing in Jerusalem, killing 16 and wounding more than 100. Meanwhile Israel had unsuccessfully attempted to kill Hamas leader Abdel Aziz Rantisi, drawing criticism from U.S. president Bush.
- *July 24:* A joint report by House and Senate Intelligence committees criticizes the FBI and CIA for not properly recognizing and dealing with reports that al-Qaeda was planning a major attack.
- *July 29:* Saudi officials demand access to the censored portion of the intelligence committee report. The withheld material is believed to implicate high Saudi officials in aiding terrorists.
- *July 29:* A Pentagon plan to learn about terrorist threats by having people buy "futures" on various events is shelved after widespread public criticism. The head of the project, former Iran-contra figure Admiral John Poindexter, will step down.
- *August 1:* A fire races through a large apartment complex that developers were completing in San Diego, causing $50 million in damages but no injuries. The Earth Liberation Front claims credit for the blaze, leaving a banner at the scene reading "If you build it, we will burn it." This is the costliest ecoterrorist attack to date.
- *August 5:* A probable suicide car bomb explodes at the J. W. Marriott hotel in Jakarta, Indonesia, killing at least 16 people and wounding 150. It is believed to be the work of Jemaah Islamiyah.
- *August 7:* A powerful car bomb badly damages the Jordanian embassy in Baghdad, killing at least 11 people and wounding 50. Although no one claims credit for the attack, many militant Iraqis had been angry at Jordan for supporting the U.S. war against Iraq.

Chronology

- *August 13:* FBI officials reveal a successful "sting" in which their agents posing as Islamic terrorists and Russian agents posing as a missile supplier allegedly got British arms dealer Hemant Lakhani to agree to set up a deal for 21 missiles.
- *August 14:* U.S. authorities announce the arrest of Riduan Isamuddin, an Indonesian also known as Hambali, who is believed to be the top al-Qaeda and Jemaah al-Islamiyah organizer in Indonesia, and suspected mastermind of numerous bombings, including the massive Bali bombing the previous year.
- *August 14:* A widespread power outage strikes parts of the northeastern United States and Ontario, Canada, darkening New York City, Detroit, Ottawa, and other cities. Although apparently not linked to terrorism, the incident highlights the vulnerability of the power grid to seemingly minor local disruptions.
- *August 15:* The government of Libya officially takes responsibility for the 1988 bombing of Pan Am Flight 103 over Lockerbie, Scotland, which took 270 lives. Libya agreed to pay $2.7 billion in compensation, to renounce terrorism, and to cooperate with investigators.
- *August 19:* A large suicide truck bomb explodes at the United Nations headquarters in Baghdad, killing at least 15 people and wounding many others. One of the dead is Sergio Vieira de Mello, the head of the UN mission in Iraq.
- *August 19:* The U.S.-backed "roadmap to peace" in Israel and Palestine meets its worst challenge yet when a suicide bomber blows up a bus filled with observant Jews returning from Jerusalem's Wailing Wall. At least 20 people are killed and more than 100 are wounded. Islamic Jihad claims responsibility, calling the attack retaliation for the killing of one of its senior operatives in an Israeli raid the preceding week. Over the next days Israel retaliates with rocket attacks targeting Hamas leaders.
- *August 25:* Two powerful car bombs hidden in taxis kill at least 45 people in Mumbai (Bombay), India, wounding more than 135 others. Although no one claims responsibility for the attacks, suspicion falls on Islamic militants who have been struggling with Hindu groups over various religious sites.
- *August 25:* A U.S. air attack in conjunction with Afghani militia and U.S. Special Operations forces destroys a camp of Taliban fighters in southeastern Afghanistan, killing as many as 50 people. Remnant Taliban forces had been regrouping and conducting attacks in recent weeks.
- *August 26:* More U.S. soldiers (140) have now been killed in Iraq since the end of "major combat" than died during the original assault. President Bush, facing mounting criticism, emphasizes the need to persevere in Iraq as part of the "war on terror."

145

- *September 9:* Seven people are killed and more than 50 wounded in a suicide bomb attack on a Jerusalem café. Hamas claims responsibility for the attack.
- *October 4:* A female suicide bomber kills 21 people and wounds 64 in a restaurant in Haifa, Israel. Islamic Jihad claims responsibility.
- *October 27:* In the largest coordinated attack to that date, Iraqi insurgents set off bombs against four targets in Baghdad, destroying a Red Cross office and damaging three police stations. Thirty-five people are killed and about 230 wounded.
- *November 11:* In Saudi Arabia, a car with suicide bombers disguised as security personnel penetrates into the 200-villa Muhaya residential complex, killing as many as 30 people and wounding at least 112. The attackers are believed to be associated with al-Qaeda. Most of the residents are from neighboring Arab countries, and it is feared that the attack marks a new front in al-Qaeda's terrorism campaign.
- *November 11:* The Supreme Court agrees to determine whether foreign nationals detained by the United States at the U.S. naval base in Guantánamo Bay, Cuba, should have access to the courts. The decision may hinge on whether Cuba or the United States exercises ultimate sovereignty over the base.
- *November 15:* Trucks filled with explosives are detonated by suicide bombers in Istanbul, Turkey, outside two Jewish synagogues. Six Jews and 17 Muslims are killed and more than 300 people wounded. The Turkish militants believed to be responsible may be working with al-Qaeda.
- *November 20:* Two more truck bombs are set off in Istanbul. One targets the British consulate, the other hits HSBC, a London-based international bank. The two attacks kill at least 26 people, including the British consul-general. More than 450 are wounded. Responsibility for the attacks is jointly claimed by al-Qaeda and an obscure group called the Great Eastern Islamic Raiders' Front (IBDA-C).
- *December 6:* Apparently because of faulty intelligence that a fugitive Taliban leader was present, nine Afghani children are killed in a U.S. air strike on a house in the small Afghan village of Hutala. The United States has been mounting major new operations against resurgent Taliban supporters.
- *December 8:* Fifteen members of the terrorist group known as November 17 are convicted in a Greek court. Prosecutors will ask for multiple life sentences for the group's leader and for a principal "hit man."
- *December 9:* In the 11th in a series of bombings in 2003 linked to the Chechnya war, a suicide bomber blows herself up in front of the National Hotel in Moscow, killing at least five people and seriously injuring 13 others.

Chronology

- **December 13:** U.S. forces capture Saddam Hussein in a hole in a farm-yard outside a village southeast of Tikrit, Iraq.

2004

- **January:** It is reported that the U.S. government will soon be using computer profiles to prescreen airline passengers into green, yellow, and red categories, according to risk.
- **January 5:** In a program called U.S. Visit, persons arriving in the United States from many foreign countries have their fingerprints and pictures taken. Officials say the information will be used to identify criminals and visa violators as well as potential terrorists.
- **January 12:** The Supreme Court refuses to consider an appeal by media and other groups challenging the withholding of information about hundreds of foreigners detained in the United States following the September 11, 2001, attacks.
- **January 20:** President George W. Bush makes the need to stay the course on the War on Terrorism a major theme of his State of the Union address. He also urges that the USA PATRIOT Act be renewed and expanded.
- **January 26:** A federal district judge in Los Angeles declares the language in the USA PATRIOT Act that bans giving "expert advice and assistance" to federally designated terrorist groups as unconstitutionally vague. She suggests a distinction between planning violent acts and helping with peaceful advocacy. The federal government is expected to appeal.
- **February 6:** Russian authorities investigate an explosion and fire that killed at least 36 people and wounded 134 in a Moscow subway car. A Chechen terrorist bomb is suspected, but no group has taken responsibility.
- **March 11:** Ten backpack bombs detonated in rapid succession kill 200 people and injure more than 1,500 in several trains and railway stations around Madrid. A tape purporting to be from al-Qaeda claims responsibility for the attacks. Authorities continue to investigate.
- **March 22:** Hamas founder and spiritual leader Sheikh Ahmed Yassin is killed by an Israeli rocket attack. Palestine militant groups vow revenge.

CHAPTER 5

BIOGRAPHICAL LISTING

This chapter provides brief biographical sketches of some of the more significant figures in the history of terrorism. More information about many of these individuals can be found on the Internet resource sites discussed in Chapter 7 and in the bibliographies in Chapter 8.

Abu Abbas (Abdul Abbas, Mohammad Abbas), leader of the Palestine Liberation Front and member of the Executive Committee of the Palestine Liberation Organization (PLO). Born shortly after the founding of Israel, Abbas grew up in Palestine refugee camps and became involved in Palestinian extremist activities in the 1960s, becoming a member of the Popular Front for the Liberation of Palestine (PFLP) and its more militant spinoff, the General Command. Abbas was best known for masterminding the *Achille Lauro* hijacking in October 1985. In a *New York Times* interview, he later expressed his relish at the death of passenger Leon Klinghoffer. Abbas became known for brutality but also for innovative (if not totally successful) methods, such as attempting to raid Israel with hot air balloons and hang gliders. He thus acquired a reputation among PLO leaders as being a loose cannon. Abbas was arrested by U.S. authorities in Iraq on April 15, 2003, and died there in U.S. custody on March 9, 2004.
Abu Daoud (nom de guerre for Mohammed Daoud Oudeh), a founder of the extremist Palestinian group Black September. He has been linked to the assassination of Jordanian prime minister Wasfi al-Tal in Cairo on November 28, 1971; the massacre of Israeli athletes at the Munich Olympics in 1972; and the assassination of U.S. ambassador Claude Noel and a Belgian diplomat at the Saudi Arabian embassy in Khartoum on March 1, 1973. In 1977, Daoud was arrested in connection with the Munich massacre, but a French court refused to extradite him to Israel and ordered him released. In 1981, he was wounded by gunmen, and speculation linked his attackers to either the Abu Nidal organization or the Israeli Mossad secret service. As of 2003, Abu

Daoud remained free, touring to promote his forthcoming book, *Memoirs of a Palestinian Terrorist.*

Abu Nidal (nom de guerre for Sabri al-Banna), one of the most notorious modern terrorists. Born in Jaffa, Palestine, al-Banna saw his family lose its holdings following the establishment of the state of Israel in 1948. Nidal joined the al-Fatah group after the Six Day War with Israel in 1967 and served with the PLO in Baghdad in the early 1970s. However, he considered the PLO to be ineffective and started a new organization, the Fatah Revolutionary Council (FRC), which was backed by Iraq as a way to counteract the Syrian-backed PLO. Eventually the council evolved into a loose association of terrorist groups known in the West as the Abu Nidal Organization. The PLO passed a death sentence against Nidal, and Nidal's FRC in turn has made several unsuccessful assassination attempts against PLO leader Yasir Arafat. Terrorists organized by Abu Nidal have conducted more than 100 attacks in nations around the world, including attacks on airport passengers in Rome and Vienna in December 1985, the massacre of worshippers in an Istanbul synagogue in 1986, and the attack on the Greek cruise ship *City of Poros* in 1988 and possibly the bombing of Pan Am Flight 103. Intense Western pressure on Nidal's backers led to Syria expelling his agents in 1987, but he continued activities from bases in Lebanon. In 2002 he was found dead in an apartment in Baghdad, Iraq. It is speculated that he may have committed suicide after plotting against the Iraqi government.

Yasir Arafat, chairman of the PLO, leader of al-Fatah, its largest constituent group, and since 1996, president of the Palestinian Authority. In the 1960s, as leader of al-Fatah, Arafat conducted guerrilla raids into Israel. In 1964, al-Fatah joined with other groups to form the PLO. During the 1970s Arafat consolidated his position as chief spokesperson for the Palestinian cause, despite opposition from more radical factions that accused him of being too moderate and too accommodating toward Israel. In 1988, Arafat announced his willingness to renounce terrorism in keeping with United Nations resolutions and to negotiate a settlement of the Palestinian question with Israel. In 1993, Arafat signed a peace agreement with the Israeli government, and in 1994, he and Israeli leaders Yitzhak Rabin and Shimon Peres were jointly awarded the Nobel Prize for Peace. By the early 2000s, however, Arafat's power was in decline. The Israelis confined him to his office. He was unable to suppress Palestinian terrorism as demanded by the United States and Israel, and corruption in the Palestine Authority remained a major problem. Arafat was increasingly ignored in the faltering peace process, and he was pressured into appointing Mahmoud Abbas (Abu Mazen) to the new office of prime minister of Palestine. With renewed violence in mid-2003, Arafat's future, like that of the whole Israel-Palestine peace process, seems dark and uncertain.

Mohamed Atta is believed to be the principal organizer of the terrorist attacks on September 11, 2001. Atta was born in Kafr El Sheikh, Egypt, the son of a lawyer. He graduated from Cairo University with a degree in architectural engineering. In 1992 Atta went to Germany and enrolled in the Technical University of Hamburg-Harburg to study urban planning, and he wrote a well-regarded thesis on the conflict between Islam and modern secularism as reflected in the architecture of Aleppo, Syria. However, in the later 1990s he evidently became a committed Islamic fundamentalist. He also apparently made contact with a number of al-Qaeda operatives and spent much of his time in 2000 in the United States, clean-shaven and dressed in American style. Apparently his attention had turned toward planning an air-based terrorist attack; later it would be reported that he had asked about getting a government loan to buy a crop-dusting plane. Atta and another future hijacker, Marwan al-Shehhi, took flying lessons and earned their basic pilot's licenses, and then took further training on Boeing 727 simulators. Gradually, through 2001 Atta is believed have assembled and coordinated the team of 19 hijackers, and on the morning of September 11, 2001, it is believed that he was at the controls of the Boeing 757 that crashed into the North Tower of the World Trade Center.

Andreas Baader, West German terrorist and cofounder of the Red Army Faction (RAF), also called the Baader-Meinhof Gang. Active in radical student politics in the 1960s, Baader committed his first terrorist act by bombing a Frankfurt department store with fellow terrorist Gudrun Ensslin in 1968. Arrested, he escaped with the aid of Ensslin and Ulrike Meinhof. They went to the Middle East and trained with other European terrorists in camps set up by the Popular Front for the Liberation of Palestine (PFLP). Returning to Germany in the early 1970s, Baader and his comrades carried out a string of bombings, kidnappings, and assassinations. In 1972, Baader and his associates were arrested by German authorities. In 1977, RAF terrorists tried to win their freedom by hijacking a Lufthansa airliner, but West German commandos freed the hostages. In despair, Baader, Ensslin, and a comrade committed suicide in their prison cells.

Menachim Begin, a leader of the Jewish Irgun terrorists in the 1940s and prime minister of Israel 1977–83. Begin's life demonstrates the complexity of the Middle East conflict. While Begin was in the Irgun's leadership, the group committed two notorious terrorist acts, the bombing of the King David Hotel and the massacre at Deir Yassin. Entering politics in the new state of Israel, he founded the right-wing Herut party and served in the Knesset (parliament) as leader of the opposition from 1948 to 1967. He helped form a national unity government in 1967–70 and became prime minister in 1977 as part of a right-wing coalition that included the Likud party. Despite his hard line against the Arabs, Begin opened the negotiations with Egypt in 1977 that under the mediation of U.S. president Jimmy Carter led to the Camp David Accords in 1978 and the 1979 Egypt-Israeli peace treaty, for which Begin shared the 1978 Nobel Peace Prize with Egyptian president Anwar Sadat. However, Begin's 1982 invasion of Lebanon to suppress continuing guerrilla activity led to political opposition at home and Begin's decision to retire in 1983.

Osama bin Laden, a Saudi multimillionaire. Bin Laden emerged at the end of the 1990s as the financial power behind terrorist actions that included the attacks on U.S. embassies in Africa. Bin Laden first became involved in conflict when the Soviets invaded Afghanistan in 1979. He moved his company and workers into the country and built the training infrastructure for the guerrilla resistance to the invasion. He and other Afghan leaders received substantial covert support from the CIA, which saw the conflict as an opportunity to mire the Soviets in an unwinnable war in Afghanistan. After the Soviets were defeated, bin Laden and his trained veterans went back to Saudi Arabia where they turned their radical Islamic focus to fighting the country's secular government. In 1994, the Saudis expelled bin Laden and his group, and he moved to Sudan, where he set up extensive bases staffed by his fellow Afghani veterans. In 1996, however, with Sudan seeking better relations with the United States, bin Laden moved again—back to Afghanistan. In February 1998, bin Laden announced a new group called the Islamic World Front for the Struggle Against the Jews and the Crusaders and declared that U.S. citizens throughout the world would be fair game for terrorist attack. In August 1998, bin Laden's terrorists bombed U.S. embassies in Nairobi, Kenya, and Dar es Salaam, Tanzania. Retaliatory U.S. attacks on a factory in Sudan that bin Laden had allegedly used for chemical weapons and on bin Laden's base in Afghanistan aroused controversy (evidence of chemical weapons in Sudan proved elusive). Although U.S. officials believed that they had weakened it through arrests in Britain, Germany, Canada, the United States, Jordan, and Pakistan, subsequent events would suggest that the true extent of bin Laden's al-Qaeda network had been underestimated. Bin Laden's ability to continually devise or sponsor new forms of terrorist attack continued to keep antiterrorist forces off balance. U.S. officials suspected that bin Laden had masterminded the October 12, 2000 attack on the U.S. destroyer *Cole*, the first use of a boat-borne bomb against a U.S. warship. However the most devastating improvisation came on September 11, 2001, when hijacked jetliners were turned into flying bombs and used to destroy the World Trade Center and badly damage the Pentagon. U.S. officials quickly declared bin Laden the "prime suspect" in the attacks. Several tapes believed to be from bin Laden surfaced in the coming months. They showed him praising the results of the attacks and calling for a continued global jihad against America. Following the military campaign by United States and Northern Alliance forces in Afghanistan, the Taliban government was destroyed and many Taliban and al-Qaeda fighters were killed or dispersed. As of early 2004 bin Laden's whereabouts remain unknown despite one of history's most intensive manhunts.

Carlos ("the Jackal," Ilyich Ramírez Sánchez), an infamous Venezuelan-born international terrorist. Carlos worked most extensively with the Popular Front for the Liberation of Palestine (PFLP) but is believed to have also coordinated efforts with the Red Army Faction, Japanese Red Army, Basque ETA, and other groups during the 1970s. He may have also had connections with the KGB and Cuban intelligence. His most successful action was probably his leadership of the PFLP kidnapping of the oil ministers of 11 nations at an OPEC meeting in Vienna, Austria, in 1975. In August 1995, Carlos was tracked down in the Sudan and extradited to France. On December 24, 1997, he was convicted of murder and kidnapping and sentenced to life in prison.

Eldridge Cleaver, U.S. Black Panther, leader of the party's most violent faction. After being released on bail following a 1968 arrest, he fled to Cuba and then to Algeria, where he sought to develop ties between the Black Panthers and Middle Eastern and African radical groups. In 1975, he returned to the United States, renounced his radical beliefs, and returned to private life. He died in 1998.

Pablo Escobar Gaviria, probably the most infamous of the Colombian drug lords of the 1980s. When Colombian president Virgilio Barco Vargas launched an all-out war against the drug cartel in late 1989, Escobar went into hiding. The cartel tried to force the government to abandon its antidrug efforts by engaging in a campaign of "narcoterrorism" that included not only bombings but also assassinations and kidnappings of government officials and wealthy persons. The terrorism did prevent the Colombian government from extraditing Escobar to the United States to face charges. In June 1991, Escobar surrendered to Colombian authorities and was housed in a luxurious prison, from which he escaped in 1992 and went underground. On December 2, 1993, a commando force trapped Escobar on a rooftop and killed him in the ensuing firefight.

Abimael Guzmán Reynoso, former professor of philosophy; founder of and major intellectual influence on Sendero Luminoso ("The Shining Path") guerrillas of Peru. He based his organization on radical Maoist principles; it became known for extreme brutality. In September 1992, Guzmán and his top lieutenants were captured by Peruvian security forces, and Guzmán was sentenced to life in prison. Sendero Luminoso subsequently lost much of its influence.

Biographical Listing

George Habash, leader and founder in 1968 of the Popular Front for the Liberation of Palestine (PFLP), a radical faction of the PLO. He was born in Lydda (now Lod, Israel) to a Greek Orthodox family. He studied medicine and earned his M.D. degree at the American University in Beirut. Under his leadership, the PFLP carried out major terrorist attacks including the hijacking of four planes over a three-day period starting September 6, 1970, which eventually backfired and resulted in Jordan expelling Palestinian guerrillas from the country. Habash and Yasir Arafat became longtime rivals, as Habash accused Arafat of being too moderate and not sufficiently grounded in leftist ideology. In 1980, Habash suffered a massive stroke; he recovered, but his health remained frail. He turned toward policy-making and away from direct involvement in terrorist activity. In 1999, Habash met with Arafat to discuss issues relating to the emerging Palestinian state. In 2000, Habash announced his retirement.

Hambali (Riduan Isamuddin) is believed to be the top leader of Jemaah Islamiyah, a terrorist group responsible for numerous attacks in Indonesia, including the massive Bali bombing in October 2002. Born in Cianjur, Indonesia, Hambali went to Afghanistan to fight in the jihad against the Soviet-backed government. He met Osama bin Laden and became part of the emerging al-Qaeda network. Returning to Indonesia, he also became a major operational leader of Jemaah Islamiyah, helping organize numerous bombings, often of Christian churches. In August 2003 Hambali was arrested by U.S. authorities working with Indonesian police.

Yaser Esam Hamdi, known as the second "American Taliban," was born in Baton Rouge, Louisiana, a fact that somewhat disconcerted American officials when they reviewed his case at the prison camp at Guantánamo Bay, Cuba. Although little is known of his background, Hamdi apparently grew up in Saudi Arabia. He had been captured by Northern Alliance forces in Afghanistan and turned over to the Americans. After his citizenship was discovered, he was then flown to a naval brig in Norfolk, Virginia. Although U.S. citizens presumably have a constitutional right to be charged and given access to legal representation, authorities have thus far held Hamdi as an "unlawful combatant," saying that he could be held without charge for the duration of hostilities. When a habeas corpus petition was filed, a federal district judge in Norfolk ordered that Hamdi be provided an attorney. However, when the government appealed, a panel of the Fourth U.S. Circuit returned the case to the lower court in July 2002, saying that sufficient deference had not been paid to the government's interest in protecting national security against terrorism.

Meir Kahane, American rabbi who founded the Jewish Defense League (JDL) in 1968. The JDL staged violent attacks on Palestinian, Arab, and other groups it perceived to be "anti-Jewish." In 1971, Kahane emigrated

153

to Israel, where he became a right-wing member of the Knesset (parliament). His party's platform called for the expulsion of all Arabs from Israel and the occupied territories. Kahane's supporters tried to intimidate Palestinian residents into leaving Israel. On November 5, 1990, Kahane was assassinated by an Egyptian Arab in New York while giving a speech to U.S. Jewish supporters.

Theodore Kaczynski, reclusive U.S. former mathematics professor known as the Unabomber. Kaczynski retreated to a Montana cabin where he built and, from 1975 to 1995, dispatched letter bombs targeting people he associated with computer and other high-tech industries. The bombs killed three persons and injured 23. Kaczynski believed that modern industrial civilization was destroying nature and alienating humanity. In 1995, he demanded that newspapers publish his antitechnology manifesto, and both the *Washington Post* and *New York Times* agreed to do so after consulting with law enforcement authorities. When Kaczynski's brother read the manifesto, he recognized the writing style as his estranged brother's. This led to Kaczynski's arrest, trial, and conviction for the Unabomber killings. After a tumultuous trial, Kaczynski pled guilty in January 1998, receiving four life sentences plus 30 years in prison. He later unsuccessfully appealed his sentence, claiming that his attorneys had not given him good counsel.

Leila Khaled, member of the Popular Front for the Liberation of Palestine (PFLP) and one of the few women to reach the front ranks of modern terrorism. Khaled played an important role in the multiple aircraft hijackings in September 1970 that became known as the Dawson's Field affair. In this incident, she was captured during an attempted hijacking in London but was released in exchange for hostages aboard a BOAC airliner at Dawson's Field. Since then, she has become a heroine to many Palestinian activists, and she has brought a strongly feminist viewpoint to the internal debates of the PFLP and related groups.

Timothy McVeigh, served with some distinction as a U.S. soldier in the Persian Gulf War, but became disillusioned and then enraged at the federal government because of its actions toward the family of Randy Weaver at Ruby Ridge, Idaho, and against the Branch Davidians at Waco, Texas. He eventually decided to strike back by setting off a fuel-oil-and-fertilizer bomb in front of the federal building in Oklahoma City. The 1995 attack, which killed 168 people, was the worst attack by domestic terrorists in American history. McVeigh was sentenced to death for the crime and was executed by lethal injection on June 11, 2001. His convicted coconspirator, Terry Nichols, is serving a life sentence.

Zacarias Moussaoui is believed to be the only surviving member of the 20-person hijacking team that carried out the September 11, 2001, attacks on the World Trade Center and Pentagon. A French citizen of Moroccan descent, Moussaoui lived for some time in the United Kingdom, little is known about his background. He was arrested on August 16, 2001, when teachers at a Minnesota flight school became suspicious at Moussaoui's interest in flying jumbo jets but not necessarily landing them. He was held at first on immigration charges, then as a material witness. He was then indicted in December 2001 for six forms of conspiracy involving the attacks themselves, air piracy, use of weapons of mass destruction, and other charges. The extensive indictment does not include a "smoking gun" tying Moussaoui to the attacks, but it represents a comprehensive outline of al-Qaeda's activities that the government believes will cumulatively prove that Moussaoui was part of a terrorist conspiracy. Some analysts believe the government's case is not very strong, and court rulings may force the government to choose between allowing Moussaoui's defense access to sensitive materials and witnesses and moving the trial to a military tribunal.

Muammar al-Qaddafi (sometimes spelled Gadafy or Khadafy), ruler of Libya since 1969. When he took power, he seemed at first to be a staunch anticommunist allied with U.S. cold war interests. But when Egypt expelled Soviet advisers in 1972, the Soviets turned to Libya and built a sustained, if volatile, relationship with Qaddafi, in which they provided weapons and aid to Libya and Qaddafi opposed Western interests. Qaddafi's chief role in terrorism has been to provide weapons (including massive amounts of explosives), training bases, and other support to the more radical Palestinian terrorist operations such as Black September, the PFLP (under George Habash), and the Abu Nidal Organization. Since 1985, the United States has imposed sanctions on Libya and lists Libya as a "terrorist state." In 1986, the United States, accusing Qaddafi of masterminding attacks on the Vienna and Rome airports, retaliated by bombing the Libyan cities of Tripoli and Benghazi. Qaddafi reportedly narrowly escaped the bombs, which killed his adopted daughter. Since then Qaddafi has kept a relatively low profile. In 1999 he appeared to be cooperating somewhat with U.S. authorities when he surrendered two Libyans accused of bombing Pan Am flight 103 over Lockerbie, Scotland, in 1988.

Sheikh Omar Abdel Rahman, Islamic fundamentalist cleric. Abdel Rahman, though blind and not a direct participant, was implicated in the assassination of Egyptian president Anwar Sadat in 1981 because he had issued an Islamic judicial decree authorizing the killing. After his acquittal, he founded a group, Jamaa al-Islami, with the purpose of overthrowing the Mubarak regime and replacing it with an Islamic state. He entered the United States and became leader of a small mosque in Jersey City,

New Jersey. Following the World Trade Center bombing in February 1993, Abdel Rahman was implicated in both the bombing and a wider conspiracy to bomb key installations in New York including the Holland and Lincoln Tunnels and the United Nations building, as well as a plot to assassinate U.S. senator Alfonse D'Amato and U.N. secretary-general Boutros Boutros-Ghali. On October 1, 1995, Rahman was convicted of directing these conspiracies; and on August 16, 1999, the conviction was upheld on appeal.

Ramzi Ahmed Yousef, Islamic terrorist and associate of Sheikh Omar Abdel Rahman. While Rahman, a blind cleric, provided theological inspiration for the New York World Trade Center bombing in 1993 and related terrorist plots, Yousef, an electrical engineer who learned to make bombs in an Afghanistan terrorist training camp, constructed and planted the bomb. Besides bombing the World Trade Center, Yousef bombed an airliner in the Philippines in December 1994 (while plotting to assassinate Pope John Paul II during his visit there). Philippine police uncovered Yousef's bomb-making operation there, but he fled to Islamabad, Pakistan. When Yousef tried to recruit South African Muslim theology student Istiaq Parker in 1995, the latter refused to smuggle a bomb into the United States and, fearing reprisal, went to U.S. authorities in Islamabad. U.S. and Pakistani agents arrested Yousef in his room in February 1995 and quickly flew him back to the United States, where he was convicted with two coconspirators and sentenced to life without parole.

CHAPTER 6

GLOSSARY

The following are some terms and events that frequently arise in the discussion of international terrorism.

active measures A Soviet euphemism for direct attempts to manipulate public opinion in western countries (such as through propaganda, disinformation, and campaigns by "front" groups), as well as support and encouragement of terrorists.

amnesty An official act of forgiveness by which a government agrees to ignore criminal offenses that have been committed by a group of people (such as a rebel force) as part of a process of peace and reconciliation.

anarchism The political philosophy asserting that government is inherently corrupt and abusive and should be replaced by arrangements arrived at through the voluntary cooperation of individuals. Starting in the 19th century, some anarchists, such as Mikhail Bakunin in Russia, advocated the use of violence and terrorism against political leaders.

ANFO (ammonium nitrate-fuel oil) A powerful explosive made by mixing ordinary fertilizer with fuel oil; used in the Oklahoma City bombing.

antiterrorism assistance (ATA) A U.S. State Department program that provides assistance to more than 40 foreign governments in the fight against terrorism, including training for border guards and customs officials and the strengthening of airport security.

assassination Deliberate murder of a politically or socially prominent person, especially when done for political purposes. It is illegal for the United States government to target individuals for assassination, but (as in the attack on the home of Libya's Muammar al-Qaddafi in 1986), military raids have been launched that might be expected to kill terrorist leaders.

attentat clause A provision of an extradition treaty in some nations that says that a nation holding the accused murderer of a head of state (or a head of state's family member) will not treat the accused as a "political" criminal and will extradite without considering any appeals on grounds of political protest or persecution.

bioterrorism   The use of biological weapons (such as disease pathogens or toxins) in terrorist attacks.

Bloody Sunday   The killing of 13 Catholic demonstrators by a British army unit in Londonderry, Northern Ireland, on July 21, 1972. The incident became a rallying cry for the IRA, which enacted bloody reprisals.

Bonn Declaration   The Joint Statement on International Terrorism, issued July 17, 1978, by Italy, France, West Germany, the United Kingdom, Canada, the United States, and Japan. The nations agreed that other nations that did not cooperate in the extradition and prosecution of aircraft hijackers would have their airlines boycotted by the signatory nations.

Camp David Accords   A peace agreement forged in 1978 and signed in 1979 between Egypt and Israel, mediated by U.S. president Jimmy Carter. As part of the agreement, Israel returned the Sinai to Egypt.

cell   The smallest unit of organization of a guerrilla or terrorist group, usually consisting of five or fewer people. Typically, members of a given cell have no knowledge of or contact with other cells, thus minimizing vulnerability to exposure or infiltration.

chatter   Intelligence term for intercepted communications and other intelligence that might indicate heightened activity by terrorist groups. Chatter sometimes results in a nonspecific threat warning or raising the designated threat level.

chemical weapons   Weapons that primarily work through the effects of toxic agents, such as nerve gas.

COINTELPRO (Counterintelligence Program)   An FBI effort to turn public opinion against political opposition groups during the 1960s and early 1970s. In 1974, a committee investigation under the leadership of Senator Frank Church found that COINTELPRO had conducted illegal surveillance and disinformation campaigns against Martin Luther King, Jr., and other dissident leaders.

commando tactics   Use of small, highly trained and motivated armed forces inserted into enemy territory. Many nations have elite antiterrorism forces trained in commando tactics, while terrorists themselves could be said to be irregular commandos.

counterinsurgency   General term for military, political, legal, economic, or other measures taken by a government to suppress or defeat revolutionaries. Counterinsurgency forces seek to gain intelligence about guerrilla activity and also to win the support of the public so it will turn against or expose the guerrillas.

counterterrorism   The attempt to prevent terrorist attacks and root out and punish terrorist leaders and groups. As with counterinsurgency, intelligence is of key importance. Use of military or paramilitary forces and extrajudicial actions is commonplace in many nations, but problematic in democratic societies that support basic civil liberties.

cyberterrorism   The damaging or compromising of computer systems by hackers working as or for terrorists. Such activities can include introducing computer viruses, stealing sensitive information, and flooding web sites with bogus information requests.

data mining   The systematic analysis of data from many sources (such as transaction records) in order to discern patterns. Such techniques have been advocated as a way to detect terrorist activity or identify persons who should be investigated further.

death squad   A vigilante, paramilitary group, often operating with the covert support of government officials or military leaders. Many right-wing Latin American governments (such as Chile under Agusto Pinochet) have used death squads to kill political opponents, usually leftist guerrillas. The killings are often indiscriminate, however.

Delta Force   The elite counterterrorist task force of the U.S. Army, established in 1977 and based in Fort Bragg, North Carolina. The Delta Force has had only limited success against terrorists. In 1980, its attempt to mount an airborne rescue of U.S. hostages in Iran failed when a U.S. helicopter and plane collided.

Dirty War   Colloquial term for the brutal program of repression undertaken by Argentina's military junta when it took power in 1976, which lasted until 1983. All types of opponents on the left and labor groups were targeted; many victims were killed and their bodies disposed of clandestinely.

disappeared   A term often used in Latin America to refer to victims of death squads and other government campaigns to eliminate opposition. Victims are kidnapped and often secretly killed, leaving their fate unknown to their families, who have not even a body to bury.

euroterrorism   Term applied to left-wing European terrorists who targeted NATO and American facilities, such as Action Directe, the Red Army Faction, and the Red Brigades.

extradition   The legal process of transferring a prisoner from the country in which he or she is arrested to the country that has placed criminal charges. Countries often resist requests for extradition of accused terrorists, either because they fear reprisals from terrorist groups or out of concern for the civil liberties of the accused.

fedayeen   Arabic term meaning commandos or guerrilla fighters.

Gaza Strip   A narrow area between Egypt and Israel, consisting of about 140 square miles. Israel occupied the area following its victory over its Arab neighbors in the 1967 Six-Day War. In 1988, the Palestine National Council declared the Gaza Strip to be part of the future independent Palestinian state, and the Intifada (uprising) of the late 1980s took place in the Gaza Strip and West Bank. Any final settlement of the Palestine issue would have to involve the Gaza Strip.

Good Friday Agreement　Irish political settlement agreed to by voters in both the Irish Republic and Northern Ireland on April 10, 1998.

Greensboro Five　Five members of the U.S. Communist Workers Party who were killed by Ku Klux Klan members and other white supremacists at a "Death to the Klan" march held in Greensboro, North Carolina, on November 3, 1979. Most of the accused killers were acquitted by an all-white jury.

guerrilla warfare　Military operations carried out by irregular forces against a government or occupying power. Guerrillas try to avoid direct, large-scale confrontations with forces that outmatch them and instead try to control the countryside and gain popular support while raiding government installations and supply convoys. While operating on a larger scale than terrorists and usually enjoying greater popular support, guerrillas frequently resort to terrorist acts such as killing people who collaborate with the government, using bombings and shootings to demonstrate that the government cannot protect the people, or extorting "taxes" from businesses or farms in areas that they control.

homeland security　Counterterrorist activities focusing on protecting the people and infrastructure within a nation rather than its facilities abroad. The United States established the unified Department of Homeland Security in 2002.

infrastructure　The facilities a society uses to provide governance, distribute resources, maintain communications, and otherwise keep a country running. Terrorists and guerrillas often attack infrastructure targets such as railroads, power plants, police stations, and perhaps in the future, computer facilities. Infrastructure can also refer to the training camps, weapons and supply caches, and other facilities used by a terrorist group.

insurgency　An armed uprising against a government, usually carried on by means of guerrilla warfare tactics.

Intifada　Arabic for "Uprising," this term refers to the spontaneous outbreak of unrest that was triggered in December 1987 by the killing of several Arabs in the Gaza Strip when their vehicle collided with an Israeli vehicle. Rumors that the killing was deliberate inflamed riots and demonstrations, and attempts by the Israeli occupation forces to suppress the demonstrations further inflamed and expanded the Intifada.

Iran-Contra Affair　The complicated interaction between members of the Reagan administration, Iran, and Nicaraguan rebels (contras). Some Reagan administration officials had sold weapons to Iran in the hope that Iran would use its influence to gain the release of American hostages in Lebanon. The profits from the weapons sales were then used to support contra rebels in Nicaragua in an attempt to circumvent restrictions on such aid passed by the U.S. Congress.

Iranian Hostage Crisis The taking of 53 hostages when the U.S. embassy in Tehran was overrun by Islamic revolutionaries on November 4, 1979. The hostages were held for 444 days. Political observers suggest that the Carter administration's inability to gain the freedom of the hostages paralyzed and weakened it, contributing to Ronald Reagan's decisive victory in the 1980 presidential election.

jihad An Arabic term usually translated as "holy war." While Islamic terrorists frequently invoke this concept to justify their violent campaigns against the enemies of Islam, some Islamic scholars believe that such use is illegitimate.

kneecapping Breaking or shooting a person's kneecaps, crippling the victim. Used by some terrorist groups in Northern Ireland and elsewhere to punish persons believed to be turncoats or collaborators.

narcoterrorism A theory that international drug traffickers and terrorists are natural allies who increasingly cooperate to achieve their ends. Proponents point to the similarities of the two groups in their clandestine nature, use of weapons, and killing and intimidation of opponents. The term is also applied to acts of terrorism carried out by drug lords, such as the Extraditables, the terrorist arm of the Colombian Medellín cartel.

nationalism The development of a national identity in culture, politics, and society. The development of such an identity by an ethnic group living in a country controlled by another group frequently results in guerrilla warfare or terrorism when the national aspirations of such a small group are not accepted by the dominant group.

necklace A burning, gasoline-soaked tire placed around the neck, which severely burns or kills the victim. Some black terrorist groups in South Africa used the necklace as a way to punish people who cooperated with the apartheid regime.

neo-Nazis Post–World War II groups that have adopted the ideology of National Socialism (Nazism) espoused by Adolf Hitler. Neo-Nazi activity is strictly banned in Germany. In the United States, under constitutional protections of freedom of speech and assembly, the small neo-Nazi groups (including some skinheads) can operate freely unless they actually engage in crimes such as vandalism or assault. Nazi symbols and doctrine are a common feature of the loosely organized racist and white supremacist network in the United States.

nom de guerre (French, literally "name of war") In terrorism, a pseudonym used by a terrorist leader, often for symbolic purposes more than for concealment. For example, Yasir Arafat used the name Abu Amar, derived from an Arabic word for "builder."

nuclear terrorism   The potential use of nuclear weapons by terrorists. Unsettled conditions in the former Soviet Union during the early 1990s fueled speculation that impoverished or disgruntled Soviet military or nuclear experts would be willing to sell their expertise or even nuclear materials or warheads to terrorist groups. By mid-2000, there seems to be little concrete sign of this happening, but the potentially devastating consequences of terrorists obtaining nuclear weapons have kept nuclear terrorism high on the agenda of counterterrorist planners.

Occupied Territories   Generally refers to the areas that came under Israeli control following the Six-Day War in 1967: the West Bank of the Jordan, the Gaza Strip between Israel and Egypt, and the Golan Heights between Israel and Syria.

Orange, Orangemen   Irish Protestants.

paramilitary   General term for forces that share many characteristics of an army (training, weapons, tactics, etc.) but are not officially constituted. Examples include death squads and some militias. Paramilitary forces have often been used as way to repress political dissidents or the general population while denying government involvement.

plastic explosive   A putty-like explosive substance manufactured under designations such as C-4 and Semtex. Easily shaped and embedded in innocuous objects, it is hard to detect, even with X rays, vapor sniffers, or other technologies. Under Muammar al-Qaddafi, Libya obtained a large amount of plastic explosive and distributed it to a variety of terrorist groups.

political risk   The likelihood of losing a foreign investment due to factors such as government confiscation of facilities, currency manipulation, or terrorist action.

postcolonial period   The period of roughly 30 years following World War II, when many developing nations that were once European colonies or protectorates gained independence.

radiological terrorism   A type of nuclear terrorism involving hypothetical bombs that would scatter radioactive material rather than producing a nuclear explosion. Such attacks might have a greater psychological than physical impact.

safe house   A house or building where a terrorist group can reside or store weapons while remaining concealed from authorities.

separatist   General term for a person or group who seeks political independence or autonomy.

Shiites   Followers of a sect that split off from the mainstream Sunni sect of Islam in the seventh century in a dispute over who would inherit spiritual leadership. Their theology and minority status (about one-tenth of the world's Muslims are Shiites) have encouraged militancy. In Iran, the only Muslim state where Shiites are the majority, this militancy has been embodied in a fundamentalist government that at least until recently aggressively promoted both fundamentalist movements in neighboring countries and terrorist action against the United States and its allies.

skinheads   A subculture of mainly young white males with shaved heads, found in the United States, Great Britain, and, to some extent, other countries in Europe. Many skinheads espouse neo-Nazi or other white supremacist ideas and attack minorities and immigrants. Established white supremacist groups such as Aryan Nations and the Ku Klux Klan have made extensive efforts to recruit skinheads as "shock troops." However there are also some left-wing, antiracist skinheads.

skyjacking   Hijacking of aircraft, a common terrorist practice in the 1960s and early 1970s. Tighter airport security has greatly reduced the incidence of skyjacking.

spillover terrorism   The spread of terrorist activity from one area (such as the Middle East) to another (such as western Europe). Many Palestinian terrorist groups forged links with western European counterparts, and each group carried out operations in the other's territory.

state terrorism   The use of terror and intimidation by a state against its own citizens. Throughout the 20th century, the number of victims of state terrorism in Germany, the former Soviet Union, China, and other countries was vastly greater than the toll taken by what are commonly considered to be terrorist groups.

state-sponsored terrorism   The support (through training, weapons, money, or provision of safe havens) of terrorism as a means to carry out a nation's foreign policy. Libya, for example, has provided extensive support to a variety of Palestinian and European terrorist groups.

Stockholm syndrome   A psychological process, first noted in four Swedish bank robbery hostages, by which hostages sometimes become sympathetic to, and identify with, their captors.

suicide bombing   Although it can refer to any attack in which the attacker is not expected to survive, the term usually describes attacks involving crashing planes or bomb-laden trucks, or walking into a crowded area while wearing a vest packed with explosives.

Sunni   The orthodox sect of Islam. Sunni Muslims are in the majority in all Islamic countries except Iran. Tension often exists between the Sunni majority and the Shiite minority.

supergrass   A term, probably derived from "snake in the grass," referring to the network of Irish informers that British authorities have been able to use to gather evidence against IRA terrorists.

Terrorism Information Awareness   This Pentagon data-mining program was originally called Total Information Awareness. It was greeted with considerable alarm by privacy and civil liberties advocates because of the potential for building dossiers on ordinary citizens through online database analysis.

threat matrix   A daily report prepared for the president by FBI and CIA specialists at the Terrorist Threat Integration Center. It provides a prioritized tabulation of intelligence indicating possible activities by terrorist groups as well as potential targets.

truth commission   A body charged with determining responsibility for atrocities committed by all sides in a conflict, usually as a part of a reconciliation or unification following a civil war or rebellion. South Africa's Truth and Justice Commission is probably the best-known example.

undetectable firearms   Guns such as the Glock-17 that are mainly plastic with few metal parts. Such guns are a problem for counterterrorism because they are hard to detect in airport X-ray screenings.

unlawful combatant   A legal designation for a person found during an armed conflict to not be following the normal rules of war, such as a terrorist attacking civilians. Such persons can be held without trial for the duration of the conflict. Applying this designation to domestic terrorism suspects has been controversial.

urban guerrillas   Guerrillas who operate within cities rather than in the countryside as do traditional guerrillas. Urban guerrilla theory is based on the works of Abraham Guillen and Carlos Marighella. Urban guerrillas emphasize terrorism as a strategy for provoking the government into repressive countermeasures and thus undermining popular support for it. As with the Tupamaros in Uruguay, this strategy has often backfired, resulting in the destruction of the guerrillas.

vigilantism   Unofficial actions taken by private groups to violently suppress criminals. Vigilantism is a common response to the failure of a country's authorities to prevent attacks by terrorist groups. For example, the Ulster Volunteer Force in Northern Ireland arose as a vigilante response to Irish Republican Army terrorism. However, vigilantes often carry out terrorism themselves and can also be used by repressive governments as death squads, targeting not only terrorists but dissidents and innocent civilians.

weapons of mass destruction (WMD)   Weapons capable of killing large numbers of people at one time, such as large conventional or nuclear bombs, chemical weapons such as nerve gases, or biological weapons such as infectious diseases or toxins. The threat of terrorists gaining access to such weapons is a major focus of modern counterterrorism.

white supremacists   Persons or groups, such as the Aryan Nations or Ku Klux Klan, who believe that the white race is superior and should dominate all other races. A related belief, white separatism, advocates a separate white state from which people of other races would be excluded.

PART II

GUIDE TO FURTHER RESEARCH

CHAPTER 7

HOW TO RESEARCH
TERRORISM

As one might expect, the events of September 11, 2001, and the subsequent foreign and domestic antiterrorism campaigns have generated large amounts of new analysis and reportage relating to regional and global terrorism. Fortunately much of the most useful material is immediately available on the World Wide Web. The text of most government documents, many scholarly works, and much of the popular press is online, ready to be retrieved via search engines or already compiled by sites that provide organized collections of Web links. For this reason this guide will emphasize online sources.

A few cautions are still in order concerning the Web. First, one cannot assume that any Web search is exhaustive. No search engine currently indexes more than a fraction of the pages available on the Web, so trying multiple search engines is always a good idea. Also, while some older papers or articles have been scanned or transcribed onto Web pages, most material found on the Web dates from the mid-1980s or later—about the time that computer-readable academic publications and full-text databases of popular periodicals became available.

Most online documents are short works: The full text of books is usually not available online, except for some historical and older works that are no longer under copyright. Therefore, the library remains a very important tool for the researcher. Fortunately, the nearly universal use of online (and often, remotely accessible) library catalogs has also made libraries easier to use.

Web pages, like all intellectual products, reflect the agenda and possible biases of their creators. Terrorism is a particularly sensitive topic, one that is intimately involved with political viewpoint. Government sources generally define terrorism very narrowly to refer to violence carried out by individuals or nongovernmental groups for political motives. Many extremist and even terrorist groups now have their own web sites. Scholars, of course, have many points of view on traditional terrorism and state terrorism. It is best to include a variety of sources and viewpoints in one's research.

TERRORISM ON THE WORLD WIDE WEB

There are a variety of government and private web sites that offer background material, news, analysis, and other material on terrorist groups, their leaders, and terrorist attacks as well as counterterrorism. The following are some of the more useful major sites, broken down by category.

GOVERNMENT SITES

There are a number of important sites for U.S. government agencies involved with intelligence, investigation and prosecution of terrorist incidents, and homeland security.

- The Department of Homeland Security coordinates most domestic counterterrorism efforts. Its home page at http://www.whitehouse. gov/homeland/ includes current statements and news, as well as the current (color-coded) terrorism threat level.
- The United States Department of State Counterterrorism Office at http://www.state.gov/s/ct/ includes links to important resources such as the official annual report "Patterns of Global Terrorism," the list of designated terrorist organizations, and statements of official government policy on terrorism.
- The Federal Bureau of Investigation (FBI) has its main page for the "War on Terrorism" at http://www.fbi.gov/terrorinfo/terrorism.htm. It includes current news about intelligence efforts, interagency cooperation, and wanted suspects.
- There is a general page for the United States Intelligence Community with links to the CIA, Defense Intelligence, and other agencies at http://www.intelligence.gov/.

GENERAL RESOURCES

A number of sites offer wide-ranging links to background and research topics relating to global terrorism. Just about any of them would make a useful jumping-off place for Web-based research.

- The California State University, Northridge, library offers "Terrorism: Research Resources" at http://library.csun.edu/llampert/terrorism/.
- *The Economist* at http://www.economist.com/countries/ offers country briefings including both background and current events. This can be very useful for getting perspective on recent developments.
- International Terrorism is a site sponsored by the International Policy Institute for Counter-Terrorism at http://www.ict.org.il/ (linked under International Terrorism). It includes "Terrorist Organization Profiles," a useful compilation that lists about 50 terrorist groups, including background, chronology of terrorist activity, and news updates, and links to articles. Other sections include "Terror Attack Database, State Sponsored Terrorism, Terrorism & Criminal Activities, Financing Terrorism, and Non-Conventional Terrorism."
- Terrorism, at the Naval Postgraduate School. Dudley Knox Library at http://library.nps.navy.mil/home/terrorism.htm provides extensive and very useful links including bibliographies, statements and reports, discussion groups and lists, federal agencies, and other Web links.
- The Terrorism Research Center at http://www.terrorism.com/ is an independent institute that offers a variety of resources including country profiles, terrorist group profiles, descriptions of terrorism-related events and attacks, and a variety of links to aspects of counterterrorism.
- Terrorist and Insurgent Organizations is a page from the Air University Library at http://www.au.af.mil/au/aul/bibs/tergps/tg98tc.htm. It is a comprehensive listing of books, research papers, articles, and periodicals on all aspects of terrorism and insurgency.

THE WAR ON TERRORISM

There are a wide variety of resource sites that offer news, links, and archives relating to the terrorist attacks of September 11, 2001, and the subsequent foreign and domestic anti-terrorism campaign.

- America at War at Washingtonpost.com, http://www.washingtonpost.com/wp-dyn/nation/specials/attacked/, provides current news and other links relating to the war on terrorism.
- America's War Against Terrorism: World Trade Center/Pentagon Terrorism and the Aftermath from the University of Michigan. Documents Center at http://www.lib.umich.edu/govdocs/usterror.html provides a variety of links on the terrorist attacks of September 11, 2001, related previous attacks, subsequent attacks, events in other countries, and background research.

- ANSER Institute for Homeland Security at http://www.homelandsecurity .org is a nonprofit institute that provides news, documents, and many links to various aspects of homeland security including government and private organizations.
- The Center for Defense and National Security Studies at http://www. cdiss.org/hometemp.htm is a U.K.-based interdisciplinary research center with research and resources focusing on issues of security and weapons proliferation, but also including material on terrorism,
- Selected Congressional Research Service (CRS) Reports are available through the Federation of American Scientists. Military Analysis Network at http://www.fas.org/man/crs/, including those related to military and national security, intelligence, and special weapons. These topics are further subdivided as appropriate by geographical region and subtopic. Reports are in PDF format.
- CRS Reports from Penny Hill Press (under the topic terrorism) at http://www.pennyhill.com/terrorism.html is a federal document distribution service, jointly operated by Penny Hill Press and Storming Media. It provides reports from the Congressional Research Service and many other agencies. Reports can be ordered individually or by description; a categorized listing and free abstracts for all reports are available online. Note that reports may also be available online for free from various sources.
- The ERRI Counter-Terrorism Archive at http://www.emergency.com/ cntrterr.htm is provided by the Emergency Response and Research Institute. It describes itself as "A Summary of World-Wide Terrorism Events, Groups, and Terrorist Strategies and Tactics." Highlights news articles and research reports on terrorism categorized by region and listed in chronological order, as well as special sections on terrorist leaders and tactics.
- Hunting bin Laden is the site for a PBS *Frontline* program at http://www. pbs.org/wgbh/pages/frontline/shows/binladen/. The program gives background on bin Laden and al-Qaeda, traces the evidence linking him to numerous terrorist attacks (culminating on September 11, 2001), and recounts the early stages of the attempt to track down the world's most wanted terrorist.
- In-Depth Special: War Against Terror from CNN.com at http://www. cnn.com/SPECIALS/2001/trade.center/index.html now serves as an archive for news (including audio and video) related to the attacks on the World Trade Center and the Pentagon, plus links to features on related topics such as Afghanistan, anthrax, bin Laden, and airport screening.
- Jane's at http://www.janes.com/ is a database service that provides access to information and articles from a variety of Jane's publications, one of the

foremost providers of military and intelligence materials to the general public. Some summaries and excerpts are free; full information requires a paid subscription. Publications related to counterterrorism include *Jane's Islamic Affairs Analyst* and *Jane's Terrorism and Security Monitor.*

- The Journalist's Toolbox: 9/11 Terrorist Attacks Index at http://www.journaliststoolbox.com/newswriting/wtccrisis.html provides links of special interest to journalists and persons interested in media coverage of terrorist events. Includes archives of coverage of the World Trade Center attack, links to documentaries, and many topical links.

- Looking for Answers is the site for the *Frontline* program from the Public Broadcasting Service at http://www.pbs.org/wgbh/pages/frontline/shows/terrorism/. It is cosponsored by the *New York Times* and provides expanded material and links for topics covered in the program, which focused on understanding the motivations and causes behind the September 11, 2001, attacks.

- National Security Archive at http://www.gwu.edu/~nsarchiv/ includes extensive source materials on United States involvement in various world crises, including the war on terrorism. See especially the link to "The September 11 Sourcebooks." Other example documents include biographies and assessments of Osama bin Laden, the report of the commission that investigated the attack on the USS *Cole*, and responses to the Kobar Towers bombings and the embassy bombings in Africa, and background on the conflict in Afghanistan.

- September 11, 2001 Resources, from the Poynter Institute, at http://www.poynter.org/column.asp?id=49&aid=3401 is an archive assembled by one of the nation's premier schools of journalism. It focuses on the coverage of the news and critical analysis of the September 11, 2001, attacks. The site includes the text of a large number of stories by journalists, indexed by topic and contributor, a collection of front pages of newspapers from the day after the attacks, and related Web links.

- September 11 Digital Archive at http://911digitalarchive.org/ is a site devoted to preserve digital text (including web logs and e-mail), imagery, video, audio, and other data relating to the attacks of September 11, 2001.

- Terrorism: Questions and Answers from the Council on Foreign Relations' page at http://cfrterrorism.org/home/ offers a "question of the day" and a detailed answer, as well as links to many other topics related to terrorist groups and the war on terrorism, and a weekly news summary.

- The U.S. Intelligence Community from Columbia University at http://www.columbia.edu/cu/lweb/indiv/dsc/intell.html is a guide to documents and resources for persons researching intelligence issues.

- War on Terrorism, sponsored by Terrorism.org, at http://www. terrorismfiles.org/ provides links to current news stories as well as background on many terrorist groups and countries and regions involved with the war on terrorism.

TERRORISM AROUND THE WORLD

A variety of sites provide general background information that is useful for understanding the context of terrorism worldwide or in a particular country or region.

- African Conflict Journal at http://www.africanconflict.org/ provides a portal for resources and discussion of current events and conflicts in Africa.

- Allafrica.com at http://www.allafrica.com is a good source for current news on developments in Africa.

- Country Profiles from the BBC at http://news.bbc.co.uk/2/hi/country_profiles/default.stm offers not only a basic summary of the background and leadership for each country but also extensive links to media within the country.

- Crisis Web, sponsored by the International Crisis Group at http://www.crisisweb.org/, highlights current developing or potential crises and provides background. Additional background can be browsed by region and country.

- Flashpoints at http://www.flashpoints.info/FlashPoints_home.html links to commentary on global issues relating to world conflict as well as to country briefings.

- Foreign Affairs. Archive and current issues for the periodical *Foreign Affairs*—http://www.foreignaffairs.org/. Includes many extensive articles relating to the war on terrorism and the situation in post-Saddam Iraq, the Middle East, and other world trouble spots.

- Israeli-Palestinian Conflict is a site from the PBS Online Newshour at http://www.pbs.org/newshour/bb/middle_east/conflict/. It includes links to current and past news stories, progress of the peace process, and essays on various aspects of the conflict.

- Middle East Report at http://www.merip.org/ offers a good selection of news and current affairs from the region.

- Mideast Web at http://www.mideastweb.org is a portal started by peace activists from a variety of backgrounds. It focuses on the peace process (both the official one and privately inspired efforts).

- Political Africa at http://www.politicalafrica.com/ provides current news about Africa (and related global issues) as well as numerous links to African news agencies.
- Sudan Net at http://www.sudan.net offers links to history, society, culture, and current events in Sudan.
- Yemen Gateway at http://www.al-bab.com/yemen/Default.htm provides many resources about current affairs in Yemen and the region. It includes an extensive set of resources on the attack on the USS *Cole* and the subsequent investigation.

SPECIAL TYPES OF TERRORISM

There are also sites devoted to particular types of terrorist threats, notably bioterrorism, as well as general response to the use of weapons of mass destruction or other large-scale terrorist attacks.

- Bioterrorism from RAND Corporation at http://www.rand.org/hot/newslinks/terrorism.html is a set of "news links" to research reports from the famed think tank.
- Bioterrorism Learning Center at http://bioterrorism.digiscript.com/ offers a variety of PowerPoint presentations on bioterrorism (including nuclear/radiological terrorism) and related disaster preparedness and response. Access is free but online registration is required.
- Disaster Mental Health at http://www.mentalhealth.org/Highlights/September2002/cmhs2/pubs.asp is a listing of publications and related links compiled by the Substance Abuse and Mental Health Administration (SAMHSA) of the U.S. Department of Health and Human Services. It includes mental health response to terrorist attacks.
- Hazardous Substances Data Bank at http://toxnet.nlm.nih.gov/cgi-bin/sis/htmlgen?HSDB lets one look up a particular substance and get information about its health effects and recommended treatment for exposure. There is also a summary of relevant toxicity studies.
- Medline Plus provides extensive resources from the National Library of Medicine (NLM). Two relevant topics include "Disasters and Emergency Preparedness" at http://www.nlm.nih.gov/medlineplus/disastersandemergencypreparedness.html and "Biodefense and Bioterrorism" at http://www.nlm.nih.gov/medlineplus/biodefenseandbioterrorism.html. Both have extensive links.
- Radiation Exposure at 23 "Radiation Exposure" at http://www.nlm.nih.gov/medlineplus/radiationexposure.html provides links to information about the effects of different types of radiation on the environment and

on living things; prevention and screening for exposure; treatment of victims; and links to a glossary, relevant organizations, and legal aspects.

LEGAL RESOURCES

There are a number of good sources for information about legislation and legal cases and issues relating to terrorism.

- FindLaw Legal News and Commentary. "Special Coverage: War on Terrorism" at http://news.findlaw.com/legalnews/us/terrorism/cases/index.html provides news stories and extensive links to terrorism-related criminal and civil cases. Categories include: Terrorism Cases Prior to September 11, Airplane/Airport Security Cases, Civil Cases, Hate Crime Cases, and Terrorist Hoax Cases.
- NCJRS Abstracts Database. Available online. URL: http://abstractsdb.ncjrs.org/content/AbstractsDB_Search.asp. Updated on August 15, 2002. This service, provided by the National Criminal Justice Reference Service, is a searchable database that has abstracts for more than 170,000 books and articles on all aspects of criminal justice. This includes thousands of publications relating to terrorism, counterterrorism, and related topics. Some abstracts include links to the full-text document.
- Terrorism Law & Policy from the JURIST Legal Education Network at http://jurist.law.pitt.edu/terrorism.htm. Provides links to terrorism-related law and policy. Major subdivisions are Terrorism and Terrorists, Counterterrorism Policy, U.S. Anti-terrorism Laws, World Anti-terrorism Laws, Civil Liberties, Bioterrorism: Legal Issues, Commentary, and Bibliography.
- The THOMAS Service of the Library of Congress under "Legislation Related to the Attack of September 11, 2001," at http://thomas.loc.gov/home/terrorleg.htm. Provides links (by bill number) to legislation, joint resolutions, and other resolutions and proposed bills related to the attacks and the war on terrorism.

CIVIL LIBERTIES GROUPS

Because antiterrorism legislation frequently raises civil liberties issues, civil liberties groups are a good source for news and advocacy materials.

The American Civil Liberties Union site at http://www.aclu.org/ has a number of issues pages that are relevant to terrorism. See, for example, the following:

Criminal Justice: http://www.aclu.org/issues/criminal/hmcj.html
Free Speech: http://www.aclu.org/issues/freespeech/hmfs.html

Immigrants' Rights: http://www.aclu.org/issues/immigrant/hmir.html
National Security: http://www.aclu.org/issues/security/hmns.html

Because proposed antiterrorism legislation often includes provisions for allowing eavesdropping, monitoring, or restrictions on private use of encryption, civil liberties groups that focus on computer-related issues are also relevant here. The Electronic Privacy Information Center (http://www.epic.org/), the Electronic Frontier Foundation (http://www.eff.org/), and the Center for Democracy and Technology (http://www.cdt.org/) are all useful for keeping up with these issues.

HUMAN RIGHTS ORGANIZATIONS

The international human rights organization Amnesty International (http://www.amnestyusa.org/) is also a good source about human rights issues, including allegations of state terrorism and of mistreatment of terrorist suspects. Another source is Human Rights Watch at http://www.hrw.org/.

ANTIHATE GROUPS

Two groups focus on terrorism and related hate crimes based on ethnicity, gender, and other biases. The Anti-Defamation League site at http://www.adl.org/ includes statistics and reports on anti-Semitic attacks. The Southern Poverty Law Center (http://www.splcenter.org) monitors the activities of the Ku Klux Klan and other racist groups. Its Intelligence Project page at http://www.splcenter.org/intelligenceproject/ip-index.html includes a list of hate groups, a list of militia groups, and a chronology of hate incidents.

TERRORIST GROUPS

As noted, many terrorist groups, guerrilla movements, political extremists, and similar organizations have their own web sites. There's an extensive listing of Separatist, Paramilitary, Military, Intelligence, and Political Organizations at http://www.cromwell-intl.com/security/netusers.html. Discretion is advised when deciding whether to visit or use sites that may be involved in the promotion of terrorist groups.

BIBLIOGRAPHIC RESOURCES

As useful as the Web is for quickly finding information and the latest news, in-depth research still requires trips to the library or bookstore. Getting the most out of the library requires the use of bibliographic tools and resources. *Bibliographic resources* is a general term for catalogs, indexes, bibliographies, and other guides that identify the books, periodical articles, and other printed resources that deal with a particular subject. They are essential tools for the researcher.

Library Catalogs

Access to the largest library catalog, that of the Library of Congress (LC), is available at http://catalog.loc.gov. This page explains the different kinds of catalogs and searching techniques available.

Yahoo offers a categorized listing of libraries at http://d4.dir.dcn.yahoo.com/reference/libraries/. Of course, for materials available at one's local public or university library, that institution will be the most convenient source.

Online catalogs can be searched not only by the traditional author, title, and subject headings, but also by matching keywords in the title. Thus a title search for *terrorism* will retrieve all books that have that word somewhere in their title. (Of course a book about terrorism may not have that phrase in the title, so it is still necessary to use subject headings to get the most comprehensive results.)

The most general Library of Congress heading is Terrorism, which can be subdivided by region or country (such as United States). Other subdivisions include:

- Terrorism and Mass Media
- Terrorism—Bibliographies
- Terrorism—Case Studies
- Terrorism—Cases
- Terrorism—Computer Network Resources
- Terrorism—Congresses
- Terrorism—Databases
- Terrorism—Directories
- Terrorism—Encyclopedias
- Terrorism—Government Policy [subdivided by country]
- Terrorism—History [many chronological and other subdivisions]
- Terrorism—Law and Legislation [subdivided by country]
- Terrorism in Literature
- Terrorism in Mass Media
- Terrorism—Moral and Ethical Aspects

- Terrorism—Political Aspects
- Terrorism—Press Coverage
- Terrorism—Prevention (i.e. counterterrorism—many subdivisions)
- Terrorism—Psychological Aspects
- Terrorism—Religious Aspects
- Terrorism—Security Measures
- Terrorism—Social Aspects
- Terrorism—Statistics
- Terrorism—Victims' Families

Related narrower terms include:

- Bioterrorism
- Bombings
- Chemical Terrorism
- Children and Terrorism
- Cyberterrorism
- Hostages
- Nuclear Terrorism
- Sabotage
- State-sponsored Terrorism
- Terrorists [many subdivisions, including Biography]
- Trials (Terrorism)

There are also some related general terms that may be relevant in some situations:

- Civil Defense—United States (for items relating to homeland security)
- Crimes Against Peace
- Genocide
- Mass murder
- National Security—United States
- Security, international
- September 11 Terrorist Attacks, 2001
- War on Terrorism, 2001–

Once the record for a book or other item is found, it is a good idea to see what additional subject headings and name headings have been assigned to it. These in turn can be used for further searching.

BIBLIOGRAPHIES, INDEXES, AND DATABASES

Bibliographies in various forms provide a convenient way to find books, periodical articles, and other materials. How far to go in one's reading depends, of course on one's research topic and goals. Some subjects, such as cyberterrorism or information warfare will not have useful materials more than a few years old. When consulting encyclopedias and handbooks, too, a researcher would generally want materials published after 1990. (The fall of the Soviet Union is a watershed between the terrorism of the cold war era and the more chaotic and diverse recent terrorism. Older books will also lack the considerable amount of information on Soviet clandestine activity that has now emerged from the archives.) The attacks of September 11, 2001, in turn represent a watershed in institutional counterterrorism. On the other hand, many older works, both scholarly and primary sources, may be vital for doing research on earlier periods of terrorist activity such as lynchings in the post–Civil War south or labor terrorists and anarchists of the 19th century.

Popular and scholarly articles can be accessed through periodical indexes that provide citations and abstracts. Abstracts are brief summaries of articles or papers. They are usually compiled and indexed—originally in bound volumes, but increasingly available online. Some examples of printed indexes that might include literature related to terrorism include:

- Criminal Justice Abstracts
- Criminal Justice Periodical Index
- Index to Legal Periodicals and Books
- Social Sciences Citation Index
- Social Sciences Index
- Sociological Abstracts

Some of these indexes, especially for recent years, are available online. Generally, they can be accessed only through a library by a cardholder, and cannot be accessed over the Internet (except by users on a college campus). Consult with a university reference librarian for more help.

Two good indexes have unrestricted search access, however. Ingentor (formerly UnCover Web) at http://www.ingentor.com contains brief descriptions of about 15 million documents from about 20,000 journals in just about every subject area. Copies of complete documents can be ordered with a credit card, or they may be obtainable for free at a local library.

Perhaps the most valuable index for topics related to criminal justice, including terrorism and hate crimes, is the National Criminal Justice Reference Service Justice Information Center, at http://www.ncjrs.org/. It offers a searchable abstract database containing 150,000 criminal justice publications, and it can be a real gold mine for the more advanced researcher.

FREE PERIODICAL INDEXES

Most public libraries subscribe to database services such as InfoTrac or EBSCO that index articles from hundreds of general-interest periodicals and some moderately specialized ones. The database can be searched by author or by words in the title, subject headings, and sometimes words found anywhere in the article text. Depending on the database used, "hits" in the database can result in just a bibliographical description (author, title, pages, periodical name, issue date, etc.), a description plus an abstract (a paragraph summarizing the contents of the article), or the full text of the article itself. Before using such an index, it is a good idea to view the list of newspapers and magazines covered and determine the years of coverage.

Many libraries provide dial-in, Internet, or Telnet access to their periodical databases as an option in their catalog menu. However, licensing restrictions usually mean that only researchers who have a library card for that particular library can access the database (by typing in their name and card number). Check with local public or school libraries to see what databases are available.

For periodicals not indexed by Infotrac or another index, or for which only abstracts rather than complete text is available, check to see whether the publication has its own web site (most now do). Some scholarly publications are putting all or most of their articles online. Popular publications tend to offer only a limited selection. Some publications of both types offer archives of several years' back issues that can be searched by author or keyword.

BOOKSTORE CATALOGS

Many people have discovered that online bookstores such as Amazon.com at (http://www.amazon.com) and Barnes & Noble.com (http://www.bn.com) are convenient ways to shop for books. A less-known benefit of online bookstore catalogs is that they often include publisher's information, book reviews, and readers' comments about a given title. They can thus serve as a form of annotated bibliography.

KEEPING UP WITH THE NEWS

It is important for the researcher to be aware of currently breaking news. In addition to watching TV news and subscribing to local or national newspapers and magazines, there are a number of ways to use the Internet to find additional news sources.

MEDIA SITES

The major broadcast and cable networks, individual television and radio stations, news (wire) services, most newspapers, and many magazines have web sites that include news stories and links to additional information. For breaking news the following are particularly useful:

- Cable News Network (CNN): http://www.cnn.com
- Reuters: http://www.reuters.com
- Associated Press (AP) wire: http://wire.ap.org/public_pages/WirePortal.pcgi/us_portal.html
- *New York Times*: http://www.nytimes.com
- *Washington Post*: http://www.washingtonpost.com/
- *Wall Street Journal*: http://online.wsj.com/public/us
- *Time* magazine: http://www.time.com
- Yahoo! maintains a large set of links to many newspapers that have websites or online editions: http://dir.yahoo.com/News_and_Media/Newspapers/Web_Directories/
- The search engine company Google provides a site at http://news.google.com/ that continuously and automatically compiles, organizes, and presents breaking news stories. One can also search the archives.

SEARCHING THE WEB

A researcher can explore an ever-expanding web of information by starting with a few web sites and following the links they offer to other sites, which in turn have links to still other sites. But because this can be a hit-and-miss way to research, some important sites may be missed if the researcher only "web surfs" in this fashion. Two other, more focused techniques can fill in the information gaps.

WEB GUIDES AND INDEXES

A web guide or index is a site that offers a structured, hierarchical outline of subject areas. This enables the researcher to zero in on a particular aspect of a subject and find links to web sites for further exploration.

The best-known (and largest) web index is Yahoo! at http://www.yahoo.com. The home page gives the top-level list of topics, and the researcher simply clicks to follow them down to more specific areas.

In addition to following Yahoo's outline-like structure, there is also a search box into which the researcher can type one or more keywords and receive a list of matching categories and sites.

Web indexes such as Yahoo! have two major advantages over undirected surfing. First, the structured hierarchy of topics makes it easy to find a particular topic or subtopic and then explore its links. Second, Yahoo! does not make an attempt to compile every possible link on the Internet (a virtually impossible task, given its size). Rather, sites are evaluated for usefulness and quality by Yahoo's indexers. This means that the researcher has a better chance of finding more substantial and accurate information. The disadvantage of Web indexes is the flip side of their selectivity: the researcher is dependent on the indexer's judgment for determining what sites are worth exploring.

To explore terrorism via Yahoo!, the researcher should click on the Society and Culture link, then Crime, then Types of Crime, then Terrorism. A variety of sites selected by the editors are available for browsing.

Yahoo's "Full Coverage" news service page on the subject of terrorism is at http://fullcoverage.yahoo.com/Full_Coverage/US/Terrorism/. In addition to news stories and related web links, it also features audio and video versions of stories that can be viewed online.

About.com (http://www.about.com) is rather similar to Yahoo!, but gives a greater emphasis to overviews or guides prepared by experts in various topics. To find information on terrorism on About.com, browse to News/Issues, Crime/Punishment then Terrorism, or enter a direct keyword search on terrorism or a relevant phrase. (Remember, with guide sites it is often a good idea to supplement browsing with a direct search to ensure the most comprehensive results.) New guide and index sites are constantly being developed, and capabilities are improving as the web matures.

SEARCH ENGINES

Search engines take a very different approach to finding materials on the web. Instead of organizing topically in a "top down" fashion, search engines work their way from the bottom up scanning through web documents and indexing them. There are hundreds of search engines, but some of the most widely used include:

- AltaVista (http://www.altavista.com)
- Excite (http://www.excite.com)
- Google (http://www.google.com)
- Hotbot (http://hotbot.lycos.com)
- Lycos (http://www.lycos.com)
- Northern Light (http://www.northernlight.com)
- WebCrawler (http://www.webcrawler.com)

Search engines are generally easy to use by employing the same sorts of key-words that work in library catalogs. There are a variety of web search tutorials available online (try "web search tutorial" in a search engine to find some). One good one is published by the Web Tools Company at http://www.thewebtools.com/tutorial/tutorial.htm.

Here are a few basic rules for using search engines:

- When looking for something specific, use the most specific term or phrase. For example, when looking for information about extradition, use the specific term "extradition", since this is the standard term. (Note that phrases should be put in quotes if you want them to be matched as phrases rather than as individual words. In this book all search terms are shown in quotes to separate them from the rest of the sentence, but that doesn't mean quotes should be used in actual searches other than for phrases.)

- When looking for a general topic that might be expressed using several different words or phrases, use several descriptive words (nouns are more reliable than verbs); for example, "international terrorism statistics." (Most engines will automatically put pages that match all three terms first on the results list.)

- Use "wildcards" when a desired word may have more than one ending. For example, terroris* matches both "terrorism" and "terrorist."

- Most search engines support Boolean (*and, or, not*) operators that can be used to broaden or narrow a search. (These operators are shown in all caps for clarity, but can usually be typed in lowercase.)

- Use AND to narrow a search. For example "chemical AND weapon" will match only pages that have both terms.

- Use OR to broaden a search: "information warfare" OR "cyberterrorism" will match any page that has *either* term, and since these terms are often used interchangeably, this type of search is necessary to retrieve the widest range of results.

- Use NOT to exclude unwanted results: "bombings NOT Israel" finds articles about bombings except those in or relating to Israel.

Because each search engine indexes somewhat differently and offers somewhat different ways of searching, it is a good idea to use several different search engines, especially for a general query. Several "metasearch" programs automate the process of submitting a query to multiple search engines. These include Metacrawler at http://www.metacrawler.com and SurfWax at http://surfwax.com. There are also search utilities that can be run from the researcher's own PC rather than through a web site. A good example is Copernic, a shareware ("try before you buy") program available for download at http://thewebtools.com/.

FINDING ORGANIZATIONS AND PEOPLE

Chapter 9 of this book provides a list of organizations that are involved with the issue of terrorism, but new organizations emerge now and then. A good place to look for information and links to organizations is the U.S. State Department, the Terrorism Research Center, and other resource sites mentioned at the beginning of this chapter. If such sites do not yield the name of a specific organization, the name can be entered into a search engine. Generally, the best approach is to put the name of the organization in quote marks such as "Terrorism Research Center."

Another approach is to take a guess at the organization's likely web address. For example, the American Civil Liberties Union is commonly known by the acronym ACLU, so it is not a surprise that the organization's web site is at www.aclu.org. (Note that noncommercial organization sites normally use the .org suffix, government agencies use .gov, educational institutions use .edu, and businesses use .com.) This technique can save time, but doesn't always work.

There are several ways to find a person on the Internet:

- Put the person's name (in quotes) in a search engine and you may find that person's home page on the Internet.

- Contact the person's employer (such as a university for an academic, or a corporation for a technical professional). Most such organizations have web pages that include a searchable faculty or employee directory.

- Try one of the people-finder services such as Yahoo People Search at http://people.yahoo.com or BigFoot at www.bigfoot.com. This may yield contact information such as e-mail address, regular address, and/or phone number.

LEGAL RESEARCH

It is important for researchers to be able to obtain the text and summary of laws and court decisions relating to terrorism. Because of the specialized terminology of the law, legal research can be more difficult to master than bibliographical or general research tools. Fortunately, the Internet has also come to the rescue in this area, offering a variety of ways to look up laws and court cases without having to pore through huge bound volumes in law libraries (which may not be easily accessible to the general public, anyway).

FINDING LAWS

Most legislation relating to terrorism is federal, since terrorism is usually national or international in scope. When federal legislation passes, it eventually becomes part of the United States Code, a massive legal compendium. Title 18 of the U.S. Code deals with crimes and criminal procedure. Part I of this title defines crimes and penalties, and can be used together with the summary in Chapter 3 of this book, "Laws and Court Cases Relating to Terrorism," to look up specific sections relating to terrorism. (Since so many new provisions and amendments have been passed, it may be better to work "backward" from the summaries of the Antiterrorism and Effective Death Penalty Act of 1996 in Chapter 3 and the complete summary in Appendix D to the existing sections of the U.S. Code.)

The U.S. Code can be searched online in several locations, but the easiest site to use is probably the web site of the Cornell University Law School at http://www4.law.cornell.edu/uscode/. The fastest way to retrieve a law is by its title and section citation, but phrases and keywords can also be used.

KEEPING UP WITH LEGISLATIVE DEVELOPMENTS

Pending legislation is often tracked by advocacy groups, both national and based in particular states. See Chapter 9, "Organizations and Agencies," for contact information.

Proposed federal legislation on terrorism often turns up as part of a large bill often called an "omnibus crime bill," although provisions can also be added to appropriations bills for defense, intelligence, or other activities.

The Library of Congress "THOMAS" web site at http://thomas.loc.gov provides access to the text and status of past, pending, and proposed legislation as well as committee reports. The Bill Summary/Status section can be searched by bill or Public Law number (if available), or using key words or phrases. A bill can also be searched under the session of Congress; each session is two years. For example, the 108th Congress is in session from 2003 to 2004.

For example, typing in the phrase "airport security" for the 108th Congress yields a list of several bills, including H.R.115, a bill: "To amend title 49, United States Code, to improve airport security by using biometric security badges, and for other purposes."

Once one is viewing the entry for a bill, one can click on various links to get a summary, find out how far along the bill is in the legislative process, get a list of the bill's sponsors, and so on.

> 1. *H.R.700 : To amend title 49, United States Code, to provide enhanced protections for airline passengers.*
> **Sponsor:** *Rep Shuster, Bud—***Latest Major Action:** *3/18/1999 House committee/subcommittee actions*
> **Committees:** *House Transportation and Infrastructure*

Clicking on the bill number brings up a screen of information that starts with the following:

> **H.R.700**
> *Sponsor: Rep Shuster, Bud (introduced 2/10/1999)*
> *Latest Major Action: 3/18/1999 House committee/subcommittee actions*
> *Title: To amend title 49, United States Code, to provide enhanced protections for airline passengers.*

Underneath this heading, a series of hyperlinks follows. Clicking on any of these links brings up the appropriate details, including the bill's current status, a summary of provisions, or the complete text of the bill.

FINDING COURT DECISIONS

If legislation is the front end of the criminal justice process, the courts are the back. The U.S. Supreme Court and state courts make important decisions every year that determine how the laws are interpreted. Like laws, legal decisions are organized using a system of citations. The general form is: *Party1 v. Party2* volume reporter [optional start page] (court, year).

Here are some examples:

Brandenburg v. Ohio, 395 U.S. 44 (1969)

Here the parties are Brandenburg (the defendant who is appealing his case from a state court) and the state of Ohio. The case is in volume 395 of the *U.S. Supreme Court Reports*, beginning at page 44, and the case was decided in 1969. (For the Supreme Court, the name of the court is omitted.)

Fierro v. Gomez 77 F.3d 301 (9th Cir. 1996)

Here the case is in the 9th U.S. Circuit Court of Appeals, decided in 1996.

A state court decision can generally be identified because it includes the state's name. For example, in *State v. Torrance*, 473 S.E.2d. 703 (S.C. 1996) the S.E.2d refers to the appeals district, and the S.C. to South Carolina.

Once the jurisdiction for the case has been determined, the researcher can then go to a number of places on the Internet to find cases by citation and sometimes by the names of the parties or by subject keywords. Some of the most useful sites are:

- **The Legal Information Institute** (LII; http://supct.law.cornell.edu/ supct/) has all Supreme Court decisions since 1990 plus 610 of what the LII considers the most important historic decisions.
- **Washlaw Web** (http://www.washlaw.edu/) has a variety of courts (including states) and legal topics listed, making it a good jumping-off place for many sorts of legal research. However the actual accessibility of state court opinions (and the formats they are provided in) varies widely.

LEXIS AND WESTLAW

Lexis and Westlaw are commercial legal databases that have extensive information including an elaborate system of notes, legal subject headings, and ways to show relationships between cases. Unfortunately, these services are too expensive for use by most individual researchers unless they are available through a university or corporate library.

MORE HELP ON LEGAL RESEARCH

For more information on conducting legal research, see the "Legal Research FAQ" at http://www.cis.ohio-state.edu/hypertext/faq/usenet/law/research/top.html. After a certain point, however, the researcher who lacks formal legal training may need to consult with or rely on the efforts of professional researchers or academics in the field.

GENERAL RESEARCH STRATEGY

It can be hard to know where to begin when there are so many kinds of information sources available. Unless one is researching a very specific topic, it is probably best to gain an overview and working knowledge of the topic by using some of the resource sites, web indexes, and guides and then pursue specific interests by using bibliographical tools (library and bookstore catalogs and periodical indexes) to obtain appropriate books, news articles, and scholarly papers. When legal research is required, having the general topic, context, and citations in hand will save time and frustration.

CHAPTER 8

ANNOTATED BIBLIOGRAPHY

This chapter presents a representative selection of books, journal and magazine articles, and web (Internet) resources relating to many aspects of terrorism. The bibliography is divided into four broad categories of materials outlined as follows:

General Background Materials
Encyclopedias, Dictionaries, and Handbooks
Bibliographies
Introductions, Overviews, and Anthologies
Theories and Perspectives

Regional Developments
Northern Ireland
Europe
Israel and Palestine
Middle East (General)
Africa
Central Asia
East and Southeast Asia
Asia-Pacific
Mexico and Latin America
United States and Canada—Indigenous Terrorism
United States and Canada—Imported Terrorism

Key Issues Related to Terrorism
Counterterrorism (Theory and Practice)
Terrorism and International Relations
Legal Prosecution of Terrorism
Terrorism and Civil Liberties
Terrorism, Media, and Popular Culture

Specific Types of Terrorism
Weapons of Mass Destruction (General)
Chemical and Biological Terrorism
Nuclear and Radiological Terrorism
Infrastructure Protection and Transportation Security
Cyberterrorism and Information Warfare

The following general principles were used for selecting materials for this bibliography:

- Utility: While most materials are for the general reader, high school age through adult, a representative sampling of more specialized or professional literature (legal, medical, and more) is also included.
- Currency: Most publications are 1998 or later (many 2001 or later) except for historical or theoretical works.
- Variety: Materials represent a wide variety of viewpoints.

Note that many of the newspaper and magazine articles listed here are available from full-text databases accessible on the Internet or through a local library, or on web sites maintained by publications. Many publications charge a few dollars for access to articles that are more than a month or so old. Of course, many libraries also keep paper copies of back issues of publications.

Internet documents in this bibliography are single documents or groups of closely related documents. A listing of wider-ranging Internet sites is included in Chapter 7, "How to Research Terrorism."

Finally, it should be noted that web addresses change frequently and sites can disappear altogether. In the entries for web material, a "downloaded" date refers to when the site was verified as existing online. "Posted" refers to either the date that the material was posted on the web or (if the material was originally in some other form) the date that the material was originally published. In general, listings are current as of mid-2003.

GENERAL BACKGROUND MATERIALS

Encyclopedias, Dictionaries, and Handbooks

BOOKS

Anderson, Ewan W. *Global Geopolitical Flashpoints: An Atlas of Conflict.* Chicago: Fitzroy Dearborn, 2000. Profiles 123 current and potential areas of conflict. For each of the relatively brief entries, there is a description of the background, relevant issues, and a detailed map. The present status of the conflict is then summarized.

Combs, Cindy C., and Martin Slann. *Encyclopedia of Terrorism*. New York: Facts On File, 2002. A comprehensive A–Z encyclopedia of concepts, organizations, persons, and events involved in the history of terrorism, including the events of September 11, 2001.

Courtois, Stephane, et al. *The Black Book of Communism: Crimes, Terror, Repression*. Cambridge, Mass.: Harvard University Press, 1999. This widely acclaimed volume tabulates the killings, terror, and repression unleashed by communist regimes throughout the 20th century. Ranging from Lenin's use of terror following the Bolshevik revolution to the bizarre policies of Pol Pot, this book is relevant to students of terrorism for both the connection between Soviet and Communist Chinese policies and the activities of terrorist groups and the use of state terrorism against internal dissent.

Kushner, Harvey. *Encyclopedia of Terrorism*. Thousand Oaks, Calif.: Sage Publications, 2003. A comprehensive A–Z encyclopedia of persons, organizations, and events relating to terrorism. Includes maps showing areas of terrorist attacks, a chronology, and a bibliography.

Nash, Jay Robert. *Terrorism in the 20th Century: A Narrative Encyclopedia from the Anarchists through the Weathermen to the Unabomber*. New York: M. Evans, 1998. A narrative history of terrorism in America during the 20th century, written in a popular journalistic style and providing useful overviews. Each of the 10 chapters describes events during a particular decade, including both domestic terrorism and attacks on U.S. interests abroad. Includes a chronology, glossary, and bibliography.

Political Risk Services. *Political Risk Yearbook, 2003*. East Syracuse, N.Y.: PRS, 2003. An eight-volume set (also available on CD-ROM and online for a fee) giving background on key political and other groups in each country and detailed assessment and rating of the risks of conflict and terrorism in each country. Regularly updated by subscription. Designed and priced primarily for corporate and academic use but may be available in large libraries.

Rudolph, Joseph R., ed. *Encyclopedia of Modern Ethnic Conflicts*. Westport, Conn.: Greenwood Press, 2003. Since much terrorism is based on ethnic and nationalist conflicts, understanding these ongoing struggles is important for the assessment of terrorist threats. This encyclopedia comprehensively describes ethnic conflicts and civil wars in the modern world. For each conflict there is a time line, introduction, historical background, the current conflict, attempts to manage the conflict, and the significance of the conflict. A bibliography also accompanies each entry.

INTERNET DOCUMENTS

"America's Response to Terrorism." The Brookings Institution web site. Available online. URL: http://www.brookings.edu/dybdocroot/fp/projects/terrorism/chronology.htm#2001. Updated July 17, 2002. A chronology of events relating to terrorist attacks on the United States, starting in 1989, with additional detail for the events of September 11, 2001, and extending through September 2002.

Beyler, Clara. "Chronology of Suicide Bombings Carried Out by Women." International Policy Institute for Counterterrorism. Available online. URL: http://www.ict.org.il/ (search for this particular article). Posted on February 12, 2003. Brief descriptions of suicide bombing attacks by females organized by country of target and then chronologically.

"Foreign Terrorist Organizations." U.S. Department of State. Office of the Coordinator for Antiterrorism. Available online. URL: http://usinfo.state.gov/topical/pol/terror/designated.htm. Posted on August 9, 2002. Lists those organizations officially designated as terrorist by the Department of State, gives background information about the organizations, and explains the legal criteria used for this designation.

"Patterns of Global Terrorism, 2002." U.S. Department of State. Available online. URL: http://www.state.gov/s/ct/rls/pgtrpt/2002/html/. Downloaded on August 1, 2003. This important annual report is the official compilation of information about terrorism-related events, statistics, anti-terrorism policy, officially designated terrorist organizations, state-sponsored terrorism, and related subjects.

"Political Science: International and Comparative Politics Reference Sources." DePaul University. Available online. URL: http://apps.lib.depaul.edu/eresource/subject_search_infotype.asp?TopicID=243&SubjectID=40. Downloaded on August 16, 2003. A list of links to bibliographies and resource guides to international and national laws, institutions, and other matters useful for researching the background of regional conflicts and terrorism. Prepared by the DePaul University Library.

"Political Science Resources on the Web." University of Michigan Documents Center. Available online. URL: http://www.lib.umich.edu/govdocs/polisci.html. Updated on January 29, 2003. This site provides a variety of links to resources on terrorism, as well as related topics such as postcolonial history, human rights, international organizations, intelligence, and peace and conflict. There are also links to other university departments and institutions involved in international affairs studies.

"Profiles of International Terrorist Organizations." International Policy Institute for Counter-Terrorism. Available online. URL: http://www.ict.org.il/ (linked under International Terrorism). Downloaded on August 15, 2003. A useful compilation that lists about 50 terrorist groups, including such information as background, chronology of terrorist activity, and news updates, along with links to articles.

"Research on Security, September 11, 2001." Louisiana State University Law Library. Available online. URL: http://l.staff.umkc.edu/lordl/ 9-11-01-library/security.htm. Posted on September 25, 2002. A guide and archival links for government statements and other documents and resources relating to the terrorist attacks, counterterrorism, civil liberties, and other areas.

"Terrorist Group Profiles." Dudley Knox Library, Naval Postgraduate School. Available online. URL: http://library.nps.navy.mil/home/tgp/ tgpndx.htm. Updated on May 5, 2003. This site includes links to the U.S. Department of State report "Patterns of Global Terrorism" starting with 1996, as well as links to terrorist group profiles and terrorist incidents.

"The World Factbook 2002." U.S. Central Intelligence Agency. Available online. URL: http://www.odci.gov/cia/publications/factbook/. Downloaded on August 15, 2003. This useful reference source provides basic information on the geography, demographics, economics, and infrastructure of each of the world's countries. It is a good first step in researching an area involved with the war on terrorism.

"The World Factbook of Criminal Justice Systems." U.S. Department of Justice. Bureau of Justice Statistics. Available online. URL: http://www.ojp. usdoj.gov/bjs/abstract/wfcj.htm. Updated on June 6, 2003. Provides a summary of the criminal justice system of each nation, including courts and criminal procedures, criminal code, law enforcement, and crime statistics.

Bibliographies

BOOKS

Alali, A. Oadasuo, and Gary W. Byrd. *Terrorism and the News Media: A Selected, Annotated Bibliography.* Jefferson, N.C.: McFarland, 1994. Contains entries for more than 600 works (print and electronic) dealing with the often symbiotic relationship between terrorism and the media. Entries are divided into three main areas: understanding terrorism, terrorism and the electronic media, and terrorism and the print media.

Babkina, A. M. *Terrorism: An Annotated Bibliography.* Commack, N.Y.: Nova Science Publishers, 1998. This bibliography covers selected books and journal articles from 1993 to 1998. Books are listed in the form of reproduced Library of Congress catalog records, with no annotation other than an occasional summary included in the cataloging. Journal articles are covered in records from the CRS (Congressional Research Service)

Public Policy Literature (PPLT) database, and the records include brief notes or summaries.

Mickolus, Edward F. *The Literature of Terrorism*. Reprint, Westport, Conn.: Greenwood Press, 1981. This volume is the beginning of what has become the most comprehensive bibliography series on terrorism (see following entries).

————. *Terrorism, 1980–1987*. Westport, Conn.: Greenwood Press, 1988. A detailed bibliography of materials on terrorism (including analytics for chapters in collections), focusing on the 1980s.

————. *Terrorism, 1988–1991*. Westport, Conn.: Greenwood Press, 1993. Continues the coverage of the preceding work and includes a chronology.

————. *Terrorism, 1992–1995*. Westport, Conn.: Greenwood Press, 1997. Continues the coverage into the 1990s, an eventful decade in the history of terrorism.

————. *Terrorism, 1996–2001: A Chronology*. 2 vols. Westport, Conn.: Greenwood Press, 2002. A detailed accounting of modern terrorist attacks through the September 11, 2001, attacks and subsequent anthrax attacks. Includes disposition of related legal cases.

Newton, Michael. *Terrorism in the United States and Europe, 1800–1959: An Annotated Bibliography*. New York: Garland, 1988. An extensive annotated bibliography of almost 6,000 early works. Begins with general works and is then organized by country with the U.S. section subdivided topically.

Prunckun, Henry W., Jr. *Shadow of Death: An Analytic Bibliography on Political Violence, Terrorism, and Low-Intensity Conflict*. Lanham, Md.: Scarecrow Press, 1995. Part I of this handbook presents a brief introduction to terrorism, its definitions, and anatomy. Part II is an annotated bibliography of terrorism broken down alphabetically by topic and by region and country. Publications covered generally range from the 1970s to the early 1990s.

Wood, M. Sandra. *Bioterrorism and Political Violence: Web Resources*. New York: Haworth Information Press, 2002. This Internet reference handbook focuses on bioterrorism but also includes sections on nuclear terrorism, the September 11, 2001, attacks, and background on political violence and Islam. There is also an introductory overview of each topic.

INTERNET DOCUMENTS

"Bibliography on Terrorism, Bioterrorism, the Middle East, and 9-11 Related Issues. Law Library Resource Xchange, LLC (LLRX.com). Available online. URL: http://www.llrx.com/features/terrorbiblio.htm. Updated on November 28, 2001. Provides a bibliography (with some light annotation) on regional background to the war on terrorism, Islam, and coping with terrorism.

Annotated Bibliography

"Congressional Research Service Documents on Terrorism." Penny Hill Press. Available online. URL: www.pennyhill.com/terrorism.html. Downloaded on August 6, 2003. A listing of Congressional Research Service reports relating to terrorism available for order online. Includes information about each document, an order number, and an abstract.

Introductions, Overviews, and Anthologies

BOOKS

Barker, Jonathan. *The No-Nonsense Guide to Terrorism.* London: Verso Books, 2003. A relatively brief but clearly written and useful guide to the history, trends, policies, and issues relating to terrorism around the world. Includes numerous sidebars with charts and quotes.

Combs, Cynthia C. *Terrorism in the 21st Century.* 3d ed. Upper Saddle River, N.J.: Prentice-Hall, 2002. Latest edition of an introductory survey geared toward college undergraduates. Discusses the anatomy of modern terrorism (the actors and their methods), the organization of national and international counterterrorist agencies, and predictions about future trends. Each discussion concisely presents and assesses the key factors.

Crenshaw, Martha, ed. *Terrorism in Context.* University Park: Pennsylvania State University Press, 1995. A collection of essays that amounts to a broad survey of the history of terrorism and its expression in many regions of the world. The first contributions deal with the origins of the concept of terrorism in early modern Europe and 19th-century anarchism. Later contributions include discussion of left-wing terrorism in Italy and West Germany, the Basque extremists in Spain, Northern Ireland, political violence in Argentina and Peru, and a variety of movements in the Middle East.

Howard, Russell D., and Reid L. Sawyer, eds. *Terrorism and Counterterrorism: Understanding the New Security Environment.* Guilford, Conn.: McGraw Hill/Dushkin, 2002. A large collection of readings (book chapters and articles) from a variety of experts. The first part deals with the nature of terrorism, models for understanding terrorism, the role of religion, weapons of mass destruction, and other forms of terrorism. The second part focuses on the strategies, approaches, organizations, and instruments that can be used to fight terrorism.

Laqueur, Walter. *No End to War: Terrorism in the Twenty-First Century.* New York: Continuum, 2003. An internationally recognized expert on terrorism distills his work into a clear exposition of the nature and definition of terrorism, what characterizes the "new terrorism," the role of Islam and

193

other religions, the relationship between terrorism and the United States, European and Israeli policies, poverty and terrorism, and questions of what makes for effective intelligence and counterterrorism.

Martin, Gus. *Understanding Terrorism: Challenges, Perspectives, and Issues.* Thousand Oaks, Calif.: Sage Publications, 2003. A comprehensive up-to-date textbook divided into four major parts: definitions and causes of terrorism, sources or motivations of terrorism, terrorist tactics and the role of the media, and options and future prospects.

Rossi, M. L. *What Every American Should Know About the Rest of the World.* New York: Penguin, 2003. Perhaps slightly marred by supercilious language, this is a useful guide to the countries involved in significant unrest, conflicts, and terrorism. Each country's entry begins with summary tables, which are followed by a résumé, "quick tour," future forecast, hot spots, and hot shots (leaders).

Violence and Terrorism, 04/05. Annual Editions. Guilford, Conn.: McGraw-Hill/Dushkin, 2004. The latest in a series of annual anthologies on the subject, the volume includes reprints of 38 articles and reports divided into 12 units: The Concept of Terrorism, Causes of Terrorism, Strategies and Tactics of Terrorism, State-Sponsored Terrorism, International Terrorism, Terrorism in America, Terrorism and the Media, Terrorism and Religion, Women and Terrorism, Countering Terrorism, Future Threats, and Trends and Projections. The volume also includes web resources. Generally there is a small amount of overlap from one annual volume to the next in material included.

White, Jonathan R. *Terrorism: An Introduction, 2002 Update.* 4th ed. Belmont, Calif.: Wadsworth, 2002. Latest edition of an introductory textbook covering the nature, scope, and expression of terrorism. Topics covered include definitions and typologies of terrorism, ways in which terrorist groups justify their activities, structure and dynamics of terrorist groups, and regional surveys of terrorism in Latin America, the Middle East, Europe, and the United States. Each regional section includes background about the ideologies, groups, and conflicts, as well as differing interpretations by experts.

Theories and Perspectives

BOOKS

Armstrong, Karen. *Islam: A Short History.* New York: Modern Library, 2000. One of the most accessible introductions to the development of Islam, a subject that has now become of vital importance to everyone. The vivid narrative runs from Mohammed to the eruption of Islam from the desert, the flowering of Islamic civilization, to its decline and subjection to Western colonialism and imperialism and the Islamic reaction against the West today.

Carr, Caleb. *The Lessons of Terror: A History of Warfare Against Civilians: Why It Has Always Failed and Why It Will Fail Again.* New York: Random House, 2002. A novelist and military historian examines the use of terror tactics throughout history, from ancient conquerors to Crusaders to the modern doctrine of "total war" that first emerged during the American Civil War. Carr argues that any short-term successes using such tactics have been bought at the price of long-term resistance and unrest. He suggests that the war on terrorism must be conducted with vigor but also with thoughtfulness and tactical discrimination if it is to have lasting success.

Chasdi, Richard J. *Serenade of Suffering: A Portrait of Middle East Terrorism, 1968–1993.* Lanham, Md.: Lexington Books, 1999. Applies a systematic analysis to the behavior of the various terrorist groups that became prominent in the Middle East during the 1970s and 1980s. Begins with a discussion of definitions, typologies, and significant variables. The book then turns to the ideological factors influencing terrorist group behavior, the process of formation and evolution of terrorist groups, and an analysis of the groups' behavior, including choice of targets and methods used.

Chomsky, Noam. *Pirates and Emperors, Old and New: International Terrorism in the Real World.* Boston: South End Press, 2003. The noted linguist and controversial political thinker gives his latest assessment of terrorism in the post–September 11 world. In his context, the actions practiced by groups such as the Palestinians is "retail terrorism," while "wholesale terrorism" in the form of bombing and other military action is practiced by powers such as the United States. Such wholesale terrorism is the response of the rich and powerful to anyone who threatens their status—and, according to this context, President Bush's war on terrorism must be seen in the same light as earlier efforts under Ronald Reagan and Bush's father.

Cragin, Kim, and Peter Chalk. *Terrorism and Development: Using Social and Political Development to Inhibit a Resurgence of Terrorism.* Santa Monica, Calif.: Rand Corporation, 2003. While it seems plausible that economic development in a country would reduce the impetus toward terrorism, the relationship between the two activities is subtle and complex. The authors examine various policies in Israel, the Philippines, and the United Kingdom, and observe the interplay between development and the peace process.

Findley, Paul. *Silent No More: Confronting America's False Images of Islam.* Beltsville, Md.: Amana Publications, 2001. The author, a congressman who has extensive experience with Middle East affairs, presents mainstream Islamic principles, beliefs, and practices and dispels common stereotypes about the religion. He points out that Muslims are an increasingly important part of the American political landscape, with a growing number of Muslims being elected to office.

Follain, John. *Jackal: The Complete Story of the Legendary Terrorist, Carlos the Jackal.* New York: Arcade, 1998. Recounts the life of Ilyich Ramirez Sanchez, better known as "Carlos the Jackal" and murderer of 83 people by his own account. A "freelance terrorist," he carried out attacks on behalf of Muammar al-Qaddafi, Saddam Hussein, Fidel Castro, and the Italian Red Brigade until he was captured and imprisoned in 1994. Based on the author's account, the Jackal appears to have been motivated far more by narcissism and hedonism than any consistent ideology.

Gilbert, Paul. *New Terror, New Wars.* Washington, D.C.: Georgetown University Press, 2003. A professor of philosophy and ethics updates his treatment of the interplay between identity, nationalism, politics, violence, and counterterror. He evaluates the ethics of military response under both the traditional "just war" theory and under newer justifications such as wars of humanitarian intervention.

Gordon, Hayim. *Quicksand: Israel, the Intifada, and the Rise of Political Evil in Democracies.* East Lansing: Michigan State University Press, 1994. The author uses the Palestinian uprising (Intifada) and Israeli response as a springboard to explore the problem of how evil can arise and flourish even in a society that proclaims and appears to implement democratic values. Classic writers on the problem of evil such as Hannah Arendt, Fyodor Dostoyevsky, and Plato are used as relevant touchstones. The author argues against the supposedly detached postmodern approach that has no room for a visceral sense of evil.

Guelke, Adrian. *The Age of Terrorism and the International Political System.* New York: I. B. Tauris, 1995. This book focuses on the origin of "the age of terrorism" as a way of thinking about small group violence during the postcolonialist cold war era of roughly 1960–90. One side of the discussion looks at how the activities of the terrorist groups reflected a transition in world politics, while the other side looks at the characterization of acts as terrorism in the media and by governments during this time. The end of the cold war has challenged the established paradigm and points to both instability and some hope for resolving conflicts.

Heymann, Philip B. *Terrorism, Freedom, and Security: Winning Without War.* Cambridge, Mass.: MIT Press, 2003. The author, a former deputy attorney general of the United States, argues that the "war" against terrorism should be conducted through mainly diplomatic, intelligence, and international legal means rather than by the military. Indeed rather than being a war focused on one or a few enemies and objectives, the battle against terrorism is ongoing and open-ended, with many fronts against a diverse array of opponents.

Juergensmeyer, Mark. *Terror in the Mind of God: The Global Rise of Religious Violence.* Updated ed. Berkeley: University of California Press, 2001. A sociologist of religion argues that it is simplistic to say that the appeal of violence or terror is not part of legitimate religion but is only the province of cults or fanatics. Rather, violence can be part of the enactment of "cosmic war"—struggles of ultimate significance that become linked with urgent political and ideological issues and are embodied in religious imagery, so that religion and violence are mysteriously and perhaps inextricably intertwined. (This updated edition adds coverage of the events of September 11, 2001.)

Kegley, Charles W., and William D. Stanley, eds. *The New Global Terrorism: Characteristics, Causes, Controls.* Upper Saddle River, N.J.: Prentice-Hall, 2002. A collection of essays by experts analyzing the new terrain of the war on terrorism. The essays are organized into three topics: the changing characteristics of emerging terrorism, causes of terrorism old and new, and principles to guide action in the new arena.

Kressel, Neil J. *Mass Hate: The Global Rise of Genocide and Terror.* Updated ed. Boulder, Colo.: Westview Press, 2002. The author, a psychologist specializing in international affairs, addresses the question of why mass terrorism and genocide reached a peak in the 20th century. Using case studies, he examines in particular the Nazi Holocaust, genocide in Rwanda, the campaign of rape and torture in Bosnia, and the bombing of the World Trade Center in New York by Islamic extremists. He suggests that while the ideologies underlying acts of terror differ, the psychological process by which leaders manipulate followers into committing them is essentially the same.

Lifton, Robert J. *Destroying the World to Save It: Aum Shinrikyo, Apocalyptic Violence, and the New Global Terrorism.* New York: Henry Holt, 1999. Psychiatrist and award-winning writer Lifton looks at the 1995 Tokyo subway nerve gas attack by the Aum Shinrikyo cult and suggests that it may be merely the tip of an iceberg. He suggests that there may be an emerging, loosely connected network of believers in apocalyptic destruction who may be able to enlist the help of psychologically vulnerable but technologically adept individuals.

Neuberger, Luisa De Cataldo, and Tiziana Valentini. *Women and Terrorism.* Translated by Leo Hughes. New York: St. Martin's Press, 1996. This Italian work deals with a largely neglected aspect of the terrorism debate: the participation of women in terrorism. Using case studies, the authors point out both the distinctive motivations of female terrorists and the stereotypes that prevent proper consideration of female terrorism by both academic researchers and the criminal justice system. Includes interview and questionnaire transcripts.

Oliverio, Annamarie. *The State of Terror.* Albany: State University of New York Press, 1998. A study of the social construction of concepts of terrorism since Niccolò Machiavelli, focusing on the conceptualization of terrorism in relation to statecraft. The *Achille Lauro* and TWA 847 hijackings, both of which took place in 1985, are used as case studies.

Pearlstein, Richard M. *The Mind of the Political Terrorist.* Wilmington, Del.: SR Books, 1991. Taking a Freudian approach to his analysis of terrorists belonging to the Weathermen, the Symbionese Liberation Army, the Baader-Meinhof Gang, and the Italian Red Brigades, the author concludes that they all suffer from a narcissistic rage that creates both self-destructiveness and violence toward others.

Reich, Walter, ed. *Origins of Terrorism: Psychologies, Ideologies, Theologies, States of Mind.* Washington, D.C.: Woodrow Wilson Center, 1990. The contributors, experts in history, religion, and behavioral science, discuss a variety of worldviews, motivations, states of mind, and goals for terrorism. They begin with the assumption that terrorism is a complex, multidimensional problem and offer diverse approaches to understanding it.

Sluka, Jeffrey A., ed. *Death Squad: The Anthropology of State Terror.* Philadelphia: University of Pennsylvania Press, 1999. A collection of papers analyzing the use of state terror, particularly quasi-official death squads, from the perspective of anthropology and the deep roots of popular culture. Areas discussed include Argentina, Spain, Northern Ireland, Punjab and Kashmir, Indonesia, and the Philippines.

Snow, Donald M. *Distant Thunder: Patterns of Conflict in the Developing World.* 2d ed. Armonk, N.Y.: M. E. Sharpe, 1997. This book provides a broad background to the kinds of conflicts that have erupted throughout the developing world, explaining how they differ from the proxy wars of the cold war era. The author goes on to look at the dynamics of insurgency and counterinsurgency, internal (civil) war, the role of the narcotics trade, the problems of counterterrorism, and a critique of the so-called New World Order.

Stern, Jessica. *Terror in the Name of God: Why Religious Militants Kill.* New York: HarperCollins, 2003. A former Fellow at the Council of Foreign Relations distills insights from her encounters with religious extremists around the world. She describes how seemingly normal people find themselves enmeshed in absolutist worldviews where they can be triggered to launch devastating attacks. She argues that the danger is increased by the willingness of certain governments to tolerate or even foster extremist groups.

Stout, Chris E., ed. *The Psychology of Terrorism.* 4 vols. Westport, Conn.: Praeger, 2002. "Outstanding academics, clinicians, and activists worldwide contributed to this multi-volume, peer-reviewed set." Titles in the set include: *A Public Understanding, Clinical Aspects and Responses, Programs and Practices in Response and Prevention,* and *Theoretical Understandings and Perspectives.*

Tanter, Raymond. *Rogue Regimes: Terrorism and Proliferation.* New York: St. Martin's Press, 1999. Examines the new landscape of foreign policy in which the polarized world of the cold war era has been replaced by the challenge of establishing an international legal order in the face of "rogue states" such as Iraq, Iran, Libya, Syria, and North Korea. Such states threaten the legal order and U.S. national security by sponsoring terrorism and producing (or trying to produce) weapons of mass destruction. The relationship between rogue states and terrorist groups (and "freelance" terrorists such as Osama bin Laden) is discussed, as well as policy options for the future.

Von Tangen Page, Michael. *Prisons, Peace, and Terrorism: Penal Policy in the Reduction of Political Violence in Northern Ireland, Italy, and the Spanish Basque Country, 1968–97.* New York: St. Martin's Press, 1998. A comparison of the effectiveness of penal systems in handling politically motivated violent offenders in three regions that have intense terrorist conflict. Because the motivations and responses of people who consider themselves to be political prisoners are different from those of conventional criminals, different approaches are required. While longer sentences, on the one hand, and the use of the "carrot" of parole, on the other, can be effective, the time may come in a terrorist conflict that concessions made as part of a "peace building" process may be needed to bring resolution to the conflict.

Wieviorka, Michel. *The Making of Terrorism.* Translated by David Gordon White. Chicago: University of Chicago Press, 1993. A comparative analysis of Italian, Peruvian, Basque, and Middle Eastern terrorist groups. The author gathered his evidence through staged confrontations and extensive interviews, using a method called "interventionist sociology." He argues that terrorism at root represents the alienation of the individual from the very ideology he or she professes as motivation.

Zulaika, Joseba, and William A. Douglass. *Terror and Taboo: The Follies, Fables, and Faces of Terrorism.* New York: Routledge, 1996. Based on the author's research into the Basque terrorist group ETA and its opponents, this book is a study of how language about terrorism is itself a weapon deployed by various players, including the government, media, academia, the arts community, and the terrorists themselves. The controlling images and thought patterns involving terrorism as portrayed in literature and the media are described. This book serves as both a look at seldom-discussed aspects of terrorism and as a specific study of the Basque situation.

Global Terrorism

ARTICLES AND PAPERS

Briggs, Rachel. "Hostage, Inc." *Foreign Policy*, July–August 2002, pp. 28–29. An economic analysis of the costs and benefits of kidnapping, an activity often used to finance terrorist groups. Returns vary, with Colombia in particular offering great rewards at minimal risk.

Canadian Security Intelligence Service. "Doomsday Religious Movements." *Terrorism and Political Violence*, Spring 2002, pp. 53–60. A survey of religious movements that focus on "Doomsday" and that have potential for carrying out terrorist activity in order to further an apocalyptic agenda. The general characteristics of the beliefs and practices of such groups are summarized. There is often a destructive spiral when authorities who lack understanding of the dynamics of such movements use inappropriate tactics. Some warning signs of dangerous groups include increased acquisition of illegal weapons, relocating to isolated rural areas, and an escalation of rhetoric.

Claridge, David. "State Terrorism? Applying a Definitional Model." *Terrorism and Political Violence*, Autumn 1996, pp. 47–63. Attempts to characterize state terrorism. States that use terrorism as an instrument of repression or social control generally pervert the judicial process, the role of the military, or both. The state uses its monopoly on violence to coerce rather than to protect rights. The author develops a model of state terrorism as similar to standard terrorism even though the actor is different. Death squads in Indonesia are discussed as an example of state terrorism.

Cox, Harvey. "Religion and the War Against Evil." *The Nation*, vol. 273, December 24, 2001, p. 29. When America was struck on September 11, many Americans instinctively turned to religion for some sort of understanding or sustenance. At the same time some right-wing religionists such as Jerry Falwell and Pat Robertson suggested that God Himself is angry at our social wickedness and thus allowed the attacks. Meanwhile the terrorists, of course, cited religion as the ultimate reason for their actions. Cox, a noted professor of divinity at Harvard University, suggests that the times call for a rapprochement or even cooperative effort between secularism (or modernity) and religion. Secularism offers a vital critique of religion's pride and power-grabbing, while religion can call modernity back from its inhuman tendencies.

Crossette, Barbara. "An Old Scourge of War Becomes Its Latest Crime." *New York Times*, June 14, 1998, pp. 1, 6. Suggests that rape is being used more frequently as a premeditated terror tactic in factional conflicts in Bosnia, Indonesia, Rwanda, and other countries. Rape is often an element in ethnic cleansing campaigns, used to instill fear and demoralize. Women's organizations are calling international attention to this trend.

Annotated Bibliography

Douglas, Susan. "Terror and Bathos." *Progressive*, vol. 60, September 1996, p. 40. Critiques the media coverage and news analysis of the TWA Flight 800 crash and the Olympic Park bombing in Atlanta. The media produces supercilious observations, indecent pressure for quick conclusions, and the need to find someone to blame.

Hoffman, Bruce. "The Confluence of International and Domestic Trends in Terrorism." *Terrorism and Political Violence*, vol. 9, no. 2, Summer 1997. The author argues that the character of terrorism changed during the 1980s and 1990s. More terrorists today are motivated by religion, and the absolute and compelling nature of religious belief tends to make religious-based terrorists more deadly and less amenable to negotiation than nationalist terrorists. Also, the "new terrorism" typified by the Unabomber and Oklahoma City bombers is amorphous and decentralized but able to use sophisticated means of attack. New terrorists are harder to identify than traditionally organized groups, and, as in the case of Aum Shinrikyo in Japan, they are not interested in taking responsibility for their actions.

Miles, Jack. "Theology and the Clash of Civilizations." *Cross Currents*, vol. 51, Winter 2002, p. 451ff. If there is indeed a clash of civilizations between Islam and the West, then the author believes that two things must happen if it is to be resolved without endless bloodshed. Within the *umma*, or world of Islam, a strong alternative to the fanatic intolerance typified by Osama bin Laden must emerge. But, equally important, the West, in which the triumph of secularism has made talk of religion almost impossible in the exercise of statecraft, must be willing to understand and engage the theological worldview and values held by Moslems.

Olcott, Martha Brill, and Bakhityar Baajanov. "The Terrorist Notebooks: During the mid-1990s a Group of Young Uzbeks Went to School to Learn How to Kill You. Here Is What They Were Taught." *Foreign Policy*, March/April 2003, pp. 30–40. The authors present excerpts from notebooks made by terrorist recruits in training, including diagrams relating to weapons, explosives, and targets, and diagrams showing the goals of global jihad. The students and their teachers seem not to be terribly literate or even knowledgeable about Islam, but the details of weapons and their uses are chillingly accurate.

Rapoport, David C. "The Fourth Wave: September 11 in the History of Terrorism." *Current History*, December 2001, pp. 419–424. Terrorism can be viewed as having undergone four phases or "waves" since the time of the French Revolution. The first wave was that of militant anarchism and revolution in the 19th century, such as against czarist Russia. The second wave, from the 1920s to 1960s, represented efforts to violently free colonies from European domination. The third wave was marked by sophisticated guerrilla tactics (such as with the Vietcong) and left-wing cell-based organizations such as the Weather Underground and Red Brigades. The fourth wave, beginning in the late 1970s, is marked by religious rather than secular political ideology, and it will prove difficult to counteract.

Ross, Jeffrey Ian. "A Model of the Psychological Causes of Oppositional Political Terrorism." *Peace and Conflict: Journal of Peace Psychology*, vol. 2, no. 2, 1996, pp. 129–141. The author develops a psychological model for terrorism. Involvement in terrorism begins with frustration generating aggression in individuals who go through a process of becoming affiliated with a group that is perceived to fulfill their needs. Once in the group, the individual has opportunities to learn terrorist methods and receives positive reinforcement or punishment. Terrorists are not simply crazy but rationally choose what they see as cost-effective ways of carrying out their agenda.

Rumrill, Clark. "Tribal Conflicts: What to Do?" *Christian Science Monitor*, July 17, 1996, p. 19. Conflicts between tribes bound together by ethnicity, religion, culture, race, or clan are often volatile and can erupt into terrorist violence. The author provides guidelines for U.S. citizens who must deal with such conflicts. They should avoid taking sides or even appearing to favor one side. Traditional U.S. values of assimilation and egalitarianism can make it hard for U.S. citizens to understand the tribal perspective and the intensity of motivations of tribal conflict. If punitive force is used by peacekeepers, it should be seen as the consequence of behavior, not an attack on any group's identity.

Schafer, John R., and Joe Navarro. "The Seven Stage Hate Model: The Psychopathology of Hate Groups." *FBI Law Enforcement Bulletin*, vol. 72, March 2003, p. 1 ff. The fight against domestic terrorism often involves the analysis of hate groups, but little is known of the psychodynamics that feed such groups. The authors suggest a seven-stage model to explain how hate-group members define themselves, target victims, then taunt them, attack them without weapons, and finally use weapons. The use of symbol and ritual is also explored; the main examples are drawn from studies of skinhead groups.

Talbot, Rhiannon. "Myths in the Representation of Women Terrorists." *Eire—Ireland*, Fall 2000–2001, pp. 165ff. A study of differences between how women terrorists are portrayed in the media and popular culture and how they have seen themselves and their activities. Generally, these portrayals have tried to separate "positive" concepts of womanhood from terrorism by minimizing the importance of women's political involvement and ascribing women's involvement in terrorism to their following the lead of men. Meanwhile, the relatively few women terrorists guilty of cold-blooded murder are tagged as "un-feminine," thus creating the "separation of 'real' women from 'real' terrorists."

Annotated Bibliography

Tierney, Michael. "Young, Gifted, and Ready to Kill." *Herald (Glasgow, UK)*, August 3, 2002, p. 8. Accounts of three young women recruits for the al-Aqsa Martyrs Brigade—a strange mixture of the "universal teenager" and committed terrorists who can be called upon any time to blow themselves up. Although still a minority, there have been a growing number of female suicide bombers.

INTERNET DOCUMENTS

Ganor, Boaz. "Defining Terrorism: Is One Man's Terrorist Another Man's Freedom Fighter?" International Policy Institute for Counterterrorism. Available online. URL: http://www.ict.org.il/articles/define.htm. Downloaded on August 15, 2003. Written by the director of the International Policy Institute for Counterterrorism, this paper explores definitions of terrorism and distinctions between terrorism and guerrilla warfare. It derives a definition of terrorism as the intentional use of, or threat to use, violence against civilians or against civilian targets, in order to attain political aims.

———. "Terror as a Strategy of Psychological Warfare." International Policy Institute for Counterterrorism. Available online. URL: http://www.ict.org.il (search for this particular article). Posted on July 15, 2002. The author, the director of the institute, emphasizes the essential psychological component of the terrorist's method and agenda. Terrorists are trying to induce paralysis or irrational behavior in the population, such as fear and risk aversion out of proportion of the actual probability of harm. This psychological effect must be taken into account as part of counterterrorist strategy. The target community must be helped to respond more rationally to the terrorist threat, and the media should be encouraged to keep things in perspective and not focus too much on details of carnage.

Ruqaiyah, Abu. "The Islamic Legitimacy of the 'Martyrdom Operations.'" International Policy Institute for Counterterrorism. Available online. URL: http://www.ict.org.il (click on links "International Terrorism," "Terrorist Organization Profiles;" "Hamas," and then find the article title listed under "Hamas—Articles" at the bottom of the page). Posted on January 1, 1997. An article originally from an Australian Islamic periodical presents a justification for "martyrdom" as opposed to suicide. According to the author, the Koran condemns suicide committed for base motives such as impatience or desperation, but actions done to further the will of Allah are not suicide, even if the actor must die as a result.

Schweitzer, Yoram. "Suicide Terrorism: Development and Characteristics." International Policy Institute for Counterterrorism. Available online. URL: http://www.ict.org.il (search for this particular article). Posted on April 21, 2000. In this lecture the author describes the distinguishing characteristics of modern suicide terrorism and recounts its development by several groups: Hezbollah, the LTTE (Tamil Tigers), radical Palestinian groups, and others. The last paragraph points in a chilling way to the later events of September 11, 2001.

REGIONAL DEVELOPMENTS

Northern Ireland

BOOKS

Bell, J. Bowyer. *Back to the Future: The Protestants and a United Ireland.* Dublin, Ireland: Poolbeg, 1996. A detailed study of the Irish Protestants and their worldview and perspective on themselves, their Catholic opponents, and the Irish state.

———. *IRA, 1968–2000: An Analysis of a Secret Army.* Portland, Ore.: Frank Cass Publications, 2000. Illuminates the workings of the IRA (Irish Republican Army) and the Northern Ireland struggle as seen through the eyes of the IRA and its opponents and based on hundreds of interviews.

———. *The Secret Army: The IRA.* 3d revised ed. New Brunswick, N.J.: Transaction Publishers, 1997. A detailed history of the Irish Republican movement and the IRA from 1916 to the 1990s, which are described as "the armed struggle transformed" and "the endgame."

Bruce, Steve. *The Edge of the Union: The Ulster Loyalist Political Vision.* New York: Oxford University Press, 1994. The author suggests that the position of the Ulster Unionists is becoming more intractable as they become increasingly isolated in the ongoing dialogue for peace in Northern Ireland. This marginalization and feeling of betrayal, together with the intractably ethnic nature of the conflict, make the prospects for a lasting peace settlement problematic.

Coogan, Tim Pat. *The IRA.* Revised and updated ed. New York: Palgrave Macmillan, 2002. A detailed but readable history of the IRA through the 1990s. It shows the ebb and flow of the organization's influence in relation to key political events, such as the treaty of Irish independence (1922), Nazi overtures during World War II, and the Bloody Sunday massacre in 1972 that revived the dormant IRA in an atmosphere of public outrage against the British. Key leaders and factional struggles within the Republican movement also receive detailed consideration.

Dillon, Martin. *The Dirty War.* New York: Routledge, 1999. A detailed account of the gruesome secret war between the British security forces and the Provisional Irish Republican Army (PIRA) during the 1970s and 1980s. As the PIRA carried out a bombing campaign in the hope of making the country ungovernable, British agencies deployed secret, illegal death squads who hunted down and murdered PIRA operatives. The PIRA responded by rooting out suspected informers, often with a bullet to the head. The implications for the limits of counterterrorism in a democratic society are disturbing.

———. *God and the Gun: The Church and Irish Terrorism.* New York: Routledge, 1998. A journalist who worked for 18 years in Northern Ireland describes the religious roots of the conflict and how historic grievances continue to motivate the violence, explored through interviews with both religious and laypeople. He argues that both religious and political leaders have failed in their moral duty to bring an end to the conflict.

———. *The Shankill Butchers.* New York: Routledge, 1999. American edition of an exposé of a Northern Ireland loyalist group that brutally murdered Catholics in Belfast. The group, which was affiliated with the paramilitary Ulster Volunteer Force (UVF), was led by Lenny Murphy, whom the author describes as a psychopath and the worst mass murderer in British history. The bitter strife between Protestants and Catholics both helped shape Murphy's rage and gave him cover to carry out his killings in a milieu where the ordinary restraints of law were not present. Murphy was eventually killed by the IRA.

English, Richard. *Armed Struggle: The History of the IRA.* New York: Oxford University Press, 2003. The author provides extensive background to help readers understand the complex aftermath of the 1998 Good Friday Agreement, where the mainstream IRA committed itself to the peace process while the militant provisionals essentially split off. The author suggests that the IRA's turning toward a campaign of violence in 1969 had marked a tragic and unproductive digression from a possible political solution.

Feldman, Allen. *Formations of Violence: The Narrative of the Body and Political Terror in Northern Ireland.* Chicago: University of Chicago Press, 1991. The author weaves oral histories from participants and victims in the Northern Ireland conflict with analysis of the narratives based on postmodernist principles and the politics of the body. The historical content is useful even for readers who do not wish to tackle the analysis.

Malone, Ed. *A Secret History of the IRA.* New York: W. W. Norton, 2003. This controversial account focuses on the activities of the conflict's most complex figure, Gerry Adams. Although Adams is best known to the world as the political face of the IRA, the author suggests that he has worked steadily and subtly to outmaneuver the militant group, possibly even tipping off the British to IRA operations while furthering the peace process and his own agenda.

McKittrick, David, and David McVea. *Making Sense of the Troubles: The Story of the Conflict in Northern Ireland.* Chicago: New Amsterdam Books, 2002. A clear overview of the conflict between Catholic and Protestant groups in Northern Ireland since the 1960s. A chronology and glossary help readers make sense of the often complex sequences of events.

O'Day, Alan, and Yonah Alexander, eds. *Dimensions of Irish Terrorism.* New York: G. K. Hall, 1994. A collection of 22 scholarly articles on several aspects of Irish terrorism (both Republican and Loyalist or Unionist). Topics include the causes of terrorist violence in Ireland, attitudes of participants, the contending groups, the impact of terrorism on the general society, and the attempts to contain or resolve the underlying crisis.

Sands, Bobby. *Bobby Sands: Writings from Prison.* Boulder, Colo.: Roberts Rinehart, 1997. Sands, the leader of IRA prisoners in Belfast's Long Kesh Prison, describes brutal treatment, prison conditions, and the hunger strike that would eventually kill him and nine other prisoners. Sands became a celebrated martyr-hero to the IRA cause. The book invites the reader to consider whether prisoners who had been convicted of brutal terrorism should themselves be terrorized by the state.

Taylor, Peter. *Behind the Mask: The IRA and Sinn Fein.* TV Books, 1997. A journalist who has spent nearly 30 years covering the "Troubles" in Northern Ireland based this book on his television documentary. He was given extensive and unprecedented access to key figures in the IRA and its political wing, Sinn Féin, thus allowing readers access to the frank opinions of people who have devoted their lives to a violent struggle.

Tonge, Jonathan. *Northern Ireland: Conflict and Change.* Upper Saddle River, N.J.: Prentice-Hall, 2002. Although this survey includes adequate historical background, it emphasizes recent events, particularly the Good Friday Agreement and the subsequent rocky peace process that was threatened by the issue of "decommissioning" weapons.

ARTICLES AND PAPERS

Hoge, Warren. "Blair Says Ulster Peace Hinges on IRA." *New York Times,* April 24, 2003, p. A11. British Prime Minister Tony Blair challenges the IRA to live up to its commitment and finally break with its violent tradition. Language offered by the IRA in exchange for consideration of issues raised by Sinn Féin had proved disappointing to the British. Blair is asking for a more specific renunciation of violence and a definite process or "decommissioning" weapons or putting them "beyond use."

———. "Sinn Féin Leader Pledges Full Disarmament of the IRA." *New York Times,* April 28, 2003, p. A2. In apparent reply to British demands, Gerry Adams of Sinn Féin offers to disarm if other parties (such as David Trimble's Unionists) also meet their obligations.

"In the Shadow of War Is Hope for Peace: The Terrorist Attacks in the U.S. Have Become the Driving Force Behind a Push to Disarm in Northern Ireland." *Time International,* vol. 158, November 5, 2001, pp. 66ff. The worldwide shock waves from the September 11, 2001, attacks have had a surprising and positive effect on the search for peace in Northern Ireland. The growing revulsion against terrorism is discrediting militant efforts and encouraging those seeking a political settlement of the conflict. The IRA is expressing willingness to "decommission" its weapons.

Openheimer, A. R. "The Countdown Begins." *Bulletin of the Atomic Scientists,* vol. 58, May–June 2002, pp. 13ff. Reports on the implementation of the procedure for "decommissioning" weapons, the factional divisions within the IRA, and the increasingly chilly attitude toward the IRA following September 11, 2001, which put more pressure on the radical Republicans to disarm. Possible attacks by the radical "real IRA" and resistance of extreme Unionists to disarmament is continuing, however, to pose obstacles.

Paul, Annie Murphy. "Dispatch from Derry." *Psychology Today,* vol. 31, November–December 1998, p. 28ff. While the April 1998 signing of a Northern Ireland peace agreement may be a hopeful sign, the psychological effects of having lived with pervasive violence and death for generations may be harder to overcome than even the political obstacles. The Catholic and Protestant cultural identities are deeply ingrained, as are the ways of keeping distance between the groups. Further, those people who have committed terrorism and are now being released on amnesty may be unable to adjust to peace.

Stevenson, Jonathan. "The Long Spoons of Ulster." *The National Interest,* Summer 2002, pp. 89ff. Following the September 11, 2001, attacks on the United States, many governments facing nationalist-inspired terrorists felt increasing urgency to try to achieve peaceful settlements before these indigenous groups forged links with the global "new terrorism" typified by al-Qaeda. The peace process in Northern Ireland has proceeded slowly, but it has been a bumpy ride. The United States asserted increased pressure on the IRA when several of its members were found to be helping train the Colombian FARC guerrillas. The author lays out what he considers to be requirements for any lasting agreement between the IRA and the Unionists.

INTERNET DOCUMENTS

"Index of/Politics/INAC." The Etext Archives. Available online. URL: http://www.etext.org/Politics/INAC/. Downloaded on August 15, 2003. Directory of "e-text" (electronic text) documents relating to Northern Ireland and the Troubles. Click on document titles to read.

"Irish History on the Web." Irish Jokes: An Alternative Web Site (personal site of Henry Kirwan). Available online. URL: http://www.users.bigpond. com/kirwilli/history/history.htm. Updated on August 2, 2003. Provides a number of useful links to resources relating to Irish history. Of particular interest for students of terrorism is the page linked under "The North and 'The Troubles.'"

"The Northern Ireland Conflict." Conflict Archive on the Internet Web Service (CAIN). Available online. URL: http://cain.ulst.ac.uk/index.html. Downloaded on August 13, 2003. This site is created by the CAIN (Conflict Archive on the Internet) Web Service. It provides extensive background and links concerning the conflict in Northern Ireland from 1968 to the present. Includes a searchable bibliographic database, glossary, list of acronyms, description of organizations, and much more.

"Sinn Féin." Sinn Féin web site. Available online. URL: http://www. sinnfein.ie/. Downloaded on August 7, 2003. Web site for the political arm of the Irish Republican movement, including background and position papers relating to peace negotiations.

Europe

BOOKS

Alexander, Yonah, and Dennis A. Pulshinsky, eds. *Europe's Red Terrorists: The Fighting Communist Organizations*. Portland, Ore.: Frank Cass Publications, 2000. Profiles left-wing European revolutionary groups such as the Red Army Faction and Red Brigades.

Alexander, Yonah, Herbert M. Levine, and Michael S. Swetnam. *ETA: Profile of a Terrorist Group*. Ardsley, N.Y.: Transnational Publishers, 2001. A profile of the Basque terrorist group Euskadi Ta Askatasuna, or ETA, including its origins, ideology, rhetoric, organization and activities, as well as its relationship to issues in recent European history.

Brinks, Jan Herman. *Children of a New Fatherland: Germany's Post-War Right-Wing Politics*. New York: St. Martin's Press, 2000. A collection of essays describing and analyzing the rise of a new right-wing politics in a reunited Germany in which divisions and new stresses from immigration persist.

Chalk, Peter. *West European Terrorism and Counter-Terrorism: The Evolving Dynamic*. New York: St. Martin's Press, 1996. Discusses the development of terrorism in Western Europe since the 1960s and the latest response of the European Union to terrorism, the "Maastricht Third Pillar." The author expresses concerns about the lack of accountability and public participation in the process of developing security and counterterrorism policies. This is part of a comprehensive critique of antiterrorism from a liberal democratic prospective.

Dartnell, Michael Y. *Action Directe: Ultra-Left Terrorism in France, 1979–1987.* Portland, Ore.: Frank Cass Publications, 1995. The author uses the story of this leftist French terrorist group to refine a more complex definition of terrorism. The group is placed within a tradition of French revolutionary "gauchiste" violence.

"Giorgio." *Memoirs of an Italian Terrorist.* New York: Carroll & Graf, 2003. An anonymous firsthand account of the Red Brigades and their bloody struggle during the 1970s. The narrator describes his gradual involvement in the underground life of a terrorist and the methodical way in which the group stalked and attacked its targets.

Kassimeris, George. *Europe's Last Red Terrorists: The Revolutionary Organization 17 November.* New York: New York University Press, 2001. A history and analysis of Greece's idiosyncratic left-wing terrorist group. The author believes the organization was so driven by personal motivations and emotion that it never achieved a coherent ideology or widespread popular support.

Naimark, Norman M. *Fires of Hatred: Ethnic Cleansing in Twentieth-Century Europe.* Cambridge, Mass.: Harvard University Press, 2002. Much terrorism in Europe has been inspired by bitter ethnic conflicts; the mid-1990s bloodbath in the Balkans is a reminder that such conflicts cannot be relegated to the first half of the century. The author offers a comparative study including the 1915 Armenian genocide, early Nazi campaigns against the Jews, Stalin's deportations, and the 1990s conflicts in Bosnia and Kosovo.

Proll, Astrid, ed. *Baader-Meinhof: Pictures on the Run 67–77.* Zurich: Scalo Verlag, 1998. Proll, who had become involved with the Red Army Faction (Baader-Meinhof Gang) in the 1970s, has assembled photographs and essays depicting the group's violent life. In retrospect she believes that the group "overestimated itself ridiculously."

ARTICLES AND PAPERS

Berger, Deidre. "Beyond Skinheads, Germany's Far Right Forms a Political Base." *Christian Science Monitor,* March 27, 1998, p. 7. Reports that right-wing parties such as France's National Front, Austria's Freedom Party, and the German League of Free Citizens are growing in power and may create a climate that encourages right-wing terrorism. Their appeal combines nationalism, anti-immigrant sentiment, and racism.

"Dangerous Stalemate: Spain and the Basques." *The Economist (U.S.),* vol. 368, July 5, 2003, p. 45. Summarizes the current status of and issues for Spain's Basque minority. Two mainstream parties, one conservative and one socialist, more or less support the status quo—a Basque region that has considerable local autonomy but remains part of Spain. The Basque nationalist party wants independence but has an ambivalent attitude toward the use of terrorism.

Ford, Peter. "Xenophobia Follows U.S. Terror: Amnesty International Says Government Curbs on Immigration Are Adding to the Anti-Arab Backlash." *Christian Science Monitor*, October 11, 2001, p. 4. Reports that both popular opinion and stringent new government rules in the wake of the September 11 attacks on the United States may be fueling violent reactions against Arabs and other immigrants.

Gutierrez, Miren. "Terror in the Pyrenees." *The Nation*, March 25, 2002, pp. 20–23. Although the Basque terrorist group ETA is still carrying on its violent campaign, it is losing legitimacy because Spanish authorities have been allowing the Basque region increasing autonomy and cultural expression. ETA uses ransom kidnappings as a major fund-raising tool, using the proceeds to finance assassinations and bombings. A brief truce between ETA and the authorities collapsed in 1999; following September 2001 the pace of government arrests of ETA units increased. An effective process toward Basque self-determination may make ETA irrelevant.

"Here's a Road Map, Perhaps; Spain and its Basques." *The Economist (U.S.)*, vol. 368, August 16, 2003, p. 46ff. Reports on the latest initiative by the Basque Nationalist party (PNV) to turn the Basque region into "a free state associated with Spain." Jose Aznar, Spain's prime minister, considers the plan to be a non-starter. The current state of popular opinion is also summarized.

Lloyd, John. "Paving the Way for the Red Brigades: The Economy Is Falling, Unemployment Is Up." *New Statesman*, vol. 131, August 19, 2002, p. 16ff. As Italians become disenchanted with right-wing premier Silvio Berlusconi, radical leftist groups may have an opportunity to push their way back onto the political stage. This may include descendants of the original Red Brigades terrorists.

O'Grady, Desmond. "The Wrong Targets: The Rise and Decline of Italian Terrorism." *America*, vol. 186, February 18, 2002, p. 19. A historical survey of terrorism by political extremists in Italy in the 1970s and 1980s. The events surrounding the kidnapping and killing of Italian Prime Minister Aldo Moro are recounted. Leftist (communist) and rightist (neofascist) extremists used each other as excuses for their acts of violence. The leftists in particular found support in the intellectual fashions of the time. Eventually the acceptance of a wider range of players in the political process diminished the urge toward terrorism.

Sciolino, Elaine, and Desmond Butler. "Europeans Fear that the Threat from Radical Islamists Is Increasing." *New York Times*, December 8, 2002, p. 32ff. Reports increased anxiety that European countries may be targeted by al-Qaeda. Extensive international terrorist networks are being uncovered in France and other European countries, but information about specific targets or plans is scant. There have also been investigations and arrests in Germany and the Netherlands.

"Terror Returns?" *The Economist (U.S.)*, vol. 351, May 29, 1999, p. 50. Reports speculation following the killing of an adviser to the Italian government that the Red Brigades terrorists, active during the 1970s, may have returned. It is unclear how large the new group using the old name may be, and whether any of the old terrorists are part of it. The manifesto issued following the killing does echo language used by earlier leftist writings, but conspiracy theories abound as to the real nature of the killers.

INTERNET DOCUMENTS

"Books About Terrorism and Human Rights in Europe." 100megsfree5.com Available online. URL: http://hotburrito.100megsfree5.com/books/ terroreurope.html. Downloaded on August 17, 2003. A well-organized and useful list that provides links to Amazon.com entries for books on terrorism and human rights in Europe.

"The Struggle of the Basque Country with the Spanish State." Basque-Red.net. Available online. URL: http://www.basque≠red.net/eng/links/ e-eheng/ehee.htm. Downloaded on August 17, 2003. A pro-nationalist page with links to history and images of the Basque conflict, atrocities committed against the Basques, arrests and repression, and related topics.

Israel and Palestine

BOOKS

Alexander, Yonah. *Palestinian Secular Terrorism: Profiles of Fatah, Popular Front for the Liberation of Palestine, Popular Front for the Liberation of Palestine-General Command, and Democratic Front for the Liberation of Palestine.* Ardsley, N.Y.: Transnational Publishers, 2003. Profiles of the major secularly oriented Palestinian terrorist groups, including the original Fatah founded by Yasir Arafat and smaller component groups of the Palestine Liberation Organization. The history, organization, ideology, and activities of each group are described.

———. *Palestinian Religious Terrorism: Hamas and Islamic Jihad.* Ardsley, N.Y.: Transnational Publishers, 2002. This volume profiles the two major religious Palestinian terrorist groups, explaining their ideology, organization, tactics, and activities.

Bell, J. Bowyer, ed. *Terror Out of Zion: The Fight for Israeli Independence*. New Brunswick, N.J.: Transaction Publishers, 1996. A definitive work on the 1943–48 period during which two Jewish extremist groups, the Irgun and the Lehi, conducted a terrorist campaign against the British occupation and then fought against Arabs who had attacked the nascent Jewish state.

Bickerton, Ian J., and Carla L. Klausner. *A Concise History of the Arab-Israeli Conflict*. 4th ed. Upper Saddle River, N.J.: Pearson Education, 2001. A comprehensive, impartial and well-illustrated textbook giving background on a century or so of conflict in Israel and Palestine, including the current peace process and its problems.

Katzman, Kenneth. *The PLO and Its Factions*. Washington, D.C.: Congressional Research Service, 2002. Also available online. URL: http://www. fas.org/man/crs/RS21235.pdf. Describes the Palestine Liberation Organization (PLO) and its component organizations, including the Fatah movement. Their role in the current Palestinian uprising (Intifada) since 2000 is discussed. The group most closely associated with terrorism is the al-Aqsa Martyrs Brigades.

Leavitt, June O. *Storm of Terror: A Hebron Mother's Diary*. Chicago, Ill.: Ivan R. Dee, 2002. A poignant account by an American turned Jewish settler as she faces daily random terrorist attacks. Over an 18-month period she and her family witness the apparent disintegration of hopes for peace.

Pearlman, Wendy. *Occupied Voices: Stories of Everyday Life from the Second Intifada*. New York: Thunder's Mouth Press, 2003. A Jewish doctoral student gives her account of six months of living among "ordinary" Palestinian people in the land controlled by Israeli forces. She lets 27 Palestinians voice their suffering and bitterness with the daily humiliations and dangers of Israeli occupation. A common theme is their sense of hopelessness yet refusal to give up what they see as the struggle for their basic rights.

Reporters Without Borders. *Israel/Palestine: The Black Book*. Sterling, Va.: Pluto Press, 2003. A compilation of accounts of human rights violations by both Israelis and Palestinians, taken from the reports of human rights groups such as Amnesty International and Human Rights Watch.

ARTICLES AND PAPERS

Avnery, Uri. "Abu Against Abu: Not Merely a Clash of Egos, but an Existential Question." *Washington Report on Middle East Affairs*, vol. 22, June 2003, pp. 9ff. The author suggests that the current power struggle between Abu Amar (better known as Yasir Arafat) and Abu Mazen, the new leader of the nascent Palestinian state, is a clash between two profound realities about the Palestinian situation. Arafat has had moral authority as the leader of the Palestinian struggle for decades. Mazen has little basis among the people, but vital connections to outside forces, particularly the United States. At the heart of the struggle is the question of whether the Intifada in which thousands have died represents a tragic waste and a failure or, rather, is finally on the verge of success. The question is whether Arafat's struggle and Mazen's efforts at state-building can cooperate.

Blanche, Ed. "Arafat Grapples with HIS 'Young Guard': The Emerging Power Struggle Within the Palestinian Leadership May Signal the End of Yasser Arafat's 50 Year Reign." *The Middle East*, September 2002, pp. 16ff. Both external pressures (such as from the United States and Israel) and Palestinians' own desire for reform are forcing Arafat to change his security apparatus, but he is being challenged by younger, more militant leaders. It is unknown whether these changes will actually allow the Palestinian leadership to stop the ongoing terrorist attacks or will instead ignite a Palestinian civil war.

Dickey, Christopher. "Inside Suicide, Inc." *Newsweek*, April 15, 2002, pp. 26–32. Details how suicide bombers in Gaza and the West Bank are recruited and trained, and how their families are rewarded. A raid on Yasir Arafat's headquarters yielding chillingly mundane ledgers listing costs for bomb-making supplies. The technique of suicide bombing tends to flourish only when there are strong, intractable motivations. Unfortunately, Israeli occupation and reaction to the attacks tends to perpetuate the conditions that facilitate recruitment of more bombers.

Fields-Meyer, Thomas. "United in Grief: Sharing the Same Land but Worlds Apart, Two Families—One Israeli, One Palestinian—Long for Peace After Each Loses a Child to an Act of Rage." *People Weekly*, vol. 48, July 7, 1997, pp. 38ff. Explores the way two families on opposite sides of the Arab-Israeli conflict are coping with the loss of children to violence. The diary of young Bat-Chen, found after her death, speaks poignantly of love and war far beyond her years. Helmi Shousha, an 11-year-old Palestinian killed by a security guard at a Jewish settlement, provides a bone marrow transplant for his ailing sister.

Gellman, Barton, and Laura Blumenfeld. "Portrait of an Assassin." *Washington Post National Weekly Edition*, November 20–26, 1995, p. 9. Portrait of Yigel Amir, who assassinated Israeli prime minister Yitzhak Rabin. It is disturbing to many Israelis that Amir came from an Orthodox upbringing and used careful reasoning from the Torah to justify killing Rabin, who had decided to surrender Israeli control of the West Bank. Amir's rejection by his fiancée may have triggered the final deed.

Prusher, Ilene R. "Budget Weddings by Hamas." *Christian Science Monitor*, July 27, 1998, pp. 1, 7. The Islamic extremist group Hamas, better known in the West for terrorist attacks, has begun promoting its public image by sponsoring low-cost weddings for Palestinians. Hamas has provided a variety of other social services in what it sees as a culture war against decadent Western practices.

INTERNET DOCUMENTS

"Israeli-Palestinian Conflict." Mount Holyoke College, International Relations Program. Available online. URL: http://www.mtholyoke.edu/acad/intrel/me.htm. Downloaded on August 17, 2003. Provides numerous links to online versions of historical documents relating to the conflict, including articles dating from 1896 to 2002 such as agreements, proclamations, letters, memos, and more. There are also links to relevant sources and organizations.

"Roadmap to Solution of Israeli-Palestinian Conflict." U.S. Department of State. Available online. URL: http://usembassy-israel.org.il/publish/press/2003/may/050101.html. Posted on April 30, 2003. The now famous "roadmap" specifies a path to "a permanent two-state solution to the Israeli-Palestinian conflict." Throughout 2003 Israeli and Palestinian authorities have struggled to implement its provisions in the face of ongoing violence. The roadmap combines mutual declarations against violence, confidence-building, building and strengthening of Palestinian security forces, and economic development.

"Sharm El-Sheikh Fact-Finding Committee Final Report." U.S. Department of State, International Information Programs. Available online. URL: http://usinfo.state.gov/regional/nea/mitchell.htm. Posted on April 30, 2001. This report, prepared by the Mitchell Committee, investigates the causes of recent violence in Israel and Palestine and formulates a number of recommended actions for Israeli and Palestinian authorities. The three essential steps, it concludes, are to end the violence, rebuild confidence, and resume negotiations.

Middle East (General)

Note: This section includes Iran and Iraq as well as regional movements and developments. For specific coverage of Afghanistan, see Central Asia. North Africa is included under Africa.

BOOKS

Appleby, R. Scott, ed. *Spokesmen for the Despised: Fundamentalist Leaders of the Middle East.* Chicago: University of Chicago Press, 1997. This collection of essays sponsored by the Fundamentalist Project of the American Academy of Arts and Sciences broadly explores a variety of fundamentalist Islamic, Jewish, and Christian movements in the Middle East. Through profiles of groups and their leaders, the authors examine both the relationship between the movements and their general religious background and the interplay between fundamentalism and social and political forces in the region.

Bergen, Peter. *Holy War, Inc.: Inside the Secret World of Osama bin Laden*. New York: Free Press, 2002. This account comes from a journalist who has painstakingly developed many contacts that he could use to find people who know the people who work with bin Laden. It reveals a broad and deep network in dozens of countries from London to remote parts of Yemen—people who are patient and highly motivated to attack the West.

Cooley, John K. *Unholy Wars: Afghanistan, America, and International Terrorism*. Sterling, Va.: Pluto Press, 1999. Details how the U.S. support for Islamic freedom fighters against the Soviet occupiers in Afghanistan later backfired as the people the United States helped train (including the now-notorious Osama bin Laden) turned their weapons and expertise against the West after defeating the Soviets. The result was a wave of destabilization in nations such as Egypt and Algeria, the conflict in Chechnya, the rise of the Taliban, and terrorist attacks on the United States itself, notably the World Trade Center bombing.

Corbin, Jane. *Al-Qaeda: In Search of the Terror Network that Threatens the World*. New York: Thunder's Mouth Press, 2002. This account is written by a BBC correspondent who has intensively pursued information about Osama bin Laden and al-Qaeda for many years, so much so that, as she explains, "for three years [bin Laden] was my screen saver." There is a strong presentation of background material as well as analysis of recent events from the war in Afghanistan. There are also many interviews with military, intelligence agents, and others who have dealt with bin Laden and al-Qaeda.

Davis, Joyce M. *Between Jihad and Salaam: Profiles in Islam*. New York: St. Martin's Press, 1999. A collection of 17 interviews with influential figures in the Muslim world, including Anwar Haddam of Algeria's Islamic Salvation Front; Hassan al Turabi, considered by some to be a spiritual successor to Ayatollah Khomeini; and Muntassir al Sayat, of a violent jihad faction in Egypt; as well as moderate or liberal leaders such as former Pakistani ambassador to the United States Abida Hussain. Valuable for providing access to the words of people not often heard directly in the West.

Gohari, M. J. *The Taliban: Ascent to Power*. New York: Oxford University Press on Demand, 2001. Describes the origins and doctrine of the Taliban, its rise to power, life in Afghanistan under Taliban rule, and relations between the Taliban, and neighboring countries, the United

Nations, and the United States. Also includes a chapter on Osama bin Laden and his attitudes.

Gold, Dore. *Hatred's Kingdom: How Saudi Arabia Supports the New Global Terrorism*. Washington, D.C.: Regnery Publishing, 2003. A former Israeli ambassador documents in detail what he charges are the extensive connections between the Saudi government and terrorist groups. He includes translations of financial documents and of sermons calling for the destruction of the Jewish state.

Harris, William W. *Faces of Lebanon: Sects, Wars, and Global Extensions*. Princeton, N.J.: Marcus Wiener, 1996. Because Lebanon has been an arena for much terrorist and counterterrorist activity, this overview of Lebanese history is useful for the student of terrorism. Part one is an overview of the religious, ethnic, and other groups whose complex interrelationships have driven much of the country's history. Part two covers that history from the beginning of the French mandate in 1920 to the end of the civil war in 1989. Part three covers the tumultuous struggle leading to the Ta'if agreement and events up to 1996.

Jaber, Hala. *Hezbollah: Born with a Vengeance*. New York: Columbia University Press, 1997. Vividly describes the secretive world of Hezbollah, viewed by many as the prototypical Islamic extremist movement. Explores the evolution of the organization since 1982 and its relationship with Syria and Iran. A prevailing theme is the tremendous devotion Hezbollah followers have to the cause, up to and including martyrdom.

Karawan, Ibrahim A. *The Islamist Impasse*. New York: Oxford University Press, 1997. In this short study the author explains the structure of Islamist movements and the strategies that states have taken in countering or restraining the influence of Islamists. The perspective is then broadened to look at regional political balances and at the response from the West. The conclusion is that the ineffectiveness of self-proclaimed Islamist states and the relatively successful strategies of moderate states have resulted in only limited effectiveness for the Islamic movement.

Katz, Samuel M. *The Hunt for the Engineer: How Israeli Agents Tracked the Hamas Master Bomber*. New York: Fromm International, 1999. A vivid inside account of how Israeli Shin Bet agents played an extended cat-and-mouse game with the Hamas bomb-maker Yehiya *Ayash*. They eventually succeeded in blowing him up with a booby-trapped cell phone.

Olson, Robert W., ed. *The Kurdish Nationalist Movement in the 1990s: Its Impact on Turkey and the Middle East*. Lexington: University Press of Kentucky, 1997. Contains nine studies of the continuing conflict between Kurdish nationalists and the Turkish government, a conflict that is little known in the West but has potentially explosive effects in neighboring countries of the Middle East.

Annotated Bibliography

Spencer, William. *The Middle East*. 9th ed. Guilford, Conn.: McGraw-Hill/Dushkin, 2003. This volume in the Global Studies series provides an overview and historical and country backgrounds for the region plus a selection of articles from the world press.

ARTICLES AND PAPERS

Abdelkarim, Riad Z. "Why Do They Hate Us? The Question That Won't Go Away." *Washington Report on Middle East Affairs*, vol. 21, March 2002, p. 84. Abdelkarim, communications director for the Council on American-Islamic Relations, gives a measured answer: There is no religious justification for the terrorist attacks, which have been condemned by all major American Muslim organizations. Most Muslims and Arabs do not hate America per se; indeed, many would like to immigrate to America. However, there are aspects of American culture, particularly as promoted by the media, which are disliked by many Muslims, and there are a minority of extremists willing to take violent action.

Eickelman, Dale F. "Bin Laden, the Arab 'Street,' and the Middle East's Democracy Deficit." *Current History*, January 2002, pp. 36–39. The author suggests that the widespread lack of democracy and free expression in the region gives the charismatic bin Laden an opportunity to recruit people who see no "legitimate" outlet for their aspirations. Ironically, while bin Laden and his key followers emphatically reject Western values, his organizational and logistical techniques are thoroughly modern. Western leaders such as British prime minister Tony Blair are just starting to engage the "Arab street" in direct dialog in their own language.

Filkins, Dexter. "Shutting Doors in Syria May Not End Militants' Attacks." *New York Times*, July 18, 2003, p. A6. Reports on the closing of the offices of Hamas and Islamic Jihad in Syria. While the Syrian government may have acquiesced to American demands and modified its overt sponsorship of terrorism, it is unclear whether the terrorist groups have stopped operating or are just operating with a lower profile.

Ford, Peter. "Why Do They Hate Us?" *Christian Science Monitor*, September 27, 2001, pp. 1ff. This question was asked by many Americans (including President George W. Bush) following the September 11, 2001, attacks. The author believes a number of decades-old U.S. policies account for much of the anger and resentment toward America in the Middle East. These include Israel's treatment of the Palestinians, sanctions against Iraq, the presence of U.S. troops in the holy places of Saudi Arabia, and the alignment of U.S. interests with repressive or secularist governments in the region. The article includes experiences of U.S. power by individuals and a chronology of U.S. policy in the Middle East.

Fried, Joseph P. "Sheikh and 9 Followers Guilty of a Conspiracy of Terrorism." *New York Times,* October 2, 1995, pp. A1, A11. Reports the conviction of Sheikh Omar Abdel Rahman and nine other militant Muslims for a conspiracy to carry out a terrorist campaign of bombings against the United States and the United Nations, in an attempt to force U.S. officials to stop supporting Israel and Egypt. Includes backgrounds of all 10 conspirators.

Gause, F. Gregory, III. "Be Careful What You Wish For: The Future of U.S.-Saudi Relations." *World Policy Journal,* Spring 2002, pp. 37–50. Relations between the United States and Saudi Arabia have become increasingly strained since September 11, 2001. Many Americans accuse the Saudis of at least tolerating terrorism, if not supporting it outright. However, the Saudi government walks a tightrope between appeasing the United States and domestic Islamic militants. According to the author, increasing U.S. pressure risks pushing Saudi Arabia into the arms of the terrorists; demanding a "free election" might well lead to victory by radical Islamic parties.

Lesch, Ann. "Osama bin Laden's 'Business' in Sudan." *Current History,* May 2002, pp. 203–209. The author suggests that Sudan's policy of welcoming displaced Islamic militants (such as bin Laden) in the early 1990s provided the terrorist leader with time and opportunity to build his international terrorist network. In turn bin Laden's construction activities brought money to help Sudan's leader Hasam al-Turabi to finance his pan-Islamic movement. Eventually, international pressure forced Sudan to expel bin Laden and his followers, who soon reestablished themselves in Afghanistan.

Levitt, Matthew A. "The Political Economy of Middle East Terrorism." *Middle East Review of International Affairs,* vol. 6, December 2002, n.p. Also available online. URL: http://www.ict.org.il (link through al-Qaida). Describes the interrelationship between funding and organization of terrorist activities. However, with increasing pressure on states that have traditionally sponsored terrorism, private organizations (especially charities) are playing a growing role in funding terrorism. "Legitimate" businesses, financial institutions, and criminal organizations also play a part.

Marquand, Robert. "The Tenets of Terror: A Special Report on the Ideology of Jihad and the Rise of Islamic Militancy." *Christian Science Monitor,* October 18, 2001, pp. 1, 10. Provides background on the various sects and movements within Islam and includes a map and summaries of Islamic extremist movements in the Middle East, Africa, and Asia.

McCarthy, Andrew C. "Prosecuting the New York Sheikh." *Middle East Quarterly,* March 1997, n.p. Also available online. URL: http://www.ict.org.il (link from International Terrorism: Terrorist Organization Profiles: Al Gama'a al-Islamiyya). Downloaded on November 25, 2003. The U.S. attorney who led the successful prosecution of Sheikh Umar Abdel Rahman for the (first) World Trade Center bombing and related conspiracies describes the background of Rahman's group and the transplanting of a jihad onto American soil. Includes a chronology.

Miller, Greg, Josh Meyer, and Michael Slackman. "Attack in Saudi Arabia; Security Push Preceded Attacks; Saudi Authorities Failed to Act on Its Requests, the U. S. Says. The Death Toll in Bombings Rises to 34." *Los Angeles Times*, May 15, 2003, p A1. Reports on the continuing impact of an al-Qaeda terror campaign in Saudi Arabia. The United States expressed its frustration with Saudi Arabia denying requests for enhanced security around U.S. facilities in the kingdom, as well as with Saudi leaders' general unwillingness to deal forthrightly with the terrorist infrastructure in their country.

Miller, Judith. "Even a Jihad Has Its Rules." *New York Times*, vol. 147, August 29, 1998, p. A13ff. Islamic terrorists often use doctrines of their faith to justify terrorism as part of a jihad (holy war) against Israel, the United States, and other enemies. But according to Peter J. Awn, professor of religion and Middle Eastern studies at Columbia University, Islam provides the jihad only as a last resort. It is to be declared only by legitimate leaders of the state or top religious leaders, not self-appointed leaders such as Osama bin Laden. The killing of noncombatants (including women and children) is forbidden.

Nedoroscik, Jeffrey A. "Extremist Groups in Egypt." *Terrorism and Political Violence*, vol. 13, no. 1, Summer 2002, pp. 47–76. A historical survey of the development of militant and terrorist groups in Egypt, dating back to the founding of the Muslim Brotherhood in 1928. This group became increasingly radical in the 1950s and 1960s and was increasingly at odds with the Egyptian government; repression caused more radical groups to spin off. The relationship between economic development and unrest in Upper Egypt is also explored in detail.

Tyre, Peg, Tara Pepper, and Mark Hosenball. "Meet the bin Ladens: They Had It All: Money, Power—and Now the Most Wanted Man on Earth. A Family Affair." *Newsweek*, October 15, 2001, p. 55. A profile of the bin Laden family, Saudis who mainly became secularized (and wealthy) businesspersons. The exception, Osama, was once viewed by the family as a "black sheep," according to the authors, but now the family is "shattered, feels abused, feels tortured."

INTERNET DOCUMENTS

"Al Qaeda Training Manual." U.S. Department of Justice. Available online. URL: http://www.usdoj.gov/ag/trainingmanual.htm. Updated on October 8, 2002. A training manual found on a computer by Manchester, England, police, later translated into English and introduced as evidence in the trial of the African embassy bombers. Some portions were excluded in order to not provide useful information to would-be terrorists.

Bin Laden, Osama, and John Miller. "Talking with Terror's Banker." *ABC News* transcript. Available online. URL: http://more.abcnews.go.com/ sections/world/dailynews/terror_980609.html. Posted on August 20, 1998. In an interview, Osama bin Laden defends the violent struggle (jihad) against the United States and its allies. He says that his goal is to "purify Muslim land of all non-believers" and claims that events show that America lacks the will to fight a protracted war. It is interesting to compare these statements with those made on the tapes produced subsequent to September 11, 2001.

Erlich, Reuven. "State-Sponsored Terrorism: Terrorism as a Preferred Instrument of Syrian Policy." International Policy Institute for Counterterrorism. Available online. URL: http://www.ict.org.il (search for this particular article). Posted on October 10, 2001. An updated study of the use of the "terror weapon" by Syria since the death of president Hafez Assad. During the 1990s Syria began to pursue terrorism indirectly through "contractors" in order to be able to simultaneously pursue advantageous diplomacy. This trend would continue during the post September 11, 2001, "war on terrorism." The article discusses details of ongoing Syrian support for terrorist groups including Hamas, Hezbollah, and the Kurdistan Workers' Party (PKK).

Johnson, David. "Who Is Osama bin Laden?" Infoplease.com. Available online. URL: http://www.infoplease.com/spot/osamabinladen.html. Downloaded on August 18, 2003. A concise summary of bin Laden's life and terrorist activity with related links.

"Kurdistan Worker's Party" (PKK). International Policy Institute for Counterterrorism. Available online. URL: http://www.ict.org.il (search for this particular article). Downloaded on August 13, 2003. A profile of the organization including history and developments through the late 1990s.

Robson, Barbara. "Iraqi Kurds: Their History and Culture." Culture Orientation web site. Available online. URL: http://www.culturalorientation. net/kurds/index.html. Posted in 1996. Prepared for refugee aid workers, this profile describes the geographical, historical, and cultural background of the Iraqi Kurds. Includes a bibliography.

Shahar, Yael. "Osama bin Ladin: Marketing Terrorism." International Policy Institute for Counterterrorism. Available online. URL: http://www. ict.org.il (linked under International Terrorism, Terrorist Organizations, and then Al-Qa'ida). Posted on August 22, 1998. Describes multimillionaire terrorist Osama bin Laden as representing "the terrorist as entrepreneur"—applying entrepreneurial planning, management, and marketing principles to delivering the "product" of terrorism.

Annotated Bibliography

"Terrorism 2002: The Strategic Environment." International Policy Institute for Counterterrorism (ICT). Available online. URL: http://www.ict.org.il (linked under International Terrorism, Terrorist Organizations, Hizballah—Articles Hizballah). Posted on March 15, 2003. This paper from an ICT conference focuses on the activities of Hizballah (Hezbolleh). Since Israeli withdrawal from Lebanon in 2000, this organization has grown in strength. Graphs are used to compare numbers of Hizballah attacks (mostly shelling) in 2000, 2001, and 2002. The author suggests that while Iran provides a great deal of support to Hizballah, the role of Syria may be even more significant; Syria has been shipping longer-range rockets to Hizballah for bombarding Israeli installations from as much as 30 kilometers away.

Africa

BOOKS

Ciment, James. *Algeria: The Fundamentalist Challenge.* New York: Facts On File, 1997. Comprehensive background to the conflict that arose in Algeria in 1992 when the government refused to recognize an election won by fundamentalist political groups. The ensuing conflict has involved both terrorist atrocities by fundamentalist extremists and severe repression by the government.

Crenshaw, Martha, Alan O'Day, and Yonah Alexander, eds. *Terrorism in Africa.* New York: G. K. Hall, 1997. A collection of essays dealing with the causes and development of terrorism in Africa. Topics discussed include the 1976 Entebbe aircraft hijacking and rescue, the development of guerrilla insurgencies (including the Mau Mau rebellion of the 1950s), and a variety of contributions dealing with South African topics, including the relationship between apartheid, terrorism, and the legal system.

Dagne, Ted. *Africa and the War on Terrorism.* Washington, D.C.: Congressional Research Service, 2002. A survey of attitudes and degree of cooperation of African nations with the U.S.-led war on terrorism. Africa is expected to become more important as the war in Afghanistan winds down and some al-Qaeda members seek refuge in nations such as Somalia.

———. *Sudan: Humanitarian Crisis, Peace Talks, Terrorism, and U.S. Policy.* Washington, D.C.: Congressional Research Service, 2002. Describes ongoing problems in Sudan, including war, instability, and state-sponsored terrorism.

Mark, Clyde R. *Libya.* Washington, D.C.: Congressional Research Service, 2003. Also available online. URL: http://www.fas.org/man/crs/IB93109.pdf. Updated on August 6, 2003. Describes the history and status of relations among the United States, Libya, and other countries in the region. These relations have been marked by Libyan participation in several serious terrorist attacks, notably the bombing of Pan Am Flight 103 over Lockerbie, Scotland. The legal proceedings and relevant UN resolutions are discussed, as are outstanding issues such as weapons proliferation.

Vines, Alex. *Renamo: Terrorism in Mozambique.* Bloomington: Indiana University Press, 1991. Discusses the chaotic situation in the late 1980s as RENAMO, an anticommunist guerrilla movement backed by South Africa, engaged a marxist government backed by the Soviets. As the South Africans disengaged and underwent their own radical transformation and the Soviet Union disintegrated, the situation became chaotic. It thus serves as a case study in what happens to a guerrilla or terrorist group when its old enemy disappears and the society begins to focus on building democracy.

ARTICLES AND PAPERS

Kaplan, David E. "On Terrorism's Trail." *U.S. News & World Report,* November 23, 1998, p. 30. Reports on the painstaking forensic and intelligence investigation by the FBI following the 1998 bombings of U.S. embassies in Kenya and Tanzania. A massive force of 375 FBI agents and experts poured into East Africa, but the real break came from questioning a man arrested while carrying a phony passport.

Meyer, Josh, and Greg Miller. "At Least 24 Die in Bombings; Blasts Rock Casablanca, Morocco, in Multiple Attacks that Are Blamed on 'International Terrorism'; No U.S. Facilities Are Targeted." *Los Angeles Times,* May 17, 2003, p. A1. Reports on what appears to be a wave of al-Qaeda bombing attacks on Morocco, closely following a similar attack in Saudi Arabia. The attacks have also raised concerns that recent counterterrorism campaigns have not substantially disrupted al-Qaeda's ability to carry out widespread, coordinated terrorist campaigns.

Peterson, Scott. "How Reporters Cheat Assassins in Algeria's War with Islamists." *Christian Science Monitor,* July 24, 1997, p. 8. The conflict in Algeria typifies the dilemma faced by journalists. On the one hand, terrorists sometimes target them as representatives of the establishment. On the other hand, authorities want to control all information and sometimes censor, expel, or even arrest journalists. The ability of a journalist to present an independent point of view often comes into question.

Thom, William. "Africa's Security Issues Through 2010." *Military Review,* July 2000, n.p. Provides a summary and prospects for stability and security in Africa during the coming decade. The decline in great power involvement may lead to more assertion of regional powers, with relatively

strong and prosperous states (such as South Africa or Nigeria) sur-
rounded by unstable states or areas of outright insurgency and civil war.
This development, of course, presents opportunities for the extension of
terrorist groups influence into the area.

INTERNET DOCUMENTS

"Somalia and the War on Terrorism." Washingtonpost.com. Available online.
URL: http://www.washingtonpost.com/wp-srv/world/somalia/front.html.
Download August 15, 2002. Interactive map and links for background on
Somalia including ties to al-Qaeda, the story of "Black Hawk Down," and
possible future U.S. military involvement.

USA Today. "Embassy Bombings." *USA Today* web site. Available online.
URL: http://www.usatoday.com/news/world/bomb000.htm. Updated on
August 7, 1999. Page of links to *USA Today* stories about the bombings of
the U.S. embassies in Kenya and Tanzania.

Central Asia

Note: This section includes Afghanistan, Pakistan, Chechnya, the former
Soviet republics, India, and Sri Lanka.

BOOKS

Ataov, Turkkaya. *Kashmir and Neighbors: Tale, Terror, and Truce*. Burlington,
Vt.: Ashgate, 2003. The author argues that the Kashmir region once had
a common culture that allowed Muslims and Hindus to live together
peaceably. However the Pakistani and Indian governments as well as insurgent groups have fomented their violent agendas, which became a
proxy war between the nuclear-armed powers.

Cronin, Richard P., and Margesson, Rhoda. *Afghanistan: Challenges and Options for Reconstructing a Stable and Moderate State*. Washington, D.C.:
Congressional Research Service, 2002. Also available online. URL:
http://www.fas.org/man/crs/RL31389.pdf. Posted on April 24, 2002. The
first part of this report provides an overview of the history of the modern
Afghan state (and sometimes, non-state) since the 1930s and through the
Soviet occupation and the rise of the Taliban in the 1990s. The second
half discusses the prospects for rebuilding Afghanistan, including both
short-term and long-term efforts and the need to negotiate with many
warlords and factions.

Jones, Owen Bennett. *Pakistan: The Eye of the Storm.* New Haven, Conn.: Yale University Press, 2002. A BBC correspondent with an intimate knowledge of the area assesses the tightrope being walked by Pakistani leader Pervez Musharraf between Islamic extremists and pressure from the United States to suppress terrorism. Jones places this question in the context of bureaucratic structure as well as religious and other forces.

Katman, Kenneth. *Afghanistan: Current Issues and U.S. Policy Concerns.* Washington, D.C.: Congressional Research Service, 2002. An update of events in Afghanistan and an overview of continuing U.S. policy objectives, including stabilization, developing the national army, humanitarian aid, and reconstruction.

LePoer, Barbara Leitch. *Pakistan-U.S. Relations.* Washington, D.C.: Congressional Research Service, 2002 Cooperation between the United States and Pakistan has been vital for the military campaign in Afghanistan and for ongoing counterterrorist operations. This report discusses the pressing issues that affect the overall relationship between the two nations, including nuclear proliferation, the activity of Pakistan-based groups in Kashmir, overall relations with India, and democratization and reform within Pakistan.

Kronstadt, K. Alan. *Pakistan-U.S. Anti-Terrorism Cooperation.* Washington, D.C.: Congressional Research Service, 2003. Also available online. URL: http://www.fas.org/man/crs/RL31624.pdf. Updated on March 28, 2003. Summarizes cooperation of Pakistan with the war on terrorism, U.S. aid to Pakistan, U.S. participation in military and law enforcement efforts against terrorists in the area, intelligence cooperation, and domestic reactions in Pakistan.

Nichol, Jim. *Central Asia's New States: Political Developments and Implications for U.S. Interests.* Washington, D.C.: Congressional Research Service, 2003. Also available online. URL: http://www.fas.org/man/crs/IB93108 .pdf. Updated on April 1, 2003. Describes the changing situation in the central Asian states including the former Soviet republics of Turkmenistan, Kazakhstan, Kyrgyzstan, Tajikistan, and Uzebekistan. Following the September 2001 attacks these states cooperated (somewhat reluctantly at first) with the U.S. war on terrorism and in particular the campaign against the Taliban and al-Qaeda in Afghanistan. The long-term prospects for stability in the region are assessed, along with the need to accommodate Russia's continuing interest in the region and specific problems such as energy resources and potential proliferation of weapons of mass destruction.

Pratap, Anita. *Island of Blood: Frontline Reports from Sri Lanka, Afghanistan, and Other South Asian Flashpoints.* New York: Penguin, 2003. More a memoir than a textbook, an Indian journalist gives vivid accounts of bloody ethnic conflicts and terrorism, with an emphasis on the Tamil Tigers of Sri Lanka.

Rashid, Ahmed. *Taliban: Militant Islam, Oil, and Fundamentalism in Central Asia*. New Haven, Conn.: Yale University Press, 2001. A Pakistani journalist gives an insider's view of the Taliban government, its oppression and corruption (including involvement in the heroin trade), its relationship to Osama bin Laden, and its role in the complex politics of the region.

Vedantam, Shankar. "A Culture Struggles with All That Defines It." *Washington Post*, March 17, 2002, pp. B1, B7. An introduction to Hindu nationalist and revivalist movements such as the Cishwa Hindu Parishad (VHP) that have in recent years targeted Muslim mosques that had been built on ancient Hindu sites.

ARTICLES AND PAPERS

Bennett, Venora. "Why Cast Me as a Criminal?" *The Times (London)*, January 31, 2003, p. 6. An interview with Chechen "freedom fighter" Akhmed Zakayev, whom the Russians once negotiated with as a leader of Chechen insurgents, but is now being pursued for extradition as a terrorist. The Russians accused him of masterminding the seizure of a Moscow theater by young Chechen suicide bombers the previous year, but there are doubts of his involvement. Following September 11, 2001, there appears to be little Western sympathy for the Chechen cause, and the conflict continues to fester.

Bonner, Raymond. "Tamil Guerrillas in Sri Lanka: How They Build Their Arsenal." *New York Times*, March 7, 1998, pp. A1, A5. The activities of the Tamil Tigers, who are waging a bloody insurrection in Sri Lanka (formerly Ceylon), are given as an example of how easy it is for terrorists, revolutionaries, and paramilitary groups to tap into a worldwide, largely unregulated market in small arms. Even heavier weapons such as grenade and missile launchers are readily available. The Tamil Tigers recently bought a large amount of explosives in Ukraine.

Cody, Edward. "Defining Terrorism Tricky for Pakistan." *Washington Post*, January 7, 2002, p. A14. Pakistan President Pervez Musharraf struggles to maintain his alliance with the U.S. antiterrorism effort—and the increased aid it brings—while managing domestic Islamic dissent. He also strives to distinguish between supporting terrorism and supporting the "legitimate" struggle of pro-Pakistani people in disputed Kashmir while trying to accommodate pressure from India and the United States.

Jayasinghe, Amal. "Tigers Emerge from the Shadows: There Are Fresh Hopes for Peace in Sri Lanka as the Island's Separatist Guerrillas Prepare for Talks." *Financial Times*, April 5, 2002, p. 17. Reports on the reopening of a major highway in Sri Lanka following a cease-fire agreement being signed by the government and the Tamil Tigers. However, some government officials believe the Tigers may be using the cease-fire as an opportunity to regroup their forces.

Kilinochchi, Alex Perry. "Tiger Country: Whatever the Outcome of Peace Talks Between Colombo and the Separatist Tigers, a Tamil Nation in all but Law Already Exists in Sri Lanka's Battle-Scarred Northeast." *Time International*, September 23, 2002. Describes the de facto emergence of a separate Tamil state in Sri Lanka, revealed as the world for the first time gains access to the area following the cease-fire. The Tigers have gained considerable support from the Tamil people, but it remains to be seen whether their prowess at war can be translated into ability to govern in peace. A chronology is included.

INTERNET DOCUMENTS

"Afghanistan." Washingtonpost.com. Available online. URL: http://www.washingtonpost.com/wp-srv/world/afghanistan/front.html. Downloaded on August 6, 2003. A basic introduction to Afghanistan and recent events there in connection with the war on terrorism. Includes an interactive map.

Behera, Navnita Chadha. "Kashmir: Redefining the U.S. Role." Brookings Institution Policy Brief #110. Available online. URL: http://www.brookings.edu/dybdocroot/comm/policybriefs/pb110.pdf. Posted in October 2002. The war on terrorism following the September 11, 2001, attacks has added new priority and direction to U.S. efforts to prevent war between India and Pakistan over their competing claims to the Kashmir region. Pakistan president Pervez Musharraf is facing a dilemma: he needs to support U.S. efforts against the Taliban and al-Qaeda in order to maintain U.S. support and counterbalance India, but the "Jihadi" groups connected with terrorism are also an important tool for the struggle to "liberate" Kashmir from India. Meanwhile, if there is to be a lasting peace, India must find some way to accommodate the aspirations of the Kashmiris.

Conetta, Carl. "Strange Victory: A Critical Appraisal of Operation Enduring Freedom and the Afghanistan War." Project on Defense Alternatives. Available online. URL: http://www.comw.org/pda/0201strangevic.html. Posted on January 30, 2002. Tallies up the achievements of the war in Afghanistan and the cost in human lives and damage. Although the Taliban was destroyed and al-Qaeda fragmented, there has been a cost in casualties, in social disruption, and possibly in the exacerbation of regional conflicts. The author asserts that some of these costs might have been avoided by undertaking a more narrowly focused military campaign accompanied by a more robust political and diplomatic effort.

"Pakistan." Washingtonpost.com. Available online. URL: http://www.washingtonpost.com/wp-srv/world/pakistan/front.html. Downloaded on August 15, 2002. Introduction to Pakistan, its support for terrorism and cooperation with the United States, and difficult relations with India. Includes an interactive map.

Swamy, Arun R. "'Déjà Vu All Over Again?' Why Dialogue Won't Solve the Kashmir Dispute." East-West Center, Asian-Pacific Issues No. 56. Available online. URL: http://www.eastwestcenter.org/stored/pdfs/api056.pdf. Posted in November 2001. Because both India and Pakistan have legitimate legal claims to Kashmir and both regimes are politically committed to prevailing, the dispute has proven to be intractable. The historical development of the dispute and the competing claims are examined. For a successful dialogue to take place, India must recognize that the Kashmir situation is of legitimate international concern and that the insurgents have some valid grievances. Pakistan, in turn, must stop fueling the insurgency and attempting to destabilize the region.

Valadi, Nojan. "The Kurds in Iran: From the Mahabad Republic Until Present." Personal web site. Available online. URL: http://www.valadi.com/Kurds.html. Downloaded on August 13, 2003. Provides an overview of the history of the Kurds, particularly in Iran. Includes a bibliography.

East and Southeast Asia

BOOKS

Chandler, David P. *The Tragedy of Cambodian History: Politics, War, and Revolution Since 1945.* New Haven, Conn.: Yale University Press, 1993. Drawing on his experience as a foreign affairs officer, interviews, and historical archives, the author unfolds in great detail the tragic history of Cambodia from the postcolonial years through the bloody excesses of the Pol Pot regime, up to 1979.

Da Cunha, Derek, ed. *Southeast Asian Affairs 1998.* New York: St. Martin's Press, 1998. In the 25th in a series of annual volumes, the authors provide overviews of conflicts and political developments in countries such as Cambodia, Indonesia, Malaysia, Myanmar (Burma), the Philippines, Singapore, Thailand, and Vietnam, as well as an analysis of regional developments.

Nanto, Dick K. *North Korea: Chronology of Provocations, 1950–2003.* Washington, D.C.: Congressional Research Service, 2003. Also available online. URL: http://www.fas.org/man/crs/RL30004.pdf. Downloaded on November 25, 2003. Summarizes North Korean actions that can be viewed as provocations, such as kidnappings, acts of terrorism, bombings, hijackings, incursions, assassination attempts, and nonviolent violations of various treaties.

Nicksch, Larry A. *Korea: Korea-U.S. Relations—Issues for Congress.* Washington, D.C.: Congressional Research Service, 2003. Summarizes current issues in U.S.–North Korean relations, including the nuclear program and nuclear weapons, the missile program, other weapons of mass destruction, and the designation of North Korea as a terrorist-sponsoring state.

ARTICLES AND PAPERS

Cha, Victor D. "Korea's Place in the Axis." *Foreign Affairs*, vol. 81, May–June 2002, p. 79. Following President Bush's declaration that North Korea is part of an "Axis of Evil," the author suggests that this uncompromising rhetoric contradicts the administration's previously announced policy of continuing to seek unconditional negotiations with the isolated communist state. This new "hawk engagement" also contradicts South Korea leader Kim Dae Jung's "sunshine policy," which attempted to address North Korea's perceived feelings of insecurity. The continuing U.S. emphasis on building a missile defense shield is likely to increase that insecurity. The author suggests that the Bush administration needs to focus more on rebuilding positive alliances in the region.

Gill, Bates. "September 11 and Northeast Asia: Change and Uncertainty in Regional Security." *Brookings Review*, vol. 20, Summer 2002, pp. 43ff. Describes changes in U.S. security relationships with Japan, China, and North Korea as a result of the new war on terrorism. Japan, whose military involvements have been limited by constitutional and other constraints, is now contemplating a more robust role for its security forces in guarding against terrorist attacks (such as on U.S. installations in the country). China has generally viewed U.S. efforts more favorably since September 11, 2001, but has remained cautious. Meanwhile, U.S. pressure on North Korea may be starting to pay off.

Malik, J. Mohan. "Dragon on Terrorism: Assessing China's Territorial Gains and Strategic Losses after 11 September." *Contemporary Southeast Asia*, vol. 24, August 2002, pp. 252ff. An extensive overview and analysis of how the war on terrorism and the assertion of U.S. power has altered many strategic balances, including those relating to China and its neighbors. The author argues that China has lost some of its recent gains as "the only great power of Asia," at the expense of such nations as India and Japan.

Mydans, Seth. "Pol Pot, Brutal Dictator Who Forced Cambodians to Killing Fields, Dies at 73." *New York Times*, April 17, 1988, p. 12. Obituary of Pol Pot, the Khmer Rouge leader who perpetrated state terrorism on a massive scale in Cambodia after his takeover of the country in 1975.

His attempt to create a radical change in society through a return to rural life resulted in the death of millions of Cambodians directly or through starvation or exposure.

Sims, Calvyn. "Poison Gas Group in Japan Distances Itself from Guru." *New York Times*, January 19, 2000. Available online. URL: http://www. nytimes.com (search for this article). Reports that the religious cult Aum Shinrikyo says that Shoko Asahara, on trial for masterminding the 1995 nerve gas attack on the Tokyo subway, will no longer be the group's leader although they will continue to follow his teachings. The group claims to be "renewing" itself but is not taking any responsibility for the attack.

INTERNET DOCUMENTS

Hwang, Balbina. "North Korea Deserves to Remain on U.S. List of Sponsors of Terrorism." Heritage Foundation, Backgrounder #1503. Available online. URL: http://www.heritage.org/Research/AsiaandthePacific/BG1503. cfm. Posted on November 19, 2001. Reviews U.S.–North Korean relations and recent events and meetings. Argues that North Korea must still be considered a sponsor of international terrorism, in part because it continues to trade with other recognized terrorist-sponsoring states. The author believes that North Korea must be evaluated in terms of its agreeing to and keeping specific agreements regarding sponsorship of terrorism and arms proliferation. (Since the time of writing, the reactivation of the North Korean nuclear program has become the most prominent issue.)

"U.S. Under Fire Over N. Korea." CNN.com Available online. URL: http://www.cnn.com/2003/US/07/15/nkorea.nukes. Posted on July 16, 2003. With North Korea busily reprocessing its nuclear materials, some experts warn that U.S. policy toward the isolated communist nation is failing, even as six nation talks are set to begin. The article includes links to a timeline and background materials.

Asia-Pacific

BOOKS

Cristalis, Irena. *Bitter Dawn: East Timor: A People's Story*. New York: Zed Books, 2002. A firsthand account of the troubled birth of the new nation of East Timor, which after a bitter insurrection was finally given its independence by Indonesia in 1999, under pressure from the United States and other nations. The region remains unstable, with inroads by Islamic extremists.

Morrison, Charles E., ed. *Asian-Pacific Security Outlook 2003*. Tokyo: Japan Center for International Exchange, available through Brookings Institution Press, 2003. Covers current developments in the region, notably the dispute over North Korea's resurgent nuclear program and the terrorist attacks in Indonesia, particularly the October 2002 Bali bombing. The security perspectives for each major country in the region are explored by a panel of experts.

Niksch, Larry. *Abu Sayyaf: Target of Philippine-U.S. Anti-Terrorism Cooperation*. Washington, D.C.: Congressional Research Service, 2002. An overview of the emerging policy and program for U.S. military aid to the Philippines to fight the Abu Sayyaf guerrilla/terrorist group.

Rabasa, Angel, and Peter Chalk. *Indonesia's Transformation and the Transformation of Southeast Asia*. Santa Monica, Calif.: RAND Corporation, 2001. Describes Indonesia's attempt to develop stable democratic institutions. The authors offer two contrasting scenarios: in one, the efforts meet with success; in the other, "centrifugal disintegration" occurs when the interests of the political elite, the military, and ethnic groups cannot be reconciled. This work is more useful for its background information than for its rather narrow military recommendations.

ARTICLES AND PAPERS

Bello, Walden. "A 'Second Front' in the Philippines: America Called On Its Former Colony to Fill the Bill for a Sequel to al Qaeda" *The Nation*, vol. 274, March 18, 2002, p. 18. A professor of sociology in the Philippines critiques the apparent rush of the U.S. administration to showcase the Philippines as a follow-on battle against al-Qaeda after Afghanistan. The Philippines government under President Arroyo is banking on massive U.S. economic and military aid, but the subsequent military campaign may easily lead to abuses of the population and increased recruitment by insurgents.

Cargata, Warren, et al. "Reprisal in East Timor." *Maclean's*, September 20, 1999, p. 30. Reports on the violence following East Timor's vote to secede from Indonesia. Pro-Jakarta militias engaged in an orgy of burning and looting, driving 200,000 people out of the province. The UN had failed to prepare, despite clear warnings of possible violence.

"Jakarta Crackdown." *Business Week*, March 25, 2002, p. 27. Reports on the recent antiterrorism efforts in Indonesia and Malaysia. After denying or minimizing the problem, Indonesian president Megawati Sukarnoputri is finally cracking down on indigenous terrorist groups and al-Qaeda operatives. However progress is much further advanced in Malaysia, where 13 terrorist leaders have been rounded up.

Pan, Philip P. "Rural Filipinos Welcome U.S. Troops; Special Forces Deployment on Southern Island Is First Since World War II." *Washington Post*, January 28, 2002, p. A13. Describes life in a rural Philippine town where farmers try to avoid being killed by the Abu Sayyaf, a Muslim extremist group. One hundred U.S. troops have arrived to help train the Philippine army, and another 500 are on the way. Public opinion supports the American effort although there are some vocal critics.

Perlez, Jane. "Group Linked to Al-Qaeda Seen Behind Jakarta Attack." *New York Times*, August 7, 2003, p. A12. Reports on the devastating car bomb attack that killed at least 16 people and wounded 150 at a Marriott hotel in Jakarta, Indonesia. It is almost certainly the work of Jemaah Islamiyah, a radical Muslim group with many active terrorist cells and close ties to al-Qaeda. The method of the attack was similar to that used in the Bali bombings the previous year.

Simon, Stephanie. "A Hostage to Her Memories, Gracia Burnham Lost Her Husband and Her Life's Work to Philippine Rebels. A Year Later, She Struggles to Make Peace with the Past and Future." *Los Angeles Times*, May 13, 2003, p. A1. Recounts the kidnapping of Gracia and Martin Burnham by Abu Sayyaf rebels in the Philippines, their life as captives, the rescue attempt in which Martin Burnham was killed, and the aftermath.

INTERNET DOCUMENTS

"Asia's Most Wanted in U.S. Hands." CNN.com. Available online. URL: http://www.cnn.com/2003/WORLD/asiapcf/southeast/08/15/hambali. capture/index.html. Posted on August 15, 2003. Reports on the capture of Hambali, also known as Risuan Isamuddin by Thai authorities. He is the top leader of the terrorist group Jemaah Islamiyah and mastermind behind numerous bombings including the devastating blast in Bali the previous year.

"The Philippines and the War on Terrorism." Washingtonpost.com. Available online. URL: http://www.washingtonpost.com/wp-srv/world/philippines/front.html. Downloaded on November 25, 2003. Interactive map and links for background to the war on terrorism in the Philippines, including description of the Abu Sayyaf terror group.

"Terrorism in Southeast Asia: Perspectives from the Region, a CSAP Round Table Discussion." Pacific Forum."Available online. URL: http://www.csis.org/pacfor/issues/v03n02.htm. Posted in December 2002. A discussion by regional experts on terrorism in Indonesia and elsewhere in the Asia-Pacific region. Includes links to background materials.

Latin America

BOOKS

Archdiocese of Guatemala. Human Rights Office. Recovery of the Historical Memory Project. *Guatemala: Never Again!* Maryknoll, N.Y.: Orbis Books, 1999. Described by the publisher as being "like a Holocaust Museum for the people of Guatemala," this is an English translation and one-volume abridgment of a massive report on the human rights abuses in Guatemala during the 1980s and continuing today. This detailed account delves not only into the physical events but the social use of terror, the profound psychological effects of brutality and fear, the methodology used by the state terrorists, historical context for the conflict, and attempts at resistance and renewal.

Bennett, John M., and Laurence Hallewell. *Sendero Luminoso in Context: An Annotated Bibliography.* Lanham, Md.: Scarecrow Press, 2000. A detailed bibliography with sections for general works on revolution and social change and on Peru, various aspects of Peruvian society and economy, periods of modern Peruvian history, and the Sendero Luminoso (Shining Path) group itself.

Chasteen, John Charles. *Born in Blood and Fire: A Concise History of Latin America.* New York: W. W. Norton, 2001. An accessible introduction to the history of Latin America, providing background for many of the conflicts that can give rise to continuing terrorism. Aspects discussed include the colonial era, effects of the Cold War, post-colonial struggles, and contemporary issues. Although recognizing continuing problems (including conflicts with U.S. policy), the author seems optimistic about the overall progress toward democracy in the hemisphere.

Corradi, Juan E., Manuel A. Garreton, and Patricia W. Fagen, eds. *Fear at the Edge: State Terror and Resistance in Latin America.* Berkeley: University of California Press, 1994. A collection of essays that explores the implications of the "culture of fear" under military regimes in Argentina, Chile, Brazil, and Uruguay from the 1960s to the 1980s. The essays, focusing on the individual countries, discuss many aspects including the perpetrators of fear, the "guardians" who protected or abetted them, the victims, the various ways people or groups fought back, literary aspects of the culture, and the possibility for justice and reconciliation.

Human Rights Watch. *Torture and Political Persecution in Peru.* New York: Human Rights Watch, 1997. Reports that, while the insurgency in Peru has wound down now that the Fujimori administration has largely defeated the rebels, the military continues to use torture against opponents, and the legal system and legislature have failed to enact effective safeguards for human rights. Meanwhile, Shining Path and MRTA insurgents continue to torture and kill opponents.

Koonings, Kees, and Dirk Kruijt, eds. *Societies of Fear: The Legacy of Civil War, Violence, and Terror in Latin America.* New York: Zed Books, 1999. A detailed study of the uses and development of political violence and terror in Latin America. The introduction discusses the concept of a *society of fear* and how it arose in the development of Latin American nations. Part I looks at civil war and low-intensity conflict in Peru and Guatemala. Part II discusses the long-term consequences of violence in terror, including case studies involving Mexico, Argentina, and Colombia. Part III examines the prospects for a transition to a democratic society and the challenges facing such transitions.

Malamud-Goti, Jaime, and Libbet Crandon Malamud. *Game Without End: State Terror and the Politics of Justice.* Norman: University of Oklahoma Press, 1996. Malamud-Goti, asked by Argentine president Raul R. Alfonsin to organize trials of the military for human rights violations, describes the proceedings and their aftermath. He believes the trials may have failed in their purpose of unequivocally condemning the perpetrators and affirming a commitment to democracy.

Marchak, M. Patricia, and William Marchant. *God's Assassins: State Terrorism in Argentina in the 1970s.* McGill–Queen's University Press, 1999. Tells the story of state terrorism in Argentina through interviews with participants on all sides, including military officers, guerrillas, journalists, union organizers, and religious workers. The interviews are amplified by additional documentation and contemporary media accounts. The failure of the Catholic Church to take a stand against the terror is examined.

Murillo, Maria, and Jesus Rey Avirama. *Colombia and the United States: War, Terrorism, and Destabilization.* New York: Seven Stories Press, 2003. Critiques U.S. policy in Colombia, which has combined the war on drugs with the war on terrorism. The authors argue that the real problem is neither drugs nor terrorism, but the inability or unwillingness of Colombia's elite to respond to demands for democracy and economic development.

O'Shaughnessy, Hugh. *Pinochet: The Politics of Torture.* New York: New York University Press, 2000. A veteran journalist uses interviews and eyewitness accounts to explore the case of Augusto Pinochet, whose widespread use of state terrorism in Chile led, after his retirement, to his arrest by Spain on charges of torturing and murdering Spanish citizens. The general's life is examined from his early career to his rise to power, his regime, and his later arrest, internment, and eventual return to Chile for health reasons. Finally, the complex maneuverings and legal implications of Pinochet's case are detailed.

Stanley, William Deane. *Protection Racket State: Elite Politics, Military Extortion, and Civil War in El Salvador.* Philadelphia: Temple University Press, 1996. Discusses the development of state terrorism and repression in El Salvador and its relationship to the country's civil war, the breakdown of social institutions, eventual mass murder, and reform.

Taussig, Michael T. *Law in a Lawless Land: Diary of a Limpieza.* New York: New Press, 2003. A noted anthropologist recounts two weeks in a Colombian village under siege by paramilitary forces. In the *limpieza*, or "cleansing," villagers are selected from lists, and then tortured and killed, with their bodies displayed as a warning to the populace.

Verbitsky, Horacio. *The Flight: Confessions of an Argentine Dirty Warrior.* New York: New Press, 1996. The author describes the state terrorism in Argentina during the 1970s, telling the story of Francisco Silingo, a junior naval officer who was enlisted by his superiors, who told him that brutal measures against dissidents were necessary to preserve the country. Victims, who became known as "the disappeared," were kidnapped, tortured, and often thrown, still living, into the sea from military aircraft.

ARTICLES AND PAPERS

Reyes, Gerardo. "Blood, Freedom in Peru, Sudden Assault Ends Four-Month Hostage Crisis. How Daring Rescue Was Carried Out." *Miami Herald*, April 23, 1997, pp. 1Aff. Describes the successful assault by Peruvian troops on the Japanese ambassador's residence in Lima, where 72 hostages were being held by Tupac Amaru rebels. All the rebels and one hostage died; the rest of the hostages were rescued.

Richter, Paul. "U.S. Debating Wider Assault on Colombia Rebels; Latin America: Officials Point to Link Between Guerrillas and Libya. Military Role Would Test Congress' Support for Campaign Against Terror." *Los Angeles Times*, February 23, 2002, p. A1. Lays out the debate over U.S. strategy in Colombia as part of the war on terrorism. On the one hand, there appear to be links between Colombian rebels and terrorists from Libya and Northern Ireland. On the other hand, the Colombian government and army seem unable to force the rebels to the peace table—thus administration officials are pushing for increased U.S. pressure. Such involvement would also signal that the U.S. war on terrorists is not restricted to Islamic groups.

Tickner, Arlene B. "Colombia and the United States: From Counternarcotics to Counterterrorism." *Current History*, February 2003, pp. 77–85. The author believes that both the war on terrorism and the war on drugs suffer from having too narrow a focus, and from engaging in policies and tactics that are too often counterproductive. The United States has not focused sufficiently on the demand of its own citizens for drugs and has tended to ignore human rights abuses and economic deprivation in its support for the Colombian government.

Vogel, Thomas T., Jr., and Matt Moffett. "Latin Leftists Make a Noisy Comeback: But with Scant Support, Radicals Seem Anachronistic." *Wall Street Journal,* January 2, 1997, p. 8. Describes the limited resurgence of leftist guerrilla activity seen in such groups as Mexico's Zapatistas and Peru's Tupac Amaru. But leftists still seem to be flailing about after the collapse of world communism. Leftist groups that have tried to enter mainstream politics have done poorly at the ballot box. In some countries, such as Colombia, leftist groups have turned to running criminal enterprises.

Zarate, Cecilia. "Human Rights Abuses in Colombia: An Interview with Javier Giraldo." *America,* vol. 178, April 4, 1998, pp. 20ff. Giraldo, a Jesuit priest and founder of a religious coalition for peace and justice, blames primarily the country's government for Colombia's violence. He says the military has had a free hand to attack all dissidents as threats to national security and has encouraged clandestine paramilitary groups and death squads. Government attempts to investigate violations of human rights have been ineffective.

United States and Canada— Indigenous Terrorism

Note: This section covers domestic terrorist and hate groups that are predominately of American origin. For foreign terrorist attacks on U.S. soil, see the next section.

BOOKS

Arnold, Ron. *Ecoterror: The Violent Agenda to Save Nature: The World of the Unabomber.* Bellevue, Wash.: Free Enterprise Press, 1997. The author describes the radical ecological agenda of ecoterrorists such as Earth First!, the Earth Liberation Front, and the Unabomber (whom he considers an ecoterrorist). Some reviewers suggest the author paints "deep ecologists" with too broad a brush.

Atkins, Stephen E. *Encyclopedia of Modern American Extremists and Extremist Groups.* Westport, Conn.: Greenwood, 2002. Provides comprehensive coverage of 275 individuals and groups that have been active since 1950, as well as entries for relevant events and concepts. The full span from left-wing revolutionaries to right-wing racist and antigovernment groups is covered.

Ayers, Bill. *Fugitive Days: A Memoir.* New York: Beacon Press, 2001. The author, an educator and former member of the Weather Underground, vividly describes how he and his associates became involved in increasingly violent action (mainly bombings) against the U.S. government during the height of the Vietnam War and how the group was devastated by the sudden death of several members in an explosives accident. An interesting aspect is the description of how the Weather Underground members learned to subtly conceal themselves from the attention of the authorities.

Barkun, Michael. *Religion and the Racist Right: The Origins of the Christian Identity Movement.* Chapel Hill: University of North Carolina Press, 1996. A study and exposé of the small but virulent Christian Identity movement. The author traces the origin of its white supremacist theology to an obscure 19th-century doctrine called British-Israelism and explains links between Christian Identity and such contemporary groups such as Aryan Nations, Posse Comitatus, and the Ku Klux Klan.

Dees, Morris. *Gathering Storm: America's Militia Threat.* New York: Harper-Collins, 1997. Describes the activities of right-wing extremists and the threat they pose to U.S. society. Dees's associates at the Southern Poverty Law Center have been investigating right-wing extremist and hate groups for many years, and his text includes descriptions of beliefs and practices from informants inside some of the more radical groups.

George, John, and Laird M. Wilcox. *American Extremists: Militias, Supremacists, Klansmen, Communists and Others.* Buffalo, N.Y.: Prometheus Books, 1996. Based on extensive interviews and study of extremist literature, the authors survey a number of groups on the U.S. political fringe, some of which have engaged in terrorist activities. While not condoning violence, the authors are somewhat sympathetic to the grievances of antigovernment groups and raise questions about abuse of power and civil liberties. They believe that such questions have often been ignored in recent years because most of today's radical groups are on the Right rather than the Left.

Hamm, Mark S. *Apocalypse in Oklahoma: Waco and Ruby Ridge Revenged.* Boston: Northeastern University Press, 1997. The author, a professor of criminology at Indiana State University, suggests that three principal elements contributed to the Oklahoma City Bombing: the right-wing, conspiracy-based ideology of the perpetrators (Timothy McVeigh and Terry Nichols), McVeigh's psychological problems and drug-induced delusions, and the government's botched and deadly raids at Ruby Ridge and Waco, which created the perpetrators' focus on vengeance.

Hewitt, Christopher. *Understanding Terrorism in America: From the Klan to al Qaeda.* New York: Routledge, 2003. This survey of terrorism and extremist violence covers roughly the second half of the 20th century and focuses primarily on indigenous terrorism (which until September 11,

2001, was responsible for about 80 percent of domestic terrorist attacks), although it also includes such groups as Puerto Rican nationalists as well as al-Qaeda operatives. Statistics and analysis of trends for each type of terrorist movement are included, as well as the political context, organizational dynamics, the motivation of individual terrorists, and an assessment of counterterrorist tactics.

Kight, Marsha, compiler. *Forever Changed: Remembering Oklahoma City, April 19, 1995.* Amherst, N.Y.: Prometheus Books, 1998. A collection of 80 accounts by survivors of the worst domestic terrorist attack in U.S. history until September 11, 2001. A moving account of the physical and emotional sufferings of the victims as they struggled to rebuild their lives.

Levitas, Daniel. *The Terrorist Next Door: The Militia Movement and the Radical Right.* New York: Thomas Dunne Books, 2002. An updated look at the American militia, Patriot, and related movements. Although these movements have generally fallen off the radar since the late 1990s, they remain a concern to terrorism experts.

Long, Douglas. *Fundamentalists and Extremists.* New York: Facts On File, 2002. This reference handbook in the Library in a Book series covers fundamentalist and extremist groups in the United States. While many fundamentalists are apolitical, religious extremism has been associated with terrorist activities in the United States such as the killing of doctors and bombing of abortion clinics. This volume includes an introduction, legal overview and cases, chronology, biographical sketches, glossary, research guidance, list of organizations, and a lengthy annotated bibliography.

Serrano, Richard A. *One of Ours: Timothy McVeigh and the Oklahoma City Bombing.* New York: W. W. Norton, 1998. A *Los Angeles Times* reporter who covered the Oklahoma City story from the bombing to conviction explores McVeigh's life, looking for clues as to what led him to the extremes of violence. A troubled childhood, career disappointments, and the hardening of antigovernment rhetoric following Ruby Ridge and Waco all played a part.

Stern, Kenneth. *A Force Upon the Plain: The American Militia Movement and the Politics of Hate.* Norman: University of Oklahoma Press, 1997. An even-handed, detailed, fact-based examination of the motivations and activities of the modern right-wing militia and Patriot movement. The relationship between militias and white supremacist, neo-Nazi, Christian Identity, and other groups is also examined.

ARTICLES AND PAPERS

Anti-Defamation League. "ADL Special Report: Armed Militias and Vigilante Justice." *Anti-Defamation League Special Report,* 1997, pp. 1–6. A report by the Anti-Defamation League (ADL) detailing incidents of violence by right-wing U.S. extremists, including robberies and bombings. According to the report, some militias, "common law" groups that establish their own "courts," and Christian Identity and other racist groups seem to be cooperating on a significant scale.

Beirich, Heidi, and Bob Moser. "From Push to Shove: Radical Environmental and Animal-Rights Groups Have Always Drawn the Line at Targeting Humans. Not Anymore." *Intelligence Report* (Southern Poverty Law Center), Fall 2002, n.p. Also available online. URL: http://www.splcenter.org/intel/intpro.jsp (search for this particular article). Posted Fall 2002. Reports on the escalating violence by ecoterrorist and radical animal rights groups. Some groups have now turned from attacking property and "liberating" laboratory animals to making direct personal threats against executives. The Earth Liberation Front (ELF) and the closely related Animal Liberation Front (ALF) are profiled. A chronology of terrorist incidents is included.

Brooke, James. "For Radical Freemen, All the Courts Are Stages." *New York Times*, vol. 146, March 26, 1997, p. A18. Describes the legal antics of the Freemen, who believe that all courts above the local level are illegitimate and noisily object to any attempt to try them for their fraudulent financial instruments. Typically, the Freemen issue bogus securities that are "backed" by judgments enacted by their own common law courts.

Ellingwood, Ken. "The Nation; Bomb Suspect's First Trial to Be Held in Alabama; Eric Rudolph will Face Charges in a 1998 Fatal Attack at a Birmingham Abortion Clinic. Lawyer for the Former Soldier Says He's No Zealot" *Los Angeles Times*, June 3, 2003, p. A14. Summarizes the charges against Rudolph, aspects of his life, and reports on the preparations for trial.

Knickerbocker, Brad. "Concerns Rise as Ecoterrorists Expand Aim: Biotech Research and Fur Farms Are the Latest Targets of Fringe Groups on the Far Left." *Christian Science Monitor*, April 3, 2000, p. 3. An update on developments in ecoterrorism. Ecoterrorists are adding genetic research facilities to their target list. Recent victims include a genetics facility (funded by the Monsanto Corporation) at the University of Michigan, a genetic engineering project at the University of Minnesota, a Boise Cascade Corporation office in Monmouth, Oregon, and a genetic seed test orchard in British Columbia.

Markels, Alex, and Scott Willoughby. "BACKFIRE: Environmentalists Had Forged an Unusual Coalition with Locals and Animal Rights Activists to Oppose Vail's Growth—Until Ecoterrorists Torched the Mountain." *Mother Jones*, vol. 24, March 1999, p. 60. In the worst ecoterrorist attack in the United States, arsonists linked to the Animal Liberation Front caused $12 million worth of damage to ski resorts in Vail, Colorado. Activists who had built a coalition opposing further expansion of the ski industry on Vail Mountain suddenly found themselves on the defensive as they faced suspicion and outrage from thousands of people who worked in the ski and tourist industry.

"Reporting on Domestic Terrorism Against Women's Health Clinics." *Anti-Abortion Violence Watch*, March 1998, pp. 1–2. Summarizes attacks on women's health clinics by antiabortion terrorists. An unusual bomb design links a Birmingham, Alabama, clinic attack with an earlier clinic bombing and with the 1996 Olympic Park bombing in Atlanta. Eric Robert Rudolph is charged with these crimes.

Richardson, Valerie. "FBI Targets Domestic Terrorists." *Insight on the News*, April 22, 2002, pp. 30–33. In the post-September 11 environment the public has become much less tolerant of environmental radicals such as the Earth Liberation Front (ELF) and Animal Liberation Front (ALF), which have engaged in extensive arson attacks against property. According to the FBI, the ALF and ELF have committed more than 600 criminal acts since 1996, resulting in damages of more than $43 million. The activists argue that their intent is different from that of true terrorists, and that they have not physically harmed anyone. However, as they widen the range of targets, it seems only a matter of time before people are hurt or killed.

Ross, Jeffrey Ian. "The Structure of Canadian Terrorism." *Peace Review*, vol. 7, no. 3/4, 1995, pp. 355–361. A history and survey of right-wing extremist organizations in Canada. Historically, the Ku Klux Klan and other U.S. racist groups have been able to establish some offshoots in Canada. Anticommunism and resentment of immigrants, as well as economic dislocation, have fueled extreme right-wing sentiment there. In general, Canadian right-wing extremism and terrorism have been more urban-centered and smaller in scope than their U.S. counterparts.

Russakoff, Dale, and Serge F. Kovaleski. "Two Angry Men." *Washington Post National Weekly Edition*, July 24–30, 1995, pp. 6–11. Portraits of Timothy McVeigh and Terry Nichols, who would be convicted of the Oklahoma City bombing. Describes their childhoods, McVeigh's fascination with guns and his army career and Nichols's desperate struggle with debt. For McVeigh, the Ruby Ridge and Waco incidents became the final justification for violent action. Also includes a chart explaining decisions that the jury had to make before sentencing McVeigh to death.

Scarf, Maggie. "The Mind of the Unabomber: Narcissism and Its Discontents." *The New Republic*, vol. 214, June 10, 1996, pp. 20ff. Presents a psychiatric profile of Theodore Kaczynski, the Unabomber, based on theories from psychiatrist Carl P. Malmquist's new book *Homicide: a Psychiatric Perspective*. The author suggests that Kaczynski fits the profile for "Narcissistic Personality Disorder." According to the American Psychiatric Association's *Diagnostic and Statistical Manual of Mental Disorders*, this condition is characterized by a "pervasive pattern of grandiosity (in fantasy or behavior), need for admiration, and lack of empathy beginning by early adulthood and present in a variety of contexts . . . an overinflated sense of uniqueness, self-importance and personal entitlement."

Smolowe, Jill. "Hidden in Plain Sight." *People Weekly*, vol. 52, July 26, 1999, pp. 88ff. Recounts the story of Kathleen Soliah, former member of the Symbionese Liberation Army who created a new life as a wife and a mother while remaining a fugitive for 23 years. She lived a typical suburban life, married to a physician and raising three daughters. She was active in community affairs. She was caught when the FBI followed a tip called in by a viewer of the "America's Most Wanted" television program.

"Terror at the Olympics." *U.S. News & World Report*, August 5, 1996, pp. 24–27. Initial reports of the bomb attack at Centennial Olympic Park in Atlanta during the 1996 summer games. Responses from officials and the public reflect fear, confusion, dismay, and resolve. Includes a map and diagram of the site.

Wells, Janet. "Animal Activists Raise the Stakes in Eco-Attacks." *San Francisco Chronicle*, April 21, 2000, pp. A1, A19. Reports on a number of recent attacks by members of the Animal Liberation Front (ALF) in California. The group, which is loosely organized into small cells, apparently maintains communication through a number of web sites. Spokesperson David Barbarash says the group's main objective is to use property damage to cause financial hardship, thus encouraging targets to stop abusing animals for research.

INTERNET DOCUMENTS

"Active Patriot Groups in the United States in 2001." Southern Poverty Law Center Intelligence Project. Available online. URL: http://www.splcenter.org/intel/intpro.jsp. Downloaded on August 16, 2003. Provides a list of 158 "Patriot" groups (these are separate from the "hate groups" also listed by the Intelligence Project) organized by state. The list includes 73 militias.

"Active U.S. Hate Groups in 2002." Southern Poverty Law Center Intelligence Project. Available online. URL: http://www.splcenter.org/intel/map/hate.jsp. Downloaded on August 15, 2003. Provides a list of 708 hate groups categorized under Klan, Neo-Nazi, Racist Skinhead, Christian

Identity, Neo-Confederate, Black Separatist, and Other. For each group, the site lists cities where it is active. Also includes a map showing the distribution of hate groups in the United States.

CNN Interactive. "Oklahoma City Bombing Trials." CNN.com. Available online. URL: http://www.cnn.com/US/9703/okc.trial/. Downloaded on April 27, 2000. Archive page of resources and background material on the trials of Timothy McVeigh and Terry Nichols. Includes coverage of the bombing, background on the convicted bombers, trial transcripts, and story behind the reporting.

CNN Interactive. "The Olympic Park Bombing." CNN.com. Available online. URL: http://www.cnn.com/US/9707/olympic.park.bombing/. Downloaded on April 27, 2000. Archive page of resources and background material on the Olympic Park bombing. Includes the story of Richard Jewell, the park security guard who was falsely accused of the bombing, and later evidence linking the attacks to Eric Robert Rudolph.

Franklin, Raymond A. "The Hate Directory." Personal web site. Available online. URL: http://www.rayfranklin.com (follow link to "The Hate Directory: Hate Groups on the Internet"). "Release 7.3" Posted on September 1, 2003. A compilation of web links to dozens of extremist or hate groups, including racist, anti-Semitic, antigay, and others, as well as mailing lists, newsgroups, IRC (Internet Relay Chat) channels, "web rings," and games with these themes. The last page is devoted to groups that are combating hate on the Net.

"Hate Incidents in 2001." Southern Poverty Law Center Intelligence Project. Available online. URL: http://www.splcenter.org/intel/intpro.jsp. Downloaded on August 15, 2003. A list of hate crimes and hate group activities, retrievable by state. Gives the location, date, and a brief description of each incident.

Gorka, Sebestyen L. "Militias and Millenarians: A Preliminary Typology." Available online. URL: http://www.terrorism.com/documents/GorkaTRC.pdf. Downloaded on April 27, 2000. A discussion paper for the Terrorism Research Center. Although the title is formidably academic, the discussion brings out important characteristics that distinguish traditional (cold war era) political terrorist groups, millenarian (apocalyptic) terrorist cults, and militias. The motivations and capabilities of, and appropriate responses to, these types of group are quite different.

Pitcavage, Mark, compiler. "Militia Watchdog." Available online. URL: http://www.militia-watchdog.org/. Updated on March 7, 2000. This site is "devoted to monitoring far right extremism in the United States." It includes news reports on militia activities, background information about militia and patriot groups, and an FAQ ("frequently asked questions" section) on the subject.

United States and Canada—Imported Terrorism

Note: This section covers the activities of foreign-based terrorist groups (such as al-Qaeda) within the United States and Canada.

BOOKS

Bernstein, Richard, and the staff of the *New York Times*. *Out of the Blue: A Narrative of September 11, 2001*. New York: Times Books, 2002. Veteran *New York Times* reporter (and former bureau chief) Richard Bernstein and his investigative staff create a detailed, interwoven account that brings together the lives of the al-Qaeda terrorists, the victims, and the many heroes who emerged on September 11, as well as describing the national reaction to the attacks.

Dwyer, Jim, et al. *Two Seconds Under the World: Terror Comes to America: The Conspiracy Behind the World Trade Center Bombing*. New York: Crown Publishers, 1994. A vivid and suspenseful account of the first World Trade Center bombing in 1993, including a moment-by-moment scenario of reconstructed events surrounding the explosion, accounts by survivors, and questions about the FBI investigation and whether authorities could have prevented the attack by responding to information they had received earlier.

Longman, Jere. *Among the Heroes: United Flight 93 and the Passengers and Crew Who Fought Back*. New York: HarperCollins, 2002. Based on extensive interviews with the families of passengers and crew of Flight 93, the author creates a vivid, detailed account of how the passengers decided to fight back against the hijackers. Many of the passengers talked with family members on air phones or cell phones before the final struggle erupted, sending the plane crashing into a Pennsylvania field. Like the firefighters and police of New York City, these passengers emerged as "ordinary American heroes" who, by thwarting the hijackers, may have saved thousands of lives.

ARTICLES AND PAPERS

Aidi, Hisham. "Jihadis in the Hood: Race, Urban Islam, and the War on Terror." *Middle East Report*, Fall 2002, pp. 36–43. The appeal of Islam to the black and other minority communities in the United States has led to fears that al-Qaeda and other Islamic terrorist groups might find numerous recruits in these communities. However, while there have been a few highly publicized cases (such as Jose Padilla), such concerns have ignored the long history of indigenous Islamic and Pan-African black movements such as the Nation of Islam. The attraction of some blacks to radical Islamic movements must also be understood in the context of alienation and economic hopelessness in their communities.

Balz, Dan, and Bob Woodward. "Bush Awaits History's Judgment; President's Scorecard Shows Much Left to Do." *Washington Post*, February 3, 2002, p. A01. (Eighth and last in a series.) By December, both President Bush and the American people were trying to assess how successful the military campaign had been. The campaign had liberated Afghanistan from the Taliban, but Osama bin Laden and many other top al-Qaeda leaders remained at large. A new emphasis had emerged: preventing the "axis of evil" (Iran, Iraq, and North Korea) from developing or obtaining weapons of mass destruction. Domestically, recriminations had begun as evidence emerged that the FBI and other intelligence agencies had significant clues before September 11 that a large terrorist attack was being planned.

———. "A Pivotal Day of Grief and Anger: Bush Visits Ground Zero and Helps Move the Country from Sorrow to War." *Washington Post*, January 30, 2002, p A01. (Fourth in a series.) Struggling with his emotions, President Bush gives a Churchill-like speech in the National Cathedral, vowing that America will overcome its sorrow and prevail. Bush then visits ground zero in Manhattan, letting people know that ""I can hear you. The rest of the world hears you. And the people who knocked these buildings down will hear all of us soon!"

———. "'We Will Rally the World': Bush and His Advisors Set Objectives, but Struggled with How to Achieve Them." *Washington Post*, January 28, 2002, p A01. (Second in a series.) On the day following the September 11 attacks, President Bush received condolences and offers of support from many nations. Bush and British Prime Minister Tony Blair form a close partnership and begin a diplomatic campaign to build support for eventual military action against the Taliban and al-Qaeda in Afghanistan.

———. "A Presidency Defined in One Speech: Bush Saw Address as Both Reassurance and Resolve to a Troubled Nation." *Washington Post*, February 2, 2002, p. A01. (Seventh in a series). Bush prepares for a pivotal speech before a joint session of Congress, where he must explain the coming war to the American people. He believes he must stress that the war will be total and last an indefinite period of time. He struggles to preserve "direct and simple" language while phrasing is fine-tuned and sometimes changed to avoid offending allied nations.

Jervis, Robert. "An Interim Assessment of September 11: What Has Changed and What Has Not?" *Political Science Quarterly*, vol. 117, Spring 2002, pp. 37ff. A lengthy assessment of changes in social and political realities following the September 11 attacks. Aspects discussed include the vulnerability of the nation and its economy, the declining relevance and power of states (as opposed to the federal government), the limitations of the ability to understand terrorist grievances that cannot be addressed, the characterization and scope of the war on terrorism and the use of war rhetoric, and the opportunity of nations to forge closer bonds against a common threat.

Whitman, David. "Day of Infamy: A Timeline of Terror." *U.S. News & World Report*, September 14, 2001, p. 18. A chronology of the events of September 11, 2001, from 7:58 A.M., when the first plane departed Boston for Los Angeles, to 10:00 P.M., when New York mayor Rudolph Giuliani ends what must have been the longest day in his life.

KEY ISSUES RELATED TO TERRORISM

Counterterrorism (Theory and Practice)

BOOKS

Alexander, Yonah. *Combating Terrorism: Strategies of Ten Countries*. Ann Arbor: University of Michigan Press, 2002. A collection of essays by experts who have worked in a variety of countries in Europe, the Middle East, Asia, and Latin America. The discussion of how terrorism is fought in countries that differ considerably in their culture and politics provides a useful perspective for Americans who tend to focus overmuch on the U.S. point of view.

Coulson, Danny O., and Elaine Shannon. *No Heroes: Inside the FBI's Secret Counter-Terror Force*. New York: Pocket Books, 1999. Coulson, the FBI agent who founded the bureau's Hostage Rescue Team, recounts his years of pursuing criminals and terrorists, including right-wing extremists and Middle Eastern bombers. He gives a vivid insider's account of events such as the Ruby Ridge and Waco incidents and the World Trade Center and Oklahoma City bombings. While acknowledging mistakes (particularly with regard to Ruby Ridge and Waco) and problems of bureaucracy and politicization in the agency, he takes an uncompromising position in favor of law enforcement.

Decker, Ronald Ray. *Bomb Threat Management*. Boston: Butterworth-Heinemann, 1998. The author, an attorney and security consultant, provides procedures and tools for security personnel to use when confronted by bomb threats. Gives examples of forms for evaluating threats, procedures for reacting to incidents, and recovering from the effects of an explosion.

Dudonis, Kenneth J. et al. *The Counterterrorism Handbook: Tactics, Procedures, and Techniques*. 2nd ed. Boca Raton, Fla.: CRC Press, 2002. The authors

Annotated Bibliography

provide systematic and practical advice about what to do before, during, and after each of many types of terrorist attacks.

Jane's Counter Terrorism. Alexandria, Va.: Jane's Information, 2002. A desktop reference to procedures and planning for a variety of possible terrorist attacks. Includes scene and incident management, personnel training, and media relations. Designed for security specialists and facilities managers.

Krouse, William J., and Raphael F. Perl. *Terrorism: Automated Lookout Systems and Border Security Options and Issues*. Washington, D.C.: Congressional Research Service, 2002. Discusses new and proposed technology and procedures for detecting known or suspected members of terrorist organizations and preventing them from entering the United States.

ARTICLES AND PAPERS

Bamford, James. "Our Best Spies Are in Space." *New York Times*, vol. 147, August 20, 1998, p. A23. Because close-knit, highly committed terrorist groups are hard for U.S. intelligence agencies to penetrate on the ground, the National Security Agency's spy satellite and computer surveillance facilities are vital to the counterterrorist effort. But the agency's biggest challenge is not in gathering data, but in sifting through the tremendous amount of information it receives.

Barnett, Thomas P. M. "The Pentagon's New Map." *Esquire*, March 2003, pp. 174–179, 227–228. A military and defense analyst argues that the U.S. attack on Iraq in 2003 is integral to a new strategy in fighting terrorism. Fundamentally, he says it is not a matter of weapons of mass destruction or similar concerns, but a fundamental disconnection between the "Core"— the part of the world where global modernity is functioning—and the dysfunctional, impoverished "Gap," which is becoming a breeding ground for the new terrorism. The latter, which includes much of the Caribbean *Rime*, Africa, the Balkans, the Caucasus, Middle East, Central Asia, and much of Southeast Asia also constitutes the fault lines along which terrorist activity moves. The article includes maps and summaries of regional developments.

"Corporate Security: Risk Returns." *Economist (U.S.)*, vol. 353, November 20, 1999, p. 78. Describes risks to companies who get involved with business in dangerous places such as Chechnya. In addition to terrorist attack, companies may face threats from criminals, litigation for failure to protect employees, and loss of reputation. To protect themselves, large corporations are developing or hiring the necessary expertise. The security industry, drawing on former police and government security agents, is flourishing.

Deutch, John M., and Jeffrey H. Smith. "Smarter Intelligence." *Foreign Policy*, January–February 2002, pp. 64–69. The struggle to improve an intelligence system widely regarded to have failed on September 11, 2001, is described by the authors, two important former CIA officials. The authors, perhaps not surprisingly, urge that the CIA be given the lead role in the new effort and that redundant counterterrorism programs in the FBI and elsewhere be eliminated. They argue that the distinction between covert intelligence action and covert military action should be removed and the combined efforts should be put under a permanent planning staff drawing on the relevant agencies. A new balancing test should be applied to the recruiting of "unsavory" sources who might have access to vital information.

Duffy, Michael, and Nancy Gibbs. "How Far Do We Want the FBI to Go?" *Time*, vol. 159, June 10, 2002, pp. 24ff. As the FBI gears up to make fighting terrorism its highest priority, it has been given broad new powers to uncover evidence. Agents can begin preliminary investigations without getting approval from headquarters, and they are free to surf web sites, chat rooms, and other public places in cyberspace. However, can the FBI change its internal culture so that it responds to, organizes, and shares information more effectively? What's more, the existing bureaucratically defensive culture is largely the result of fear of recriminations from Congress, and the civil liberties implications of the agency's new powers might well bring such scrutiny.

Hersh, Seymour M. "Missed Messages: Why the Government Didn't Know What It Knew." *New Yorker*, June 3, 2002, pp. 40–48. According to the author, the problem for the United States was not that intelligence agencies did not know there were strong indications of a terrorist threat before September 11, 2001—rather, they did not have a way to evaluate and act upon the information they were receiving. The FBI under Robert Mueller now faces a need to revamp antiquated computer systems and, as he has said, "refocus our mission and our priorities."

Isikoff, Michael, and Daniel Klaidman. "The Hijackers We Let Escape." *Newsweek*, June 10, 2002, p. 20. The authors question why the United Stated permitted two suspected terrorists, Nawaf Alhazmi and Khalid Almihdhar, to enter the United States after attending an al-Qaeda summit in Malaysia. In what may be the biggest intelligence failure of all, the CIA did not pass information about the terrorists to the Immigration and Naturalization Service, which could have denied them entry, or the FBI, which could have tracked them to learn more about their mission, which it turned out was attending a flight school and then flying a jet into the Pentagon on September 11. The FBI believes that if they had known about these two terrorists being in the country, they could have unraveled the entire plot.

Klare, Michael T. "Waging Postindustrial Warfare on the Global Battlefield." *Current History*, vol. 100, December 2001, pp. 433ff. The author suggests that September 11, 2001, has changed modern warfare as radically as had Pearl Harbor (naval air power) and Hiroshima (nuclear weapons). Al-Qaeda's attack on America typifies "postindustrial warfare," through the use of irregular forces and unconventional tactics. The author also discusses the related subjects of guerrilla and insurgent warfare. He asserts that economic globalization has created poverty and social/cultural disruption, thus supplying new grievances for terrorists.

Miller, Judith. "Planning for Terror but Failing to Act." *New York Times*, December 30, 2001, pp. A1ff. An extensive account that outlines what the government knew about Osama bin Laden and al-Qaeda before September 11. Bin Laden was perceived to be a major threat (particularly after the 1998 embassy bombings) and repeated proposals for dealing with him in a more systematic way were considered, but none came to fruition. Additionally, evidence arising from the activities of Ramzi Yousef and the first World Trade Center bombing, in 1993, was not used effectively, and investigations petered out.

Ratnesar, Romesh, and Michael Weisskopf. "How the FBI Blew the Case: The Inside Story of the FBI Whistle-Blower Who Accuses Her Bosses of Ignoring Warnings of 9/11." *Time*, vol. 159, June 3, 2002, pp. 24ff. Provides background on the whistle-blower Coleen Rowley, who as a youngster wanted to be an FBI agent and became a pioneer as a woman agent. Her memo provides a devastating critique of the FBI's failure to recognize and properly follow up on the suspicious flight school activities of Zacarias Moussaoui, who is now awaiting trial as the "20th hijacker." The Rowley memo eventually led to a promise of reform and non-reprisal by FBI director Robert Mueller.

Reynolds, Maura. "Poindexter Expected to Resign in Futures Market Controversy; Ex-Reagan Aide Leads the Pentagon Unit That Devised Unusual Plan to Predict Terrorist Attacks." *Los Angeles Times*, August 1, 2003, p. A20. Reports on the furor that erupted when a Pentagon think tank proposed creating a "futures market" to tap into the ability to predict terrorist attacks and other events. Pentagon officials quickly backpedaled when the idea was attacked in the media and by various Democrats; Poindexter, who had been a senior security adviser to President Reagan and a key figure in the Iran-Contra scandal, evidently became a casualty of the uproar.

Serrano, Richard A. "100 Terrorist Attacks Thwarted, U.S. Says; Success Is Linked to Detainee Interrogations. Targets Are Said to Include Embassies, a U.S. Base in Europe and Cargo Ships at Gibraltar." *Los Angeles Times*, January 11, 2003, p. A12. Summarizes high-profile cases in which U.S. officials believe they had successfully detected and thwarted terrorist plots against embassies, ships, and other targets. However, many of the cases lack specific targets. The CIA claims to have detained more than 3,000 al-Qaeda operatives in more than 100 countries from September 2001 to the beginning of 2003.

Smith, Paul J. "Transnational Terrorism and the al Qaeda Model: Confronting New Realities." *Parameters*, vol. 32, Summer 2002, pp. 33ff. Describes al-Qaeda's ambitious plans (including an aborted 1995 plan to bomb multiple airliners), the weaknesses that it exploits in Western societies, and its "multi-cellular terror model" with a horizontal structure of 24 organizations combined with a vertical structure culminating in Osama bin Laden. Al-Qaeda is a truly international organization that has penetrated many organizations, including Islamic charities.

"A Systematic Failure; George Bush and September 11." [not attributed]. *The Economist*, May 25, 2002, n.p. While it is not reasonable to think the president had definite knowledge of an attack and failed to act, administration characterizations of what was known or could be known are problematic. For example, the possibility of using hijacked airliners as missiles should have been considered, given that two previous plots to crash aircraft into the Eiffel Tower and CIA headquarters had been foiled. There were also reports received by the FBI stating that suspicious individuals had enrolled in flight schools.

Thachuk, Kimberley L. "Terrorism's Financial Lifeline: Can It Be Severed?" *Strategic Forum*, May 2002, n.p. Also available online. URL: http://www.ndu.edu/inss/strforum/SF191/sf191.htm. Posted in May 2002. Describes the ways in which terrorists can raise and distribute funds. The decline in direct state sponsorship of terrorists (mainly due to U.S. pressure) means that terrorist groups are turning increasingly to illicit activities (such as drug selling) and money laundering. Although the approaches of organized criminals and terrorists are somewhat similar, the latter emphasize secrecy, decentralization, and the use of multiple layers to conceal their intent. The traditional system of *havala* provides an anonymous alternative for Islamic terrorists to transfer funds. Suggested policies for fighting terrorist funding are suggested, but their limitations are also acknowledged.

Van Natta, Don, Jr. "Report Calls U.S. a Top Target for Terror Attack Within a Year." *New York Times*, August 17, 2003, p. A9. Reports on the results of a terrorism risk analysis by World Markets Research Center, Inc. The company has created a World Terrorism Index to help its clients (mostly major corporations) evaluate the risk of terrorism to their facilities. The latest report shows the United States as being likely to have another attack comparable to the September 11, 2001, events. The United States is ranked fourth in overall risk of major terrorist attacks, behind only Colombia, Israel, and Pakistan. Despite its characterization as an "axis of evil" country, North Korea is 186th and last because it has a regime so repressive that it is very unlikely that terrorists could operate against the country.

Annotated Bibliography

INTERNET DOCUMENTS

Armond, Paul de. "Rock, Paper, Scissors: Counter-terrorism, anti-terrorism, and terrorism." Public Good project, NorthWest Citizen. Available online. URL: http://www.nwcitizen.com/publicgood/reports/rockpaperscissors/. Posted in 1997. The author distinguishes between antiterrorism, which is a broad political strategy of combating terrorism through strengthening democracy, and counterterrorism, which is a military response that treats the fight against terrorism as a low-intensity military conflict. The circumstances under which antiterrorist and counterterrorist options are available vary with the nature of the terrorist threat and the structure of the target state. Responses to right-wing and millenarian terrorism in the contemporary United States are used as an example

"Counterterrorist Organization Profiles." Terrorism Research Center. Available online. URL: http://www.terrorism.com/modules.php?op=modload&name=CTGroups&file=index. Downloaded on August 10, 2003. Offers descriptions of counterterrorist, special operations, and hostage rescue/response units around the world, with additional links.

Terrorism and International Relations

BOOKS

Hanson, Victor Davis. *An Autumn of War: What America Learned from September 11 and the War on Terrorism*. New York: Anchor Books, 2002. The author, a classics professor and columnist for National Review Online, presents a collection of essays written during the months following the attacks. In them, he explores the idea of war coming to America from a military historical perspective and argues that September 11 is the latest chapters in the West's long struggle against barbarism. He describes how Americans of different classes and backgrounds responded to the challenge. His conservative analyses challenge leftist critics of the war effort.

Kumamoto, Robert D. *International Terrorism and American Foreign Relations, 1945–1976*. Boston: Northeastern University Press, 1999. Describes how confrontation with three terrorist movements helped shape the approach of American diplomacy toward regional conflicts. The author looks at Jewish extremists' attacks against the British government in Palestine, 1945–48; the revolt of Algerian nationalists against France, 1954–62; and the Palestinian jihad against Israel and American interests, 1968–76. He argues that America's response to terrorism became flexible and moderated as it took into account cold war alignments, relations with allies, domestic politics, and other concerns.

Mahajan, Rahul. *The New Crusade: America's War On Terrorism*. New York: Monthly Review Press, 2002. The author, a peace activist, offers a comprehensive critique of the "war on terrorism." He explores what he says is systematic distortion by government officials and the media of the reasons for the terrorist attack and the American war aims, as well as events in Afghanistan. The "war on terrorism" is put in the context of ongoing American foreign policy that has protected elite interests while leading to the deaths of thousands of innocent people.

Perl, Raphael, and Kenneth Katzman. *State-Supported Terrorism*. Washington, D.C.: Congressional Research Service, 2002. An updated review of policies and issues with regard to U.S. treatment of states whose governments sponsor or support terrorism.

Rich, Paul B., and Richard Stubbs, eds. *The Counter-Insurgent State: Guerrilla Warfare and State Building in the Twentieth Century*. New York: St. Martin's Press, 1997. A collection of papers dealing with the relationship between political development, insurgency, and counterinsurgency in various parts of the world. Areas covered are the Philippines, Malaysia, Sri Lanka, Algeria, Mozambique, Peru, Northern Ireland, and Afghanistan. Overall, the authors suggest that governments able to respond to insurgency by creating broad-based programs of social and economic reform are more likely to be able to contain insurgent violence.

Scraton, Phil, ed. *Beyond September 11: An Anthology of Dissent*. Sterling, Va.: Pluto Press, 2002. An anthology of personal accounts and political dissents by critics of the U.S. war on terrorism, including Noam Chomsky, Robert Fisk, and Naomi Klein. The varied critiques include challenges to the legal basis of the government's actions, deconstruction of language used to justify the war against terrorism, and criticism of the media, especially the lack of coverage of civilian deaths in Afghanistan.

Strauss, Steven D. *The Complete Idiot's Guide to World Conflicts*. Indianapolis, Ind.: Pearson Education, 2002. Somewhat irreverent, but a good basic overview of the major conflict areas in the Middle East and North Africa, Central and Southern Asia, Asia and the Pacific, Europe, South America and Latin America, and North America. Includes a list of organizations and a bibliography.

ARTICLES AND PAPERS

Choharis, Peter. "The Rule of Law: Indispensable to a Wider War." *Washington Post*, January 6, 2002, p. B01. The author, an expert on international law, argues that if the United States is to expand its war effort it must show that its actions have legitimacy under widely accepted international law. Only this procedure will keep allies on board, particularly those among the moderate Islamic nations. However, while the case against the Taliban was straightforward, the new argument that nations can be attacked for "supporting terrorism" or for posing a future threat is more problematic. Thus far the United Nations has not authorized the use of force in such situations.

Crenshaw, Martha. "Why America? The Globalization of Civil War." *Current History*, December 2001, pp. 425–432. Recent terrorist attacks should be placed in the context of a long-term reaction to the global power of the United States. Religious fanatics and secular insurgents alike see the United States as moving toward world domination. Examples are drawn from Central and South America, the Middle East, Western Europe, and Asia. In the Middle East, the Soviet invasion of Afghanistan and the Gulf War of 1990–1991 were pivotal events in defining opposition. During the 1990s religious-based terrorism became ascendant, but it has gained much of its fuel from oppressive conditions of U.S.-backed regimes.

Eisendrath, Craig. "U.S. Foreign Policy After September 11." *USA Today*, May 20, 2002, pp. 12–14. The author suggests an alternative to the largely unilateral U.S. war on terrorism. Such an alternative would include a ready UN deployment force, an international criminal court, economic and social development that would change the conditions that often breed terrorism, and enforcement of human rights. These alternatives were also possible at the dawn of the Cold War in the later 1940s but were largely rejected.

Hoffmann, Stanley. "Why Don't They Like Us? How America Has Become the Object of Much of the Planet's Genuine Grievances—and Displaced Discontents." *The American Prospect*, vol. 12, November 19, 2001, pp. 18ff. The author suggests that the virulence that erupted on September 11 must be understood in the context of a collapse of the old world of states, diplomats and soldiers and a new world in which movements of "ordinary" people are driving much of the conflict and change in the world. Although the United States retains dominant power, it finds itself dealing with governments that no longer represent the people and is thus out of touch with the powerful emerging currents such as that in the Islamic world. The alliance of American with globalist forces further complicates matters. America can reduce terrorism by altering its approach to the world and thus the negative images it has for many people around the world.

Legal Prosecution of Terrorism

Note: This section deals with works that focus on the investigation and prosecution of terrorist suspects. For broader issues arising from new antiterrorism legislation, see the next section.

Global Terrorism

BOOKS

Ackerman, David. *Suits Against Terrorist States*. Washington, D.C.: Congressional Research Service, 2002. Describes legislation and issues relating to the ability of American victims of terrorism to sue states that sponsor the attacks. Discusses the payment of judgments and the use of frozen assets.

Bazan, Elizabeth B. *Assassination Ban and E.O. 12333: A Brief Summary*. Washington, D.C.: Congressional Research Service, 2002. Discusses the applicability of the executive order banning assassination (direct targeting of foreign leaders) to the current war on terrorism.

Chadwick, Elizabeth. *Self-Determination, Terrorism, and the International Humanitarian Law of Armed Conflict*. Boston: M. Nijhoff, 1996. Focuses on terrorism conducted as part of a popular struggle for self-determination, a complex area that often blurs the distinction between terrorism and guerrilla war. Discusses the problem of applying international humanitarian law to such actions and the broader question of the strategy behind such terrorism and the failure of states to deter it.

Doyle, Charles. *The USA PATRIOT Act: A Legal Analysis*. Washington, D.C.: Congressional Research Service, 2002. Provides a detailed analysis of the new law, which includes far-reaching extensions of federal law enforcement and investigation powers with regard to terrorism.

Elsea, Jennifer. *Terrorism and the Law of War: Trying Terrorists as War Criminals Before a Military Commission*. Washington, D.C.: Congressional Research Service, 2001. Discusses principles, precedents, issues, and considerations involved in treating terrorists as war criminals and trying them for violating the laws of war.

Fisher, Louis. *Military Tribunals: The Quirin Precedent*. Washington, D.C.: Congressional Research Service, 2002. Discusses the procedures used in the military tribunal that tried eight German saboteurs during World War II and the issues and precedents arising from the Supreme Court appeal in *Ex Parte Quriin*.

Halstead, T. J. *Monitoring Inmate-Attorney Communications: Sixth Amendment Implications*. Washington, D.C.: Congressional Research Service, 2001. Describes the interim order authorizing prisons to monitor conversations between suspects and their attorneys when "reasonable suspicion" exists that the communications may facilitate terrorism. Discusses relevant Sixth Amendment issues.

ARTICLES AND PAPERS

Cohen, Adam. "Rough Justice: The Attorney General Has Powerful New Tools to Fight Terrorism. Has He Gone Too Far?" *Time*, vol. 158, December 10, 2001, pp. 30ff. Describes a number of civil liberties issues arising from the new initiatives and powers being used by the Justice Department against terrorism suspects. The most controversial is the proposed use of military tribunals that bypass many key protections of the regular courts, but there is also the danger that broad powers (such as being able to hold persons without charges or conduct secret proceedings) first used against noncitizen terrorist suspects might be extended to citizens and beyond the context of terrorism. Finally, there is the question of whether the balance of powers between the executive and judiciary branches may be dangerously tilted toward the former if the courts are unable or unwilling to review cases involving extraordinary powers in "wartime."

Gerstein, Josh. "Under Charge—The Real 9/11 Civil Liberties Problem." *The New Republic*, April 22, 2002, p. 22. The holding of suspects without charges and the carrying out of secret legal proceedings are the two most serious civil liberties issues arising from the war on terrorism. Recently, the government has started holding persons indefinitely as "material witnesses," such as Anwar Almirabi, who was held at first only for a visa violation but now has been in prison for seven months. The secrecy of the proceedings and the lack of access to communications facilities for most prisoners makes it very difficult to defend such cases, and thus far the appeals courts have generally not scrutinized them.

Johnston, David. "A Plea Suited to Both Sides." (Traces of Terror: News Analysis). *New York Times*, July 16, 2002, p. A1. John Walker Lindh's plea bargain gained him an expected 20-year sentence in a climate where a jury might well have sentenced him to life. But it also rid the government of a case with weak evidence and that might reveal mistreatment.

Meyer, Josh, and John-Thor Dahlburg. "QUEST FOR SECURITY; Florida Professor Charged in Terrorism Case; Sami Al-Arian Is Accused Along with Seven Others of Supporting a Palestinian Group Linked to Suicide Bombings. Four are Still at Large." *Los Angeles Times*, February 21, 2003, p. A5. Reports on the prosecution of a professor and three accused co-conspirators charged with racketeering, extortion, obstruction of justice, and other offenses in connection with allegedly aiding the Palestinian Islamic Jihad. The prosecution illustrated the growing use of foreign intelligence surveillance not previously permitted as evidence in domestic cases. Professor al-Arian has denied the charges and sued the university for discrimination.

Selye, Katharine. "Judge Questions Detention of American in War Case." *New York Times*, August 14, 2002, p. A1ff. Despite the great deference of the appeals court to the government's wartime interest, federal district judge Robert G. Doumar remains skeptical about the legality of holding Yaser Hamdi without charges or access to an attorney. Judge Doumar is called upon to determine whether a bare statement from a government official is sufficient to brand Hamdi an "enemy combatant" without legal rights.

Selye, Katherine Q. "War on Terror Makes for Odd Twists in Justice System. Flexible Rules Raise Constitutional Issues." *New York Times,* June 23, 2002, pp. 16ff. A survey of recent cases that expose the contradictory processing of terrorism suspects. While two Americans (Yaser Hamdi and Jose Padilla) are held in military brigs without access to lawyers, two foreigners (Zacarias Mossaoui and Richard Reid) are provided the protections of the normal courts. Following the plea bargain for John Walker Lindh, the intentions of prosecutors with regard to the other cases remain uncertain.

Serrano, Richard A. "Two Guilty in Terrorism Trial; Jury in Detroit Convicts the Arab Immigrants of Aiding Terror in the First Major Case Tied to 9/11. Two Others Are Cleared of Conspiracy Charges." *Los Angeles Times,* June 4, 2003, p. A1. Reports the conviction in Detroit of two North African immigrants in the first major criminal trial resulting from post-September 11, 2001, investigations. Charges included conspiracy to provide material resources to terrorists and to misuse visas and other documents. The jury spent a week sorting the complex charges, and seemed to act with due deliberation.

INTERNET DOCUMENTS

Dorf, Michael C. "What Is an 'Unlawful Combatant,' and Why It Matters." FindLaw Corporate Counsel Center. Available online. URL: http://writ. corporate.findlaw.com/dorf/20020123.html. Posted on January 23, 2002. The author argues that neither al-Qaeda nor Taliban fighters meet the requirements for treatment as prisoners of war under the Geneva Convention. It is plausible to classify them as "unlawful combatants" and detain them until the (indefinite) cessation of hostilities. However, even if they were deemed prisoners of war, they could also be held.

Human Rights Watch. "Legal Issues Arising from the War in Afghanistan and Related Anti-Terrorism Efforts." Available online. URL: http://www. hrw.org/campaigns/september11/ihlqna.htm. Posted on August 15, 2002. A series of questions and answers about the applicability of international humanitarian and human rights law to the prosecution of the war on terrorism. Topics include the nature of international humanitarian law, the use of law enforcement versus military action, how persons captured can be prosecuted or treated, and what forms of warfare are lawful.

Legal Information Institute. "LII Backgrounder on National Security Law and Counter-Terrorism." Available online. URL: http://www.law.cornell. edu/background/warpower/. Downloaded on August 10, 2003. Provides references to the legal underpinnings of the war on terrorism and legislation and executive orders subsequent to September 11, 2001. Divided into sections for the executive, legislative, and judicial branches.

U.S. Department of State. "International Conventions and Other Treaties Relating to Terrorism." Available online. URL: http://www.state.gov/r/pa/ho/pubs/fs/6093.htm Posted on November 6, 2001. Gives titles and links to terrorism-related treaties of which the United States is a signatory.

Terrorism and Civil Liberties

BOOKS

Cole, David, and James X. Dempsey. *Terrorism and the Constitution: Sacrificing Civil Liberties in the Name of National Security* 2d ed. Los Angeles: First Amendment Foundation, 2002. Discusses the impact of federal antiterrorist laws and policies on civil liberties. Parts I and II discuss the implications of FBI investigations of groups such as Amnesty International and Earth First! during the 1980s and early 1990s, the investigation of supporters of leftist insurgencies in Central America, and the agency's attempt to enlist the aid of librarians in tracking potential terrorists. Part III is devoted to the 1996 Antiterrorism Act and the 2001 USA PATRIOT Act, discussing their core provisions and their implications.

Etzioni, Amitai, and Jason H. Marsh, eds. *Rights vs. Public Safety After 9/11*. Lanham, Md.: Rowman and Littlefield, 2003. A collection of essays on the civil liberties issues raised by the campaign against terrorism. Contributors include Attorney General John Ashcroft, Senator Patrick Leahy, and advocates and legal scholars such as Laurence H. Tribe and Richard A. Posner. Both pro and con views are given on issues such as immigrant rights, racial profiling, freedom of the press vs. national security, and the justification for going to war against Iraq. There is also discussion of proposed national service and other communitarian approaches to national security.

Ewing, Alphonse B., ed. *The USA Patriot Act*. Hauppage, N.Y.: Nova Science Publishers, 2003. This collection of articles includes general legal analysis of the law and discussions of its implications for the Internet community.

Freeman, Michael. *Freedom or Security: The Consequences for Democracies Using Emergency Powers to Fight Terror*. Westport, Conn.: Praeger, 2003. A comparative study of the effects of use of emergency powers in democracies that are facing terrorist or insurgent attack. The examples explored are Northern Ireland and the IRA, Uruguay and the Tupamaros, Canada and the FLQ, and Peru and the Shining Path. Lessons drawn from these situations are applied to the effort to develop new antiterrorist policies in the United States after September 11, 2001. The first question is whether emergency powers are truly effective (they were not in many cases). If effective, what is the tradeoff between benefits and abuses? Only in the case of Canada versus the FLQ did the author find the optimal outcome.

Higgins, Rosalyn, and Maurice Flory. *Terrorism and International Law.* New York: Routledge, 1997. A comprehensive collection of documents, including laws and treaties, reflecting the response of the British, French, and international legal systems to terrorism. Includes a discussion of the extent and existing limitations of international cooperation against terrorism.

Leone, Richard C., and Greg Anrig, Jr., eds. *The War on Our Freedoms: Civil Liberties in an Age of Terrorism.* New York: Public Affairs, 2003. The contributors describe various aspects of what they see as the precipitous loss of civil liberties in the United States following September 11, 2001. Aspects discussed include the lack of public debate on the issue, the ignoring of fundamental constitutional principles, treatment of prisoners at Guantánamo Bay, invasions of privacy, attacks on the rights of immigrants, the new racial profiling, government secrecy, restrictions on the media during military conflict, and efforts of lawyers to defend rights.

Reisman, M., and Chris T. Antoniou. *The Laws of War: A Comprehensive Collection of Primary Documents on International Laws Governing Armed Conflict.* New York: Vintage Books, 1994. Because terrorist acts often arise during wars (particularly civil war and ethnic conflicts), this useful collection of sources on the law of armed conflict is also relevant to the student of terrorism.

Smith, Alison M. *National Identification Cards: Legal Issues.* Washington, D.C.: Congressional Research Service, 2002. Summarizes the legal background and controversy over the proposed use of some form of uniform national identification, perhaps incorporating biometric data.

Smith, Marcia S. et al. *The Internet and the USA PATRIOT Act: Potential Implications for Electronic Privacy, Security, Commerce, and Government.* Washington, D.C.: Congressional Research Service, 2002. Summarizes the application of the USA PATRIOT Act with regard to electronic commerce, security, and privacy.

Stevens, Gina Marie. *Privacy: Total Information Awareness Programs and Related Information Access, Collection and Protection Laws.* Washington, D.C.: Congressional Research Service, 2003. Also available online. URL: http://www.fas.org/irp/crs/RL31730.pdf. Updated on March 21, 2003. Describes the Total Information Awareness (later renamed Terrorist Information Awareness) program, a proposed effort to use data-mining technology on a massive scale to ferret out patterns suggesting terrorist-related activity. The issues raised by this effort are explored in relation to a variety of existing federal laws protecting various forms of personal information.

Annotated Bibliography

ARTICLES AND PAPERS

Beown, Andrew. "The Price of Liberty." *New Statesman*, vol. 128, February 19, 1999, pp. 41ff. A case in which a jury awarded $100 million to people who were threatened when publishers of an extremist antiabortion web site called the Nuremberg Files posted their names and addresses raises issues of free speech, as does a British site called Hansard Report containing Northern Irish Protestant leader Ian Paisley's list of Republicans accused of murdering Protestants in 1975. The author believes the threats to those listed are quite real but that the alternative of censorship is even worse.

Berkowitz, Bill. "AmeriSnitch." *The Progressive*, vol. 66, May 2002, pp. 27ff. A critique of Attorney General John Ashcroft's promotion of Neighborhood Watch programs expanded to watch for terrorists, and the proposed TIPS (Terrorist Information and Prevention System), which is supposed to enlist workers such as mail carriers, utility workers, and train conductors to watch for suspicious activity. Civil liberties groups are beginning to speak out against the idea of "turning the information society into an informant society."

Davis, Derek H. "The Dark Side to a Just War: The USA PATRIOT Act and Counterterrorism's Potential Threat to Religious Freedom." *Journal of Church and State*, vol. 44, Winter 2002, pp. 5ff. An evaluation of the effects of the PATRIOT Act on civil liberties, free expression, and religious freedom. The author is particularly concerned with the impact on faith groups who may find themselves defined as terrorists according to secret criteria, and in a process that necessarily involves the government determining the boundaries of permissible religious activity.

Demmer, Valerie L. "Civil Liberties and Homeland Security." *The Humanist*, vol. 62, January–February 2002, pp. 7ff. A critique of the USA PATRIOT Act, particularly its impact on First Amendments rights of expression and association. Russ Feingold, a Democrat from Wisconsin and the only senator to vote against the bill, is quoted as follows: "Of course there is no doubt that, if we lived in a police state, it would be easier to catch terrorists. If we lived in a country that allowed the police to search your home at any time for any reason; if we lived in a country that allowed the government to open your mail, eavesdrop on your phone conversations, or intercept your email communications; if we lived in a country that allowed the government to hold people in jail indefinitely based on what they write or think, or based on mere suspicion that they are up to no good, then the government would no doubt discover and arrest more terrorists. But that probably would not be a country in which we would want to live. And that would not be a country for which we could, in good conscience, ask our young people to fight and die. In short, that would not be America."

Dreyfuss, Robert. "Colin Powell's List: The Targeting of 'Terrorist' Groups Harks Back to Earlier Repression of Dissent." *The Nation*, vol. 274, March 25, 2002, p. 16. The proliferation of government lists that designate foreign terrorist organizations threatens to stifle dissent in a maze of regulations that leave people who simply want to express political views uncertain as to where they stand. Historically, the lists conjure up earlier periods of repression, such as the post–World War I "Red Scare" and the McCarthy hysteria of the 1950s. Further, the criteria by which some organizations are listed but others are not remain unclear.

Egelko, Bob. "ABA Panel Assails Plan to Monitor Detainees' Lawyers; They Say Pentagon Rules Threaten Rights." *San Francisco Chronicle*, August 9, 2003, p A5. The president of the nation's largest legal organization proposes that the organization squarely oppose the proposed rules for conducting trials of terrorism suspects before military tribunals. Under these rules conversations between lawyers and clients could be monitored. Although the contents of conversations could not be used at trial, many defense attorneys feel such monitoring would fatally undermine the ability of lawyer and client to speak freely, and thus compromise representation. Another organization, the National Association of Criminal Defense Lawyers, had already declared that defense attorneys who submitted to the rules would be violating their ethical duties to their clients.

Kandra, Anne. "National Security vs. Online Privacy: The New Antiterrorism Law Steps Up Electronic Surveillance of the Internet." *PC World*, vol. 20, January 2002, pp. 37ff. The author expresses concern about provisions of the new USA PATRIOT Act as they apply to Internet use. E-mail and web activities of persons unrelated to a particular investigation might be "swept up," and the secret technology for Internet surveillance (formerly known as "Carnivore") remains obscure but troubling.

Kopel, David B., and Joseph Olson. "Bipartisan Reign of Terror." *Liberty*, July 1996. Available online. URL: http://www.libertysoft.com/liberty/features/54kopel.html. Posted in July 1996. Discusses the elements of the 1996 Antiterrorism and Effective Death Penalty Act as proposed by the U.S. administration and as passed. While a broad coalition of civil liberties groups were able to remove some of the most intrusive provisions, the final bill compromises basic rights of association, privacy, and due process.

Lichtblau, Eric. "Justice Dept. Lists Use of New Power to Fight Terror." *New York Times*, May 21, 2003, p. A1. The Justice Department makes its first detailed accounting of how it is employing the enhanced powers it received under the PATRIOT Act. Marking a departure from earlier constraints, intelligence gathered abroad is now being used by prosecutors to determine whether to bring criminal charges against suspects. Hundreds of secret search warrants have been issued, and more than 50 people have been detained without charges as material witnesses (most others were released after 90 days or less).

Martin, Kate. "Intelligence, Terrorism, and Civil Liberties." *Human Rights*, vol. 29, Winter 2002, pp. 5–7. Traditionally, the United States has separated foreign intelligence from intelligence gathering for law enforcement purposes, as in the separate roles for the CIA and FBI. However, since September 11, 2001, there has been great pressure to expand the CIA's involvement in domestic intelligence gathering. The last time this happened was in the 1960s and 1970s, when domestic left-wing activists were targeted and there were numerous civil liberties violations. There needs to be much more attention to how intelligence can be pursued in a way that safeguards the nation from serious threats without threatening civil liberties.

McGee, Jim. "Fighting Terror with Databases; Domestic Intelligence Plans Stir Concern." *Washington Post*, February 16, 2002, p. A27. Federal authorities are building powerful new investigative tools by linking databases containing information about, for example, immigrants and resident aliens. Local police are being given increased access to information from federal agencies, and often carrying out interviews on their behalf. As a sort of pilot program, 5,000 Middle Eastern men who share some characteristics with the September 11 hijackers have been "voluntarily" interviewed. Some civil libertarians believe that an open-ended database system may suck in thousands of innocent citizens and subject them to harassment and employment difficulties, and serve to deter legitimate political dissent as happened in the 1950s and 1970s.

Oder, Norman. "Libraries, Universities Meet with Lawyers on Patriot Act: Questions about Patron Confidentiality Heating Up; After TV Controversy, ALA Issues Distancing Statement." *Library Journal*, vol. 117, January 2002, p. 16. Library and academic organizations meet with the Justice Department to discuss the implications of the new USA PATRIOT Act for information about patrons' library use. The American Library Association is preparing specific guidelines for dealing with subpoenas and other government demands, and for determining their legality. One difficult area is determining when a library is allowed to tell a patron that his or her records have been requested by the government; another problem is potential conflicts with state confidentiality laws that may be superceded.

Padgett, Tim, and Rochelle Renfor. "Fighting Words: Can a Tenured Professor Be Fired for His Pro-Muslim Views? In a Post–Sept. 11 America, All Bets Are Off." *Time*, vol. 159, February 4, 2002. Describes the case of Sami al-Arian, a computer science professor at the University of South Florida who was dismissed for expressing stridently anti-Israel and pro-Intifada views. The university argues that death threats against the professor were creating a security risk, while angry alumni might stop donating to the institution. Al-Arian is fighting the dismissal with the support of civil liberties groups.

Peabody, Bruce G. "In the Wake of September 11: Civil Liberties and Terrorism." *Social Education*, vol. 66, March 2002, pp. 90ff. Considers three major civil liberties issues raised by executive and legislative action after September 11: expanded power to eavesdrop between prisoners and their attorneys, the possible use of military tribunals, and the ability to deport aliens "reasonably believed" to be connected to terrorist organizations, or to hold them indefinitely without trial.

Schmitt, Richard B. "Planned Sequel to Patriot Act Losing Audience; as Congressional Critics of 'Sneak-And-Peek' Searches Gain Ground, the Justice Department May Shelve Requests for Expanded Powers." *Los Angeles Times*, July 29, 2003, p. A 14. Reports that growing opposition to expanded investigative and prosecutorial powers (such as "sneak and peak" searches that can be done secretly) may lead to the withdrawal of the proposals dubbed "PATRIOT 2."

INTERNET DOCUMENTS

American Civil Liberties Union. "Section-by-Section Analysis of Justice Department Draft 'Domestic Security Enhancement Act of 2003,' also Known as Patriot Act II." Available online. URL: http://www.aclu.org/ SafeandFree/SafeandFree.cfm?ID=11835&c=206. Posted on February 14, 2003. Provides analysis and criticism of the proposed new antiterrorism legislation. It is suggested that the legislation would diminish personal privacy, diminish government accountability, undermine rights on the basis of persons' mere association with certain groups, and strip immigrants of most rights.

Constitutional Rights Foundation. "America Responds to Terrorism." Available online. URL: http://www.crf-usa.org/terror/America%20 Responds%20to%20Terrorism.htm. Downloaded on November 17, 2003. A series of online lessons designed to help teachers and students deal with feelings and concerns arising from the September 11, 2001, attacks. Includes sections on media awareness and critical thinking, civil liberties issues (with historical background), Islamic issues, and international law and organizations. There is also a link to a related page on the war in Iraq.

"Democracy, Human Rights, and Labor." U.S. Department of State. Available online. URL: http://www.state.gov/www/global/human_rights/ index.html. Downloaded on April 27, 2000. This is the main page for the State Department's Bureau of Democracy, Human Rights, and Labor Affairs. It includes news items and reports including a link to the annual reports on human rights, which are organized by region and then by country. Significant human rights abuses are described and characterized.

Electronic Privacy Information Center. "Critical Infrastructure Protection and the Endangerment of Civil Liberties: An Assessment of the President's Commission on Critical Infrastructure Protection (PCCIP)." Available online. URL: http://www.epic.org/security/infowar/epic-cip.html. Posted in 1998. A 1998 report discussing the Clinton administration's Commission on Critical Infrastructure Protection, which was created to assess vulnerabilities to terrorist attack in water, transportation, communications, and other areas. According to the author, the commission's recommendations regarding computer security, eavesdropping, encryption, and related areas pose a threat to privacy and other civil liberties.

Terrorism, Media, and Popular Culture

BOOKS

Hachten, William A., and James Francis Scotton. *The World News Prism: Global Media in an Era of Terrorism*. 6th ed. Ames: Iowa State University Press, 2002. The goals and effects of terrorism are intimately related to the dynamics of world media coverage. An increasingly global media and new alternative channels (such as al-Jazeera and the Internet) gives terrorist groups more direct access to the public. Including the worldwide response to the attacks of September 11, 2001, this revised textbook also includes the role of the Internet, global information distribution channels, and public diplomacy and information warfare carried out by competing governments.

Nacos, Brigitte L. *Mass-Mediated Terrorism: The Central Role of the Media in Terrorism and Counterterrorism*. Lanham, Md.: Rowman and Littlefield, 2002. The author points out the increasing sophistication of terrorists in creating maximum media coverage for their actions, as well as for transmitting fear through the media. For that reason effective counterterrorism requires an equally sophisticated strategy for dealing with the mass media following a terrorist attack.

Tuman, Joseph S. *Communicating Terror: The Rhetorical Dimensions of Terrorism*. Thousand Oaks, Calif.: Sage Publications, 2003. An up-to-date survey of the uses of terrorism as a form of communication addressed not just to the immediate victims but to both the target society and the terrorist's own constituents and competitors. Considerations include definitions and characterizations of terrorism, the use of symbolism, terrorism in public debate, and the relationship between terrorism and the media.

ARTICLES AND PAPERS

Miller, Henry K. "Fatal Attraction; Che Guevara, Carlos the Jackal, Andreas Baader: These Are the Faces of Radical Terrorist Chic. Henry K. Miller Examines the Myths." *New Statesman*, October 28, 2002, n.p. Also available online. URL: http://www.findarticles.com (search for this particular article). The author explores "terrorist chic" and the portrayal of terrorists and rebels in popular music, movies, and culture. Movies examined include a new film about German Red Army Faction terrorist Andreas Baader.

Nacos, Brigitte. "Accomplice or Witness? The Media's Role in Terrorism." *Current History*, April 2000, pp. 174–178. Explores the fundamental problem that the free press, which properly must give extensive coverage to terrorist attacks and threats, is also fulfilling the goals of terrorists who want to achieve recognition and publicity for their cause(s) as well as spreading fear. In addition, new media, ranging from handheld video cameras to the Internet, is making it easier for small terrorist or radical groups to spread their messages.

Smolkin, Rachel. "Thinking About the (No Longer) Unthinkable: When News Breaks, the Journalistic Instinct Is to Respond Quickly and in Force. But Are the Rules Different When the News Is a Chemical, Biological, or Radiological Attack?" *American Journalism Review*, vol. 25, May 2003, pp. 52ff. The realities of such terrorist attacks require that journalists not follow their instinct to run to a story. Experts suggest that reporters take a cautious, observant approach. The different types of toxic agents and recommended responses are explained.

Taylor, Philip. "Spin Laden." *The World Today*, December 2001, pp. 6–8. The author suggests that the media can sometimes exacerbate misperceptions at home and anger toward the United States abroad and thus contribute to terrorism and unrest. For example, the Internet spread rumors such as that "4,000 Jews failed to turn up for work at the World Trade Center" the morning of September 11. Footage of a Palestinian celebration during the 1991 Gulf War was mistakenly labeled as showing them celebrating the attacks on the World Trade Center in 2001. To many Islamic fundamentalists in the Middle East, global broadcast networks such as CNN have become not neutral sources of news but symbols of American imperialism. To counter such negative images and rhetoric, the United States needs to have a serious, wide-ranging program of public diplomacy that can reach not only local elites but the person in the street.

INTERNET DOCUMENTS

Hamblen, Jessica. "How the Community May be Affected by Media Coverage of the Terrorist Attack." National Center for PTSD. Available online. URL: http://www.ncptsd.org/facts/disasters/fs_media_disaster.html. Updated on May 14, 2003. Describes the results of a study of the effects of media coverage of the 1995 Oklahoma City bombing. The study found no correlation in adults between hours of exposure to coverage of the attack in people seeking mental health services six months later and increases in post–traumatic stress disorder (PTSD) symptoms. However, children watching more coverage of the attack did report more PTSD symptoms. It is unclear, however, whether children more disturbed by the attack therefore watched more coverage.

SPECIFIC TYPES OF TERRORISM

Weapons of Mass Destruction (General)

BOOKS

Brackett, D. W. *Holy Terror: Armageddon in Tokyo.* New York: Weatherhill, 1996. The author, a foreign correspondent specializing in Asia, looks at the Aum Shinrikyo cult and its activities, which he characterizes as "ultraterrorism"—terrorism using weapons of mass destruction. He argues that terrorism based on religious fanaticism is a growing threat, particularly coupled with the ability to produce weapons such as nerve gas. He suggests that the United States must develop a comprehensive intelligence and response system to cope with the threat.

Carus, W. Seth. *Bioterrorism and Biocrimes: The Illicit Use of Biological Agents Since 1900.* Washington, D.C.: Center for Counterproliferation Research, 2002. A survey of more than 270 alleged worldwide cases of the use of pathogens by terrorists and criminals in the 20th century. As of the time of original writing (about 1998), interest in this threat was high but actual incidences were relatively rare. However, in 2001 the as yet unsolved anthrax attacks were added to the 1984 Rajneeshee cult's activities as the only confirmed instances of bioterrorism attacks within the United States. The types of agents used are also tabulated.

Laqueur, Walter. *The New Terrorism: Fanaticism and the Arms of Mass Destruction.* New York: Oxford University Press, 1999. The author, one of the foremost experts on terrorism, argues that terrorism is taking a new and dangerous form. Traditional terrorist groups, motivated by coherent ideology or nationalism, are giving way to tiny, idiosyncratic groups driven by fanaticism, apocalyptic visions, or the desire for simple vengeance. At the same time, weapons of mass destruction (chemical, biological, even nuclear) are becoming more available, and the complex information systems at the heart of the modern economy have also become vulnerable to "cyberterrorism."

Schram, Martin. *Avoiding Armageddon: Our Future, Our Choice.* Basic Books, 2003. A companion book to the Public Broadcasting Service (PBS) series of the same name, it focuses on the vast supply of unsecured weapons of mass destruction that may be quite readily available to terrorists and interviews a variety of experts about how to prevent or respond to potentially devastating attacks.

Stern, Jessica. *The Ultimate Terrorists.* Cambridge, Mass.: Harvard University Press, 1999. Despite its ominous title, this introduction calmly and concisely places in perspective the threat of terrorism using weapons of mass destruction. The author suggests that the threat is real and the effects of a chemical or biological attack could be grave, especially when the effects of panic are added to the initial damage. However, there are a variety of commonsense approaches that can minimize the threat.

ARTICLES AND PAPERS

Neuman, Johanna. "Mass Evacuations Present Massive Problems; As The Nation Faces the Threat of Terrorism, Public Officials Are Reviewing Disaster Responses for Clues on How Best to Empty a City." *Los Angeles Times,* May 11, 2003, p. A28. The threat of the use of weapons of mass destruction by terrorists is spurring cities to revise their evacuation plans. The fundamental problem is that too many people are likely to move at once, overwhelming the roads. In many cases mass evacuation might make the situation worse.

"The Terror Next Time? Nuclear, Chemical and Biological Threats." *The Economist (US),* October 6, 2001, n.p. Modern industrial society creates huge amounts of hazardous substances (more than 850,000 sites in the United States alone). However, terrorists face considerable difficulty obtaining the material and creating a weapon (such as a bomb) that would disperse it in the most effective way. Possible state sponsors of nuclear, chemical, or biological terrorism are also discussed.

INTERNET DOCUMENTS

"Mental Health Aspects of Terrorism." U.S. Department of Health and Human Services. Substance Abuse and Mental Health Services Administration. Center for Mental Health Services. Available online. URL: http://www.mentalhealth.org/publications/allpubs/KEN-01-0095/default.asp. Downloaded on August 7, 2003. This document gives a basic outline of typical psychological reactions to terrorist attacks and suggested do's and don'ts for helping victims cope with the disaster.

Chemical and Biological Terrorism

BOOKS

Burke, Robert. *Counter-Terrorism for Emergency Responders.* Boca Raton, Fla.: Lewis Publishers, 2000. A handbook for paramedics, police, firefighters, and others who are first on the scene and may have to deal with an increasing number of chemical or biological terrorist attacks. The book provides step-by-step procedures for assessing and containing a situation and for aiding victims.

Cole, Leonard A. *The Eleventh Plague: The Politics of Biological and Chemical Warfare.* New York: W. H. Freeman, 1997. Discusses recent developments in biological and chemical warfare, particularly as they emerged in the Persian Gulf War with Iraq in 1991 and the terrorist nerve gas attack on a Tokyo subway in 1995. The author suggests that difficulties in detecting and preventing use of chemical and biological agents by rogue states or terrorist groups will prove to be formidable. The book ends with discussion of a proposal to minimize the threat through a multilayered web of detection, defensive efforts, and active response.

Cook, Michelle Stem, and Amy F. Woolf. *Preventing Proliferation of Biological Weapons: U.S. Assistance to the Former Soviet Union.* Washington, D.C.: Congressional Research Service, 2002. Describes the extent and capabilities of biowar-related facilities in the former Soviet Union and U.S. programs aimed at preventing diversion of materials or workers from these facilities to terrorist groups or rogue nations.

Frist, Bill. *When Every Moment Counts: What You Need to Know About Bioterrorism from the Senate's Only Doctor.* Lanham, Md.: Rowman and Littlefield, 2002. A useful guide written in lay language. It describes the various agents that might be encountered (including pathogens, toxins, and chemical agents) as well as the threat to the food and water supply and the preparations needed to better protect the nation.

Jennings, Christopher. *Biological and Chemical Weapons: Criminal Sanctions and Federal Regulations.* Washington, D.C.: Congressional Research Service, 2001. Discusses applicable regulations and criminal law applicable to biological and chemical weapons (some are also applicable to nuclear, radiological, or other regulated substances).

Redhead, C. Stephen, and Donna U. Vogt. *Bioterrorism: Legislation to Improve Public Health Preparedness and Response Capacity.* Washington, D.C.:

Congressional Research Service, 2002. Summarizes new bioterrorism preparedness legislation in the House and Senate in 2002, as well as new funding for bioterrorism defense.

Stevens, Nye. *Anthrax in the Mail.* Washington, D.C.: Congressional Research Service, 2002. Assesses the ability of the U.S. Postal Service to deal with bioterrorism threats such as the anthrax distributed by mail in fall 2001.

Tierno, Philip M. *Protect Yourself Against Bioterrorism.* New York: Pocket Books, 2002. This compact handbook is geared to answering common questions about each of the types of pathogens and toxins that might be used in a bioterrorist attack. The operation, symptoms, diagnosis, and recommended treatment are given for each agent.

Venzke, Ben N., ed. *First Responder Chem-Bio Handbook.* Tempest Publishing, 1998. A succinct, practical guide to dealing with chemical or biological attacks. Topics include assessment, treatment, decontamination, and precautions for workers on the scene.

ARTICLES AND PAPERS

Ban, Jonathan. "Agricultural Biological Warfare: an Overview." Chemical and Biological Arms Control Institute. Available online. URL: http://www. cbaci.org/arenaban.PDF. Posted on June 2000. Gives a historical overview of attacks on agricultural facilities in war, such as German agents using anthrax to sabotage draft and food animals in the United States and several other countries. Agricultural resources were also targeted in various ways by France and Japan; the United States and Britain have extensively researched and tested various agents but have not deployed them. (The United States stopped stockpiling and development of offensive biological weapons in 1969.) The use of agriculture-based attacks and sabotage by non-state groups (such as terrorists) and the potential risks and consequences of such attacks are also explored.

Eban, Katherine. "Waiting for Bioterror: Is Our Health System Ready?" *The Nation,* December 9, 2002, pp. 11–18. Despite the new interest in defense against bioterrorism following September 11, 2001, and the anthrax attacks, the root problem remains: The healthcare system and public health infrastructure are woefully ill-funded and under-equipped to deal with a major attack such as a smallpox epidemic. Too often attention and funding are focused on exotic technology instead of the basics. Case studies include Las Vegas and Atlanta.

Gellman, Barton. "Al Qaeda near Biological, Chemical Weapons Production." *Washington Post,* March 23, 2003, p. A1. According to documents recently recovered by U.S. forces, al-Qaeda's program to develop chemical and biological weapons appears to be considerably more advanced than had been suspected.

Gewin, Virginia. "Agriculture Shock." *Nature*, January 9, 2003, pp. 106–108. The author suggests that using diseases to target agriculture and animal husbandry could cause severe damage to a nation's food supply. Capabilities for monitoring and quickly detecting the introduction of pathogens are being improved in the United States and Europe. It remains questionable whether terrorists would be attracted to such low-profile forms of attack.

Holloway, Harry C., et al. "The threat of biological weapons: prophylaxis and mitigation of psychological and social consequences." *JAMA, the Journal of the American Medical Association,* vol. 278, August 6, 1997, pp. 425ff. Explores the psychological and social consequences of a biological attack. Panic, post–traumatic stress disorder, depression, and survivor guilt are all likely psychological effects. The invisible nature of the microbial threat increases fear. Social consequences might include a breakdown of institutions and loss of trust and cooperation. Psychiatric casualties among survivors must be promptly treated.

LaPorte, Ronald E. et al. "Towards an Internet Civil Defence Against Bioterrorism." *Lancet Infectious Diseases* 2001, vol. 1, pp. 125–127. The authors suggest that in developing an effective defense against bioterrorism, planners look toward the traditional model of civil defense, where citizens were expected to take considerable responsibility for watching for and appropriately reacting to threats. The Internet offers a new way to allow millions of people to watch for potential bioterrorist activity. Schools and existing organizations (as well as online communities) could be the nucleus for such a system.

Rashbaum, William K. "Sniffing New York's Air Ducts for Signs of Terror." *New York Times*, April 22, 2003, p. A1. Reports that a specially trained unit of National Guard soldiers have fanned out through the city, testing for radiation and chemical and biological agents in office complexes, hotels, malls, and other areas where the public gathers. Each soldier has been trained in a particular specialty. The team also uses a computer model that can predict the dispersion of an agent under various conditions.

INTERNET DOCUMENTS

"American Anthrax Outbreak of 2001." University of California, Los Angeles. School of Public Health. Department of Epidemiology. Available online. URL: http://www.ph.ucla.edu/epi/bioter/detect/antdetect_intro. html. Downloaded on December 9, 2003. This site compiles detailed epidemiological studies of the anthrax cases of late 2001 that arose from

Global Terrorism

a still-unsolved terrorist attack or attacks. There is an overview of the differing roles of "disease detectives" (epidemiologists, particularly at the
National Centers for Disease Control) and police detectives, which have
had to cooperate in addressing the anthrax attacks. There is also a listing
of the specific incidences of the disease and different possible interpretations of the origin and spread of the pathogen.
"Firefighting: Terrorism." Available online. URL: http://www.about.com
(click on jobs/careers, firefighting and emergency services, and then terrorism). Downloaded on April 27, 2000. Links to information about biological and chemical weapons and terrorist attacks, as well as general
resources on terrorism.
Friedlander, Arthur M. "Anthrax." Available online. URL: http://www.
nbc-med.org/SiteContent/HomePage/WhatsNew/MedAspects/
CH-22electrv699.pdf. Downloaded on August 15, 2002. A chapter from
Medical Aspects of Chemical and Biological Warfare. Describes the organism,
its epidemiology, pathology, and possible effects, diagnosis, and treatment.
Rega, Paul, and Donald McConnaughy. "History of Bioterrorism."
Bioterry.com (authors' personal site). Available online. URL: http://www.
bioterry.com/History_of_Biological_Terrorism.asp. Posted in 2001. A
chronology of biological warfare and bioterrorism excerpted from the authors' *Biological Terrorism Response Manual.*
Tucker, Jonathan B. "Historical Trends Related to Bioterrorism: An Empir-
ical Analysis." *Emerging Infectious Diseases.* Special Issue. vol. 5,
July–August 1999. Available online. URL: http://www.cdc.gov/ncidod/
EID/vol5no4/tucker.htm. Updated on July 1, 1999. An analysis of a database from the Chemical and Biological Weapons Nonproliferation Project at the Monterey Institute's Center for Nonproliferation Studies. A
total of 415 incidents from 1900 to January 31, 1999, are classified according to materials used (chemical, biological, radiological), type of
event (conspiracy to acquire, possession, threat, hoax, etc.), type of terrorist organization involved, motivation, and other factors. In general,
motivation seems to have shifted from protest to separatist sentiment, retaliation, revenge, or apocalyptic prophecy. Symbolic buildings and the
general population are more likely to be targeted.

Nuclear and Radiological Terrorism

BOOKS

Lee, Rensselaer W. *Smuggling Armageddon: The Nuclear Black Market in the
Former Soviet Union and Europe.* New York: St. Martin's Press, 1998. The

author, an associate with the Foreign Policy Research Institute, investigates and documents the potential and actual illegal movement of nuclear material in Russia. Desperate economic conditions, chaos, and opportunism have combined to create a worrisome situation. While many reports of nuclear smuggling turn out to be bogus or unsubstantiated, the possibility that organized crime or terrorists could gain access to some of the former Soviet Union's huge stockpile of nuclear materials or even warheads cannot be dismissed. Efforts by the United States and other governments to cope with the threat are incomplete and poorly coordinated.

Medalia, Jonathan. *Nuclear and Radiological Terrorism*. Washington, D.C.: Congressional Research Service, 2001. Discusses nuclear capabilities that might be available to terrorists (including radiological "dirty bombs") and international programs to better secure and reduce stockpiles of nuclear weapons and materials.

ARTICLES AND PAPERS

Gellman, Barton. "Fears Prompt U.S. to Beef Up Nuclear Terror Detection." *Washington Post*, March 3, 2002, pp. A1, A18. The possibility that al-Qaeda may be close to using some sort of nuclear or radiological weapon of mass destruction has led to a stepping up of efforts to detect such weapons and thwart attacks. These efforts include increased use of radiation sensors, particularly at borders and around key installations, as well as having an army Delta Force unit on standby.

Keller, Bill. "Nuclear Nightmares." *New York Times*, May 26, 2002, Section 6, pp. 22ff. The author describes a variety of devastating scenarios involving terrorist attacks with nuclear weapons or dispersing radioactive material via a "dirty bomb" or even an aerosol device. All of them were suggested by various American or Russian experts, and introduce a discussion of how to deter, detect, or prevent them.

Kluger, Jeffrey. "Defusing the Terror." *Time*, vol. 159, June 24, 2002, p. 30ff. Using a question-and-answer format, the author explains what a "dirty" nuclear bomb is and what its effects would be. Such a weapon uses a conventional explosion to scatter radioactive material. It is likely to cause only minimal casualties (mainly from the explosion), but fear of radiation would enhance its psychological and economic effects.

Kluger, Jeffrey. "The Nuke Pipeline: The Trade in Nuclear Contraband Is Approaching Critical Mass. Can We Turn Off the Spigot?" *Time*, vol. 158, December 11, 2001, pp. 40ff. Smugglers of weapons-grade uranium and other radioactive materials have been arrested trying to sell the stuff. The main source is Russia, which has more than 100 military facilities, 80 decommissioned nuclear submarines, as well as power plants, all with nuclear material that is being poorly guarded. Although the United States and Russia have been cooperating to try to get a handle on nuclear material, the Bush administration has reduced funding for the program.

Richelson, Jeffrey. "Defusing Nuclear Terror." *Bulletin of the Atomic Scientists*, vol. 58, March–April 2002, pp. 38ff. Describes the capabilities of the NEST (Nuclear Emergency Search Team). The NEST would first evaluate the credibility of the threat (such as by determining the level of knowledge of nuclear weapons demonstrated by a terrorist group). Teams could then use sensors in aircraft and disguised vehicles to track down nuclear bombs or radioactive material and then destroy or disarm the bomb. Since its formation in 1975, NEST has investigated approximately 100 cases of possible nuclear terrorism, and has actually deployed personnel to the scene in up to 20 or so of these cases.

INTERNET DOCUMENTS

"Effect of Nuclear Weapons and Nuclear War." Trinity Atomic Web Site. Available online. URL: http://nuketesting.enviroweb.org/nukeffct/index. html. Updated on June 8, 2002. Describes how various types of nuclear explosions develop and expand and their effects on people and the environment. While originally developed as a way to understand the devastating effects of nuclear war, the principles also apply to nuclear explosions set off by terrorists, although these are likely to be smaller and not involve multiple detonations.

Infrastructure Protection and Transportation Security

BOOKS

Abel, Amy, and Mark Holt. *Terrorism: Electric Utility Infrastructure*. Washington, D.C.: Congressional Research Service, 2002. Discusses the physical and cybernetic vulnerability of the complex grid of interlocking components that make up the electrical power system.

Behrens, Carl E. *Nuclear Powerplants: Vulnerability to Terrorist Attack*. Washington, D.C.: Congressional Research Service, 2002. Discusses vulnerability of nuclear plants to different forms of terrorist attack, including seizure of facilities by armed terrorists and crashing a hijacked airliner into a power plant. Also discusses relevant legislative proposals.

Copeland, Claudia, and Betsy Cody. *Terrorism and Security Issues Facing the Water Infrastructure Sector*. Washington, D.C.: Congressional Research

Service, 2002. Assesses the adequacy of security for the nation's water supplies and discusses the development and funding of new measures.

Frittelli, John. *Port and Maritime Security: Overview and Issues.* Hauppage, N.Y.: Nova Science Publishers, 2003. Discusses issues relating to current maritime security legislation, including monitoring and tracking information about cargo and improving the physical security of port facilities.

Morgan, Daniel. *Aviation Security Technologies and Procedures: Screening Passengers and Baggage.* Washington, D.C.: Congressional Research Service, 2001. Describes aviation security issues including technology, funding, and congressional oversight. Outlines proposals in Congress and administration actions since the September 11 attacks.

Rothberg, Paul F. *Hazardous Materials Transportation: Vulnerability to Terrorists, Federal Activities, and Options to Reduce Risks.* Washington, D.C.: Congressional Research Service, 2001. Assesses the risks of terrorist attack or diversion of the more than 800,000 hazardous materials shipments made each day—mostly by truck. Describes preventive measures.

———. *Pipeline Security: Industry and Federal Efforts and Associated Legislation.* Washington, D.C.: Congressional Research Service, 2002. Discusses the efforts of owners to better secure natural gas pipelines and storage facilities as well as congressional efforts to improve pipeline security.

Shea, Dana A. *Critical Infrastructure: Control Systems and the Terrorist Threat.* Washington, D.C.: Congressional Research Service, 2003. Also available online. URL: http://www.fas.org/irp/crs/RL31534.pdf. Updated February 21, 2003. Discusses the vulnerabilities of industrial control systems to terrorist attack and suggested measures, including uniform security standards and encrypting data used in control systems.

ARTICLES AND PAPERS

Gathright, Alan. "No-Fly List Ensnares Innocent Travelers." *San Francisco Chronicle,* June 8, 2003, p. A1. Reports that a problematic algorithm called Soundex is leading to the detaining of innocent persons whose names may sound similar to those of people on the terrorist watch list. The American Civil Liberties Union reported that at least 339 passengers have been so detained since September 11, 2001, and all turned out to be "false positives," with no arrests made.

Homer-Dixon, Thomas. "The Rise of Complex Terrorism." *Foreign Policy,* January–February 2002, pp. 52–62. The author suggests that unlike the relatively "simple" act of blowing up a building or crashing a plane into it, future "complex" terrorist attacks will be characterized by more subtle, distributed attacks against infrastructure such as power generation and distribution systems. Such physical or information-based attacks can be called "weapons of mass disruption." Additionally, as shown on September 11, many presumably innocuous facilities and objects contain potentially devastating materials, ranging from liquefied natural gas to chemical plants. Terrorists mounting "complex" attacks will also focus on maximum psychological effect, using sudden, unpredictable, bizarre tactics.

Janofsky, Michael. "Armed Pilots? Many Travelers Are Gun-Shy." *New York Times*. July 12, 2002, p. A1. The reporter asks travelers what they think about the idea of allowing airline pilots to have firearms in the cockpit. Many oppose arming pilots out of fear of stray bullets, concern that terrorists might obtain the gun, or a general antipathy toward firearms. Supporters note that pilots are trained, responsible individuals who are already responsible for the life of all aboard. A few opponents of firearms suggest that stun guns be used instead.

Rao, Ed, and Frank Binzoni. "Do Detection Technologies Fly?" *Security Management*, vol. 45, October 2001, p. 95. Overview and evaluation of a variety of baggage scanning technologies and the effectiveness of screeners using them.

Satchell, Michael. "Everyone Empty Your Pockets?" *U.S. News & World Report*, April 1, 2002, p. 18. Because of opposition to profiling, U.S. airports basically treat each passenger as an equal threat, and then overlay random closer inspections. Besides inconveniencing the public, this policy makes it easier for terrorists to slip "under the radar" since scrutiny is diluted. Use of non-profile information (such as watch lists) can help, and profiles aren't foolproof, since terrorists can learn how to avoid them.

Senkowsky, Sonya. "Building Better Biosensors: If You Think You're Nervous in Airports These Days, You Should Talk to Fred Milanovich." *BioScience*, vol. 52, April 2002, pp. 332ff. Describes the work of Fred Milanovich, program leader for chemical and biological national security at Lawrence Livermore National Laboratory. His team is trying to find ways to thwart terrorists who might surreptitiously spread deadly pathogens in a public place—particularly an airport, where travelers might spread the disease for thousands of miles. The potential solution is a "biodetector" that, like a smoke alarm, would give instant warning as soon as a pathogen is detected. Building a detector that is fast and accurate enough is difficult, but two technologies—immunoassay and DNA-based polymerase chain reaction (PCR) might be confined and refined sufficiently.

Wilson, Jim. "Blowing Up a 747: A Dramatic Test Proves that Simple Improvements Can Checkmate Bomb-Wielding Terrorists." *Popular Mechanics*, vol. 174, October 1997, pp. 56ff. The British Civil Administration has tested an improved aircraft cargo container that can contain the force of a bomb exploding inside, protecting the plane carrying it. The container is made from material similar to that used in bulletproof vests.

Annotated Bibliography

Wood, Daniel B. "Remote Screening Gains, But Will It Help?" *Christian Science Monitor*, July 8, 2002, n.p. Also available online. URL: http://www.csmonitor.com/2002/0708/p03s01-usgn.html. Posted in July 2002. The shooting attack at Los Angeles International Airport on July 4, 2002, has renewed interest in developing ways to screen people before they enter the secure area of the airport—perhaps before entering terminals or other crowded public areas. Ironically, one of the largest such programs under development is in Los Angeles, which would screen all passengers at a central facility before transporting them to the various terminals. Supporters of the idea believe that it would improve efficiency and the ability to contain incidents, while critics suggest that it would just relocate the vulnerability.

INTERNET DOCUMENTS

Sirhal, Maureen. "Critical Infrastructure Operators Lack Key Information." Government Executive.com. Available online. URL: http://www.govexec.com/dailyfed/0802/081302td1.htm. Posted on August 13, 2002. A report from the FBI's National Infrastructure Protection Center, which conducted simulations to test the ability of various government and private installations (including utilities and communications companies) to recover from damage to their systems. The study found that many organizations had inadequate contingency plans that failed to account for such things as the loss of telephone and Internet connectivity. They also lacked reliable backup communications systems.

Cyberterrorism and Information Warfare

BOOKS

Hildreth, Steven A. *Cyberwarfare*. Washington, D.C.: Congressional Research Service, 2001. Discusses current U.S. policies and efforts to combat the threat of foreign agents or terrorists mounting attacks on the American information infrastructure. Includes a glossary.

Sofaer, Abraham D., and Seymour E. Goodman, eds. *Transnational Dimension of Cyber Crime and Terrorism*, Stanford, Calif.: Hoover Institution Press, 2001. A distinguished panel of experts assess the potential for crime, vandalism, and terrorism, particularly against the Internet infrastructure that now carries billions of dollars worth of economic activity.

Verton, Dan. *Black Ice: The Invisible Threat of Cyberterrorism*. New York: McGraw Hill/Osborne Media, 2003. A well-organized picture of the threatening potential for terrorist hacking is derived from numerous interviews

273

with experts as well as indications of what terrorist groups are trying to do with and to our technological infrastructure.

ARTICLES AND PAPERS

Gellman, Barton. "Cyber-Attacks by Al Qaeda Feared: Terrorists at Threshold of Using Internet as Tool of Bloodshed, Experts Say." *Washington Post*, June 27, 2002, p. A1. Terrorists may be studying and preparing to target the digital distributed control systems (DCS) that control systems such as those that distribute oil, water, and gas. The most devastating attack might be a combination of a direct physical attack (such as a bombing) and an indirect cyber-attack that would cripple medical, firefighting, or other response capabilities. In Australia, a hacker named Vitek Boden demonstrated his ability to take control of a sewage treatment system, gaining access to all its functions.

Green, Joshua. "The Myth of Cyberterrorism: There Are Many Ways Terrorists Can Kill You—Computers Aren't One of Them." *Washington Monthly*, vol. 34, November 2002, pp. 8ff. In this contrary view the author points out that there have been no recorded instances of terrorists killing anyone with computers, and that the real computer security problems involve criminals and malicious hackers, not terrorist groups. The critical control systems are largely isolated from unauthorized remote access.

Levy, Stephen, and Brad Stone. "Hunting the Hackers." *Newsweek*, vol. 135, February 21, 2000, p. 38. Describes the "denial of service" attacks by hackers who paralyzed major e-commerce sites such as Yahoo! and eBay. While the hackers were not linked to terrorist groups, the attack underscores the vulnerability of the "new economy" to cyberattack.

Piazza, Peter. "Who's Winning the Cyberwars? Hackers and Terrorists Are Constantly Developing New Exploits, Which Government and Industry Must Defend Against." *Security Management*, vol. 46, December 2002, pp. 71ff. Surveys the new awareness of vulnerability that swept through government and industry following September 11, 2001, and how it was reflected in efforts to assess the vulnerabilities of information systems and "harden" them. A variety of organizational and technical measures are being taken, and growing resources are being dedicated to the problem.

Wallace, Bill. "Security Analysts Dismiss Fears of Terrorist Hackers: Electricity, Water Systems Hard to Damage Online." *San Francisco Chronicle*, June 30, 2002, p. A11. While many experts say concerns about cyberattacks are reasonable, terrorists would have a hard time attacking the control systems for power plants, water systems, and other critical facilities. This is because these systems are not directly accessible via the Internet.

Annotated Bibliography

Whitelaw, Kevin. "Terrorists on the Web: Electronic 'Safe Haven': Guerrillas Use Guns, Bombs, and Home Pages." *U.S. News & World Report*, vol. 124, June 22, 1998, p. 46. Although most observers focus on the potential of terrorist groups to attack computer systems, the other side of the story is the growing extent to which such groups are using the information superhighway to spread their message and coordinate their efforts. ELN in Colombia, the Zapatistas in Mexico, and Hezbollah in Lebanon all have extensive web sites. Trying to force such groups off the Internet would violate the freedom of expression that is at the heart of the new medium. Sample web addresses are included.

INTERNET DOCUMENTS

Borland, John, and William Church. "Analyzing the Threat of Cyberterrorism." *Techweb News*. Available online. URL: http://www.techweb.com (search news index for this particular article). Posted September 25, 1998. In an interview with John Borland, William Church, managing director of a company that monitors computer infrastructure problems, says that while individual hackers and crackers have attacked or exploited information systems, sometimes for criminal purposes, terrorist groups have not yet adopted such techniques. Terrorists generally put their trust in weapons they understand such as bombs. Most terrorists also prefer weapons that cause direct, sensational damage.

Collin, Barry C. "The Future of CyberTerrorism: Where the Physical and Virtual Worlds Converge." 11th Annual Symposium on Criminal Justice Issues. Available online. URL: http://afgen.com/terrorism1.html. Downloaded on August 25, 2003. A conceptual outline of the modes of cyberterrorism—how the physical and virtual worlds are connected by computer and control systems, how cyberterrorists can target this interface, their goals and possible scenarios, and the difference between terrorists and ordinary "crackers."

CHAPTER 9

ORGANIZATIONS AND AGENCIES

Following are listings for organizations and agencies involved with terrorism-related issues. These include government agencies, academic research institutes, and civil liberties and human rights organizations.

American Civil Liberties Union (ACLU)
URL: http://www.aclu.org
E-mail: aclu@aclu.org
Phone: (212) 549-2500
125 Broad Street, 18th floor
New York, NY 10004-2400
Founded in 1920, the ACLU conducts extensive litigation on constitutional issues including privacy and free speech. This focus often brings the group into conflict with much antiterrorism legislation.

Amnesty International
URL: http://www.amnesty.org (international)
URL: http://www.aiusa.org (U.S.)
E-mail: admin-us@aiusa.org
Phone: (202) 544-0200
Washington Office
600 Pennsylvania Avenue, SE
5th Floor
Washington, DC 20003
This worldwide human rights group publicizes human rights abuses around the world and seeks to mobilize world opinion against oppressive governments. Since human rights abuses are often related to terrorism and counterterrorism, this organization's reports and other resources can be quite useful.

Anti-Defamation League (ADL)
URL: http://www.adl.org
E-mail: webmaster@adl.org
Phone: (202) 452-8320
(Washington, D.C., office)
Anti-Defamation League
823 United Nations Plaza
New York, NY 10017
Based on its focus on combating anti-Semitism and the numerous terrorist attacks on Jews, the ADL generally takes a strong position in support of antiterrorism legislation. For example, the group filed an amicus brief supporting the government in *Humanitarian Law Project v. Reno*, arguing that provi-

sions of the 1996 Antiterrorism and Effective Death Penalty Act prohibiting U.S. citizens from giving any kind of aid to government-designated terrorist groups was reasonable and necessary because there is no way to separate "peaceful" aid from aid that furthers a group's violent agenda. The ADL has a web page at http://www.adl.org/main_terrorism.asp that provides periodic reports on international and domestic terrorism.

Brookings Institution
URL: www.brookings.org
E-mail: brookinfo@brook.edu
Phone: (202) 797-6000
1775 Massachusetts Avenue, NW
Washington, D.C. 20036
This venerable think tank produces reports and conferences. It takes a generally liberal, activist-government approach to public policy issues. It has undertaken a major project on "Terrorism and American Foreign Policy" to provide analysis and recommendations in the wake of the September 11, 2001, attacks.

Cato Institute
URL: www.cato.org
E-mail: Web form
Phone: (202) 842-0200
1000 Massachusetts Avenue, NW
Washington, DC 20001-5403
The Cato Institute is a libertarian policy think tank that generally advocates individual liberty and strict limitations on government power. Cato has been critical of a number

of the post–September 11 government initiatives. See its terrorism resource page at http://www.cato.org/current/terrorism/index.html.

Center for Democracy and Technology
URL: http://www.cdt.org
E-mail: webmaster@cdt.org
Phone: (202) 637-9800
1634 I Street NW
Suite 1100
Washington, DC 20006
Civil liberties group that works to "promote democratic values and constitutional liberties in the digital age." Has a "Counter-Terrorism Issues Page" at http://www.cdt.org/policy/terrorism/ that includes links to news about legislation relating to terrorism, particularly wiretapping and computer surveillance.

Center for Strategic and International Studies (CSIS)
URL: www.csis.org
E-mail: webmaster@csis.org
Phone: (202) 887-0200
1800 K Street, NW
Suite 400
Washington, DC 20006
This center publishes books, reports, and periodicals dealing with foreign policy and national strategy. Relevant topics include arms control, nuclear proliferation, and homeland security.

Centre for the Study of Terrorism and Political Violence (St Andrews University)

URL: http://www.st-andrews.ac.
uk/academic/intrel/research/
cstpv/
E-mail: CSTPV@st-andrews.ac.
uk
Phone: 44 (0)1334 76161

**Department of International
Relations
University of St Andrews
St Andrews, Fife
KY16 9AL
United Kingdom**
A Scottish academic research cen-
ter that provides an extensive data-
base and links at its web site.

**Council on American-Islamic
Relations (CAIR)**
URL: www.cair-net.org
E-mail: cair@cair-net.org
Phone: (202) 488-8787
453 New Jersey Avenue, SE
Washington, DC 20003
Relations between the Islamic and
other communities in the United
States came under increased strain
after the September 11, 2001, attacks. CAIR condemns the attacks
while advocating for tolerance and
nondiscrimination toward American Muslims.

Derechos Human Rights
URL: http://www.derechos.org/
E-mail: hr@derechos.org
Phone: 34 91 526-7502
P.O. Box 156037
Madrid 28080 Spain
Described as "the first Internet-
based human rights organization,"
Derechos publicizes, investigates,

and works to end human rights
abuses around the world. Its regional pages (such as the one for
Africa) provide useful reports and
links to human rights issues by
country.

**Electronic Frontier Foundation
(EFF)**
URL: http://www.eff.org
E-mail: ask@eff.org
Phone: (415) 436-9333
1550 Bryant Street
Suite 725
San Francisco, CA 94103-4832
Organization formed in 1990 to
maintain and enhance intellectual
freedom, privacy, and other values
of civil liberties and democracy
in networked communications. It
publicizes and campaigns against
antiterrorism legislation that it
considers repressive or threatening
to privacy. The group publishes
newsletters, Internet guidebooks,
and other documents; provides
mailing lists and other online fo-
rums; and hosts a large electronic
document archive.

**Electronic Privacy Information
Center (EPIC)**
URL: http://www.epic.org
E-mail: info@epic.org
Phone: (202) 544-9240
666 Pennsylvania Avenue, SE
Suite 301
Washington, DC 20003
EPIC was established in 1994 to
focus public attention on emerging
privacy issues relating to the na-
tional information infrastructure.

Some of these issues, such as the Clipper Chip and the Digital Telephony proposal, have arisen from antiterrorism legislation. The organization publishes the *EPIC Alert* newsletter and leads campaigns on privacy issues.

Federation of American Scientists
URL: http://www.fas.org/
E-mail: fas@fas.org
Phone: (202) 546-3300
1717 K Street, NW
Suite 209
Washington, DC 20036
The Federation of American Scientists provides research and advocacy on many issues involving the use (or abuse) of science and technology. Its Intelligence Resource Program page at http://www.fas.org/irp/threat/terror.htm offers a variety of links to FAS reports and other resources relating to intelligence and counterterrorism.

Human Rights Watch
URL: http://www.hrw.org/
E-mail: hrwnyc@hrw.org
Phone: (212) 290-4700
350 Fifth Avenue
34th Floor
New York, NY 10118-3299
A group dedicated to investigating and publicizing human rights violations around the world and working for reforms that strengthen human rights. Its web site offers access by region and country to reports on human right abuses, as well as offering the group's annual World

Report and an extensive catalog of publications.

Humanitarian Law Project
URL: http://hlp.home.igc.org
Phone: (310) 836-6316
8124 West Third Street
Suite 105
Los Angeles, CA 90048
Supports legal protection for international humanitarian efforts. Became involved with the debate and subsequent litigation over the Antiterrorism Act of 1996, because the law includes a provision prohibiting U.S. citizens from giving humanitarian aid to or through groups that the federal government has designated as terrorist. In 1998, the project filed a suit, *Humanitarian Law Project v. Reno*, seeking to overturn that provision.

Institute for Security Technology Studies
URL: http://www.ists.dartmouth.edu/ISTS
E-mail: Stacy.Kollias@Dartmouth.EDU
Phone: (603) 646-0700
Dartmouth College
45 Lyme Road
Suite 200
Hanover, NH 03755
A government-funded institute at Dartmouth College, focusing on "cyber-security and information infrastructure protection research." Includes links to information about cyberterrorism and its relationship to the September 11 and subsequent attacks.

279

International Association for
  Counterterrorism & Security
  Professionals
URL: http://www.iacsp.com/
P.O. Box 10265
Arlington, VA 22210
An organization for professionals
involved with security and coun-
terterrorism issues. Has two mem-
ber publications, the *Journal of
Counterterrorism & Security* and the
Counterterrorism & Security Report.
Pages on the web site include Ter-
rorism Watch, which summarizes
recent news developments, Terror
Info Bank, and an archive of se-
lected articles from the organiza-
tion's publications.

International Policy Institute for
  Counter-Terrorism
URL: http://www.ict.org.il/
E-mail: services@ict.org.il
ICT
Interdisciplinary Center Herzlia
P.O. Box 167
Herzlia, 46150
Israel
A research institute and think tank
in Herzliya, Israel, primarily con-
cerned with developing public pol-
icy and strategies to deal with
terrorism as a global issue. Offers
publications and holds conferences.
The web site includes news updates
and background data about terror-
ist groups and attacks.

Southern Poverty Law Center
URL: http:/www.splcenter.org
E-mail: Web form
Phone: (334) 956-8200

400 Washington Avenue
Montgomery, AL 36104
This organization monitors the activities of Ku Klux Klan and other
hate groups as well as Patriot
groups and militias. Its projects
have included Klanwatch (founded
in 1981) and the Militia Task Force
(1995). The home page for the Intelligence Project, which monitors hate groups, is at URL:
http://www.splcenter.org/intel.
The organization also publishes
the quarterly *Intelligence Report*
available at the web site, and it also
conducts tolerance education.

Terrorism Research Center
http://www.terrorism.com/
  welcome.htm
E-mail: TRC@terrorism.com
Phone: (877) 635-0816
An independent organization conducting research and providing
public information on terrorism
and related issues. The organization's web site provides extensive
resource links.

United States Department of
  Homeland Security
URL: http://www.dhs.gov
E-mail: Web form
Washington, D.C. 20528
The Department of Homeland Security (DHS) was established in
2002 as a single, coordinated effort
for protecting the territory of the
United States from terrorists. The
new department has incorporated
a number of existing agencies
(such as the Coast Guard, U.S. Im-

migration, and the Secret Service) and new agencies (such as the Transportation Security Administration) as well as coordinating efforts with intelligence agencies such as the FBI and CIA. The DHS issues terrorism alerts and provides resources for research and implementation in many areas including transportation and infrastructure security.

United States Department of Health and Human Services Centers for Disease Control and Prevention Bioterrorism Preparedness and Response Network 1600 Clifton Rd. Atlanta, GA 30333 URL: http://www.bt.cdc.gov/ Phone: (800) 311-3435
The Centers for Disease Control and Prevention has, like many other federal agencies, undertaken new initiatives to assess and deal with the threat of biological terrorism. Its Bioterrorism Preparedness and Response web page includes links to background information, news, official statements, and emergency services. Procedures for notification in case of actual or threatened biological attacks are outlined.

United States Central Intelligence Agency (CIA) URL: www.cia.gov/ E-mail: Web form Phone: (703) 482-0623 Central Intelligence Agency

Office of Public Affairs Washington, DC 20505
The Central Intelligence Agency is responsible for obtaining and analyzing intelligence relating to foreign threats against the United States, including terrorist activities. It provides analysis for the executive and policymakers as well as engaging in various clandestine activities. The CIA also provides educational resources to the public, including the *CIA World Factbook*.

United States Department of Justice Federal Bureau of Investigation (FBI) URL: http://www.fbi.gov Phone: (202) 324-5520 935 Pennsylvania Avenue, NW Washington, DC 20535
The FBI investigates incidences of terrorism and compiles data on domestic terrorism.

United States Department of State URL: http://www.state.gov/s/ct E-mail: publicaffairs@panet. us-state.gov Phone: (202) 647-4000 2201 C Street, NW Washington, D.C. 20520
The U.S. State Department provides a variety of resources dealing with foreign affairs, including annual reports on human rights abuses and terrorism. The above web site provides an index to these resources.

United States Department of State
Counterterrorism Office
URL: http://www.state.gov
E-mail: Web form
Phone: (202) 647-6575
Public Information
Bureau of Public Affairs
Room 2509

U.S. Department of State
2201 C Street, NW
Washington, DC 20520
This office coordinates antiterrorism efforts with foreign governments and provides reports and advisories to the general public. It is a good source of official information.

PART III

APPENDICES

APPENDIX A

STATISTICS ON TERRORISM

Most of the following statistics are excerpted from the Department of State publication *Patterns of Global Terrorism 2002*. This publication may be browsed online at http://www.state.gov/s/ct/rls/pgtrpt/2002.

ATTACKS AGAINST U.S. CITIZENS OR FACILITIES

ATTACKS ON AMERICANS BY REGION (2002)

The pie chart "Total Anti–U.S. Attacks by Region, 2002" breaks down attacks on U.S. citizens and facilities in 2002 by region. As has been generally true, by far the largest number of such attacks occurred in Latin America.

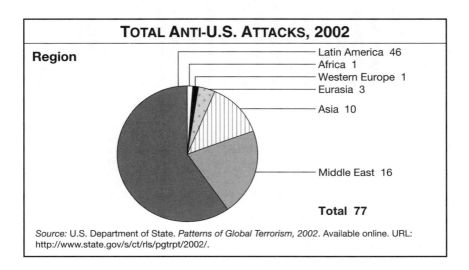

TOTAL ANTI-U.S. ATTACKS, 2002

Region

Latin America 46
Africa 1
Western Europe 1
Eurasia 3
Asia 10
Middle East 16

Total 77

Source: U.S. Department of State. *Patterns of Global Terrorism, 2002*. Available online. URL: http://www.state.gov/s/ct/rls/pgtrpt/2002/.

TOTAL TERRORIST ATTACKS, 1981–2002

The graph "Total International Terrorist Attacks, 1981–2002" indicates the total number of terrorist attacks worldwide from 1981 through 2002. The number of attacks peaked in the late 1980s the overall trend in the 1990s was downward, there was an upward spike in 1999 and 2000. The effectiveness of the global war on terrorism might be suggested by the 2002 figures, which is by far the lowest in the past two decades.

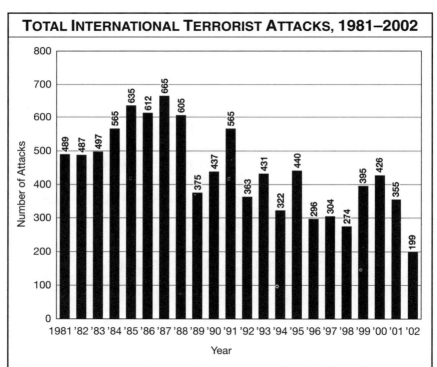

TOTAL INTERNATIONAL TERRORIST ATTACKS, 1981–2002

Note: In past years, serious violence by Palestinians against other Palestinians in the occupied territories was included in the database of worldwide international terrorist incidents because Palestinians are considered stateless people. This resulted in such incidents being treated differently from intraethnic violence in other parts of the world. In 1989, as a result of further review of the nature of intra-Palestinian violence, such violence stopped being included in the U.S. government's statistical database on international terrorism. The figures shown above for the years 1984 through 1988 have been revised to exclude intra-Palestinian violence, thus making the database consistent.

Source: U.S. Department of State. *Patterns of Global Terrorism, 2002.* Available online. URL: http://www.state.gov/s/ct/rls/pgtrpt/2002/.

Appendix A

FREQUENCY OF ATTACKS BY REGION, 1997–2002

The graph "Total International Attacks by Region, 1997–2002" breaks down the total number of international terrorist attacks by region for the years 1997–2002. The relatively high total for western Europe predominately reflects activity in Northern Ireland. Although it has not received as much media coverage as the Middle East, Latin America has had the most attacks, many in Colombia.

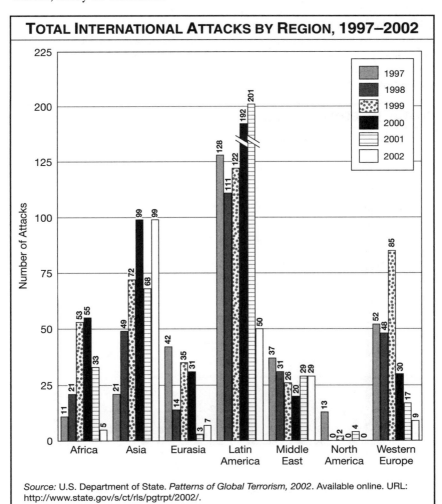

TOTAL INTERNATIONAL ATTACKS BY REGION, 1997–2002

Source: U.S. Department of State. *Patterns of Global Terrorism, 2002*. Available online. URL: http://www.state.gov/s/ct/rls/pgtrpt/2002/.

287

SEVERITY OF TERRORISM BY REGION, 1997–2002

The graph "Total International Casualties by Region, 1997–2002" breaks down the casualties caused by international terrorist attacks by region for the years 1997–2002. (Note the "scale break" marks indicating some of the higher figures are not drawn to scale.) It is hard to draw conclusions from this data because just a few incidents or situations can cause disproportionate numbers of casualties. If one excludes the two "spikes" in Africa (caused by the bombings of two U.S. embassies in 1998) and Asia in 1995, and the 2001 spike in North America from the September 11 attacks, the Middle East tends to have the most casualties, followed by western Europe (which is primarily accounted for by Northern Ireland). In most years except 2001 there are actually very few victims of international terrorism (that is, terrorism not of domestic origin) in the United States.

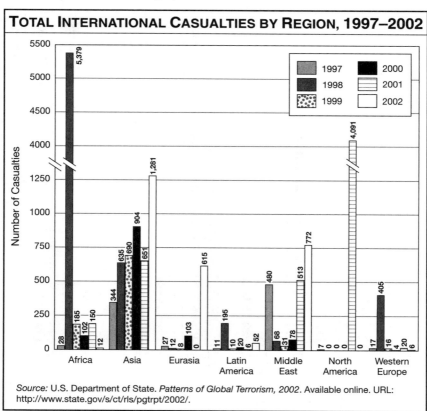

TOTAL INTERNATIONAL CASUALTIES BY REGION, 1997–2002

Source: U.S. Department of State. *Patterns of Global Terrorism, 2002.* Available online. URL: http://www.state.gov/s/ct/rls/pgtrpt/2002/.

Appendix A

TYPES OF TERRORIST ATTACKS (2002)

The pie chart "Total Anti-U.S. Attacks by Type of Event, 2002" breaks down the attacks against U.S. citizens and facilities by type. Clearly, the bomb remains the weapon of choice.

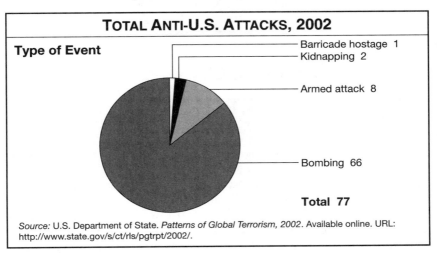

TOTAL ANTI-U.S. ATTACKS, 2002

Type of Event

Barricade hostage 1
Kidnapping 2
Armed attack 8
Bombing 66
Total 77

Source: U.S. Department of State. *Patterns of Global Terrorism, 2002.* Available online. URL: http://www.state.gov/s/ct/rls/pgtrpt/2002/.

WHO GETS HURT (2002)

The pie chart "Total Anti-U.S. Attacks, 2002" breaks down terrorist victims according to their status. Most U.S. victims in 2002 were businesspeople.

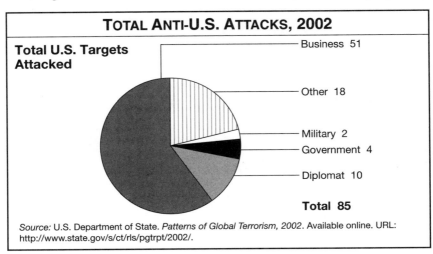

TOTAL ANTI-U.S. ATTACKS, 2002

Total U.S. Targets Attacked

Business 51
Other 18
Military 2
Government 4
Diplomat 10
Total 85

Source: U.S. Department of State. *Patterns of Global Terrorism, 2002.* Available online. URL: http://www.state.gov/s/ct/rls/pgtrpt/2002/.

APPENDIX B

———————

THE GEOGRAPHY OF TERRORISM

Following are five maps showing areas of the world where there have been persistent clashes between ethnic groups as well as campaigns of violence by both indigenous and global terrorist groups. These are not the only parts of the world where terrorism is a problem. For example, in Northern Ireland until recently, and in Colombia and other parts of Central and Latin America, there is also significant terrorist activity, and the potential for such activity remains even within Europe and North America. However, in the regions featured here geography plays a particularly important role.

Each map is numbered to show some particularly significant areas or events.

TERRORISM IN ISRAEL AND PALESTINE, AS OF EARLY 2004

Israeli-occupied with current status subject to the Israeli-Palestinian Interim Agreement. Permanent status to be determined through further negotiation.

Israeli-occupied area

✪ The United Nations and most governments do not recognize Jerusalem as the capital of Israel.

UNDOF Zone United Nations Disengagement Observer Force

UNIFIL Zone United Nations Interim Force in Lebanon

LEBANON
UNIFIL Zone
Qiryat Shemona
UNDOF Zone
Nahariyya
GOLAN HEIGHTS
'Akko
SYRIA
Haifa
Lake Tiberias
Nazareth
'Afula
Hadera
Janin
Netanya
Tulkarm
Jordan R.
Nablus
WEST BANK ②
Tel Aviv-Yafo
Ramallah
Jericho
Ashdod
Rehovot
Jerusalem ✪ ①
Ashqelon
Qiryat Gat
Bethlehem
Hebron ③
Dead Sea
GAZA STRIP ④
Gaza
Khan Yunus
'Arad
Beersheba
Dimona
Yeroham
Nizzana
Mediterranean Sea
⑤

JORDAN

N E G E V

EGYPT

N

0   30 miles
0   30 km

Elat
Gulf of Aqaba

1. Claimed as a cultural capital and sometimes political capital by both Israelis and Palestinians, the ancient city of Jerusalem is frequently rocked by suicide bombings and other attacks.

2. The West Bank contains major Palestinian towns and refugee camps. Plans to turn over control of its cities to the Palestinian Authority are uncertain as violence continued into 2004.

3. As of early 2004 Hebron was part of the Palestinian area, but it has many established Jewish settlements and is subject to frequent attacks. A disturbed Jewish gunman massacred Palestinians in the marketplace in 1997. In 2002

the Israeli army invaded Hebron looking for terrorist bases.

4. The tiny Gaza Strip is the other major Palestinian area. It is densely populated with refugees who have few resources. Hamas has mounted rocket attacks from this area into nearby Israeli towns, with Israeli forces retaliating and personally targeting Hamas leaders in 2003. However, a possible truce between Israel and Hamas may be emerging as of early 2004.

5. Tel Aviv, the capital of Israel, has also been the target of terrorist bombings.

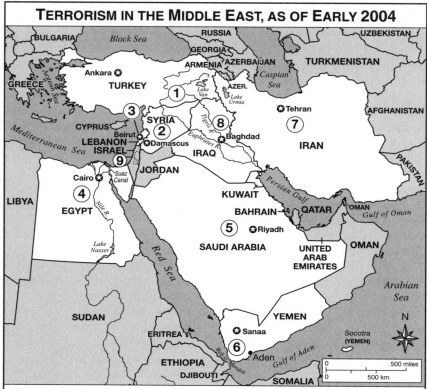

TERRORISM IN THE MIDDLE EAST, AS OF EARLY 2004

1. In southeastern Turkey the Kurdistan Workers Party (PKK) has waged a violent Kurdish separatist struggle. Turkey also has an interest in restraining the emergence of an independent Kurdish state in northern Iraq. In November 2003 al-Qaeda and local militant groups began to target symbols of "foreign" presence in Istanbul, including Jewish synagogues, the British consulate, and an international bank.

2. Syria sponsored terrorism starting in the 1970s, but following September 11, 2001, became more circumspect. It still supports Hezbollah and other groups, but it has provided some cooperation against al-Qaeda and may be seeking more normal relations with the United States.

3. A battleground between Israel and Syria in the 1980s, Lebanon was the scene of a devastating bombing of a U.S. Marine barracks in 1983.

4. Egypt's relatively moderate and secular government has often been attacked by militant Islamic groups.

5. Saudi Arabia's oil makes it vital to American interests, and it has been an ally in the U.S. effort against terrorism and the first Gulf War in 1990–91. However, prominent Saudi

families have been accused of supporting Saudi-born Osama bin Laden and other terrorists.

6. Poor but strategically located, Yemen was the site of the bombing attack on the U.S. warship *Cole* in 2000 in the port of Aden. In 2002 U.S. forces used drone aircraft to hunt al-Qaeda suspects.

7. Iran has become somewhat more moderate since the heyday of its Islamic revolution under Ayatollah Khomeini, and it has cooperated somewhat with the United States since September 11, 2001. However, the possible development of nuclear weapons by Iran has recently become a more urgent issue.

8. In April 2003 the United States invaded Iraq and overthrew Saddam Hussein. However, rebuilding the country has proved difficult, and both Baathist loyalists and terrorist groups seem to be launching increasingly effective attacks against U.S. forces. An unstable Iraq could become a major regional problem.

9. There have been numerous terrorist incidents and Israeli reprisals in the ongoing struggle over the status of Palestine. For more details, see map on p. 291.

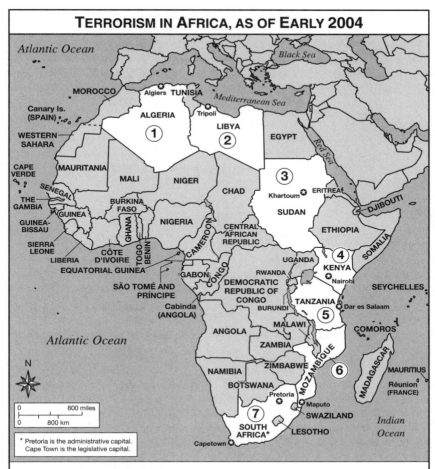

TERRORISM IN AFRICA, AS OF EARLY 2004

Atlantic Ocean

Black Sea

MOROCCO

Algiers ✪ TUNISIA

Mediterranean Sea

Canary Is.
(SPAIN)

ALGERIA

Tripoli

1

LIBYA

2

EGYPT

WESTERN
SAHARA

Red Sea

CAPE
VERDE

MAURITANIA

MALI

NIGER

CHAD

3

Khartoum ✪

ERITREA

DJIBOUTI

SENEGAL

THE
GAMBIA

GUINEA

BURKINA
FASO

SUDAN

SOMALIA

GUINEA-
BISSAU

NIGERIA

ETHIOPIA

SIERRA
LEONE

GHANA

CENTRAL
AFRICAN
REPUBLIC

LIBERIA

CÔTE
D'IVOIRE

TOGO

BENIN

CAMEROON

UGANDA

KENYA

4

EQUATORIAL GUINEA

GABON

CONGO

RWANDA

Nairobi ✪

SEYCHELLES

SÃO TOMÉ AND
PRÍNCIPE

DEMOCRATIC
REPUBLIC OF
CONGO

TANZANIA

Dar es Salaam

Cabinda
(ANGOLA)

BURUNDI

5

Atlantic Ocean

MALAWI

COMOROS

ANGOLA

ZAMBIA

N

ZIMBABWE

MOZAMBIQUE

6

MADAGASCAR

MAURITIUS

NAMIBIA

BOTSWANA

Pretoria ✪

Maputo

SWAZILAND

Réunion
(FRANCE)

0 — 800 miles
0 — 800 km

7

SOUTH
AFRICA*

LESOTHO

*Indian
Ocean*

Capetown ✪

* Pretoria is the administrative capital.
Cape Town is the legislative capital.

1. Algeria was the scene of one of the first major postcolonial conflicts in the 1950s. It continues to be the site of violence as armed Islamists fight the military-backed government.

2. Libya under Muammar al-Qaddafi was a major sponsor of terrorism, notably the bombing of Pan Am Flight 103 in 1988. In 2003, however, Libya agreed to settle claims and renounce terrorism.

3. A factory in Khartoum, Sudan, was bombed by the United States in 1998 as retaliation for the embassy attacks and in an attempt to destroy facilities allegedly manufacturing chemical weapons.

4. On August 7, 1998, the U.S. embassy in Nairobi, Kenya, was destroyed by a terrorist truck bomb. The attack was soon linked to Osama bin Laden and al-Qaeda.

5. The U.S. embassy in Dar es Salaam, Tanzania, was struck at virtually the same time.

6. Mozambique was the scene of a bitter civil war in the 1970s and 1980s, with terrorist atrocities on all sides. However, relative peace was established in the 1990s.

7. South Africa is another relative success story. The apartheid era saw state terrorism by the government and some terrorism by the African National Congress (ANC) and more extreme liberation groups. After the election of Nelson Mandela in 1994, there was no bloodbath but rather a difficult process of reconciliation.

TERRORISM IN CENTRAL ASIA, AS OF EARLY 2004

RUSSIA

Astana

Ishim R.

Irtysh R.

KAZAKHSTAN

Lake Zaysan

Lake Balqash

Lake Alaköl

④

Aral Sea

Syr Darya

Ili R.

Ural R.

Caspian Sea

UZBEKISTAN

Bishkek

Lake Ysyk Köl

AZERBAIJAN

Tashkent

KYRGYZSTAN

CHINA

TURKMENISTAN

Amu Darya

Ashgabat

Dushanbe

TAJIKISTAN

occupied by CHINA

① Kabul

Kashmir

IRAN

AFGHANISTAN

③

N

Islamabad

②

PAKISTAN

INDIA

Persian Gulf

Gulf of Oman

| 0 | | 600 miles |
| 0 | | 600 km |

1. Afghanistan under the Taliban became the main refuge for Osama bin Laden in the 1990s. Following September 11, 2001, U.S. and Northern Alliance forces destroyed the infrastructure of the Taliban and al-Qaeda and a new government was established, but remnant terrorist forces may be gathering strength.

2. Pakistan under Pervez Musharraf became a somewhat reluctant ally in the war against terrorism.

3. In the Kashmir region militant Islamic groups backed by Pakistan fight for independence from India. Because both Pakistan and India have nuclear weapons, the consequences of full-scale war could be dire. However, in early 2004 Pakistan agreed to stop supporting Islamic militants in Kashmir in return for peace talks with India aimed at settling the Kashmir dispute.

4. Kazakhstan, Turkmenistan, Uzbekistan, Kyrgyzstan, and Tajikistan have varying but significant amounts of oil and other resources, making them a potential battleground between Russian, Western, and Islamist forces.

TERRORISM IN SOUTHEAST ASIA, AS OF EARLY 2004

1. In Mindanao in the southern Philippines, the Abu Sayyaf terrorist group has been active, pursuing kidnappings and other attacks. There has also been a longstanding separatist campaign by the Moro National Liberation Front and Moro Islamic Liberation Front. The United States has pledged an increasing amount of military and economic support.

2. East Timor was the scene of a bitter and bloody struggle that finally ended in independence in May 2002.

3. The Moluccas are also a hotbed of Islamic separatism and fighting between Muslims and Christians.

4. A huge blast in Bali in 2002 was quickly linked to the increasingly powerful and troublesome Jemaah Islamiyah, which has ties to Osama bin Laden's al-Qaeda.

5. Under the notorious Pol Pot during the 1970s, Cambodia was the scene of state terrorism that killed several million people.

APPENDIX C

EXCERPTS FROM "PATTERNS OF GLOBAL TERRORISM, 2002"

Released by the Office of the Coordinator for Counterterrorism April 30, 2003

ANTITERRORISM ASSISTANCE PROGRAM

Congress authorized the Antiterrorism Assistance (ATA) Program in 1983 as part of a major initiative against international terrorism. Since that time ATA has provided training for over 31,000 students from 127 countries. The ATA Program provides training and related assistance to law-enforcement and security services of selected friendly foreign governments. Assistance to the qualified countries focuses on the following objectives:

Enhancing the antiterrorism skills of friendly countries by providing training and equipment to deter and counter the threats of terrorism. Strengthening the bilateral ties of the United States with friendly, foreign governments by offering concrete assistance in areas of mutual concern. Increasing respect for human rights by sharing with civilian authorities modern, humane, and effective antiterrorism techniques.

ATA courses are developed and customized in response to terrorism trends and patterns. The training can be categorized into four functional areas: Crisis Prevention, Crisis Management, Crisis Resolution, and Investigation. Countries needing assistance are identified on the basis of the threat, or actual level of terrorist activity they face.

Antiterrorist assistance and training, which begins with a comprehensive, in-country assessment, can take many forms, including airport security, crime-scene investigations, chemical and biological attacks, and courses for first responders. Most of this training is conducted overseas to maximize its effectiveness, and even more courses are being conducted in country under ATA's new "Fly-Away" concept.

Appendix C

ATA programs may also take the form of advisory assistance, such as police administration and management of police departments, how to train police instructors or develop a police academy, and modern interview and investigative techniques. Equipment or bomb-sniffing dogs may also be included in the assistance package.

The post-September 11 era has shifted the focus of ATA outreach to the newly identified frontline nations. These include Algeria, Armenia, Azerbaijan, Bangladesh, Djibouti, Egypt, Georgia, India, Indonesia, Jordan, Kazakhstan, Kenya, Kyrgyz Republic, Malaysia, Morocco, Oman, Uzbekistan, and Yemen. The United States delivered 80 courses to these frontline nations in 2002.

ATA has also identified specific areas in which courses will be added or expanded to enhance the antiterrorism capabilities in frontline and other countries. These include medical response to mass casualties, advanced police tactical intervention, physical security, border controls, and operations to deal with weapons of mass destruction such as mail security, customs/immigration inspection, disaster response, and urban search and rescue.

The ability of the United States to assist friendly governments with mastering the detection and prevention of terrorist activities will clearly enhance the mutual security of all the participating nations. Detecting and eliminating terrorist cells at the root before their violence can cross borders and oceans will ensure a safer world for all nations.

In the wake of the September 11 attacks, government officials of these frontline countries expressed greater interest in receiving antiterrorism assistance. ATA has increased efforts to familiarize ambassadors, regional security officers, and other US officials with the program offerings. The success of these efforts is evidenced by the fact that every frontline nation has requested antiterrorist assistance in some form. US diplomats report that the ability of the United States to offer immediate, specific, and intensive training, along with technical tools and equipment, has succeeded in breaking down barriers and building trust.

ATA is responding to the growing demand for training and services, not only by expanding course selection, but also by pursuing development of the Center for Antiterrorism and Security Training (CAST). ATA is already offering training at the Louisiana State Police Academy (Baton Rouge, Louisiana), the DOE Nonproliferation and National Security Institute (Albuquerque, New Mexico), the FBI Academy (Quantico, Virginia), and in the Washington, DC metropolitan area.

REWARDS FOR JUSTICE PROGRAM

The Rewards for Justice Program is one of the most valuable US Government assets in the fight against international terrorism. Established by the 1984 Act to Combat International Terrorism, Public Law 98-533, the Program is administered by the US Department of State's Bureau of Diplomatic Security.

Under the Program, the Secretary of State may offer rewards of up to $5 million for information that prevents or favorably resolves acts of international terrorism against US persons or property worldwide. Rewards also may be paid for information leading to the arrest or conviction of terrorists attempting, committing, and conspiring to commit, or aiding and abetting in the commission of such acts.

The USA Patriot Act of 2001 authorizes the Secretary to offer or pay rewards of greater than $5 million if he determines that a greater amount is necessary to combat terrorism or to defend the United States against terrorist acts. Secretary Powell has authorized a reward of up to $25 million for information leading to the capture of Usama Bin Ladin and other key al-Qaida leaders.

In November 2002, the State and Treasury Departments announced a $5 million rewards program that will pay for information leading to the disruption of any terrorism financing operation.

Diplomatic Security has fully supported the efforts of the private business sector/citizens to establish a Rewards for Justice Fund, a nongovernmental, nonprofit 501 C (3) charitable organization administered by a group of private US citizens. One hundred percent of all donated funds will be used to supplement reward payments only. Diplomatic Security has forged a strong relationship with the private business and US citizen representatives of the Rewards for Justice Fund. Diplomatic Security has embarked on a much closer relationship with the US public and private business in the US Government's continuing efforts to bring those individuals responsible for the planning of the September 11 attacks to justice and preventing future international terrorist attacks against the United States at home or abroad.

INTERNATIONAL TERRORISM: US HOSTAGES, US POLICY

The US Government will make no concessions to individuals or groups holding official or private US citizens hostage. The United States will use every appropriate resource to gain the safe return of US citizens who are held hostage. At the same time, it is US Government policy to deny hostage takers the benefits of ransom, prisoner releases, policy changes, or other acts of concession.

BASIC PREMISES

It is internationally accepted that governments are responsible for the safety and welfare of persons within the borders of their nations. Aware of both the hostage threat and public security shortcomings in many parts of the world, the United States has developed enhanced physical and personal security programs for US personnel and established cooperative arrangements with the US private sector. It has also established bilateral assistance programs and close intelligence and law-enforcement relationships with many nations to prevent hostage-taking incidents or resolve them in a manner that will deny the perpetrators benefits from their actions. The United States also seeks effective judicial prosecution and punishment for hostage takers victimizing the US Government or its citizens and will use all legal methods to these ends, including extradition. US policy and goals are clear, and the US Government actively pursues them alone and in cooperation with other governments.

US GOVERNMENT RESPONSIBILITIES WHEN PRIVATE US CITIZENS ARE TAKEN HOSTAGE

Based upon past experience, the US Government concluded that making concessions that benefit hostage takers in exchange for the release of hostages increased the danger that others will be taken hostage. US Government policy is, therefore, to deny hostage takers the benefits of ransom, prisoner releases, policy changes, or other acts of concession.

At the same time, the US Government will make every effort, including contact with representatives of the captors, to obtain the release of hostages without making concessions to the hostage takers.

Consequently, the United States strongly urges US companies and private citizens not to accede to hostage-taker demands. It believes that good security practices, relatively modest security expenditures, and continual close cooperation with embassy and local authorities can lower the risk to US citizens living in high-threat environments.

The US Government is concerned for the welfare of its citizens but cannot support requests that host governments violate their own laws or abdicate their normal enforcement responsibilities.

If the employing organization or company works closely with local authorities and follows US policy, US Foreign Service posts can be involved actively in efforts to bring the incident to a safe conclusion. This includes providing reasonable administrative services and, if desired by local authorities and the US entity, full participation in strategy sessions. Requests for US Government technical assistance or expertise will be considered on a case-by-case basis. The full extent of US Government participation must await an analysis of each specific set of circumstances.

The host government and the US private organizations or citizen must understand that if they wish to follow a hostage-resolution path different from that of US Government policy, they do so without US Government approval. In the event a hostage-taking incident is resolved through concessions, US policy remains steadfastly to pursue investigation leading to the apprehension and prosecution of hostage takers who victimize US citizens.

LEGAL CAUTION

Under current US law, 18 USC 1203 (Act for the Prevention and Punishment of the Crime of Hostage Taking, enacted October 1984 in implementation of the UN convention on hostage taking), seizure of a US citizen as a hostage anywhere in the world is a crime, as is any hostage-taking action in which the US Government is a target or the hostage taker is a US national. Such acts are, therefore, subject to investigation by the Federal Bureau of Investigation and to prosecution by US authorities. Actions by private persons or entities that have the effect of aiding or abetting the hostage taking, concealing knowledge of it from the authorities, or obstructing its investigation may themselves be in violation of US law.

US TERRORISM LISTS:
PREVENTION, PUNISHMENT, PRESSURE

The US Government has established four primary counterterrorism "lists" to serve as tools in the fight against terrorism: The State Sponsors of Terrorism, Foreign Terrorist Organizations (FTO), Executive Order 13224, and the Terrorist Exclusion (TEL) list. Each list has its individual mechanisms, but they all serve to prevent terrorism, punish terrorists and their supporters, and pressure changes in the behavior of designated states and groups.

Because these lists are a means to fight terrorism, rather than an end in themselves, they are not designed or intended to be immutable. The US Government encourages states and organizations to take the necessary actions to get out of the terrorism business. The bar for a state or group being removed from a US terrorism list is and must be high—it must end all involvement in any facet of terrorism, including passive support, and satisfy all US counterterrorism concerns.

STATE SPONSORS OF TERRORISM

The Secretary of State is authorized to designate a government as a "State Sponsor of Terrorism" if that government "has repeatedly provided support for acts of international terrorism." United States law requires the imposition of various sanctions on a state so designated. A number of US laws and sanctions affect countries whose governments have been designated as state sponsors of terrorism. The four main categories of sanctions include a ban on arms-related exports and sales; restrictions on exports of dual-use items;

Appendix C

prohibitions on official US Government economic assistance (except humanitarian assistance), including a requirement that the US Government oppose multilateral bank assistance; and imposition of miscellaneous trade and other restrictions, including a prohibition on imports and liability in US courts for officials of that country that engage in terrorist activity. Inclusion on the State Sponsors of Terrorism list also targets a country for other sanctions laws that penalize persons and countries engaging in certain trade with state sponsors. Currently, there are seven countries on the list: Cuba, Iran, Iraq, Libya, North Korea, Sudan, and Syria.

FOREIGN TERRORIST ORGANIZATIONS (FTOS)

The Secretary of State is authorized to designate as FTOs groups that conduct international terrorism and threaten the interests of the United States. Designation allows the US to block designees' assets in US financial institutions; criminalizes witting provision of material support to designated groups; and blocks visas for members of FTOs without having to show that the individual was involved in specific terrorist activities. FTO designation also sends a strong signal that any group that engages in terrorism regardless of its purported goals will be condemned and penalized for its actions. (The list of FTOs can be found in Appendix B [of "Patterns of Global Terrorism, 2002"].)

EXECUTIVE ORDER 13224–TERRORIST FINANCING

President Bush signed Executive Order 13224 on 23 September 2001, to give the US Government a strong tool for eliminating the financial supporters and networks of terrorism. EO 13224 enables the US Government to block designees' assets in any financial institution in the United States or held by any US person. It also expands US Government authority to permit the designation of individuals and organizations that provide support or financial or other services to, or associate with, designated terrorists. EO 13224 designations have allowed the US Government, as well as Coalition partners acting in concert, to block tens of millions of dollars intended to bankroll the murderous activities of al-Qaida and other terrorist groups.

A complete listing of individuals and entities covered under EO 13224 can be found at: www.ustreas.gov/offices/enforcement/ofac/sanctions/terrorism.html

USA PATRIOT ACT: TERRORIST EXCLUSION LIST

President Bush on 26 October 2001 signed into law a comprehensive counterterrorism bill (Public Law 107-56, also known as USA PATRIOT). The new law strengthened enforcement tools and made improvements to the last major terrorism bill, the Antiterrorism and Effective Death Penalty Act of 1996. The Patriot USA Act also created a Terrorist Exclusion List (TEL) with immigration consequences for groups named therein. Designation on the TEL allows the US Government to exclude or deport aliens who provide material assistance to, or solicit it for, designated organizations, giving the Department of State and US law-enforcement agencies a critical tool for bolstering homeland security.

TERRORIST EXCLUSION LIST DESIGNEES
Designated on 5 December 2001

- al-Ittihad al-Islami (AIAI)
- al-Wafa al-Igatha al-Islamia
- 'Asbat al-Ansar
- Darkazanli Company
- Salafist Group for Preaching (Call) and Combat (GSPC)
- Islamic Army of Aden
- Libyan Islamic Fighting Group
- Maktab al-Khidamat
- al-Hamati Sweets Bakeries
- al-Nur Honey Center
- al-Rashid Trust
- al-Shifa Honey Press for Industry and Commerce
- Jaish-e-Mohammed
- Jamiat al-Ta'awun al-Islamiyya
- Alex Boncayao Brigade (ABB)
- Army for the Liberation of Rwanda (ALIR)–a.k.a. Interahamwe, Former Armed Forces (EX-FAR)
- First of October Antifascist Resistance Group (GRAPO)–a.k.a. Grupo de Resistencia Anti-Fascista Premero de Octubre
- Lashkar-e-Tayyiba (LT)–a.k.a. Army of the Righteous
- Continuity Irish Republican Army (CIRA)–a.k.a. Continuity Army Council
- Orange Volunteers (OV)
- Red Hand Defenders (RHD)

- New People's Army (NPA)
- People Against Gangsterism and Drugs (PAGAD)
- Revolutionary United Front (RUF)
- al-Ma'unah
- Jayshullah
- Black Star
- Anarchist Faction for Overthrow
- Red Brigades-Combatant Communist Party (BR-PCC)
- Revolutionary Proletarian Nucleus
- Turkish Hizballah
- Jerusalem Warriors
- Islamic Renewal and Reform Organization
- The Pentagon Gang
- Japanese Red Army (JRA)
- Jamiat ul-Mujahidin (JUM)
- Harakat ul-Jihad-I-Islami (HUJI)
- Allied Democratic Forces (ADF)
- Lord's Resistance Army (LRA)

Designated on 6 November 2002

- Al Taqwa Trade, Property and Industry Company Ltd.
- Bank Al Taqwa Ltd.
- Nada Management Organization
- Youssef M. Nada & Co. Gesellschaft M.B.H.
- Ummah Tameer E-Nau (UTN)
- Loyalist Volunteer Force (LVF)
- Ulster Defense Association
- Afghan Support Committee
- Revival of Islamic Heritage Society (Pakistan and Afghanistan offices— Kuwait office not designated)

Source: http://www.state.gov/s/ct/rls/pgtrpt/2002/

INDEX

Locators in **boldface** indicate main entries. Locators followed by *b* indicate biographical listings, by *g* indicate glossary entries, by *c* indicate chronology entries, by *t* indicate tables or graphs, and by *m* indicate maps.

Index

Index

Index

Index

311

Index

Index